Using
Quicken 3
for Windows

Set Up Security

Name: Deluxe Checks
Symbol: DLX (optional)
Type:
Goal: Growth (optional)

Est. Annual Income($): 0.00 (per share)

OK
Cancel

Linda A. Flanders

Use   New   Edit   Del   Mark

Calendar

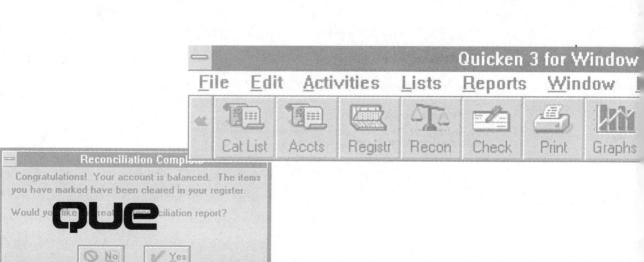

Quicken 3 for Window

File   Edit   Activities   Lists   Reports   Window

Cat List   Accts   Registr   Recon   Check   Print   Graphs

Reconciliation Complete

Congratulations! Your account is balanced. The items you have marked have been cleared in your register.

Would you like to create a reconciliation report?

que

No   Yes

Using Quicken 3 for Windows

Library of Congress Catalog No.: 93-86244

ISBN: 1-56529-457-2

95 94 93   4 3 2 1

Interpretation of the printing code: the rightmost double-digit number is the year of the book's printing; the rightmost single- digit number, the number of the book's printing. For example, a printing code of 93-1 shows that the first printing of the book occurred in 1993.

This book is based on Quicken Version 3 for Windows.

Publisher: David P. Ewing

Director of Publishing: Michael Miller

Managing Editor: Corinne Walls

Marketing Manager: Ray Robinson

Dedication

To Scott, Jade, Jordan, and Ali

Credits

Publishing Manager
Don Roche, Jr.

Acquisitions Editor
Nancy Stevenson

Product Director
Joyce J. Nielsen
Jim Minatel
Steven M. Schafer

Production Editor
Susan Shaw Dunn

Copy Editors
Jo Anna Arnott
Judy Brunetti
Robin Drake
Lorna Gentry
Thomas Hayes
Patrick Kanouse
Susan Pink
Brad Sullivan

Technical Editor
Janice A. Snyder

Book Designer
Amy Peppler-Adams

Cover Designer
Jean Biesesi

Indexers
Michael Hughes
Joy Dean Lee
Suzanne Snyder

Production Team
Angela Bannan
Claudia Bell
Danielle Bird
Charlotte Clapp
Teresa Forrester
Joelynn Gifford
Michelle Greenwalt
Carla Hall
Tim Montgomery
Ryan Rader
Caroline Roop
Dennis Sheehan
Amy L. Steed
Tina Trettin
Sue VandeWalle
Mary Beth Wakefield
Donna Winter
Michelle Worthington

Editorial Assistant
Jill Stanley

Composed in *Stone Serif* and *MCPdigital*
by Que Corporation.

About the Author

Linda A. Flanders is a certified public accountant with a bachelor of science degree in accounting from Indiana University. She has worked in public accounting for Arthur Andersen & Co. and in corporate taxation for Mayflower Group, Inc. She is the author of *Using QuickBooks for Windows, Using TurboTax, Using Microsoft Money 2.0,* and several other Que books.

Acknowledgments

Thanks to all those at Que, who continually strive to make their products the best.

Trademarks

All terms mentioned in this book that are known to be trademarks or service marks have been appropriately capitalized. Que cannot attest to the accuracy of this information. Use of a term in this book should not be regarded as affecting the validity of any trademark or service mark.

Quicken is a registered trademark of Intuit, Inc.

Contents at a Glance

Managing Quicken

Putting Quicken To Use

Appendixes

Table of Contents

5 Writing and Printing Checks

6 Using the Register

II Getting the Most from Quicken for Windows   227

15 Monitoring Your Investments 367

16 Budgeting with Quicken 415

17 Saving for the Future with Quicken   433

IV Analyzing Your Finances with Quicken   453

18 Creating and Printing Reports   455

23 Using Quicken in Your Small Business   573

Appendixes   605

A Installing Quicken 3 for Windows   607

Introduction

If you're like most people, your personal bookkeeping takes you hours and hours each month. You probably sit down three to four times a month to pay bills, each time gathering paperwork, writing checks, entering checks and deposits into your checkbook register, calculating your bank account balance, and addressing envelopes. Then, when your monthly bank statement arrives, you must sit down again to perform the tedious task of balancing your checkbook by checking off cleared transactions, adding outstanding deposits and checks, and performing the reconciling calculations.

After you endure all these ordeals, heaven forbid if your bank account balance doesn't agree with the bank's! That crisis means spending even more time trying to find the error(s). All these tasks, just to keep your financial records in some semblance of order. But keeping your financial records in order is a task that you *can't* overlook nor trust to an outdated or ineffective financial system.

If you invest your money in any type of securities, you absolutely must keep track of your investments, or you won't know whether your investment strategies are paying off. If your focus is on income-producing investments, you need to monitor those investments to make sure that the income yields are maximized. If your focus is on growth investments, you need to monitor those investments to make sure that they are growing at a satisfactory level. No matter what your focus, you need to monitor your investments to make sure that they don't dwindle away. Of course, you can entrust this process to your investment advisor or broker, but you will want to be on top of things to make sure that the experts are doing their job with *your* money.

And everyone is trying to get ahead and save for the future. But how do you know how much you will need to send your kids to college or to retire in the lifestyle that you've always dreamed of? Certainly, many financial consultants or planners are more than willing to work with you and devise a savings scheme to take care of all your future concerns—but not without a price.

Quicken 3 for Windows is your solution to the boring and long process of bookkeeping and financial management and the necessary—but sometimes complex—task of monitoring your investments. Quicken even can help you devise a savings strategy for retirement *and* college for the kids.

With Quicken, you can speed up your record-keeping activities and have a little fun, too. By using windows that resemble what you're used to seeing on the desktop (checks, check registers, bank statements, and so forth), you quickly and easily can enter your financial transactions, print checks, reconcile your bank account, create budgets, and generate reports and graphs so that you can analyze your finances more easily. Quicken for Windows' investment features help you track each of your investments so that you easily can manage your portfolio. And Quicken's financial planners can be of great help in determining your future financial needs.

To truly have a handle on your finances, you must keep track of your income and expenses so that you know how much money is coming in and how much is going out. Quicken helps you do that. To make informed decisions about spending, you must know exactly where you are (financially) at any given time. If you want to take a vacation to Europe or buy a new car, for example, you immediately know what you can afford. Quicken helps you make these decisions by presenting the financial data that you need in a format that is meaningful to you. That's what this book is really about: making better financial decisions by using financial information—financial information that Quicken can help you collect, store, and use.

In this age of supertechnology, you can accomplish on a computer almost anything you do behind a desk. Bookkeeping and financial management are no exception. With a well-designed software package, you can perform all your financial activities, including tracking your investments, in far less time and with far less frustration.

If you are considering the installation of a personal or small-business accounting package like Quicken, if you have decided to install Quicken and want a little extra help, or if you already have begun using Quicken and want a reference source that goes beyond the information provided in the user's manual, *Using Quicken 3 for Windows* will help. This text includes a wealth of information about Quicken for Windows Version 3 and about managing your personal or small-business finances.

After you read this introduction, you will know what Quicken for Windows Version 3 is and whether the program suits your needs. This introduction also identifies the contents of each chapter.

Author's Testimonial

You may think that most computer-book authors learn many programs but use only a few. Well, you're right. And the programs that we authors end up using are the programs that have proven to work the best. Because we do learn numerous programs so that we can write about them and tell users, like yourself, the ins and outs of the program, we have a better-than-average feel for which programs work the way they're supposed to and will save us the most time.

As a CPA, I'm particularly interested in financial programs, like Quicken for Windows. The last thing that I want to do is spend more time than I have to with financial tasks, such as writing checks, balancing the checking account, preparing a budget, updating investment accounts, and so forth. But as a CPA, I'm extremely critical of software publishers that promote their products as the "only financial software" that I'll need and then fall short of the mark. Many do.

Quicken, however, meets all my expectations for a financial software package, and then some. I've been using Quicken for five years (beginning with Quicken for DOS, of course). And with each new version of the program, Quicken keeps getting better and better. (As a matter of preference for the Windows environment, I switched from Quicken for DOS to Quicken for Windows, but for those of you who continue to use DOS software, Quicken for DOS offers the same activities that you'll find in Quicken for Windows.)

I use Quicken for all my financial needs. I probably save the most time by using preprinted checks to write checks. At any given time, I may have 25 checks to write and print. With Quicken, I can perform this task almost effortlessly and in little time. I also appreciate the tasks I can perform with Quicken that used to take hours, such as reconciling my bank account at the end of the month, preparing a budget and then comparing actual to budget data, gathering tax information in April, putting together financial statements, and updating my investment account values. With Quicken I can do all these things while the sun is still shining—no more late nights spent with calculators and spreadsheets!

I welcome you to the world of Quicken and encourage you to learn everything you can about the program. In time, you'll be using Quicken for all your financial needs, too.

What Is Quicken for Windows?

Quicken for Windows is a computer-based bookkeeping system you can use to manage your personal or business finances. Quicken for Windows is developed for use with Microsoft Windows. Windows is an environment surrounding DOS, the disk operating system. With Windows, you can accomplish the same tasks that you can with DOS but through the use of a graphical user interface (GUI), which provides visual choices and options for performing tasks. With Windows programs, all your choices can be visible, which provides you with easier access to program features.

When working in a Windows program, you can load other programs and quickly switch from one to another. Within the same application (like Quicken for Windows), you can display multiple windows so that you can work faster and easier.

Used in the simplest way, Quicken maintains your check register for you by deducting payments and adding deposits to your checking account balance. Quicken eliminates the possibility of you overdrawing your account because of an arithmetic error.

The real value of Quicken, however, stems from several other features the program provides:

■ Quicken enables you to use your computer and printer to generate checks, which is a real time-saver if you find yourself writing many checks at home every month.

■ Quicken enables you to use the information stored in your Check Register to report on your income and expenses, track tax deductions, and compare your actual income and expenses to what you originally budgeted.

■ You can use Quicken to perform bookkeeping for most personal and business assets and liabilities, including personal investments, business receivables, personal credit lines and mortgages, and business payables.

With these extra features, individuals can track and manage their finances closely, and many small businesses can use Quicken as a full-fledged accounting package. (Quicken enables you to generate personal and business income statements, balance sheets, and cash-flow statements.)

New Features in Quicken 3 for Windows

If you have used earlier versions of Quicken for Windows (or Quicken for DOS), you will want to know what Quicken 3 for Windows has in store for you. Quicken for Windows features new to Version 3 are indicated throughout this book by a special icon, just like the one in the margin next to this paragraph. The following is a list of the new features in Quicken 3 for Windows:

- *Quicken Financial Calendar.* Quicken includes a Financial Calendar that you can use to schedule transactions due in the future. You can view transactions in the calendar format so that you quickly can see what's due and when. Quicken Reminders pop up on-screen to tell you when a transaction is due. Refer to Chapter 14, "Scheduling Future Transactions," to learn how to use this new feature.

- *Calendar notes.* Quicken takes on a more personal look with notes or reminders that you can make to yourself in the new financial calendar. You never will forget a birthday or any other special event if you use Quicken's new calendar note feature. Learn about calendar notes in Chapter 14, "Scheduling Future Transactions."

- *Pop-up field calculator.* Now making quick calculations is easier than ever with the new pop-up calculator. You can do quick math in the amount field in the register. See Chapter 7, "Using Quicken Shortcuts," to learn how to use the pop-up field calculator.

- *Pop-up calendar.* You can use Quicken's new pop-up calendar to enter dates in all date fields. Refer to Chapter 7, "Using Quicken Shortcuts," to learn how to enter dates with the pop-up calendar.

- *Refinance Planner.* In just seconds, you can calculate how feasible (or unfeasible) refinancing your home is with the new Refinance Planner. The Refinance Planner computes the difference in your monthly payment at various interest rates and how long it will take to recover the closing costs incurred when you refinance your mortgage. See Chapter 10, "Tracking Loans," to learn how to use the Refinance Planner.

- *Investment forms.* New on-screen forms make entering investment transactions quicker and easier. Quicken includes forms for buying and selling securities, recording investment income and margin loans, re-deeming U.S. savings bonds and treasury bills, selling short, option trading, and so forth. Chapter 15, "Monitoring Your Investments," explains how to enter investment transactions with the new forms.

■ *Specifying which lots of shares you're selling.* In Quicken 3 for Windows, you can identify which shares of securities you are selling if you have multiple lots bought at different times. You learn how to specify which lots you are selling in Chapter 15, "Monitoring Your Investments."

■ *Viewing your portfolio for investment accounts.* To see your investment accounts in a clearer and more complete format, you can switch be-tween different views of your portfolio. Each portfolio view gives differ-ent measures of investment performance, such as estimated income, market value, investment yield, and so forth. Learn about portfolio views in Chapter 15, "Monitoring Your Investments."

■ *Examining portfolio detail with QuickZoom.* You can see the detail behind transactions in a portfolio view of an investment account using the QuickZoom feature. Chapter 15, "Monitoring Your Investments," ex-plains how to use QuickZoom for investment accounts.

■ *Measuring investment performance and value.* By using the new portfolio views, you can see up to 18 measures of your investment performance: estimated income, actual dollars of income, percent of income, market value, market value change, percent of market value, actual dollars invested, percent of investment, investment yield, percent of invest-ment yield, percent of cost, average cost, last price, actual return, return on investment, actual gain or loss, percent of gain or loss, and internal rate of return. Refer to Chapter 15, "Monitoring Your Investments," for an explanation of these new investment performance measures.

■ *Setting up accounts with deferred-tax status.* You can establish an account as tax-deferred so that you can track IRAs, 401(k), Series EE Savings Bonds, and so forth. See Chapter 3, "Defining Your Accounts," to learn how to set up an account with deferred-tax status.

■ *QuickReport.* In many windows in Quicken 3 for Windows, you can get a quick transaction listing for the selected payee, for example, by using the new QuickReport feature. Refer to Chapter 6, "Using the Register," and Chapter 18, "Creating and Printing Reports," to learn about the new QuickReport feature.

- *Aligning checks more easily.* Quicken 3 for Windows has improved the check alignment feature to minimize the number of misprinted checks. See Chapter 5, "Writing and Printing Checks," to learn how to align checks in Quicken 3 for Windows.

- *New reports.* Quicken 3 for Windows includes the new Missing Checks and Comparison reports. Refer to Chapter 18, "Creating and Printing Reports," to learn about the new reports in Quicken 3 for Windows.

- *Viewing reports with percentages.* In Quicken 3 for Windows, you can view report data as percentages. Chapter 18, "Creating and Printing Reports," shows you how to use the new percentage display option for reports.

- *Easier report customization.* Customizing reports is quicker and easier in Quicken 3 for Windows. See Chapter 18, "Creating and Printing Reports," to learn how to customize reports.

- *Select report date ranges by name.* Rather than enter dates for reports, you can use Quicken 3's named date ranges, such as year-to-date, to define report periods. See Chapter 18, "Creating and Printing Reports," for more on date ranges.

- *Viewing sample reports on-screen.* Quicken 3 for Windows shows you the report layout and appearance on-screen before it's created. Refer to Chapter 18, "Creating and Printing Reports," to learn about sample reports.

- *Printing range of pages in reports.* Rather than print all pages in a report, you can specify a range of pages to print. See Chapter 18, "Creating and Printing Reports," to learn how to print a range of pages.

- *Copying reports to Windows Clipboard.* Quicken 3 for Windows makes transferring report data to other programs easy. Just copy the report to the Windows Clipboard and then paste it to a spreadsheet or word processing program. Copying report data is explained in Chapter 18, "Creating and Printing Reports."

- *Register button bar.* Registers in Quicken 3 for Windows include a button bar that contains buttons for common commands, such as deleting, copying, or inserting transactions. See Chapter 6, "Using the Register," to learn how to use the button bar.

■ *Maximizing the Register.* You now can maximize any Register window so that the Register fills the screen and makes your work a little easier. Refer to Chapter 6, "Using the Register," to learn how to maximize the Register.

■ *Copying, pasting, and inserting transactions in Registers.* Now you can copy a transaction from a Register and paste it in another Register. You also can insert a new transaction anywhere in the Register. See Chapter 6, "Using the Register," to learn how to insert a new transaction. Chapter 7, "Using Quicken Shortcuts," shows you how to copy and paste transactions in Registers.

■ *Improved QuickFill.* Quicken 2 for Windows introduced QuickFill, which helps speed up data entry in Quicken by searching all memorized transactions for a transaction that matches the first characters that you type. When a match is found, QuickFill shows you the details from the matching transaction. You can accept the transaction or edit it. See Chapter 7, "Using Quicken Shortcuts" to learn about the improved QuickFill feature in Quicken.

■ *Storing percentages in split transactions.* Now, when you have Quicken memorize a split transaction, you can save the split line as a percentage of the total transaction. See Chapter 7, "Using Quicken Shortcuts" to learn how to store percentages in split transactions.

■ *Financial Planning Graph and Worksheet.* The new Financial Planning Graph shows you the state of your accounts for the next two years. You use the graph to help you plan for vacations, major purchases, or investments. You can change the graph with the Financial Planning Worksheet to analyze "what-if" scenarios. Refer to Chapter 14, "Scheduling Future Transactions," to learn about the Financial Planning Graph and Worksheet.

■ *Savings Goal account.* Quicken 3 for Windows includes a special account that you can set up to track your savings. See Chapter 17, "Saving for the Future with Quicken," to learn how to create a Savings Goal account and monitor your savings.

■ *Graph subcategories.* You now can include subcategories, as well as categories, in graphs. Refer to Chapter 19, "Using Graphs To Analyze Your Finances," to learn how to graph subcategories.

- *Easier setup for loans.* Loans are easier to set up and edit. Quicken 3 for Windows displays the Set Up Loan dialog box, which includes fields for all information needed to amortize a loan. Chapter 10, "Tracking Loans," explains how to set up a loan in Quicken for Windows.

- *Handling alternative loan calculation methods.* By using Quicken 3's Loan Planner, you can amortize a loan with variable interest rates, balloon payments, prepayment of principal, and negative amortization. Quicken 3 for Windows also handles Canadian amortization. See Chapter 10, "Tracking Loans," to learn how to amortize loans using alternative loan calculation methods.

- *Budgeting selected categories with AutoCreate.* The AutoCreate Budget feature was new in Quicken 2 for Windows. Now you can select budget categories and use AutoCreate to enter budget amounts only for those categories. Chapter 16, "Budgeting with Quicken," shows you how to use AutoCreate to budget selected categories.

- *Printing and copying budget spreadsheets.* Now you can print your budget spreadsheet and copy the budget spreadsheet to the Windows Clipboard for use in another program. See Chapter 16, "Budgeting with Quicken," to learn how to perform these activities.

- *Improved Qcards.* Quicken 2 for Windows introduced Qcards to teach you how to use Quicken as you go. Now Qcards are improved. You can move Qcards to a different location on-screen or remove Qcards when you're up to speed in Quicken. Chapter 2, "Learning Your Way around Quicken for Windows," explains how to use Qcards for help; Chapter 21, "Customizing Quicken," explains how to move or close Qcards.

- *Pasting check logos.* If you have your own logo that you want to appear on printed checks, with Quicken 3 for Windows you can paste the logo artwork into Quicken to be printed on your checks. Refer to Chapter 5, "Writing and Printing Checks," to learn how to paste logos in Quicken.

- *Customizing the Iconbar.* Quicken 3 for Windows enables you to re-arrange the Iconbar so that the buttons displayed are the ones you use the most. See Chapter 21, "Customizing Quicken," to learn more about customizing the Iconbar.

- *Automatic backup option.* You no longer will forget to back up your Quicken data; the program automatically prompts you to back up your files at regular intervals. Read Chapter 20, "Managing Your Quicken Files," to learn about automatically backing up your files.

■ *Changing register colors and fonts.* You can change the color and fonts used in Quicken registers. See Chapter 21, "Customizing Quicken," to learn how to change the appearance of Quicken's registers.

■ *Sorting the reconciliation list.* When reconciling your bank account, you can sort the reconciliation list (list of uncleared bank transactions) by date, if that's how they appear on your bank statement. Uncleared transactions in the reconciliation list are now separated into debits and credits. Refer to Chapter 8, "Reconciling Your Bank Account," for more on the reconciliation list.

■ *Recording additional information for accounts.* Now, in addition to the standard account information, you can record additional information for accounts, such as a bank's address and phone number. See Chapter 3, "Defining Your Accounts," to learn how to enter extra detail for accounts.

■ *Exporting or importing lists.* You can transfer your lists of accounts, categories, classes, and memorized transactions to new files. See Chapter 20, "Managing Your Quicken Files," to learn how to transfer lists.

■ *Canadian categories.* For Canadian users of Quicken, the program now includes categories for GST and PST in the standard category list. See Chapter 4, "Organizing Your Finances," for more on Canadian categories.

When To Use Quicken for Windows

Answering the question *When should I use Quicken for Windows?* depends on whether you are using the program for personal or small-business purposes. If you are considering Quicken for personal use, four factors indicate that Quicken represents a good investment of your time and money:

■ When check-writing and checking account record-keeping take more time than you want to spend. Quicken does most of the work related to keeping your checkbook: recording transactions, writing checks, reconciling account balances, and maintaining the check register. Because

Quicken does the work for you, the program saves you a tremendous amount of time.

- When you need to track your tax deductions carefully. Quicken tracks the amounts you spend on tax-deductible items. At the end of the year, totaling your charitable contribution deductions is as simple as printing a report.

- When you want to budget income and expense amounts and compare what you earn and spend with what you budgeted. Budgets, contrary to their reputation, aren't equivalent to financial handcuffs that prevent you from enjoying life. Budgets are tools that enable you to identify your financial priorities. They help you monitor your progress in organizing your financial life so that you can meet your financial objectives. Quicken makes budgeting easy.

- When you want to monitor and track personal assets (such as investments) and personal liabilities (such as your mortgage and credit card debt).

If you are considering Quicken for business, three factors indicate that Quicken represents a good investment of your time and money and a reasonable accounting alternative:

- You don't need or want to use a small-business accounting package that requires double-entry bookkeeping. Packages such as DacEasy, Peachtree, and others require that you use double-entry bookkeeping. If you aren't familiar with double-entry bookkeeping, you probably can spend your time better in ways other than learning accounting methods. Quicken provides a single-entry, easy-to-use accounting system. Quicken's category and transfer accounts provide an easy way to meet the double-entry requirement without the added difficulty of entering transactions in journals and then posting transactions to a general ledger.

- You don't need a fancy billing and accounts receivable system. Quicken enables you to perform record-keeping for accounts receivable. If you have fewer than two dozen transactions a month, Quicken provides a satisfactory solution.

> **Note**
>
> If your transactions are voluminous, you may want to consider a full-fledged accounts receivable package that prepares invoices, calculates finance charges, and easily handles high volumes of customer invoices and payments. You may want to use QuickBooks for DOS or QuickBooks for Windows, Intuit's new software for small businesses.

■ You don't need an automated inventory record-keeping system. Although Quicken enables you to track other assets, such as inventory, the program doesn't enable you to track the number of units of these other assets—only the dollars.

What This Book Contains

Using Quicken for Windows 3 consists of 23 chapters (divided into 6 parts) and two appendixes. The following sections provide an overview of what each chapter discusses.

> **Note**
>
> If you read the book from cover to cover, you may notice a little repetition in some places. Repetition is inevitable because the book also serves as a reference.

Part I: Learning Quicken for Windows

Part I, "Learning Quicken for Windows," includes eight chapters that, as the title implies, help you learn the basics of Quicken so that you can perform most tasks.

Chapter 1, "Preparing To Use Quicken for Windows," guides you through the steps you need to take before you start using Quicken for Windows, including ordering any preprinted forms you will need, learning to use the system, choosing a starting date, and setting up Quicken to print (if you haven't printed with other Windows applications).

Chapter 2, "Learning Your Way around Quicken for Windows," gives you a quick introduction to the mechanics of actually working with the program. You learn how to start the program, use the menu bar and the Iconbar to choose commands and options, tap into Quicken's on-line help feature, and exit the program when your work is finished. If you already have started using Quicken for Windows, you may want to skim this material.

Chapter 3, "Defining Your Accounts," walks you through the steps to set up the accounts that you will use in Quicken, such as your bank or checking account, credit card accounts, and so forth. The chapter also describes a few basic concepts you need to know from the start if you will be using Quicken for more than just a single bank account.

Chapter 4, "Organizing Your Finances," discusses one of Quicken's optional and most powerful features—the capability to categorize and classify your income and expenses. The categories make it easy to determine tax deductions, the amounts spent for various items, and the types of income that go into your bank accounts. The classes also enable you to look at specific groups of categories, such as expenses relating to specific clients, jobs, or properties. Chapter 4 defines Quicken's categories and classes, describes why and when you should use them, shows the predefined categories provided within Quicken, and explains how to use these categories. The chapter also outlines the steps for adding, deleting, and modifying your own categories and classes.

Chapter 5, "Writing and Printing Checks," describes one of Quicken's core features—the capability to print checks. The chapter includes instructions for completing the Write Checks window, where you provide the information Quicken needs to print a check. You also learn how to record, review, edit, and print checks. Not everyone wants or needs to use Quicken to print checks, but if you do, Chapter 5 is the place to start.

Chapter 6, "Using the Register," explains the steps for using Quicken's fundamental feature—its Register. This chapter gives a complete explanation of what the Register is, what information it contains, and how to use it. If you're not going to use Quicken to print checks, you need to understand how to use the Register so that you can enter your manual transactions in the program.

Chapter 7, "Using Quicken Shortcuts," describes how to use the special Quicken features to speed up your work in Quicken. This chapter describes some of the special Quicken features that, although not essential, can make check-writing faster and the Quicken Register easier to use.

Chapter 8, "Reconciling Your Bank Account," discusses one of the important steps you can take to protect your cash and the accuracy and reliability of your financial records. This chapter first reviews the reconciliation process in general terms and then describes the steps for reconciling your accounts in Quicken, correcting and catching errors, and printing and using the reconciliation reports that Quicken creates.

Part II: Getting the Most from Quicken for Windows

Part II, "Getting the Most from Quicken for Windows," consists of Chapters 9 through 13. In these chapters, you learn how to use Quicken for Windows to its maximum potential.

Chapter 9, "Managing Your Credit Cards," explains how to use Quicken's Credit Card Register to record credit card purchases and payments and reconcile your account against your credit card statements. And if you have a Quicken for Windows VISA card, Chapter 9 shows you how to set up an IntelliCharge account so that you can receive your credit card statements on disk or by modem.

Chapter 10, "Tracking Loans," explains how to use Quicken to keep track of amortized loans. You learn how to set up loans (such as mortgages, home equity loans, car loans, and so forth), make loan payments, refinance a loan, and delete a loan when it's paid in full. Quicken 3 for Windows handles variable interest rate loans and alternative loan calculation methods, including Canadian amortization. In Chapter 10, you also learn how to use Quicken's Loan Planner to compute loan variables (payment, principal, interest rate, and term).

Chapter 11, "Managing Your Assets and Other Liabilities," describes some of the special features that Quicken 3 for Windows provides for personal use. You can track cash and other assets (such as real estate), as well as liabilities (such as a non-amortized loan to a friend). Recording all your assets and liabilities in Quicken completes your financial picture so that you can assess your net worth at any given time.

Chapter 12, "Using Quicken To Prepare for Income Taxes," is a short but important chapter. This chapter tells you how to make sure that the financial records you create with Quicken for Windows provide the information you need to prepare your federal and state income tax returns. The chapter also briefly discusses the general mechanics of passing data between Quicken and an income tax preparation package, such as TurboTax.

Chapter 13, "Paying Your Bills Electronically," describes how you can use Quicken to pay your bills electronically by using the CheckFree service. Electronic payment isn't for everybody, but if you're a Quicken user, you should at least know what's involved and whether it makes sense for you.

Part III: Planning for the Future with Quicken

Part III, "Planning for the Future with Quicken," consists of Chapters 14 through 17. These chapters show you how to use Quicken beyond the basics to plan for your future financial needs.

Chapter 14, "Scheduling Future Transactions," shows you how to use Quicken's new Financial Calendar to schedule bills to be paid in the future. Using the Financial Calendar helps you avoid paying bills late and also helps you schedule your cash flows for future needs. You learn how to use the Financial Planning Worksheet to project your future cash flows and gauge your progress towards future goals.

Chapter 15, "Monitoring Your Investments," describes the Investment Register that Quicken provides for investors. With Quicken 3 for Windows, entering investment transactions is easier using new on-screen forms for buying and selling securities, recording investment income, selling short, buying and redeeming U.S. savings bonds, and numerous other activities. If you want to monitor your investments and stay on top of their performance, read through Chapter 16 to see the tools and options that Quicken provides specifically for managing investments.

Chapter 16, "Budgeting with Quicken," discusses one of Quicken's most significant benefits—budgeting and monitoring your success in following a budget. This chapter reviews the steps for budgeting, describes how Quicken helps with budgeting, and provides some tips on how to budget more successfully. If you aren't comfortable with the budgeting process, Chapter 16 should give you enough information to get started. If you find budgeting an unpleasant exercise, the chapter also provides some tips on making budgeting a more positive experience.

Chapter 17, "Saving for the Future with Quicken," explains how to use Quicken's new Savings Goal account to earmark funds to save toward specific goals. This chapter also shows you how to use three of Quicken's financial planners: the Investment Savings Planner, the Retirement Planner, and the College Planner. Quicken's financial planners help you play out "what-if" scenarios to see results quickly.

Part IV: Analyzing Your Finances with Quicken

Part IV, "Analyzing Your Finances with Quicken," shows you how to use Quicken to analyze your finances through the use of reports and graphs. Part IV consists of Chapters 18 and 19.

Chapter 18, "Creating and Printing Reports," shows you how to sort, extract, and summarize the information contained in the Quicken Registers by using the Reports options. Quicken's reports enable you to gain better control over and insight into your income, expenses, and cash flow.

Chapter 19, "Using Graphs To Analyze Your Finances," describes the Quicken graph feature. If you want to see relationships between your income and expenses, assets and liabilities, actual and budget amounts, and investment portfolios, read Chapter 19 to learn about the various graphs that you can create on-screen and print.

Part V: Managing Quicken for Windows

Part V, "Managing Quicken for Windows," shows you how to manage your Quicken files and customize the Quicken program. Part V consists of Chapters 20 and 21.

Chapter 20, "Managing Your Quicken Files," describes how to take care of the files that Quicken uses to store your financial records. This chapter describes how to back up and restore your Quicken files, make copies of the files, and purge from the files information you no longer need.

Chapter 21, "Customizing Quicken," describes how to change program preferences to customize, or fine-tune, Quicken's operation.

Part VI: Putting Quicken for Windows To Use

Part VI, "Putting Quicken for Windows To Use," moves away from the mechanics of using Quicken's features and tells how to use Quicken as a financial-management tool. This section of the book consists of Chapters 22 and 23.

Chapter 22, "Using Quicken for Home Finances," discusses how you can use Quicken for personal financial record-keeping. Using any software—particularly, a financial-management program—is more than mechanics. This chapter answers questions about where Quicken fits in for home users, how Quicken changes the way you keep your personal financial records, and when you should use Quicken options.

Chapter 23, "Using Quicken in Your Small Business," covers some of the special techniques and procedures for using Quicken in business accounting. This chapter begins by discussing the overall approach to using Quicken in a business. Next, the following basic accounting tasks are detailed: tracking receivables, tracking payables, tracking inventory, accounting for fixed assets, preparing payroll, and job costing.

Appendixes

Using Quicken 3 for Windows also provides two appendixes.

Appendix A, "Installing Quicken 3 for Windows," discusses the hardware and software requirements to use Quicken for Windows and shows you how to install the Quicken 3 for Windows program.

Appendix B, "Using QuickPay with Quicken," explains how to use the QuickPay payroll utility program with Quicken for Windows.

Conventions Used in This Book

A number of conventions are used in *Using Quicken 3 for Windows* to help you learn the program. The following examples for these conventions can help you distinguish the different elements in *Using Quicken 3 for Windows*.

CPA TIPS: Helpful Financial Advice

This book includes CPA tips, formatted the way this paragraph is formatted, to provide advice that will help you better manage your finances.

Tip
A paragraph in the margin (like this one) suggests an easier or alternative way to execute a procedure in Quicken.

Note

This paragraph format indicates additional information that may help you avoid problems or that should be considered in using the described features.

Caution

The paragraph format warns you of problems you may encounter when you are learning how to use Quicken.

The following special typefaces are used in this book:

Type	Meaning
italics	New terms or phrases when initially defined
boldface	Information you are asked to type, and letters that appear underlined on-screen in Quicken menu and dialog box options
`monospaced type`	Direct quotations of words that appear on-screen or in a figure

Names of menus and dialog boxes are shown with the initial letter capitalized. Commands and options also appear with initial capital letters (such as Open and Print).

Ctrl+Enter indicates that you press and hold the Ctrl key while you press the Enter key. Other key combinations, such as Shift+Tab and Alt+H, are performed in the same manner.

Part I

Learning Quicken for Windows

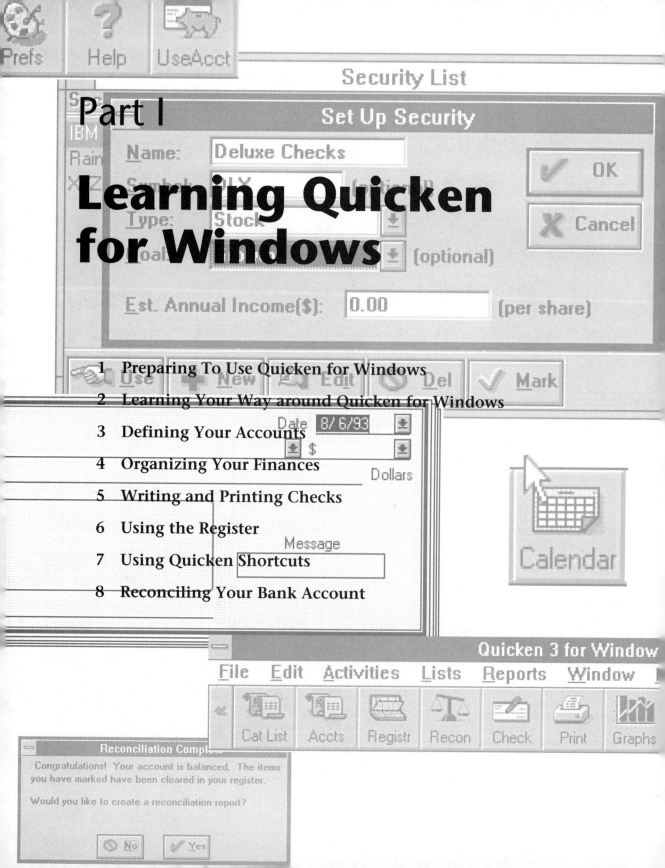

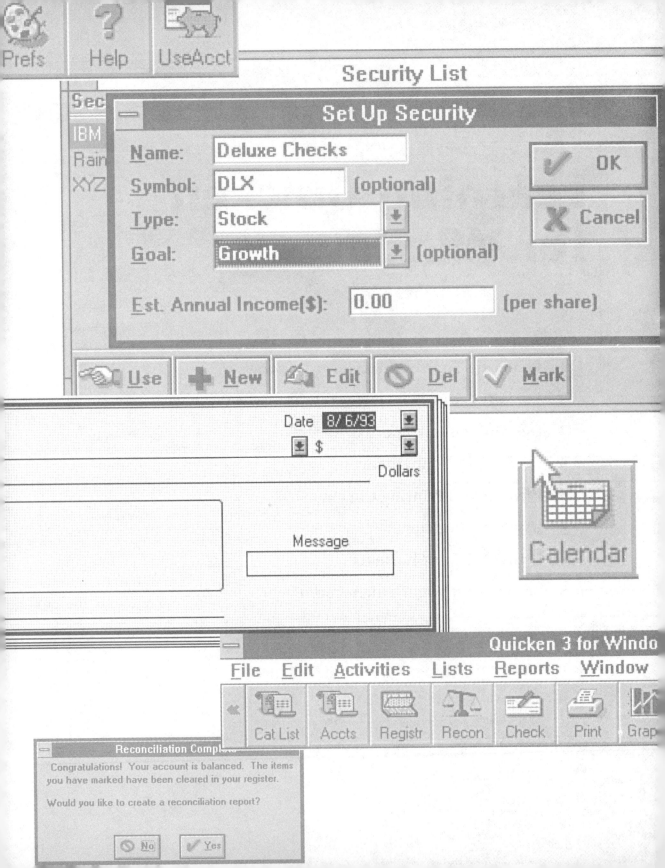

Chapter 1

Preparing To Use Quicken for Windows

Preparing to use Quicken for Windows isn't difficult. If you are new to computers, however, a little hand-holding and emotional support never hurts. Chapter 1 walks you through the steps for preparing to use Quicken for Windows. Don't worry that you may not know enough about computers, Quicken for Windows, or computer-based accounting systems. Simply follow the instructions and steps described in this chapter.

Choosing a Conversion Date

Choosing a conversion date is a critical decision you must make before you can enjoy the advantages of an automated accounting system. The *conversion date* is the day on which you stop using your old manual system and begin using your new Quicken system. The more frequently you expect to use Quicken, the more important is the conversion date.

Perhaps you don't intend to use Quicken to summarize income and expense transactions or to monitor how closely you are sticking to a budget; all you really want is a tool to help you maintain your checkbook and produce checks. If so, the conversion date isn't so important.

If you intend to use Quicken to organize your income-tax deductions, calculate business profits, or plan budgets, however, you should designate a clean accounting cutoff point for the date you begin keeping records with Quicken. From the conversion date forward, Quicken handles all your accounting information. Before the conversion date, your old accounting system still provides your accounting information.

In this chapter, you learn how to do the following:

- Choose a conversion date (the best date to start using Quicken to automate your finances)

- Start Quicken 3 for Windows for the first time and set up your Quicken system

- Order checks and other supplies from Intuit

- Prepare to print in Windows

Pick a natural cutoff date that makes switching from one system to another easy. Often the best time to begin a new accounting system is at the beginning of the year or your fiscal year. All income and expense transactions for the new year are then recorded in the same place. Picking a good cutoff date may seem trivial, but having all your tax deductions for one year recorded and summarized in one place can save you valuable time and effort.

Note

No matter which date you decide to use to begin your Quicken system, at any time you can enter transactions dated before your start date. Quicken automatically places previous transactions in the proper date order in the Register. Refer to Chapter 6, "Using the Register," to learn how to enter transactions in the Register.

Tip
To start using Quicken at the beginning of the month, first take time to summarize your accounting information from the old system. Make sure that you don't record the same transaction twice or forget any altogether.

If you can't start using Quicken at the beginning of the year, the next best time is at the beginning of a month. If you do start at the beginning of a month, you must combine your old accounting or record-keeping information with Quicken's information to get totals for the year. When calculating tax deductions, for example, you must add the amounts Quicken shows to whatever your old system shows.

The worst time to begin using Quicken is in the middle of a month. With no natural cutoff point, you are even more likely than at the beginning of a month to count some transactions on both systems and to forget to record others in either system.

Caution

Two common errors are possible after you choose an accounting cutoff date: you may record the same income or expense transaction in both systems and therefore count the transaction twice when you combine the two systems to get your annual totals, or you may neglect to record a transaction in one system because you think you recorded it in the other system. Your records will be wrong if you make either error. To ensure that you have entered the appropriate transactions in Quicken, be sure to review the transactions in the Register against those in your manual system.

> **CPA TIP: Document Your Deductions**
>
> If you use data from your manual system and your Quicken system to complete your income tax return, make sure that you keep adequate worksheets and documentation for any items you deduct. If audited, you want your documentation to show clearly that you added amounts from your manual system to your Quicken system to arrive at your deductions.

Starting Quicken 3 for Windows

You can start Quicken in one of two ways. The easiest way is to start Quicken when you start Windows. Rather than type **win** at the DOS prompt (which just starts Windows), type **win qw** to start Windows and cause Windows to start Quicken.

Another way to start Quicken is from the Quicken program group window (after you start Windows). If the Quicken program group window is displayed, you can start Quicken by double-clicking the Quicken icon (quickly click the left mouse button twice in a row). You also can start Quicken by highlighting the Quicken icon and pressing Enter.

The first time you start Quicken, a dialog box appears to ask whether you want to learn more about Windows by seeing the Windows Tutorial. If you are a new Windows user, choose Yes to view the Tutorial. Otherwise, choose No. If you aren't running Windows 3.1 or using a VGA monitor, Quicken doesn't present the Windows Tutorial.

After you view the Windows Tutorial or choose No, Quicken asks whether you want to see the Quicken Tutorial for an introduction to Quicken. If you are a new Quicken user, choose Yes to view the Quicken Tutorial. Otherwise, choose No. If you aren't using a VGA monitor, Quicken doesn't present the Quicken Tutorial.

Next, the First Time Setup dialog box appears (see fig. 1.1). If you have used previous versions of Quicken for Windows or Quicken for DOS, you can choose Cancel at the First Time Setup dialog box. Previous Quicken users can begin using Quicken 3 for Windows by simply selecting a Quicken file from the File menu.

If you've never used Quicken before, the first-time setup procedure enables you to create a new data file and select the categories that you want to use in Quicken.

Fig. 1.1

The First Time Setup dialog box appears the first time you start Quicken 3 for Windows.

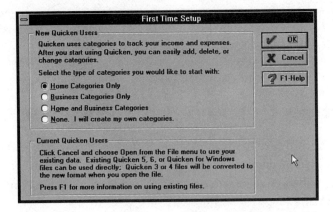

Setting Up Your Quicken System

If you're new to Quicken, you can set up your system quickly by selecting a predefined category list (the list of categories that you want to use to classify your income and expenses) and creating your first account (usually a bank account). If you have used Quicken before (Windows or DOS), setting up your Quicken system is simple; just show Quicken where your previous version data file is and open the file. Quicken automatically updates files from previous versions of Quicken for use in the new version.

If you previously used Quicken for DOS or previous versions of Quicken for Windows, read the section "Setup for Current Quicken for Windows Users" or "Setup for Quicken for DOS Users" later in this chapter. If you are new to Quicken, proceed with the next section.

Note

As you begin to use Quicken, notice the message boxes that appear on-screen. These boxes, called *Qcards*, are brief help messages that appear at places you are likely to need help entering information. You learn more about Qcards in Chapter 2, "Learning Your Way around Quicken for Windows."

Setup for New Quicken Users

If you're new to Quicken, you need to establish your Quicken data file, select the categories that you want to use in Quicken, and set up your first account. When you start Quicken the first time, a data file named QDATA.QDT is created automatically. Quicken stores all your accounts, categories, classes, and memorized transactions in this file. (Chapter 20, "Managing Your Quicken Files," further explains your Quicken files.) You can change the name of this file by renaming the file. Refer to Chapter 20 to learn how to rename Quicken files.

A *category* describes and summarizes common income and expenses, such as salary, insurance, utilities, and so on. Categories group your income and expenses so that Quicken can classify your transactions for reporting, graphing, budgeting, and income-tax purposes. In simple terms, categories describe where your money comes from and where it goes. (Chapter 4, "Organizing Your Finances," describes Quicken's categories in more detail.)

Accounts in Quicken are similar to the accounts you use to keep track of your transactions—such as checking, savings, and credit card accounts.

For new users of Quicken, set up your system by following these steps:

1. In the First Time Setup dialog box (refer to fig. 1.1), select the predefined categories that you want to use. Quicken includes three predefined sets of categories, for home, business, and for both home and business. If you want to use Quicken's categories, you can tell Quicken to use one of the predefined category lists. If you don't want to use one of Quicken's predefined category lists, you can choose None and then create your own list.

   ### Caution

   Now is the only time you can choose to use one of the predefined category lists. After your data file is created, you can't go back and change to another of these category lists. Be sure to choose the category list that works best for you. If you plan to use Quicken in your business, make certain that you choose Business Categories Only instead of Home Categories Only so that you don't need to modify the list completely to make it appropriate for business use.

   Select Home Categories Only if you want to use Quicken's home categories. Select Business Categories Only if you want to use business categories. If you want to use Quicken to track your personal and business activities within the same file, select the Home and Business Categories option button. If you don't want to use either category list, select None.

> **Note**
>
> When you select None, you must create your own list if you plan to use categories to classify your transactions in Quicken. Chapter 4, "Organizing Your Finances," explains how to add categories.

2. Choose OK or press Enter. Quicken displays the Select Account Type dialog box so that you can create your first account in Quicken (see fig. 1.2).

Fig. 1.2
Use the Select Account Type dialog box to create an account in Quicken. Usually, the first account you create is a bank account for your checking account.

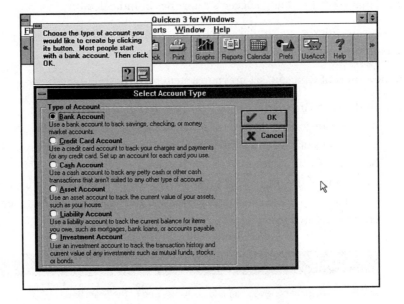

3. Choose the account type that you want to create by choosing the appropriate option button in the Select Account Type dialog box. To create a bank account, for example, choose the Bank Account option button.

4. Choose OK or press Enter. The New Account Information dialog box appears (see fig. 1.3).

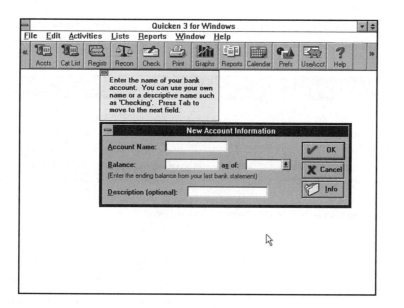

Fig. 1.3

Use the New Account Information dialog box to enter information about the new account that you are creating.

> **Note**
>
> Usually, you will create a bank account first so that you can begin using Quicken for your checking account activities. Chapter 3, "Defining Your Accounts," further explains the account types in Quicken. There, you will find a complete explanation of each account type and when it should be used.

5. In the Account Name text box, type the new bank account name, using up to 15 characters (including spaces). You can't use the following characters in an account name:

> :] [/ | ^

For example, type your bank's name, such as **First National**, or just use the name Checking.

Press Tab to move to the next text box.

6. In the Balance text box, enter the starting account balance by typing the dollar amount (no dollar sign is necessary). For example, to enter $1,345.89, type **1345.89**.

For bank accounts, this dollar amount is your current account balance according to your records. For best results, use the ending balance from your last bank statement as the starting balance. You must enter a balance, even if it is 0.

> **Caution**
>
> When you enter the ending balance from your last bank statement as the starting balance in your bank account, you must enter all uncleared transactions in the Bank Account Register. In other words, you must include all transactions that haven't cleared through your bank account by the current date (the date you start using Quicken). If you overlook these transactions, you will have difficulty reconciling your account. Chapter 6, "Using the Register," explains how to use the register.

7. Press Tab to move to the As Of text box and type the date on which the balance you entered is correct. You also can click the drop-down arrow to display Quicken's mini-calendar and select the appropriate As Of date. (Refer to Chapter 7, "Using Quicken Shortcuts," to learn how to use the Quicken calendar.) If you use the ending balance from your last bank statement, enter the statement date in the As Of text box.

8. (Optional) If you want, press Tab to move to the Description text box and type a description of the account, using up to 21 characters. For example, you might want to include an account number or a short phrase that describes the account, like **Checking**, **Savings**, or **Money Market**. The account's description appears next to the account name in the Account list.

9. When the information in the New Account Information dialog box is complete, choose OK or press Enter to create the account.

Tip
Now that you have set up your first account, review Chapter 2 for a complete explanation of Quicken fundamentals.

Quicken displays the register for the account that you just created. Figure 1.4 displays the Bank Account Register for the bank account named *First National*, described as a *Checking account*.

> **Note**
>
> All transactions relating to your bank account are entered in the Bank Account Register, such as checks, deposits, and ATM withdrawals.

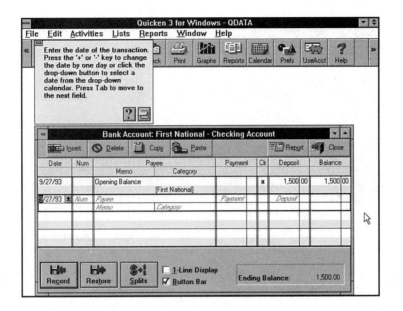

Fig. 1.4
The Bank Account Register appears after you create a bank account.

Setup for Current Quicken for Windows Users

If you have been using Quicken for Windows Version 1 or 2, you quickly can upgrade the current version of your program to Version 3. When you install Quicken 3 for Windows (see Appendix A), the program converts previous version files to Quicken 3. Your Quicken 1 or 2 files, however, aren't changed in any way. You still may use Quicken 1 or 2 files after installing Quicken 3 for Windows.

Before you can begin using Quicken 3 for Windows after it's installed, you must show Quicken where your data files are located and open the data file that you want to use. After you open your data file in Quicken, your system is set up and you're ready to begin using the new version of Quicken.

To set up your Quicken system with previous Quicken for Windows version data files, follow these steps:

1. Choose File from the menu bar at the top of the Quicken screen. Quicken displays the File menu, shown in figure 1.5.

2. From the File menu, choose Open. You also can choose the File Open command by pressing Ctrl+O. Quicken displays the Open Quicken File dialog box (see fig. 1.6).

Fig. 1.5
The File menu includes the Open command so that you can open other Quicken files.

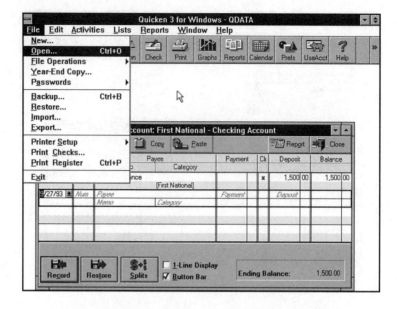

Fig. 1.6
The Open Quicken File dialog box lists all other Quicken files. You can change the directory and/or the drive where Quicken looks for data files.

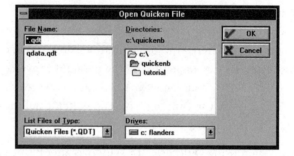

3. In the File Name list box, choose the Quicken for Windows Version 1 or 2 file that you want to use. If necessary, change the directory in the Directories list box by double-clicking the directory name. Also, if necessary, change the drive where Quicken looks for data files in the Drives drop-down list box. Note that Quicken automatically selects Quicken Files (*.QDT) as the type of files to locate in the List Files of Type drop-down list box.

Quicken opens the file that you selected. You're now ready to use Version 3 of Quicken for Windows.

Setup for Quicken for DOS Users

If you have been using Quicken for DOS Version 5 or 6, your existing files are updated automatically when you install Quicken 3 for Windows. Quicken reads your existing Quicken 5 or 6 files directly and converts your data, but doesn't change your data. You still can use Quicken for DOS files after installing Quicken 3 for Windows.

If you have been using Version 3 or 4 of Quicken for DOS, Quicken updates your files when you open them; however, you can't reopen updated files with Quicken 3 or 4 after you use them with Quicken 3 for Windows.

Before you can begin using Quicken 3 for Windows after it's installed, you must show Quicken where your data files are located and open the data file that you want to use. After you open your data file in Quicken, your system is set up and you're ready to begin using the new version of Quicken for Windows.

To set up your Quicken system with Quicken for DOS (Version 3, 4, 5, or 6) files, follow these steps:

1. Choose File from the menu bar at the top of the Quicken screen. Quicken displays the File menu (refer to fig. 1.5).

2. From the File menu, choose Open. (You can also select the File Open command by pressing Ctrl+O.) Quicken displays the Open Quicken File dialog box (refer to fig. 1.6).

3. From the File Name list box, select the Quicken for DOS file that you want to use. If necessary, change the directory in the Directories list box by double-clicking the directory name. Also, if necessary, change the drive where Quicken looks for data files in the Drives drop-down list box. Note that Quicken automatically selects Quicken Files (*.QDT) as the type of files to locate in the List Files of Type drop-down box.

Quicken opens the file that you selected. You're now ready to use Quicken Version 3 for Windows.

Ordering Check Forms and Other Supplies

You don't need to use Quicken for Windows to print your checks to benefit from the program, but Quicken's check-writing feature is a time-saver. The time saved, however, doesn't come cheaply. Expect to pay between $40 and $90 for 250 computer check forms. Usually, you will spend more for check forms in the course of a year than you originally spent for the Quicken software.

Obviously, you want to make sure that you make the right decision about ordering checks. Two situations merit the expense of check forms: you write many checks at home or at work (more than two dozen each month), or you plan to use Quicken for Windows for a business and want the professional appearance of computer-printed checks.

> **Note**
>
> You still will use manual checks (those you write by hand) even if you choose to use Quicken check forms. Home users, for example, need manual checks for trips to the grocery or the department store. And business owners need manual checks for unexpected deliveries that require immediate cash payments (when access to a computer isn't available).

If you decide to use Quicken to print checks, you must order preprinted check forms for every bank account for which you want computer-printed checks. The least expensive and easiest source of preprinted check forms is Intuit, the manufacturer of Quicken. Intuit offers laser and continuous-feed checks. You also can order from Intuit other supplies, such as deposit slips, double-window envelopes, and stationery.

To order from Intuit, complete and mail the order form included in the Quicken for Windows package. Intuit prints checks with your name and address at the top of the check and the bank and account information at the bottom. Or choose the Order Supplies option from the Activities menu (described later in this chapter) to generate an order form for the checks and any additional supplies you need. You can also fax your order for checks and supplies to Intuit at (415) 852-9146.

Deciding Which Checks To Use

When you order preprinted checks, you make choices about size, style, or color, and you decide whether the check is multipart or has voucher stubs. Intuit offers continuous-feed check forms and laser check forms. Table 1.1 summarizes your options for continuous-feed forms; table 1.2 shows options for laser forms.

CPA TIP: Choosing a Starting Number for Preprinted Checks

When choosing a starting number for your computer checks, consider two points. First, start the computer-printed check form numbers far enough away from your manual check numbers so that the numbers don't overlap or duplicate (duplications can cause confusion in your record-keeping and reconciliations). Second, start your computer-printed checks with a number that quickly shows you whether you wrote a check manually or with Quicken. For example, if your manual checks start with the number 1 (like 14356), you might start your computer checks with the number 5 (like 55000).

Table 1.1 Quicken Check Form Options for Continuous-Feed Printers

Name	Colors	Form Size (inches)	Number of Parts	Comments
Antique Standard	Tan	3 1/2 x 8 1/2	1	*Antique* refers to parchment background; printed three to a sheet
Classic Standard	Blue or Green	3 1/2 x 8 1/2	1, 2 or 3	Printed three to a sheet
Prestige Standard	Gray	3 1/2 x 8 1/2	1 or 2	You can choose blue, green, or maroon accent stripe; printed three to a sheet
Prestige Voucher	Gray	7 x 8 1/2	1 or 2	You can choose blue, green, or maroon accent stripe; larger form size due to voucher stub
Classic Voucher	Blue or Green	7 x 8 1/2	1, 2, or 3	8 1/2 x 10 1/2 sheets
Antique Wallet	Tan	2 13/16 x 6	1	Has a 2 1/2-inch check-size stub; overall form width is 8 1/2 inches
Classic Wallet	Blue or Green	2 13/16 x 6	1	Has a 2 1/2-inch check-size stub; overall form width is 8 1/2 inches

Table 1.2 Quicken Check Form Options for Laser Printers

Name	Colors	Form Size (inches)	Number of Parts	Comments
Standard	Blue or Green	3 1/2 x 8 1/2	1	8 1/2-by-11-inch sheets, each with three-check forms, fit into printer paper tray
Voucher	Blue or Green	3 1/2 x 8 1/2	1 or 2	8 1/2-by-11-inch sheets, each with one-check form, fit into printer paper tray
Antique Wallet	Tan	2 13/16 x 6	1	Has a 2 1/2-inch check-size stub; overall form width is 8 1/2 inches
Classic Wallet	Blue or Green	2 13/16 x 6	1	Has a 2 1/2-inch check-size stub; overall form width is 8 1/2 inches

CPA TIP: Using Quicken To Print Checks

Printing checks with Quicken assures that you don't fall behind in entering your financial transactions. When you write manual checks, putting off entering transactions for those checks in Quicken for Windows is easy. As a result, you may find that you have several transactions to enter in Quicken at one time if you let yourself fall behind.

You are on your own when selecting the color, size, and lettering style of your check forms. The following discussion, however, offers some hints about choosing the number of parts your check form can have and about deciding whether you want a voucher stub (or a copy of the transaction) on your checks.

The number of parts in a check refers to the number of printed copies. With a one-part check, only the actual check form that you sign is printed. With a two-part check, a copy is printed at the same time as the original. With a three-part check, you get two copies plus the original.

Multipart forms probably aren't necessary for most home uses. In a business, however, you can attach the second parts to paid invoices as a fast and convenient way of keeping track of which checks paid which invoices. You can place the third copy of a check in a numerical sequence file to help you identify the payee more quickly than you can by using the check number alone.

Note

If you use multipart checks, keep in mind that the check forms may wear out your dot-matrix printer's head (the points that strike the printer ribbon and cause characters to be printed) or may cause your laser or inkjet printer to run out of ink more quickly. Check your printer's multipart form rating by referring to your printer manual. Verify that your printer is rated for at least the number of parts you want to print.

The voucher stub, also called the *remittance advice*, is the blank piece of paper attached to the check form. The voucher stub, which is approximately the same size as the check form, provides extra space for you to describe, or document, the reason for writing the check. You also can use this area to show any calculations involved in arriving at the total check amount. You can use the voucher stub space to describe how an employee's payroll amount was calculated, for example, or to define the invoices for which that check was issued. As with multipart checks, voucher stubs probably make more sense for business use rather than home use.

If you are unsure about which check forms to choose, try Quicken's starter kit. The starter kit costs about $35 as of this writing and includes 250 checks to give you a chance to experiment with preprinted check forms.

Using Quicken To Order Supplies

Quicken includes an Order Supplies option (from the Activities menu) that you can use to generate an Intuit Supplies Order Form. Intuit phone numbers also are displayed, for additional information about Quicken supplies. When you select this option, Quicken prints a three-page order form. Complete the order form and mail it to

> Intuit Supplies
> P.O. Box 51470
> Palo Alto, CA 94303

Be sure to enclose your check or money order if you are paying by either method.

Preparing To Print

If you have been printing reports or documents using other Windows applications, you're ready to print checks, reports, lists, and graphs with Quicken. See Chapter 5, "Writing and Printing Checks"; Chapter 18, "Creating and Printing Reports"; and Chapter 19, "Using Graphs To Analyze Your Finances," to learn how to customize printer settings, use other printers, or choose a different paper size and orientation.

> **Note**
>
> If you haven't printed from a Windows application, you must set up Windows to use your printer or printers before you can print from Quicken.

To set up Windows to use your printer(s), follow these steps:

1. Type **win** at the DOS prompt and press Enter to start the Windows program.

2. Make sure that the Program Manager window is active. If it isn't, double-click the Program Manager icon or press Ctrl+Esc to display the Windows Task List. From the Windows Task List, choose Program Manager, or use the arrow keys to highlight Program Manager and press Enter.

3. From the Program Manager, locate the Control Panel icon (usually in the Main group). Double-click the Control Panel icon to display the Control Panel window.

4. From the Control Panel window, double-click the Printers icon to display the Printers dialog box.

5. Examine the printer shown in the Default Printer box to see whether the correct default printer and printer port (such as LPT1) appears. If it doesn't, select a printer from the Installed Printers list box and choose the Set As Default Printer button.

6. If you want to install other printers to use with Quicken for Windows, choose the Add button and select a printer name from the List of Printers. Choose Install and follow the on-screen instructions.

Summary

This chapter described the steps you take in preparing to use Quicken. You learned the following:

- How to choose the conversion date, or the date that you should start using Quicken

- How to start Quicken the first time after you install the program

- How to set up your Quicken system if you're a new user, current Quicken for Windows user, or a Quicken for DOS user

- How to order preprinted checks that you use to write checks with Quicken (you can use your Quicken program to generate order forms to order checks and other supplies from Intuit)

- How to set up Windows to print from your Quicken application

Now you are ready to begin using Quicken. Before you start writing checks, entering actual checks and deposits, or reconciling accounts, however, take a few minutes to review the next chapter. Chapter 2, "Learning Your Way around Quicken for Windows," covers the basics of using Quicken and makes getting the most from Quicken that much easier. You learn your way around the Quicken application window, how to choose menu commands and options using the mouse and keyboard, how to switch between Quicken windows, and how to get help when you need it.

Learning Your Way around Quicken for Windows

Now that you have your Quicken system set up, you're ready to learn the basics of the Quicken program. Quicken 3 for Windows is easy to use, especially when you begin by learning the operations described in this chapter.

Starting Quicken

In Chapter 1, you learned how to start Quicken for the first time. You start your second session almost the same way; however, you don't have to bother with selecting categories or opening your Quicken file this time.

> **Note**
>
> When you exit Quicken, the file that you were using is saved and reopened the next time that you start the program.

To start Quicken, follow these steps:

1. At the DOS prompt, type **win** and press Enter.

2. From the Windows opening screen, move the mouse pointer to the Quicken icon in the Quicken group window.

3. Double-click (press the left mouse button twice in quick succession) the Quicken icon to start the program. (Mouse operations are explained in more detail later in this chapter.)

Quicken starts and opens the last file that you used.

In this chapter, you learn how to do the following:

- Start the program

- Use the mouse and keyboard

- Use quick keys

- Use Quicken menus

- Use the Iconbar

- Arrange the desktop

- Use Qcards for step-by-step help

- Use Quicken's on-line Help system

- Exit Quicken when your work is finished

Reviewing the Quicken Application Window

When you start Quicken, the Quicken application window and the Quicken file that you last used opens automatically. (Refer to Chapter 20, "Managing Your Quicken Files," to learn how to open other Quicken files.) The Quicken application window appears, as you see in figure 2.1. (Note that other windows may appear on-screen, depending on which windows were open when you last used Quicken.) Before you begin to learn your way around Quicken for Windows, review the Quicken application window.

Fig. 2.1

The Quicken application window appears when you start the program. Included in the Quicken application window are the title bar, menu bar, and Iconbar.

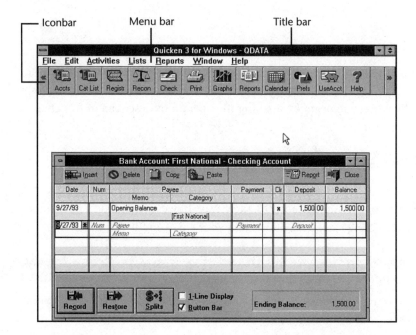

At the top of the window is the *title bar*. Title bars are a common element in all Windows programs. The title bar indicates which program you are using and the file name. In figure 2.1, `Quicken 3 for Windows - QDATA` appears in the title bar. You're working in Quicken 3 for Windows and using the QDATA file.

Under the title bar, the Quicken *menu bar* appears. The menu bar includes seven menus with commands and options for performing activities in Quicken. Using the menu bar is explained in the section "Using Quicken Menus" later in this chapter.

The next row of icons is called the *Iconbar*. The Iconbar contains icons (or pictures) that represent Quicken commands or options. Selecting commands or options from the Iconbar is much easier than selecting the same commands or options from the menu bar. Using the Iconbar is discussed later in the section "Using the Quicken Iconbar."

In the following sections of this chapter, you learn how to move around the Quicken application window and how to choose the commands and options that you use to perform activities in Quicken.

Working with the Mouse and Keyboard

Quicken, as with most Windows programs, works equally well with a mouse or the keyboard to move around the screen or choose commands. The mouse probably makes learning and searching through the program menus easier. Sometimes, however, using a combination of the mouse and keyboard is the most efficient way to work within Quicken.

Using the Mouse

Reference to the mouse was made when you started Quicken for the first time. With a mouse you can open menus, choose commands, and perform other operations. You probably noticed that the mouse pointer on-screen is in the shape of an arrow. Actually, the shape of the mouse pointer can change depending on the operation you are performing.

Following is a list of basic mouse shapes that you will see on-screen:

Mouse shape on-screen	Operation
Arrow pointer	Selects or chooses menus, commands, or options
I-beam	Moves the cursor or selects text to be edited
Hourglass	Waits while the program works
Double-sided arrow	Resizes the window

To move the mouse pointer around the screen, move the mouse on your desk or mouse pad in the same direction that you want the mouse pointer to move. When you have moved the mouse pointer to where you want it, you can follow any of these procedures:

■ *Click*. Press the left mouse button once.

■ *Double-click*. Press the left mouse button twice in quick succession.

■ *Drag*. Hold down the left button and move the mouse on your desk or mouse pad.

Throughout this book, the preceding terms are used to explain how to select menus, commands, and options with a mouse.

Using the Keyboard

You enter text and numbers into Quicken text boxes and fields by using the keys on the keyboard. You also can use the keyboard to choose menus, commands, and options. You learn how to use the keyboard to choose menu commands in the section "Using Quicken Menus" later in this chapter.

Using Quick Keys

Quick keys can save you steps in choosing menus, commands, or options when using the keyboard. Quick keys usually combine the Ctrl, Alt, or Shift key with a letter key or a function key, but also may be a single function key. Quick keys are listed to the right of the command or option name in the menu, as shown in figure 2.2.

> **Note**
>
> Throughout this book, instructions for using the Ctrl, Alt, or Shift key with another key appear as Alt+*letter* (as in Alt+F, for example). This notation indicates that you press and hold the first key while you then press the second key. If the second key is a letter key, the key you press can be in upper- or lowercase.

Table 2.1 lists the quick keys that you can use in Quicken to access menus, select commands and options, and move more quickly within the program.

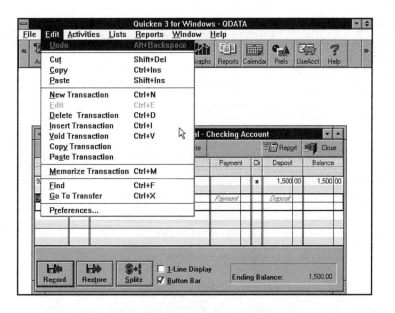

Fig. 2.2
Quick keys are listed next to the menu command or option. Use quick keys to select menu commands and options from the keyboard.

Learning Quicken

Table 2.1 Quick Keys To Perform Quicken Functions

Quick Key	Function
Ctrl+A	Displays the Account list
Ctrl+B	Backs up the current file
Ctrl+C	Displays the Category & Transfer list
Ctrl+D	Deletes a transaction or split line
Ctrl+E	Edits a transaction or split line
Ctrl+F	Finds a transaction
Ctrl+H	Sets up a loan
Ctrl+I	Inserts a transaction
Ctrl+J	Schedules a transaction
Ctrl+K	Displays the Financial Calendar
Ctrl+L	Displays the Class list
Ctrl+M	Memorizes a transaction
Ctrl+N	Goes to a new transaction line
Ctrl+O	Opens a file

(continues)

Table 2.1 Continued	
Quick Key	**Function**
Ctrl+P	Prints the current Register or checks
Ctrl+R	Uses the Register
Ctrl+T	Recalls a memorized transaction
Ctrl+U	Changes the Investment Register to Portfolio View
Ctrl+V	Voids a transaction
Ctrl+W	Displays the Write Checks window
Ctrl+X	Goes to a transfer transaction
Ctrl+Y	Displays the Security list
Alt+Backspace	Undoes the last edit
Shift+Del	Removes the selected transaction to the Windows Clipboard
Ctrl+Ins	Copies the selected transaction to the Windows Clipboard
Shift+Ins	Pastes the transaction from the Windows Clipboard
F1	Gets help on current window or menu

Using Quicken Menus

Quicken operates through commands and options. You access Quicken commands from separate menus contained in the menu bar at the top of the Quicken application window. Quicken commands are used to initiate an operation or procedure within the program, to display another menu of commands, or to display dialog boxes to select options. Options define how certain Quicken operations and procedures are performed and enable you to make selections.

Figure 2.3 shows the Quicken menu bar, which contains seven different menus: File, Edit, Activities, Lists, Reports, Window, and Help. These menus contain various Quicken commands. When you select a menu name from the menu bar, the menu is pulled down and displayed below the menu bar.

Menu bar

Fig. 2.3
The menu bar has seven menus that include commands and options to perform activities in Quicken.

Learning Quicken

Accessing Menus from the Menu Bar

To access menus from the Quicken menu bar, follow one these procedures:

- Place the mouse pointer on the name of the menu that you want to pull down and then click the menu name. To choose the File command on the menu bar, for example, place the mouse pointer on the word File and click.

- Press Alt to display the highlight bar, use the right- and left-arrow keys to move the highlight bar to the menu name on the menu bar that you want to select, and then press Enter.

  or

  Press the Alt in combination with the underlined letter in the menu name within the menu bar. For example, press Alt+F to access the File menu.

When you access a menu from the menu bar, Quicken displays the pull-down menu, as shown in figure 2.4.

Choosing Menu Commands and Options

You can use the mouse or the keyboard to choose commands from a menu. To choose commands from a menu by using the *mouse*, place the mouse pointer on the command that you want to choose and click.

To choose commands by using the *keyboard*, use one of the following procedures:

- Use the up- and down-arrow keys to highlight the command you want to choose, and then press Enter.

- Press the underlined letter within the command name. To choose the Delete command from the Edit menu, for example, press D.

Tip
A quick way to view all the Quicken pull-down menus, or lists of commands, is to use the right- and left-arrow keys to move the highlight bar from one menu name to another when one pull-down menu is displayed.

Fig. 2.4
A pull-down menu
appears when you
select a menu
name from the
menu bar.

Pull-down
menu

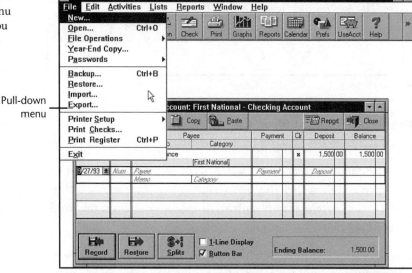

Note

Throughout the remainder of this book, the term *choose* relates to using the keyboard or mouse to choose a menu, command, or option. "Choose **File**," therefore, indicates that you should press Alt+F or click the word **File** on the menu bar.

Tip
You can choose
some commands
by using quick
keys. Quick keys
are listed to the
right of the command in the
menu. (Quick keys
are listed earlier in
this chapter in the
section "Using
Quick Keys.")

When a command from a pull-down menu is followed by ... (an ellipsis), Quicken displays another window or dialog box when you choose this command. When you choose the P**r**eferences... command from the Edit menu, for example, Quicken displays the Quicken for Windows Preferences dialog box (see fig. 2.5).

Removing Menus from the Screen

If you don't want to select a command or option from a pull-down menu on-screen, follow one of these procedures:

■ Click the menu name in the menu bar.

■ Press Esc to remove the menu; however, the highlight bar remains in the menu bar until you press Esc again.

Learning Quicken

Fig. 2.5
The Quicken for Windows Prefer-ences dialog box appears when you choose the Preferences... command from the Edit menu.

Using the Quicken Iconbar

Quicken displays an Iconbar beneath the menu bar at the top of the screen. The Iconbar contains icons (or pictures) along with text (or labels) so that you can select a Quicken window, list, or activity quickly.

> **Note**
>
> You can select icons from the Iconbar only by using the mouse. You can't use the keyboard to select an icon.

By default, the Iconbar contains the icons listed in table 2.2.

Table 2.2 The Default Icons on the Iconbar	
Icon	**Function**
Accts	Displays the Account list
Cat List	Displays the Category & Transfer list
Registr	Displays the Register for the current account
Recon	Displays the opening window to reconcile an account
Check	Displays the Write Checks window
Print	Prints the current Register or checks
Graphs	Displays the Create Graphs dialog box
Reports	Displays the Create Reports dialog box

(continues)

Table 2.2 Continued	
Icon	**Function**
Calendar	Displays the Financial Calendar
Prefs	Displays the Quicken for Windows Preferences dialog box
UseAcct	Opens the account that has been assigned to this icon
Help	Displays the Help window for the current Quicken window or menu

To select a function from the Iconbar, simply point to the icon with the mouse pointer and click.

Scrolling the Iconbar

If all the icons in the Iconbar aren't visible, you can scroll the Iconbar left or right by clicking the left- and right-arrow buttons at each end of the Iconbar (see fig. 2.6).

Fig. 2.6
Scroll through the icons in the Iconbar by clicking the left and right arrow buttons at each end of the Iconbar.

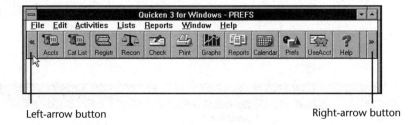

Left-arrow button   Right-arrow button

Changing the Iconbar Display

If you want to continue to display the Iconbar but want to change its size so that more of the application window is visible, you can choose to show only icons, only text, or icons and text.

To change the Iconbar display, follow these steps:

1. Choose Edit on the menu bar. Quicken displays the Edit menu.

2. From the menu, choose Preferences or press R.

   Quicken displays the Quicken for Windows Preferences dialog box, shown earlier in figure 2.5.

3. Choose the Iconbar preference button. Quicken displays the Customize Iconbar dialog box, shown in figure 2.7.

Fig. 2.7
Use the Customize
Iconbar dialog box
to change the
display of the
Iconbar. Select to
show icons only,
text only, or icons
and text.

Learning Quicken

4. Select the Show Icons check box if you want icons displayed on the Iconbar. Quicken enters a check mark in the check box (or removes an existing check mark). Quicken displays the change on the Iconbar.

    Select the Show Text check box if you want text displayed on the Iconbar. Quicken enters a check mark in the check box (or removes an existing check mark). Quicken displays the change on the Iconbar.

    If you want icons *and* text shown in the Iconbar, select the Show Icons and Show Text check boxes. (By default, Quicken shows icons and text in the Iconbar.) Quicken displays the change on the Iconbar.

5. Choose OK.

6. Choose Done in the Quicken for Windows Preferences dialog box.

> **Note**
>
> You can customize the Iconbar by adding icons, editing and deleting existing icons, setting up an icon to open a specific account, or setting up an icon to enter a specific transaction. Refer to Chapter 21, "Customizing Quicken," to learn how to customize the Iconbar.

Switching Between Windows

If you now are working with one Quicken window (such as the Write Checks window) and want to switch to another Quicken window (such as the Register window), the program saves your work in the current window.

To switch to another window, choose **Window** on the menu bar. Quicken lists all open windows, by number, in the lower part of the **Window** menu. Click the window that you want to switch to; you also can press the under-lined number of the window that you want to switch to.

You also can switch between windows by clicking the title bar of the window you want to switch to.

A third option for switching between windows involves the Control menu box. The Control menu box is the small box in the upper left corner of a window's title bar. When you click this box or press Alt+space bar, the Con-trol menu appears. The Control menu contains options for manipulating and switching windows. To switch to another Quicken window, select the Ne**x**t command from the Control menu or press Ctrl+F6.

Arranging the Desktop

The *desktop* refers to the way your screen now is arranged with respect to open windows and their position within the screen. You can arrange open windows in a cascading (or overlapping) format. If you have windows that have been reduced to icons, you also can arrange the icons within the Quicken screen. You also can clear your screen by closing all windows. Op-tions from the **Window** menu are used to arrange your desktop.

After you have the desktop the way you want it, with certain windows open and in the position you want them, you can save the desktop so that each time you open your Quicken file, windows and their position are exactly the same as the previous work session.

Arranging Windows and Icons

You can arrange windows in a cascade. If you're working in the Write Checks window, for example, you can open the Bank Account Register for your checking account and have it displayed behind (cascade) it. When you cas-cade windows, the window that appears on top is the active window.

To cascade windows, choose **Cascade** from the **Window** menu. Figure 2.8 shows how Quicken windows appear when they are cascaded. Notice that the Write Checks window is the active window because it appears on top.

You also can arrange icons (windows that you have reduced to a small picture by clicking the down arrow in the upper right corner of the window) hori-zontally at the bottom of the screen. To arrange icons, choose Arrange **I**cons from the **Window** menu.

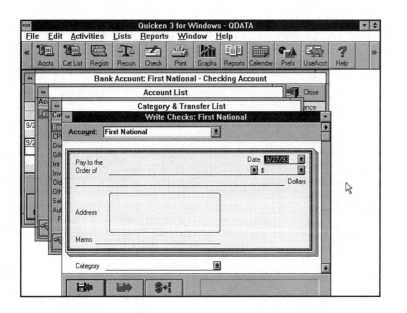

Fig. 2.8
Cascade Quicken windows by choosing Cascade from the Window menu.

Learning Quicken

Closing Windows

If you want to clear your screen, you can close all open windows and all windows that have been reduced to icons. To do so, choose Close All Windows from the Window menu.

Saving the Desktop when Exiting

As you work in Quicken, you may prefer to have the same windows open each time you start the program. You can instruct Quicken to save the open windows and their positions so that each time you start Quicken, the same windows are opened and in the saved position. You also can instruct Quicken to save the desktop automatically as it is displayed when you exit.

To save the current desktop to be displayed each time your Quicken file is opened, follow these steps:

1. Open the windows that you want to save and arrange them the way you want on the desktop.

2. Choose Preferences from the Edit menu or click the Prefs button from the Iconbar. Quicken displays the Quicken for Windows Preferences dialog box.

3. Choose the Desktop preference button to display the Save Desktop dialog box, shown in figure 2.9.

Fig. 2.9

With the Save Desktop dialog box, you can save the current desktop or save the desktop automatically as it appears when you exit Quicken.

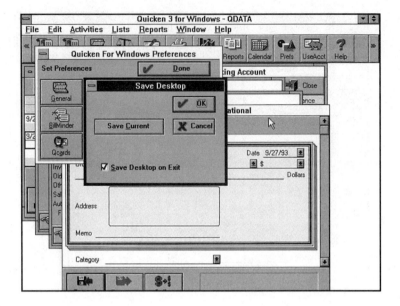

4. Choose the Save Current button.

5. Choose OK to save the current desktop.

To have Quicken automatically save the desktop as it appears when you exit the program, follow these steps:

1. Choose Preferences from the Edit menu or click the Prefs button on the Iconbar. Quicken displays the Quicken for Windows Preferences dialog box.

2. Choose the Desktop preference button to display the Save Desktop dialog box (refer to fig. 2.9).

3. Select the Save Desktop on Exit check box.

4. Choose OK.

Note

When you save the desktop, Quicken saves the desktop only in the current file. To save the desktop in other Quicken files, open each file and then select the appropriate desktop setting, as explained earlier.

Getting Help

Quicken provides a significant amount of on-screen help for users. Almost anytime you get stuck, you can turn to Quicken for help.

For beginning users, Quicken provides Qcards that serve as on-screen "cues" to help you with each item in a window or dialog box. The Qcard appears within a window or next to a dialog box and explains each part of the window or dialog box as you go.

On-screen information provides step-by-step help with Quicken windows so that you know the exact procedure for performing an activity. You can access the Quicken Help system at any time from almost any window.

If you want a brief tutorial on Quicken, you can take the Quick Tour. In the Quick Tour, you can select from 9 topics that each give a general overview of the program. If you're uncomfortable with Windows, you also can take the Windows tutorial.

These help options are described in the following sections.

Using Qcards

Quicken provides help and tips on various fields in a window or dialog box in rectangular boxes called *Qcards*. Qcards are on-screen cues to help you fill out each item in a window or dialog box. As you move from item to item, Quicken displays the appropriate Qcard for the current field. Each Qcard presents Help for the current field and, when applicable, shows the page number to turn to in the Quicken *User's Guide* for more information. Figure 2.10 shows the Qcard for the Date field in the Register.

The display of Qcards doesn't interfere with entering information or data in windows or dialog boxes. Qcards always are displayed within the current window or next to the current dialog box and don't prevent you from seeing the current field.

From a Qcard, you can access the Help system for additional help with the current window by clicking the question mark icon (refer to fig. 2.10). Quicken displays the Help window when you click the question mark icon.

To see where information for the current field or window is covered in the Quicken *User's Guide*, click the Notebook icon (refer to fig. 2.10).

Learning Quicken

Fig. 2.10
The Qcard for the
Date field in the
Register window.

Close button
Qcard

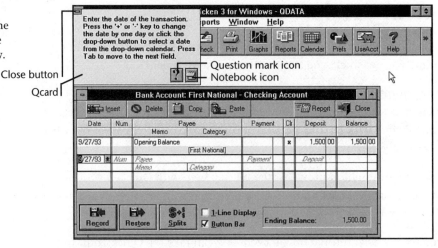

After you become comfortable with Quicken, you may want to turn off the
Qcard feature. You can remove Qcards from the current window or turn off
the Qcard feature completely so that Qcards are never displayed as you work
in Quicken. These options are discussed in the following sections.

Removing Qcards in the Current Window

You can turn off or remove Qcards from the current window without turning
off Qcards for other windows or dialog boxes by clicking the Close button at
the top left corner of the Qcard (refer to fig. 2.10).

Turning Off Qcards throughout the Program

If you're feeling comfortable with Quicken and don't need the added help
from the Qcards for any window or dialog box, you can turn the Qcards feature off (disable it) so that Qcards no longer appear.

To turn off Qcards throughout the program, follow these steps:

1. Choose Preferences from the Edit menu or click the Prefs button from
   the Iconbar. Quicken displays the Quicken for Windows Preferences
   dialog box.

2. Choose the Qcards preference button. Quicken displays the Qcard Preferences dialog box, shown in figure 2.11.

3. The status line reads Currently, ALL Qcards are ON. Choose the Qcards
   Off button. The status line changes to Currently, ALL Qcards are OFF.

4. Choose OK.

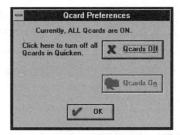

Fig. 2.11
The Qcard Preferences dialog box to turn the Qcard feature on or off.

If you need to turn Qcards back on, access the Qcard Preferences dialog box again, choose the Qcards On button, and then choose OK.

Using Quicken's On-Line Help System

Quicken's on-line Help system assists with menu commands and options, provides definitions of financial and Quicken terms, explains Quicken procedures (like writing checks or reconciling a bank account), and gives tips for using the program.

To get help information from the Help system, choose Quicken Help from the Help menu. Quicken displays the Welcome to Quicken 3 for Windows Help window on the left side of the screen and the Help Contents window on the right (see fig. 2.12).

Tip
Rather than choose Quicken Help from the Help menu, you can press F1 to access the Help system and display directions for the current window or dialog box.

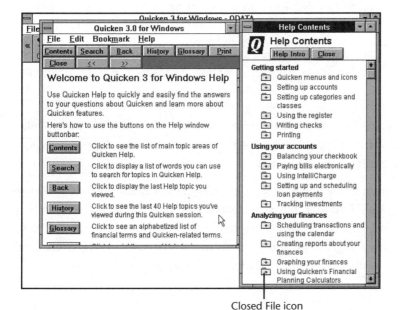

Closed File icon

Fig. 2.12
When you select Quicken Help from the Help menu, Quicken displays the window on the left that explains how to use the Help system and another window with a list of Help topics.

A window similar to the window on the left side of the screen in figure 2.12 appears each time you access the Quicken Help system. The Help Contents window (shown on the right in fig. 2.12) appears when you access the Help system when the desktop has no open Quicken windows, or when you select the Contents command button under the menu bar at the top of the Help window. (Help command buttons are explained later in this section.)

Using the Help Contents Window

The Help Contents window groups help topics into four general areas:

- Getting started

- Using your accounts

- Analyzing your finances

- Having Quicken work for you

To select a topic from the Help Contents window, follow these steps:

1. Click the Closed File icon to the left of the topic (refer to fig. 2.12). Quicken re-displays the Help Contents window and breaks out the topic that you selected into several subtopics.

Notice the Open File icon to the left of the topic that you selected, as shown in figure 2.13. A Page icon appears next to each subtopic.

2. Click the Page icon next to the subtopic that you want to view. Quicken displays the Help window (to the left) with information about the subtopic that you selected.

Figure 2.13 shows the Help window and the Help Contents window when you select the topic `Quicken menus and icons` and the subtopic `Choosing menu commands and clicking icons`.

To return to the original topics list in the Help Contents window, click the Help Intro button in the Help Contents window. Quicken displays a Help Intro message and instructs you to `click here`. The mouse pointer changes to a pointed finger when you point to the words `click here`. The Help Contents window displays the original topics with Closed File icons.

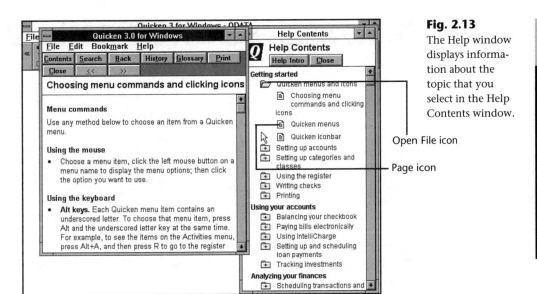

Fig. 2.13
The Help window displays information about the topic that you select in the Help Contents window.

Using the Help Window

The Help window is where Quicken displays help information on the topic that you select in the Help Contents window or on the current window or dialog box when you access the Help system. If, for example, the current window is the Write Checks window and you access the Help system (by pressing F1 or by clicking the Help button on the Iconbar, for instance), Quicken displays help information for writing checks in the Help window.

The Help window contains a menu bar at the top. The menu bar contains the menus listed in table 2.3.

Table 2.3 Help Window Commands

Menu	Commands	Description
File	Open	Opens a new Help file
	Print Topic	Prints the topic now in the help screen
	Print Setup	Sets printer options
	Exit	Exits the Help system and saves any annotations or bookmarks

(continues)

Table 2.3 Continued		
Menu	**Commands**	**Description**
Edit	Copy	Copies the text of the Help screen in the Windows Clipboard
	Annotate	Enables you to add your own notes or comments on the current help topic
Bookmark	Define	Enables you to place bookmarks at help topics
Help	Using Help	Accesses the How to Use Help window
	About Help	Displays copyright information

The Help window also includes nine command buttons that you can use to maneuver through the Quicken Help system. Not all command buttons are active at any given time; active command buttons are highlighted. Table 2.4 lists the command buttons and their functions.

Table 2.4 Help Window Command Buttons	
Command Button	**Function**
Contents	Displays the Help topics
Search	Displays a dialog box to use to define the Help topic you are looking for
Back	Returns to last Help topic displayed
History	Lists the Help topics that you have viewed in the order they were selected
Glossary	Displays an alphabetized list of financial terms and Quicken terms
Print	Prints the contents of the open Help window
Close	Closes the open Help window
<<	Displays the preceding Help window
>>	Displays the next Help window

To select a command button, place the mouse pointer on the button and click or press the Alt key in combination with the underlined letter in the command button name. To choose the **B**ack command button, for example, press Alt+B.

The help information displayed in Help windows often includes additional topics that you can select to see more information. Additional topics appear in green and are underlined. To select a topic from within a Help window, place the mouse pointer (your mouse pointer changes to the shape of a pointed finger when you point to an underlined topic) on any of the under-lined topics and click. Quicken displays the information on the topic that you selected in the Help window.

Closing Help Windows

After you finish reviewing a Help window or the Help Contents window, click the Close button. You also can close Help windows by selecting Close from the Control menu, by pressing Alt+F4, or by double-clicking the Control menu box.

Using the Tutorials

Quicken includes two tutorials that you can use to get a general overview of the Quicken program and the Windows program.

To view the Quicken Tutorial, follow these steps:

1. Choose Tutorials from the Help menu. Quicken displays the Tutorials submenu, shown in figure 2.14.

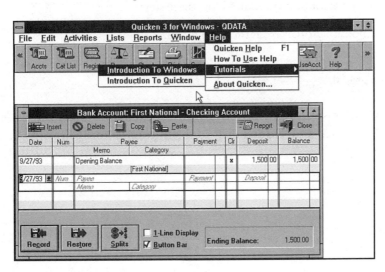

Fig. 2.14

You can choose to view the Quicken Tutorial or the Windows Tutorial from the Tutorials submenu.

Tip
To move forward
in the Tutorial,
click the right
arrow button; to
back up, click the
left arrow.

2. Choose Introduction To Quicken. Quicken displays the Quick Tour screen (see fig. 2.15).

3. Choose the topic button that you want to view. Quicken displays information on the topic that you selected.

4. When you're finished with Quick Tour, return to the Quick Tour screen (by choosing the Topics button) and choose Exit.

Fig. 2.15
The Quick Tour
screen includes
nine topics from
which you can
choose to get an
overview of the
activities per-
formed in
Quicken.

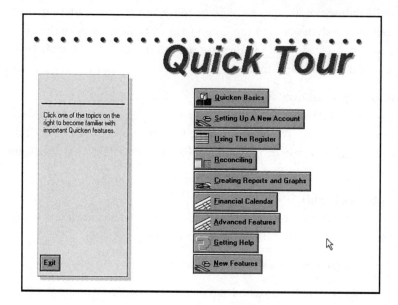

To view the Windows Tutorial, follow these steps:

1. Choose Tutorials from the Help menu.

2. Choose Introduction To Windows. Quicken begins the Windows Tutorial.

Follow the on-screen instructions to proceed with the Windows Tutorial. To exit the tutorial, press Esc and then press Y to confirm that you want to leave the tutorial.

Exiting the Program

After you finish working in Quicken, you need to exit the program so that you don't risk losing or damaging any of your financial data. To exit Quicken and to save your file, choose Exit from the File menu. Your Quicken file is saved automatically.

Caution

Don't exit Quicken by turning off your computer—otherwise, data from your current work session may not be saved!

CPA TIP: Back Up Your Files Before Exiting

No matter what level of computer experience you have, keeping backup copies of your company files is *always* advisable. You can back up your Quicken files each time you exit the program by choosing **B**ackup from the **F**ile menu. Refer to Chapter 20, "Managing Your Quicken Files," for more information on backing up your files before exiting Quicken.

Summary

In this chapter, you got a general view of Windows programs and also learned how to get around in Quicken. You learned the following:

- Your way around the Quicken for Windows application window

- About Quicken menus

- How to select menu commands and options using the mouse and keyboard

- How to use quick keys to select menu commands and options

- How to use the Quicken Iconbar buttons to choose menu commands and options, and how to change the Iconbar display

- How to arrange windows and icons and how to save the desktop so that Quicken remembers which windows to open each time you start the program

- How to use Qcards, Quicken's on-line Help system, and the Quicken and Windows Tutorials for guidance when you need it

- How to exit Quicken

If you need to define more than one bank account to use with Quicken, you now should read Chapter 3. If you need only one bank account defined, you are ready to learn the fundamentals of actually working with Quicken: setting up categories, writing and printing checks, using the register, and reconciling your bank account. These operations are covered starting in Chapter 4.

Chapter 3
Defining Your Accounts

If you followed the steps outlined in Chapter 1, "Preparing To Use Quicken for Windows," you already have defined one account (probably a bank account) as part of setting up your Quicken system. But you may have more than one checking account, one or two savings accounts, and even certificates of deposit for which you will keep records with Quicken. If you want to use Quicken to track more than one account, you need to define these accounts in Quicken. You then can use Quicken to record transactions in the accounts and track transfers between accounts.

You can add other Quicken account types (Credit Card, Cash, Asset, Liability, and Investment accounts) to your Quicken file so that you can record and track all your financial activity—not just transactions that occur in a bank account. These account types are explained in general later in this chapter, and more specifically in later chapters. This chapter also gives you some tips on creating accounts—information that should make working with multiple accounts easy.

Quicken stores accounts in the Account list, which includes the account name, account type, account description, number of transactions entered in the account, account balance, and number of checks to print (for bank accounts only). From the Account list, you can select to use an account, add a new account, edit an existing account, or delete an account.

In this chapter, you learn about the following:

- Quicken account types

- How to decide which accounts to add to your Quicken file

- How to add another account and add extra detail about an account

- How to access the Account list

- How to edit and delete accounts

- How to select an account to use

Defining Account Types

Before you go any further, you should learn a little more about accounts and the types of accounts that you can use in Quicken. A Quicken account is similar to the accounts you use to keep track of your transactions—such as checking, savings, and credit card accounts. You use other types of accounts to track the value of your assets and investments or the principal balance of your liabilities or debts. The types of accounts you can add and use in Quicken are as follows:

- *Bank account.* This account type is the most commonly used. Use bank accounts to set up your checking, savings, or money market accounts.

- *Credit Card account.* This type of account keeps track of your credit card activity, including purchases, payments, other credits, finance charges, and credit card fees. With Quicken for Windows, you can set up an IntelliCharge account to track your Quicken VISA card activity electronically. Chapter 9, "Managing Your Credit Cards," has more information about credit card accounts.

- *Cash account.* A Cash account keeps track of your cash expenditures, such as the cash you spend on vacations or dining out, or your business's petty cash fund. Chapter 11, "Managing Your Assets and Other Liabilities," has more information on how to use cash accounts.

- *Asset account.* Use this account type to record and track the value of the things you own, such as your home or auto, or your business's accounts receivable and fixed assets. You learn more about other asset accounts in Chapter 11, "Managing Your Assets and Other Liabilities."

    You also can set up an asset account as a Savings Goal account to keep track of money you want to put aside for a goal. You learn about setting up a Savings Goal account in Chapter 17, "Saving for the Future with Quicken."

- *Liability account.* Use this account type to record and track the debts you owe, such as the mortgage on your home or other outstanding loan balances. For a business, you can use the other liability account type to track accounts payable or a credit line with the bank. Chapter 10, "Tracking Loans," explains liability accounts used to track amortized loans in Quicken. Chapter 11, "Managing Your Assets and Other Liabilities," has more information on liability accounts for other types of loans.

- *Investment account.* Use Investment accounts to track your investments, such as stocks, bonds, and mutual funds. The investment account is an advanced feature in Quicken, so be sure to read Chapter 15, "Monitoring Your Investments," to learn about this account type.

You need only one account to start using Quicken: your bank account, the account from which you write checks and make deposits. If you're just learning Quicken, don't worry about setting up additional accounts. Chapters 4 through 8 explain how to enter transactions and write and print checks from your bank account. As you get up to speed with Quicken, start adding other accounts to your Quicken system to complete your financial picture.

Deciding Which Accounts To Add

When you first set up accounts for Quicken, adding accounts can get out of hand. You can define Quicken accounts for every checking account you have, regardless of whether the account is active. You also can define Quicken accounts for each of your savings accounts, credit union accounts, money market accounts, and perhaps even accounts for certificates of deposit. Rather than indiscriminately define accounts for every bank account you have, consider a few ideas and rules for determining which of your accounts should be Quicken accounts:

- If you want to write checks on the account by using Quicken, you must define a Quicken Bank account.

- If you want to use Quicken's reconciliation feature to explain differences between your records and the bank's, credit union's, or brokerage house's statement, you must define a Bank account.

- If you have transactions in an account that you want to include in Quicken's tax reports or profit-and-loss statements, you must define a Quicken account. You can have, for example, charitable contributions or mortgage interest transactions in separate Bank accounts.

The following factors indicate that you probably *don't* need to define a bank, credit union, or brokerage house account as a Quicken account:

- If you don't have any deposits into or withdrawals from the account other than interest income or bank service fees, your monthly statement will suffice for your financial records.

- If you have only a handful of transactions a month (fewer than a dozen) and none represents an account transfer from or to an account for which you will use Quicken, you probably don't need to track the account in Quicken. This choice, however, is a matter of personal preference.

- If you otherwise wouldn't track an account, you probably shouldn't bother to put the account into Quicken—even if you have the best of intentions about becoming more diligent in your record-keeping.

CPA TIP: Measuring Your Net Worth

If you want to measure your *net worth* (assets minus liabilities), you should add a Quicken account for each of your assets and liabilities. You can have, for example, an account with only a few transactions per month but with a large balance. If you don't set up a Quicken account to record these transactions, the account balance (which represents an asset or a liability) won't be reflected in your net worth in Quicken Net Worth reports.

Adding an Account

You need to define or identify accounts for each account you want to track with Quicken. You defined only one account when you set up your Quicken system, but you can have as many as 255 accounts in a data file, and you can have multiple files. (Chapter 20, "Managing Your Quicken Files," discusses files in more detail.) Quicken stores all your accounts in the Account list (see fig. 3.1), which you can access by clicking the Acct button on the Iconbar. If you have more than one Quicken file, a separate Account list is included in each file. The Account list is explained in more detail later in this chapter.

Accounts are sorted alphabetically by account type. Bank accounts appear first in the Account list, followed by Credit Card accounts, Cash accounts, Asset accounts, Liability accounts, and Investment accounts.

Fig. 3.1
The Account list shows all the accounts added to your Quicken file. Quicken can store up to 255 accounts in the Account list.

When you add an account, you define it by entering the account name, the balance in the account as of the date that you add the account, and a brief description of the account. In Quicken 3 for Windows, you can add even more information about an account, such as the bank name, bank account number, and contact person. Now you can store in your Quicken system all the information that you need about your accounts.

Defining the Account

When you add an account to the Account list in your Quicken file, you must define the account by entering the account name, account balance, the date of the account balance, and (optionally) a brief description.

To define and add an account to the Account list, follow these steps:

1. Click the Accts button on the Iconbar, and then choose the New button; or choose the Create New Account option from the Activities menu. Quicken displays the Select Account Type dialog box, shown in figure 3.2.

2. Select the account type you want to add by choosing the appropriate option button in the Select Account Type dialog box. To create a Bank account, for example, choose the Bank Account option.

3. Choose OK or press Enter. The New Account Information dialog box appears (see fig. 3.3).

4. In the Account Name text box, type the new account name using up to 15 characters. You can use letters, spaces, and any symbols in the account name except the following:

   :] [/ | ^

Fig. 3.2

The Select Account Type dialog box includes the six different account types in Quicken.

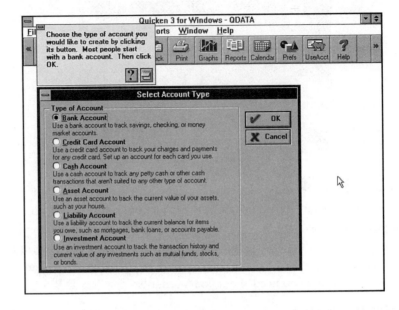

Fig. 3.3

Use the New Account Information dialog box to enter information about the new account you are creating.

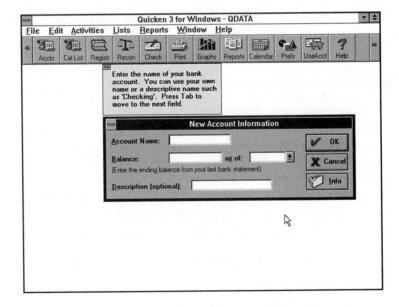

CPA TIP: Naming Accounts

Remember that you have only 15 spaces for the account name. Use an abbreviation of the bank's name; *First National* could become *1stNatl*, for example. This way, you have room for the last four digits of the account number. You then can distinguish accounts easily, as the following example shows:

> 1stNatl-1234 for a checking account
> 1stNatl-3272 for a savings account
> 1stNatl-7113 for CDs

5. Press Tab to move to the **B**alance text box and type the starting account balance. For Bank accounts, this dollar amount is your current account balance according to your records.

Don't use commas or dollar signs when you type the balance. If the starting balance for an account is zero, you must type 0.

Tip
For best results, use the ending balance from your last bank statement as the starting balance.

Note

Although you can enter a starting balance for an account from any source (not just your bank statement), Quicken recommends that you use the ending balance from your last bank statement as your starting balance. Make sure, however, that you reconcile your account with that statement before you rely on the amount the bank states you have in the account.

Caution

When you enter the ending balance from your last bank statement as the starting balance, you must enter all uncleared transactions in the Bank Account Register. In other words, you must include all transactions that haven't cleared through your bank account by the current date (the date you start using Quicken). If you overlook these transactions, you will have difficulty reconciling your account. Chapter 6, "Using the Register," explains how to enter transactions in the Register.

6. Press Tab to move to the **A**s Of text box and type the date on which the balance you entered is correct, using the *mm/dd/yy* format. You can also enter the date by clicking the down arrow and selecting a date from Quicken's mini-calendar. (Refer to Chapter 7, "Using Quicken

Tip

You can press the + (plus) and – (minus) keys to move the current date ahead and back one day.

Shortcuts," to learn more about the mini-calendar.) If you use the ending balance from your last bank statement in step 5, enter the statement date (the ending or cutoff date) in the As Of text box.

7. (Optional) If you want, press Tab to move to the Description text box and type a description of the account, using up to 21 characters.

> **Note**
>
> If you want to enter additional information about an account you are defining (such as the bank name, account number, contact person's name, and telephone number), choose the Info button in the New Account Information dialog box. The next section teaches you how to enter additional information for an account.

8. When the information in the New Account Information dialog box is complete, choose OK or press Enter to add the account. Quicken displays the Bank Account Register for the account that you just created. Figure 3.4 shows the Bank Account Register for the bank account named *First National*, described as a *Checking Account*.

If you want to add more accounts, repeat steps 1 through 8.

Fig. 3.4

The Bank Account Register appears after you create a bank account.

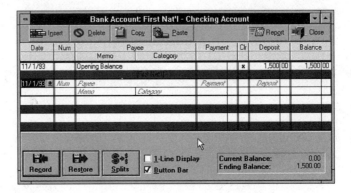

Entering Additional Account Information

In Quicken 3 for Windows, you can enter additional information for each account in the Account list. Use Quicken to store information about accounts, like the account number, contact person, and telephone number.

To enter additional account information, follow these steps:

1. Define the account by filling in the New Account Information dialog box (refer to fig. 3.3), as explained in the preceding section.

2. Choose the Info button. Quicken displays the Additional Account Information dialog box, as shown in figure 3.5.

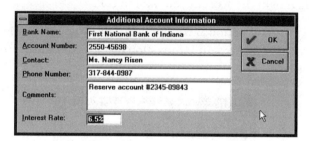

Fig. 3.5
The Additional Account Information dialog box enables you to enter extra detail for accounts.

3. Press Tab to move to the text box that you want to complete in the Additional Account Information dialog box. How much information you enter here is up to you. Enter as little or as much as you like.

4. After you enter the information that you want to add for the account, choose OK or press Enter to save the information.

Editing Existing Accounts

After you add an account to the Account list in your Quicken file, you can change the account name, the account description, or any of the additional information about the account that you have entered. You may want to make such changes if, for example, you originally described the account incorrectly. Or you may want to edit an account name and description if you have transferred the account in total to a new account number, or even a new bank. When you are editing an account, Quicken doesn't allow you to change the account type, balance, or As Of date after you add the account.

Tip
If you need to change the starting balance or date for an account, you can edit the Opening Balance transaction that Quicken enters in the Register for the account. Chapter 6 explains how to edit transactions in the Register.

> **Note**
>
> If you need to change the account type for an account that you have added, you first must delete the account and then re-create the account using the correct account type. Deleting accounts is explained later in this chapter.

To edit an account, follow these steps:

1. Select Account from the Lists menu or choose the Accts button on the Iconbar. Quicken displays the Account list (refer to fig. 3.1).

2. Scroll the Account list by clicking the arrows on the scroll bar on the right side of the list (or by using the up- and down-arrow keys), and then highlight the account you want to edit.

3. Choose the Edit button at the bottom of the Account list. Quicken displays the Edit Account Information dialog box for the account that you selected (see fig. 3.6).

Fig. 3.6
The Edit Account Information dialog box contains the account information that you can edit.

4. Press Tab to move to the text box you want to edit. Type over the existing characters or use the Backspace or Del key to remove characters.

5. If you want to edit any additional information you may have entered for an account, choose the Info button. Make the necessary changes in the Additional Account Information dialog box (refer to fig. 3.5) and choose OK. Quicken returns to the Edit Account Information dialog box.

6. Choose OK or press Enter to save your changes to the account and return to the Account list.

To edit additional accounts, repeat steps 2 through 6.

Deleting Accounts

You can delete an existing account from the Account list. Perhaps you closed an account or decided that an account wasn't worth tracking with Quicken. To delete an account, follow these steps:

1. Select Account from the Lists menu or choose the Accts button on the Iconbar. Quicken displays the Account list (refer to fig. 3.1).

2. Scroll the Account list by clicking the arrows on the scroll box on the right side of the list or by using the up- and down-arrow keys, and then highlight the account that you want to delete.

3. Choose the **D**el button at the bottom of the Account list. Quicken displays the Deleting Account dialog box, with the name of the account you are deleting (see fig. 3.7). Quicken requires confirmation for you to delete an account to ensure that you don't mistakenly delete an account with important data.

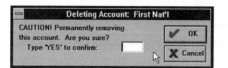

Fig. 3.7
Quicken displays the Deleting Account dialog box when you delete an account.

4. To delete the selected account, type **yes** and then choose OK or press Enter.

   If you don't want to delete the account, choose Cancel or press Esc; Quicken displays an information dialog box telling you that the account was not deleted. Choose OK to return to the Account list.

> ## Caution
>
> When you delete an account, you delete the account description and any transactions you have recorded in the account. Make sure that you really want to delete the account before taking the steps to do so.

Selecting an Account To Use

When you start working with multiple accounts, you need to tell Quicken which account you want to use. Suppose that you decide to use Quicken to track a savings and a checking account. Whenever you enter a savings account deposit, you need to make sure that you record the deposit in the savings account and not in the checking account. Similarly, if you withdraw money from the checking account, you need to make sure that the withdrawal is correctly recorded in your checking account and not in the savings account. To record account activity correctly, you first must select the appropriate Quicken account to use.

To select an account to use, follow these steps:

Tip
Entering all transactions for an account at one time is more efficient than entering them randomly. Consider collecting several transactions for an account and then recording them at one time.

1. Select Account from the Lists menu or choose the Accts button on the Iconbar. Quicken displays the Account list (refer to fig. 3.1).

2. Scroll the Account list by clicking the arrows on the scroll box on the right side of the list or by using the up- and down-arrow keys, and then highlight the account you want to use.

3. Choose the Use button at the bottom of the Account list. Quicken displays the Register for the account that you selected. (You learn about the Register and how to enter transactions in Chapter 6, "Using the Register.")

Summary

In this chapter, you learned about the accounts that you will be using in Quicken. You learned the following:

■ About Quicken account types and how to determine which accounts you need to add to your Quicken file

■ How to add another account to your Quicken file—specifically, bank accounts

■ About Quicken 3 for Windows' new feature that enables you to add extra detail about an account

■ How to edit and delete existing Quicken accounts

■ How to select the account that you want to use

Chapter 4 shows you how to set up Quicken so that you can classify your transactions into income and expense categories and subcategories. You learn how to work with the Category & Transfer list and how to modify the list if needed. Chapter 4 also shows you how to use classes in Quicken to add a extra dimension to your income and expense tracking system.

Chapter 4

Organizing Your Finances

Before you can manage your finances successfully, you need a system that tracks your income and expenses. To help you track these elements, Quicken uses *categories*. By classifying your income and expenses in categories, you see exactly where your money comes from and where it goes. This information is a vital component of effective financial management and planning. You must know your sources of income and your spending habits before you can gain control of your finances.

You also can use *subcategories* in Quicken to divide a category into smaller categories that provide a more detailed accounting of your income and expenses.

Categories and subcategories, therefore, enable you to monitor the money flowing into and out of accounts. By assigning categories and subcategories to transactions, you can summarize the information in a Register and track tax deductions easily.

Classes are used to organize your finances by more than just income and expenses. Using classes in Quicken enables you to specify the information a transaction covers. Classes are an extension of categories and specify who, where, what, and when. If, for example, you want to track expenses for a rental property you own, you can create and assign a class for expense transactions relating to the property.

This chapter goes into depth on the subject of categories, subcategories, and classes, and how you can use categories to organize your finances and track your income and expenses.

This chapter goes into depth on the subject of categories, subcategories, and classes, and how you can use categories to organize your finances and track your income and expenses.

You learn how to do the following:

- Add categories and subcategories to the Category & Transfer list

- Rearrange categories and subcategories

- Merge categories and subcategories

- Use the new QuickReport feature to see a report of all transactions for a category

- Work with classes and subclasses

Working with Categories

Categories enable you to group *income* and *expense* items that flow into and out of accounts. Income or deposits into an account can stem from earned wages from a full-time job, interest income, dividends, revenues from a part-time business, and so on. Expenses or payments can stem from rent, food, transportation, clothing, business expenses, and so on. By grouping each payment from and each deposit into an account, Quicken easily adds the totals for each kind of payment and deposit. You then can see exactly how much each category contributes to the cash flow.

You may find, for example, that cash flows into and from your account are like the cash flows summarized in table 4.1. The information shown in table 4.1 is valuable because categorizing your inflows and outflows is the first step in beginning to manage personal or business finances.

Table 4.1 Examples of Personal Cash Flows	
Deposits	**Amount**
Wages from job	$35,000
Interest	$ 500
Dividends	$ 500
Business revenue	$12,300
Total Deposits	$48,300

Withdrawals	Amount
Housing	$20,000
Food	$ 4,000
Transportation	$ 4,000
Clothing	$ 2,500
Business Expenses	$ 8,500
Total Withdrawals	$39,000
Cash Flows	$ 9,300

CPA TIP: Cash Inflows Aren't Always Income

Not all cash inflows represent income, and not all cash outflows represent an expense. If you sell stock, for example, the proceeds from the sale aren't considered income. Income from the sale is determined by subtracting the cost basis of the stock from the net sales proceeds (if the result is negative, you incur a loss).

Medical insurance reimbursements also aren't considered income; instead, they offset your medical expense. If you pay $100 to a doctor, for example, you enter a transaction in the Register for $100 and assign the Medical category to the transaction. If you later receive an $80 reimbursement from your medical insurance company, the $80 isn't income; instead, it offsets the $100 medical expense transaction that you previously entered. Your net medical expense is $20 ($100–$80).

CPA TIP: Cash Outflows Aren't Always Expenses

If you pay $15,000 for a car, this amount isn't considered an expense. You should enter a transaction in your Bank Account Register for the $15,000 check you write to the car dealer, but rather than assign a category to the transaction, assign an account. In this example, you probably would set up an Asset account for your new automobile (perhaps called *Auto*) and enter the Asset account in the Category field. In essence, this transaction transferred funds from your bank account to another asset account (the account called *Auto*). Transfer transactions like this are explained in Chapter 6, "Using the Register."

Categories enable you to do the following:

- Track and tally income-tax deductions for individual retirement accounts, mortgage interest deductions, charitable contributions, and so on

- Break down checking account deposits and payments into groups of similar transactions so that you can summarize income and expenses

- Budget income and expenses and compare budgeted amounts with actual amounts

If you want to use Quicken for a business, the predefined categories enable you to prepare most of the reports you need for managing business finances. These reports include the following:

- A business profit-and-loss statement that resembles and performs most of the calculations required to complete the federal income tax form Schedule C (which reports the profits or losses from a business or profession)

- Income and cash-flow statements on monthly and annual basis that enable you to understand cash flows and measure business profits or losses

- Accounts receivable reports by customer so that you can track how much each customer owes

- Accounts payable reports by vendor so that you can track how much you owe to each vendor

- Job/project reports that show you the net income for each job or project you set up in Quicken

- Employee payroll reports that track wages paid to each employee and related payroll deductions

 - Comparison reports so that you can analyze your progress from period to period

If any of the reports listed look like benefits you want to enjoy as part of using Quicken, you will want to use Quicken's categories. How involved or complicated the use of these categories becomes depends on your goals.

Quicken doesn't require that you assign categories to transactions. If you want to make sure that you assign a category to all your transactions so that your income and expenses are accurately accounted for, you can turn on the **W**arn Before Recording Uncategorized Transactions preference. When this preference is turned on, Quicken displays a message each time you try to record a transaction in the Register or Write Checks window without a category. You must confirm that you don't want to assign a category to the transaction before you can record the transaction. To learn how to turn on the **W**arn Before Recording Uncategorized Transactions preference, refer to Chapter 21, "Customizing Quicken."

CPA TIP: Assign Categories to Every Transaction

If you want your Quicken system to track each item of income and each expense, make sure that you assign a category, subcategory, or other Quicken account to every transaction you enter. Turning on the **W**arn Before Recording Uncategorized Transactions preference helps you remember to do so.

Building a List of Categories

The information you want to track determines the various categories you want to use to group similar payments or deposits. The following basic rules apply when building a list of categories:

- If you want to use categories for tallying and tracking income tax deductions, you need a category for each deduction. Refer to Chapter 12, "Using Quicken To Prepare for Income Taxes," to learn more about creating categories for tax deductions.

- If you want to use categories to summarize cash inflows and outflows, you need a category for each income or expense account you want to use in the summaries. To account for your work expenses and your spouse's work expenses, you need categories for both sets of expenses.

- If you want to use categories to budget—so that at a later date, you can compare what you budgeted and what you actually spent—you need a category for each comparison you want to make. To budget entertainment expenses and clothing expenses, for example, you need categories for both.

Tip
Access the Category & Transfer list by clicking the Cat List button on the Iconbar.

By applying these rules, you can build a list of the categories you want to use. As an aid in creating the list, table 4.2 shows the category list that Quicken provides for home use. Table 4.3 shows the category list Quicken provides for business use.

Table 4.2 Predefined Home Category List			
Category	**Description**	**Tax Related?**	**Type**
Bonus	Bonus Income	x	Income
CCP	Canadian Pension Plan	x	Income
Div Inc	Dividend Income	x	Income
Gift Received	Gift Received	x	Income
Int Inc	Interest Income	x	Income
Invest Inc	Investment Income	x	Income
Old Age Pension	Old Age Pension	x	Income
Other Inc	Other Income	x	Income
Salary	Salary Income	x	Income
Auto	Automobile Expenses		Expense
Fuel	Auto Fuel		Subcategory
Loan	Auto Loan Payment		Subcategory
Service	Auto Service		Subcategory
Bank Chrg	Bank Charge		Expense
Charity	Charitable Donations	x	Expense
Cash	Cash Contributions	x	Subcategory
Non-Cash	Non-Cash Contributions	x	Subcategory
Childcare	Childcare Expense		Expense
Christmas	Christmas Expenses		Expense
Clothing	Clothing		Expense
Dining	Dining Out		Expense
Dues	Dues		Expense

Category	Description	Tax Related?	Type
Education	Education		Expense
Entertain	Entertainment		Expense
Gifts	Gift Expenses	x	Expense
Groceries	Groceries		Expense
GST	Goods and Service Tax	x	Expense
Home Rpair	Home Repair & Maint.		Expense
Household	Household Misc. Expense		Expense
Housing	Housing		Expense
Insurance	Insurance		Expense
Int Exp	Interest Expense	x	Expense
Invest Exp	Investment Expense	x	Expense
Medical	Medical Expenses	x	Expense
Doctor	Doctor & Dental Visits	x	Subcategory
Medicine	Medicine & Drugs	x	Subcategory
Misc	Miscellaneous		Expense
Mort Int	Mortgage Interest Exp	x	Expense
Other Exp	Other Expenses		Expense
PST	Provincial Sales Tax	x	Expense
Recreation	Recreation Expenses		Expense
RRSP	Reg Retirement Sav Plan		Expense
Subscriptions	Subscriptions		Expense
Supplies	Supplies		Expense
Tax	Taxes	x	Expense
Fed	Federal Tax	x	Subcategory
Medicare	Medicare Tax	x	Subcategory
Other	Misc. Taxes	x	Subcategory

(continues)

Learning Quicken

Table 4.2 Continued			
Category	**Description**	**Tax Related?**	**Type**
Prop	Property Tax	x	Subcategory
Soc Sec	Soc Sec Tax	x	Subcategory
State	State Tax	x	Subcategory
Tax Spouse	Spouse's Taxes	x	Expense
Fed	Federal Tax	x	Subcategory
Medicare	Medicare Tax	x	Subcategory
Soc Sec	Soc Sec Tax	x	Subcategory
State	State Tax	x	Subcategory
Telephone	Telephone Expenses		Expense
UIC	Unemploy. Ins. Commission	x	Expense
Utilities	Water, Gas, Electric		Expense
Gas & Electric	Gas and Electricity		Subcategory
Water	Water		Subcategory

Table 4.3 Predefined Business Category List			
Category	**Description**	**Tax Related?**	**Type**
Other Inc	Other Income	x	Income
Rent Income	Rent Income	x	Income
Ads	Advertising	x	Expense
Bus. Insurance	Insurance (not health)	x	Expense
Bus. Utilities	Water, Gas, Electric	x	Expense
Business Tax	Taxes & Licenses	x	Expense
Car	Car & Truck	x	Expense
Commission	Commissions	x	Expense
Freight	Freight	x	Expense
GST	Goods and Service Tax	x	Expense

Category	Description	Tax Related?	Type
Int Paid	Interest Paid	x	Expense
L&P Fees	Legal & Prof. Fees	x	Expense
Meals & Entertn	Meals & Entertainment	x	Expense
Office	Office Expenses	x	Expense
PST	Provincial Sales Tax	x	Expense
Rent on Equip	Rent-Vehicle,mach,equip	x	Expense
Rent Paid	Rent Paid	x	Expense
Repairs	Repairs	x	Expense
Returns	Returns & Allowances	x	Expense
Supplies, bus.	Supplies	x	Expense
Travel	Travel Expenses	x	Expense
Wages	Wages & Job Credits	x	Expense

Learning Quicken

Consider these lists as starting points. The predefined Home category list provides a long list of income and expense categories that you may find useful for your home finances. Depending on the situation, some categories you don't need may be provided, and other categories you do need may be missing. Similarly, the predefined Business list provides income and expense categories you may find useful in business accounting. If you apply the rules described earlier for devising categories, you should have no problem when using the predefined lists as starting points for constructing a category list that works well for you.

Categories act as building blocks in classifying data the way you want it. You can use the following categories to calculate the tax-deduction and budgeted items shown in table 4.4:

> Mortgage interest
>
> Mortgage principal
>
> Mortgage late-payment fees
>
> Credit card late-payment fees
>
> Property taxes

Tip

For Canadian users of Quicken, the predefined list of categories includes categories for GST (Goods and Service Tax) and PST (Provincial Sales Tax).

CPA TIP: Reviewing the Category List for Redundancies

After you complete the list, review the categories for any redundancies produced by two of the rules calling for the same category. For home use of Quicken, for example, you can add a category to budget for monthly individual retirement account (IRA) contributions. You also can add a category to tally IRA payments because these payments represent potential tax deductions. Because both categories are the same, cross one category off the list.

Sometimes overlapping or redundant categories aren't as easy to spot. A tax deduction you need to calculate may be only a small part of a budgeting category, or a budgeting amount you need to calculate may be only a portion of a tax-deduction category. You need to detail categories so that each represents separate tax deduction or budgeting categories.

Table 4.4 Personal Budget and Tax Categories

Items	Categories Used
Late fees (a budgeted amount)	Mortgage late-payment fees Credit card late-payment fee
Housing (a budgeted amount)	Mortgage principal Mortgage interest Property taxes
Mortgage interest (deduction)	Mortgage interest Mortgage late-payment fees
Property taxes (deduction)	Property taxes

Setting Up Categories

When you create a new file in Quicken, you can choose to use the defined Home or Business categories from the Create Quicken File dialog box as the foundation of the Category & Transfer list (see fig. 4.1). Chapter 20 describes how to create new files.

If you select the Home option, Quicken copies its predefined list of Home categories (as listed in table 4.2) to the Category & Transfer list in your file. If you select the Business option, Quicken copies its predefined list of Business categories that you saw in table 4.3 to your list.

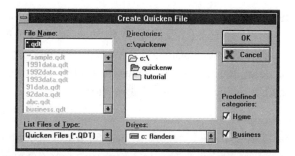

Fig. 4.1
In the Create Quicken File dialog box, you can specify which predefined category list you want to set up in your new file: Home, Business, or both.

Learning Quicken

Note

Quicken enables you to specify which categories are tax-related (a taxable income item or a tax-deductible expense) so that you easily can summarize your tax items to prepare your income tax return. Setting up categories as tax-related also enables you to export your Quicken data to a tax preparation program. See Chapter 12, "Using Quicken To Prepare for Income Taxes," to learn how to make tax time easier with Quicken.

Quicken stores the predefined categories that you select to use (Home or Business) in the Category & Transfer list (see fig. 4.2). The Category & Transfer list also is where Quicken stores all the subcategories and accounts in your Quicken file. Accounts are listed after the alphabetical listing of income and expense categories (income categories are listed before expense categories). Quicken provides a separate Category & Transfer list for each file.

The Category & Transfer list not only lists the categories, subcategories, and accounts, but also shows the category type (income or expense), the account type (bank, cash, investment, and so on), the category or account description, and whether the category or subcategory is tax-related.

Tip
Access the Category & Transfer list by choosing Category & Transfer from the Lists menu.

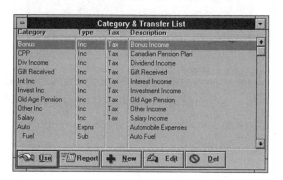

Fig. 4.2
The Category & Transfer list stores the categories and subcategories that you use to classify transactions.

You can use the Category & Transfer list to select a category, subcategory, or transfer account to assign to a transaction. You also can use the list to add, edit, or delete categories and subcategories, change a category to a subcategory (and vice versa), and create a QuickReport that lists all transactions assigned to the highlighted category or subcategory.

Adding a Category

You can add categories to the Category & Transfer list by accessing the list and adding a category directly to the list, or you can type the new category name in the Category field while entering a transaction in Quicken.

> **Note**
>
> This chapter describes the steps to add a category directly to the Category & Transfer list. Because you don't learn about entering transactions until the next few chapters, wait until then to learn about adding categories while entering transactions. (See Chapter 5, "Writing and Printing Checks," and Chapter 6, "Using the Register.")

Tip
You also can access the Category & Transfer list by clicking the Cat List button on the Iconbar.

To add a category to the Category & Transfer list, follow these steps:

1. Choose Category & Transfer from the Lists menu (or press Ctrl+C) to access the Category & Transfer list (refer to fig. 4.2).

2. Choose New to display the Set Up Category dialog box, shown in figure 4.3.

Fig. 4.3
In the Set Up Category dialog box, you can set up income or expense categories or a subcategory.

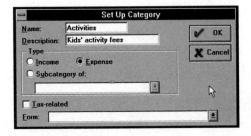

3. Type the category name you want to use in the Name text box. Category names can contain up to 15 characters and can include any character except the following:

        :] / [| ^

4. (Optional) If you want, press Tab to move to the Description field and type a brief description of the category that you are adding. You can use up to 25 characters to describe the new category.

5. In the Type section, select the appropriate option to designate the category as an income or expense category. Select the Income option button for income categories or the Expense option button for expense categories. If you're adding a subcategory, select the Subcategory Of option (adding subcategories is covered later in this chapter).

6. (Optional) If you need to specify the category as tax-related, select the Tax-Related check box. The Tax-Related check box determines whether the category you are adding is a taxable income or tax-deductible expense item.

If you specify that a category is tax-related by selecting the check box, Quicken includes that category in tax reports. You then can use tax reports to accumulate transactions that are assigned to tax-related categories to help you prepare your personal or business income tax return.

If you want to assign a tax form to your tax-related category, continue with step 7; otherwise, skip to step 8.

7. (Optional) If you are setting up a category to report a specific kind of taxable income or tax deduction, click the arrow next to the Form drop-down list box to display the list of tax forms and schedules that you can assign to this category (see fig. 4.4). Scroll the list and select the tax form or schedule that the category pertains to. If, for example, you're adding a category for an itemized deduction, such as tax preparation fees, select Schedule A: Tax preparation fees.

> **Note**
>
> Quicken does not display the Form drop-down list box in the Set Up Category dialog box automatically. You first must select the Use Tax Schedules with Categories preference in the General Preferences dialog box. (Access the General Preferences dialog box by clicking the Prefs button on the Iconbar and then choosing the General preference button.)

Fig. 4.4
From the Form drop-down list box, select the tax form or schedule to assign to the category that you are adding.

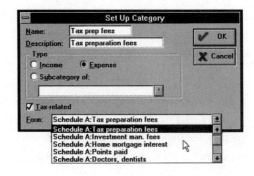

8. When the Set Up Category dialog box is complete, choose OK to save the category information and add the category to the Category & Transfer list. Quicken inserts the new category name in its proper alphabetical order.

> **Note**
>
> Generally, you have plenty of room for as many categories as you need. The precise maximum number, however, depends on the computer's available memory, the length of the category names and descriptions, and the other information stored in memory. You usually have room for about 150 categories with 384K of memory and more than 1,000 categories with 512K of memory.

Deleting a Category

You also may want to delete categories, because you don't use a particular category or because you added the category incorrectly. Deleting categories is even easier than adding categories.

To delete a category, follow these steps:

1. Choose Category & Transfer from the Lists menu, click the Cat List button on the Iconbar, or press Ctrl+C to access the Category & Transfer list (refer to fig. 4.2).

2. Use the scroll box to move up and down in the Category & Transfer list and highlight the category that you want to delete.

   You also can select a category by typing the first letter of the category name to move the section of the list that contains all categories starting with that letter. For example, to move to the category Subscriptions, press S.

Tip
To move quickly to the top or bottom of the Category & Transfer list, press Home to move to the beginning of the list or End to move to the end of the list.

3. When the item you want to delete is highlighted, choose Del. Quicken displays a warning, telling you that you are about to delete a category permanently.

> **Caution**
>
> You can't delete a category that has subcategories. If you need to delete a category with subcategories, first change its subcategories into categories *or* move the subcategories to another category. Changing and moving subcategories is explained later in this chapter.

4. To remove the category from the category list, choose OK. If you don't want to remove the category, press Cancel.

After you delete a category, you can't use the category unless you add it again. If you assigned previous transactions to the deleted category, Quicken removes the category from the Category field in the transaction (that Category field becomes blank). Transactions assigned to the category that you delete are not deleted. You need to return to the Register and assign a new category to any blank Category field. (Chapter 6 explains how to use the Register.)

Editing a Category

You also can edit a category. Suppose that you run a business and use Quicken to account for, among other things, the wages you pay. Further, suppose that the Wages category was always used for employees working in Washington state. If you create a new category named OR_WAGES to account for the wages you pay to employees working in Oregon, you may want to change the name of the Wages category to WA_WAGES to reflect the change in the significance of the account.

The steps for editing a category roughly parallel the steps for adding one. To edit a category, follow these steps:

1. Choose Category & Transfer from the Lists menu, click the Cat List button on the Iconbar, or press Ctrl+C to access the Category & Transfer list (refer to fig. 4.2).

2. Use the scroll box to move up and down in the Category & Transfer list and highlight the category that you want to edit.

3. Choose Edit to display the Edit Category dialog box, shown in figure 4.5.

Fig. 4.5
The Edit Category dialog box shows the category information that you can edit.

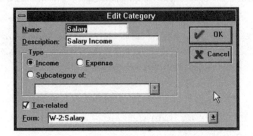

4. Press Tab to move to the text box that you want to edit and then type over the existing information. If necessary, change the Income, Expense, or Subcategory setting by selecting the appropriate option button in the Type section. You also can change a category's tax status by selecting the Tax-Related check box to enter or remove the check mark. Change the tax form or schedule by selecting a new form or schedule from the Form drop-down list box.

5. To save the changes to the category, choose OK or press Enter.

Using Subcategories

If you decide to use categories as building blocks to classify your income and expenses, you need to know about subcategories. Taking the first row of the data from table 4.4, suppose that you create a category called LateFees to track late-payment fees. You then can set up two subcategories of the category LateFees called LMortgage for late mortgage fees and LCredit for late credit-card fees (the *L* stands for *late*.) Then, when you record a transaction to pay late fees on your mortgage, you can assign the subcategory LMortgage to the transaction. When you record a transaction for late fees on your credit card, assign the subcategory LCredit to the transaction. You can design reports so that all your subcategories are shown or just the categories.

When only categories are shown, Quicken shows the sum of all transactions assigned to their subcategories as the category total. In the example, you could show a subcategory line for LMortgage and LCredit to see just how much was spent on late fees for each, or you could lump the LMortgage and LCredit subcategories together and show their total in the category line LateFees.

Adding a Subcategory

You add a subcategory to the Category & Transfer list in much the same way you add a category. To add a subcategory to the Category & Transfer list, follow these steps:

1. Choose Category & Transfer from the Lists menu, click the Cat List button on the Iconbar, or press Ctrl+C to access the Category & Transfer list (refer to fig. 4.2).

2. Choose New to display the Set Up Category dialog box (refer to fig. 4.3).

3. Type the subcategory name you want to use in the Name text box. Subcategory names can contain up to 15 characters and can include any character except the following:

   :] / [| ^

4. (Optional) If you want, press Tab to move to the Description field and then type a brief description of the subcategory that you are adding. You can use up to 25 characters to describe the new category.

5. In the Type section, select the Subcategory Of option.

6. Click the arrow next to the Subcategory Of drop-down list box to display the list of categories. Scroll the list to select the category to which you are adding the subcategory.

7. (Optional) Subcategories can be specified as tax-related in the same way as categories. If you need to specify the subcategory as tax-related, refer to steps 6 and 7 earlier in the section "Adding a Category."

8. When the Set Up Category dialog box is complete, choose OK to save the subcategory information and add the subcategory to the Category & Transfer list.

Quicken inserts the new subcategory name under the category to which it pertains, or its parent category. If a category has more than one subcategory, Quicken places the new subcategory within the other subcategories in its proper alphabetical order.

Editing and Deleting Subcategories

You can edit a subcategory at any time. When you change a subcategory name, all previous transactions assigned to that subcategory also are changed. To edit a subcategory, follow the same steps for editing a category, as explained earlier in this chapter.

You also can delete a subcategory if you no longer need it. When you delete a subcategory, Quicken permanently removes it from the Category & Transfer list. Previous transactions assigned to the subcategory that you subsequently delete are merged into the parent category. If, for example, you assign transactions to the subcategory Movies, under the category Entertainment, and then delete the Movies subcategory, Quicken assigns all those transactions to the category Entertainment.

To delete a subcategory, follow the same steps for deleting a category, as explained earlier in this chapter.

Rearranging Categories and Subcategories

After you establish your category list and add categories and subcategories, you can change categories to subcategories and vice versa. You can change a category to a subcategory (*demote* a category), change a subcategory to a category (*promote* a subcategory), or move a subcategory under another category (so that it has a different parent category). You may decide, for example, to make the category Auto Fuel a subcategory of the category Auto. You can make this change so that Quicken changes the previous transactions assigned to these categories.

Changing Categories and Subcategories

To change a category to a subcategory (demote a category), or to change a subcategory to a category (promote a subcategory), follow these steps:

1. Choose Category & Transfer from the Lists menu, click the Cat List button on the Iconbar, or press Ctrl+C to access the Category & Transfer list (refer to fig. 4.2).

2. Use the scroll box to move up and down in the Category & Transfer list and highlight the category or subcategory that you want to change.

3. Choose Edit to display the Edit Category dialog box.

4. To change a category to a subcategory, select the Subcategory Of option button. Then choose the arrow in the drop-down list box to display the list of categories and subcategories and select the new parent category.

   To change a subcategory to a category, select the Income option button or the Expense option button.

5. Choose OK or press Enter.

Moving a Subcategory to Another Category

You can change the parent category for a subcategory by moving the subcategory to another category. You may want to move a subcategory called Auto Lease, for example, from the Auto category to the Lease Expense category.

To move a subcategory to another category, follow these steps:

1. Choose Category & Transfer from the Lists menu, click the Cat List button on the Iconbar, or press Ctrl+C to access the Category & Transfer list.

2. Use the scroll box to move up and down in the Category & Transfer list and highlight the subcategory that you want to move.

3. Choose Edit to display the Edit Category dialog box.

4. Choose the arrow in the Subcategory Of drop-down list box to display the list of categories and subcategories and select the new parent category.

5. Choose OK or press Enter. Quicken repositions the subcategory under the new parent category in the Category & Transfer list.

Merging Categories and Subcategories

You can merge one category or subcategory into another. You may want to merge the Int Inc (Interest Income) category into the Invest Inc (Investment Income) category if you find that you aren't really using the former category, for example. When you merge two categories or subcategories, Quicken assigns the category or subcategory name that you retain (in this case, Invest Inc) to each transaction that was assigned to the merged category or subcategory (Int Inc).

Before you can merge a category into another category, you first must change the category that you want to merge into a subcategory. To merge a subcategory into another subcategory, make the subcategory that you want to merge a subcategory of the subcategory that you want to retain. If the subcategory that you are merging has its own subcategories, its subcategories follow its parent subcategory as you change it to a subcategory of another subcategory. (Quicken enables you to create a subcategory of another subcategory, a subcategory of a subcategory of a subcategory, and so forth.) If, for example, you have a subcategory named Condo Exp and want to merge it with a subcategory named Condo Repairs, you first must make the subcategory Condo Exp a subcategory of Condo Repairs.

Figure 4.6 shows how categories and subcategories are listed in the Category & Transfer list. Notice how categories and subcategories appear in outline format with a category listed first, followed by its subcategory (indented to the right). A subcategory of a subcategory is indented to the right a little farther.

To merge a category or subcategory, follow these steps:

1. Choose **C**ategory & Transfer from the Lists menu, click the Cat List button on the Iconbar, or press Ctrl+C to access the Category & Transfer list (refer to fig. 4.6).

2. Use the scroll box to move up and down in the Category & Transfer list and then highlight the category or subcategory that you want to merge.

Fig. 4.6
The Category & Transfer list arranges categories and subcategories in outline format.

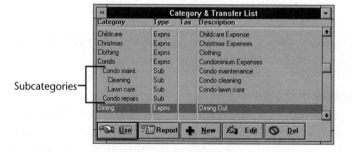

3. Choose Edit to display the Edit Category dialog box.

4. If you are merging a category into another category, change the category that you don't want to retain into a subcategory of the category that you want to keep. Follow the steps given earlier in the section "Changing Categories and Subcategories."

If you are merging a subcategory into another subcategory, change the subcategory that you don't want to retain into a subcategory of the subcategory that you want to keep.

5. After you change the category or subcategory in step 4, highlight the subcategory that you don't want to keep.

6. Choose Del. Quicken displays a message that deleting the subcategory merges the subcategory with its parent (category or subcategory).

7. Choose Yes to merge the subcategory with its parent.

Using QuickReport for Instant Category Reports

If you want a quick report of all transactions that have been assigned to a category or subcategory, you can use Quicken 3's new *QuickReport* feature. When you use QuickReport, Quicken lists all transactions (in all accounts) assigned to the selected category or subcategory through the current date. Quicken shows the date, account, check number (if applicable), description, memo, category or subcategory name, cleared status, and amount for each transaction in the list.

To see a QuickReport for categories and subcategories, follow these steps:

1. Access the Category & Transfer list by choosing Category & Transfer from the Lists menu, clicking the Cat List button on the Iconbar, or pressing Ctrl+C.

2. Highlight the category or subcategory for which you want a list of transactions.

3. Choose the Report button at the bottom of the Category & Transfer list (see fig. 4.7).

Quicken quickly filters all transactions and displays only those that have been assigned to the category or subcategory that you select. Figure 4.8 shows the QuickReport for the Auto Fuel category.

4. To remove the QuickReport from your screen, choose Close at the top of the report.

Fig. 4.7
You can display an instant report for any category or subcategory from the Category & Transfer list by clicking the Report button.

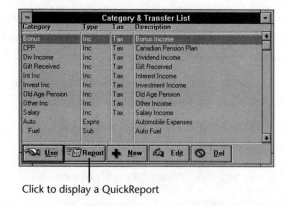

Click to display a QuickReport

Fig. 4.8
The QuickReport feature displays a report of all transactions for a single category or subcategory.

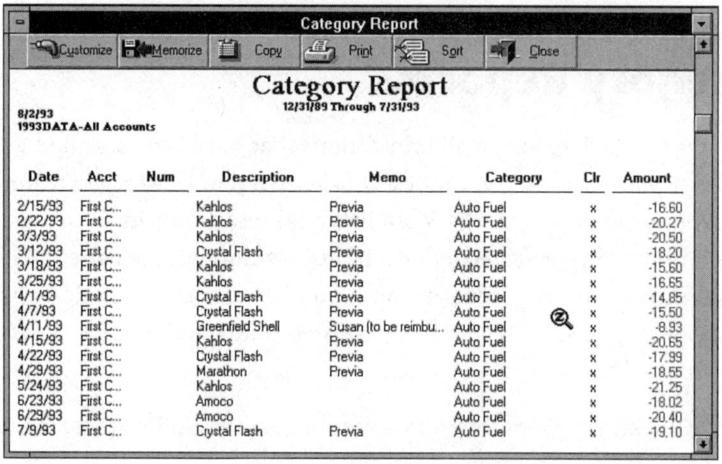

You can change the report settings by using the buttons at the top of the QuickReport screen. You also can print the QuickReport by choosing the Print button; however, you first must make sure that the report settings in Quicken are set for your printer. Chapter 18, "Creating and Printing Reports," explains how to change report settings and enter printer settings.

Printing the Category & Transfer List

Occasionally, you may want a printed copy of the Category & Transfer list. You also may want to review the list with a tax advisor at his office to verify that you are tracking all tax deduction categories, or you may want to keep a paper copy of the list as an aid to entering transactions.

Until now in Quicken, you haven't printed any lists, checks, or reports. Before you can print from Quicken, you must set up the program to print to your printer. Quicken includes different printer settings for lists (Report/Graph Printer Setup) and checks (Check Printer Setup). This section shows you how to set up Quicken quickly to print lists (or reports). To learn how to customize printer settings, refer to Chapter 18, "Creating and Printing Reports."

To set up Quicken to print lists, follow these steps:

1. From the File menu, choose Printer Setup and then choose Report/Graph Printer Setup. Quicken displays the Report Printer Setup dialog box, shown in figure 4.9.

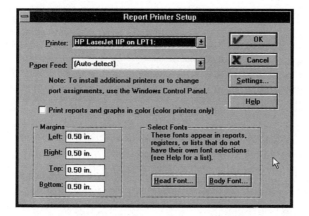

Fig. 4.9
The Report Printer Setup dialog box tells Quicken which printer you are using, the type of paper you use, the report margins, and the type fonts.

2. Select your installed printer from the Printer drop-down list.

3. Quicken uses Auto-detect to determine whether your printer is continuous-feed or page-oriented. If the paper feed setting isn't correct, select the appropriate paper feed for your installed printer from the Paper Feed drop-down list.

4. If you are using a color printer and want to print the Category & Transfer list in color, select the Print Reports and Graphs in Color check box. You must have an installed color printer to use this option.

5. If necessary, set the Left, Right, Top, and Bottom margins by entering larger or smaller values than the preset values that Quicken uses.

6. If you want to change the type font for the heading or body of the Category & Transfer list, choose Head Font or Body Font. Quicken

displays the Report Default Headline Font dialog box or the Report
Default Font dialog box, from which you can change the font type, font
style, and font size. When the head and/or body fonts are the way you
want them, choose OK or press Enter to return to the Report Printer
Setup dialog box.

7. You also can change other print settings, such as the paper tray, paper
size, orientation, and number of copies. To change these settings,
choose Settings. Quicken displays a dialog box for your installed
printer. Make the necessary changes and then choose OK or press Enter
to return to the Report Printer Setup dialog box.

8. Choose OK or press Enter to save the printer settings.

To print a copy of the Category & Transfer list, follow these steps:

1. Click the Cat List button on the Iconbar (or press Ctrl+C) to display the
Category & Transfer list.

2. Choose Print List from the File menu (or press Ctrl+P). Quicken displays
the Print Report dialog box, shown in figure 4.10.

3. In the Print To section, select where you want the Category & Transfer
list printed. By default, Quicken selects the Printer option to print to
your printer. You also can save the Category & Transfer list to an ASCII
Disk File, a Tab-delimited Disk File, a 123 (.PRN) Disk File, or preview
the list on your Screen.

Fig. 4.10
The Print Report
dialog box appears
when you press
Ctrl+P from the
Category & Trans-
fer list.

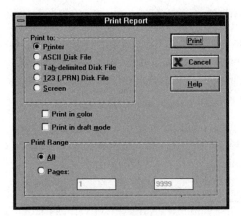

4. Select the Print in Color check box to print the Category & Transfer list in color. You must have an installed color printer to print the list in color.

5. Select the Print in Draft Mode check box, if desired. Your printer must support draft mode printing to be able to print a draft copy.

6. Next, set the print range: select All to print all pages of the Category & Transfer list, or select Pages and specify which pages you want to print.

7. Choose Print or press Enter to begin printing the Category & Transfer list.

Working with Classes

Categories and subcategories group revenues and expenses by the type of transaction. You can categorize income transactions, for example, as gross sales, other income, and so on. You can categorize expense transactions as car and truck expenses, supply expenses, utilities, and so on. But you may want to slice the data in other ways. You also may want to see income or expenses by job or project, by salesperson or product line, and by geographic location or functional company areas.

Classes add a second dimension to the income and expense summaries that categories provide. Non-business use of Quicken probably doesn't require this second dimension. Business owners, however, can find Quicken's classes a powerful way to view financial data from a second perspective.

In addition to using two categories (Product and Service) to track income, you can use classes to determine which salespeople actually are booking the orders. With three salespeople, use these three classes: Joe, Bill, and Sue. In addition to seeing the sales of company products and company services, you also can see things such as the sales Bill made, the product sales Joe made, and the service sales Sue made. In effect, you have two perspectives on this income—the kind of income (which appears as a product or service) and salesperson (which appears as Joe, Bill, or Sue). Table 4.5 shows these perspectives.

Table 4.5 Two Perspectives on Income			
Kind of Income	**Salespeople Booking Orders**		
	Joe	**Bill**	**Sue**
Product	Joe's product sales	Bill's product sales	Sue's product sales
Service	Joe's service sales	Bill's service sales	Sue's service sales

Note

The basic problem with classes is that they don't give you a way to budget. You can't budget by classes, for example. This problem may not seem too important to you right now, but before you begin to use classes, review Chapter 16, "Budgeting with Quicken." Business users also should benefit by reading Chapter 23, "Using Quicken in Your Small Business."

Defining a Class

The first step in using classes is to define the classes you want to use. The classes you choose depend on how you need or want to view the financial data you collect with Quicken. Unfortunately, giving specific advice on picking appropriate classes is difficult, and Quicken doesn't provide predefined lists of classes (as it does for categories). Classes usually are specific to the particular personal or business finances. You can follow one rough rule of thumb, however; look at the kinds of questions you now ask but can't answer by using categories alone.

A real-estate investor may want to use classes that correspond to individual properties. A law firm may want to use classes that represent each partner or each client. Other businesses have still different views of financial data. After you define the classes you want to use, you are ready to add the classes in Quicken. You can add as many classes as you want.

To add a class, follow these steps:

1. Choose Class from the Lists menu (or press Ctrl+L) to display the Class list (see fig. 4.11). The Class list includes an alphabetical listing of all classes set up in Quicken.

2. Choose New to display the Set Up Class dialog box, shown in figure 4.12.

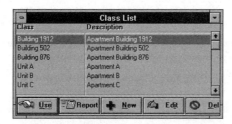

Fig. 4.11
You can select to use a class, add a new class, edit a class, or delete a class from the Class list.

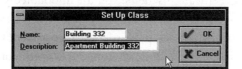

Fig. 4.12
The Set Up Class dialog box is used to define a new class.

3. In the Name text box, type the name you want to use for the class. Class names can contain up to 15 characters, including spaces. You can't use the following characters:

   :] / [| ^

4. (Optional) If desired, press Tab to move to the Description text box and type a description for the class.

5. Choose OK or press Enter. Quicken adds the class to the Class list in alphabetical order.

You also assign a class to a transaction as you enter the transaction in Quicken (see Chapters 5 and 6). The class that you want to assign to a transaction is entered in the Category field, after the category name. Note, however, that you don't have to assign a category to a transaction to assign a class to the transaction.

To assign a class to a transaction, access the Class list (as explained in the preceding steps) and select the class name from the list, or type a forward slash (/) in the Category field for the transaction and begin typing the class name. Note that as you begin typing the class name, Quicken's QuickFill feature searches the Class list for the class name that matches the first few characters that you type and then enters the rest of the class name for you.

Note

You can add a class to the Class list *on the fly*, or as you enter a transaction in Quicken. Just type the new class name in the Category field (after the forward slash). When the name isn't found in the Class list, Quicken asks whether you want to add it. You then can define the new class and immediately return to the transaction so that you can assign the new class to the transaction.

Editing and Deleting Classes

If you start defining classes, you also need to know how to edit and delete these classes. The classification scheme you use undoubtedly can change over time. Suppose that you are a real-estate investor and use classes to track properties. You probably buy and sell properties over a period of time. Alternatively, if you are a bookkeeper for a law firm, the lawyers working at the firm probably change over a period of time. Both examples indicate a need for editing classes. The steps for editing and deleting are simple and familiar if you previously edited or deleted categories.

To edit a class, follow these steps:

1. Choose Class from the Lists menu (or press Ctrl+L) to display the Class list (refer to fig. 4.11).

2. Use the scroll box to move through the Class list and highlight the class that you want to edit.

3. Choose Edit to display the Edit Class dialog box, which includes the class name and description.

4. Press Tab to move to the text box that you want to change and then type over the existing information.

5. Choose OK or press Enter to save the changes to the class.

To delete a class, follow these steps:

1. Choose Class from the Lists menu (or press Ctrl+L) to display the Class list (refer to fig. 4.11).

2. Use the scroll box to move through the Class list and highlight the class that you want to delete.

3. Choose Del. Quicken warns you that you are about to delete a class permanently.

4. Choose OK or press Enter to complete the deletion; choose Cancel or press Esc to cancel the deletion.

Using QuickReport for Instant Class Reports

If you want a quick report of all transactions that you have assigned to a class, you can use Quicken 3's new *QuickReport* feature. When you use QuickReport, Quicken lists all transactions (in all accounts) assigned to the selected class through the current date.

To see a QuickReport for a class, follow these steps:

1. Access the Class list (refer to fig. 4.11) by pressing Ctrl+L.

2. Highlight the class for which you want a list of transactions.

3. Choose Report at the bottom of the Class list.

   Quicken quickly filters all transactions and displays only those that have been assigned to the class that you select.

4. To remove the QuickReport from your screen, choose Close at the top of the report.

Using Subclasses

If you use classes to add another dimension to the reporting and recording process, you also may want to use subclasses. *Subclasses* are classes within classes. If you use a geographical scheme to create classes, the classes may be states. Within each state, you may choose to use subclasses corresponding to portions of the state. A class called Washington, for example, may have the subclasses E. Washington and W. Washington. California, another class, may have the subclasses N. California (excluding the Bay Area), Bay Area, S. California (excluding Los Angeles County), and Los Angeles County.

You don't actually add subclasses to the Class list. Instead, you set up a class name for each item that you want to function as a subclass. Then, when you assign a subclass to a transaction (see Chapter 5 and Chapter 6), type the class, a colon (:), and then the subclass. When assigning the class California and the subclass Bay Area to a transaction, for example, enter the following in the Category field:

   California:Bay Area

You edit and delete subclasses by following the same procedures as for classes.

Caution

If you have assigned a subclass to transactions, you may not be able to display a QuickReport when you select that transaction from the Class list and then choose the Report button.

CPA TIP: Using Subclasses for Sales Tax

Subclasses are helpful for sales taxes based on a state, county, or city with different tax rates for each jurisdiction or if you must report sales within each jurisdiction.

Summary

Quicken's categories and classes give you a means to organize your finances to give you the information that you need. In this chapter, you learned the following:

- How to build your list of categories by adding categories, and how to edit and delete existing categories from the predefined category list

- How to create and use subcategories

- How to use the new QuickReport feature to get an instant report of all transactions for any one category or subcategory, as well as all transactions assigned to a class

- How to set up Quicken to print reports and lists

- How to add, edit, and delete classes and subclasses

The next four chapters in Part I, "Learning Quicken for Windows," describe the basics of using Quicken and cover such tasks as recording financial transactions with Quicken, printing Registers, writing and printing checks, reconciling your bank account, and so on. These chapters don't cover as much about business and personal accounting topics as they do about using the Quicken system.

After you finish reading the chapters in this part of *Using Quicken 3 for Windows*, you will be well acquainted with the mechanics of using the Quicken program. That knowledge is essential to turning Quicken into a tool you can use for business or personal financial management.

Chapter 5

Writing and Printing Checks

With Quicken's check-printing feature, you can write checks and pay bills faster and more efficiently than you ever thought possible. You can pay bills faster because Quicken provides a collection of shortcuts and timesaving techniques that automate and speed up check writing and bill paying. You can pay bills more efficiently because Quicken helps you keep track of the bills coming due and provides categories with which you can classify the ways you are spending your money.

The check-writing feature in Quicken is one of the program's most powerful tools. Writing checks with Quicken not only saves you valuable time, but spares you from having numerous opportunities to make clerical errors. When you write a check using Quicken, you simply enter the information in a check facsimile window (the Write Checks window), and Quicken takes it from there. The program records the check in the Check (Bank Account) Register, adjusts your account balance, and adds the transaction amount to the appropriate category, which you specify when you write a check. From this point, you must print the check, sign it, put the check in an envelope (Intuit even provides window envelopes for checks), and mail it.

Displaying the Write Checks Window

You need to display the Write Checks window when you want to do the following:

- Write checks

- Postdate checks

This chapter describes the basics of writing and printing checks with Quicken. The following topics are discussed:

- Using the Write Checks window

- Writing and recording checks

- Reviewing and editing checks

- Deleting and voiding checks

- Postdating checks

- Splitting a check transaction by assigning more than one category

- Printing checks

■ Review checks that you haven't printed

■ Edit or delete checks that you haven't printed

■ Print checks

If you use Quicken to print checks, use the Write Checks window to enter check information. Manual checks that you write are entered in the Check Register (see Chapter 6, "Using the Register").

> **Note**
>
> You can't write a check from any other type of account other than a Bank account. The Bank account that you use usually will be your checking account.

To display the Write Checks window, shown in figure 5.1, use one of the following methods:

■ Choose Write Checks from the Activities menu.

■ Click the Check button on the Iconbar.

■ Press Ctrl+W.

Fig. 5.1
The Write Checks window resembles an actual check.

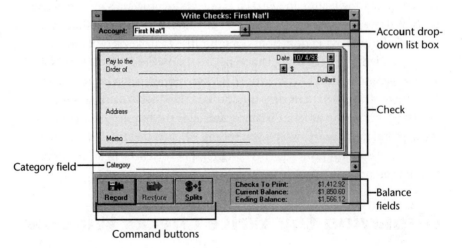

Reviewing the Write Checks Window

You use the Write Checks window to collect the information you use to print checks. After collecting the information, Quicken records the check in the Register for the account you're using.

The Write Checks window includes the following items:

- *The Account drop-down list box*. Select the checking account from which you want to write a check from this list box.

- *The actual check*. Enter the date, payee, amount, and memo (optional). If you select the Allow Entry of Extra Message on Check preference, an additional field appears on the check so that you can enter an informational message. (You learn how to select this preference later in the section "Setting Check Preferences.")

> **Note**
>
> Check numbers aren't entered in the Write Checks window; you specify the check numbers when you print checks. The steps for completing checks are described later in the section "Writing a Check."

- *Category field*. Assign a category, subcategory, class, subclass, or transfer account to a check transaction in this field.

- *Command buttons*. Use the command buttons to record the check, restore the information in an edited check, or open the Splits window so that you can assign more than one category to the check.

- *Balance fields*. These fields show the total amount of the checks that you have written but not yet printed, the current balance in the checking account (as of the current date) before checks are printed, and the ending balance in the account after the checks are printed. You can't make entries to the balance fields in the Write Checks window.

Moving around the Write Checks Window

You easily can move from check to check in the Write Checks window by using the scroll bar on the right side of the window. Just click the down arrow to move to the next check, or click the up arrow to move to the preceding check.

Use the scroll box to move quickly through checks in the Write Checks window. First, point the mouse pointer at the scroll box. Then press and hold down the left mouse button as you drag (move) the scroll box up or down the scroll bar. As you are scrolling, Quicken displays a date box to the left of the scroll box. The date shown in the date box represents the date of the check that will be displayed when you release the scroll box.

You also can use the keyboard to move from check to check and from field to field in the Write Checks window. The following keys help you move around the Write Checks window quickly and easily:

Press	To Move
Tab	Forward one field
Shift+Tab	Backward one field
Home	Beginning of current field
Home Home	Beginning of first field in current check
End	End of current field
End End	End of last field in current check
Ctrl+→	Forward one word within a field
Ctrl+←	Backward one word within a field
PgUp	To the preceding check written
PgDn	To the next check written or a blank check
Home (3 times)	To the first check written (but not yet printed)
End (3 times)	To a blank check
End (3 times) and PgUp	To the last check written

Writing a Check

The mechanics of writing a check with Quicken closely resemble those for manually writing a check. The only real difference is that Quicken's Write Checks window makes the process easier. With Quicken, writing a check means you simply complete the Write Checks window. You fill in as many as seven fields: Date, Pay to the Order of, $ (Amount), Address, Memo, Category, and Message. After you write the check, you're ready to record and print the check.

To write a check, follow these steps:

1. Choose the Write Checks option from the Activities menu, click the Check button on the Iconbar, or press Ctrl+W to display the Write Checks window (refer to fig. 5.1).

2. If the correct checking account isn't shown in the Account drop-down list box, click the down arrow to display a list of bank accounts and select the checking account from which you want to write a check.

3. Press Tab to move to the Date field and type the date of the check. Enter the date in the *mm/dd/yy* format (such as **5/11/94**).

> **Note**
>
> The first time you write a check in the current Quicken session, the program fills the Date field with the system date (the current date according to your computer's internal memory). After you write your first check using the Write Checks window, Quicken fills the Date field with the last date used.
>
> You can change the date by typing over the existing date or by pressing the + (plus) and – (minus) keys to change the date one day at a time. To change the existing date of 5/11/94 to 5/13/94, for example, press the + key twice.

Tip

To use Quicken 3 for Windows' new pop-up calendar to enter dates in the Write Checks window, just click the arrow in the Date field.

4. Press Tab to move to the Pay to the Order Of field, where you enter the name of the person or business (called the *payee*) that the check pays. Type the name you want to appear on the check. Because you have space for up to 40 characters, you shouldn't have any problem fitting in the payee's name.

> **Note**
>
> The QuickFill feature makes entering payees and transactions fast and easy. When you type a few characters of the payee name, Quicken searches all previous entries in the Check Register, plus your memorized transactions, for a transaction with a payee name that begins with the characters you type. (Memorized transactions represent stored transaction information from previously entered transactions.) When a transaction is found, QuickFill fills in the rest of the payee name for you. If this payee is the one you want, press Tab; QuickFill fills in the rest of the check for you—the check amount; memo (if used); and category, subcategory, or transfer account. Chapter 7, "Using Quicken Shortcuts," explains how to use QuickFill and memorized transactions.
>
> If the check that QuickFill completes for you is the way you want it, you're ready to record the check (go to step 10). If the amount is different, continue with step 5 to learn how to enter or edit check amounts.

Tip

Quicken also provides a drop-down list box in the Pay to the Order Of field that you can use to select a payee. Quicken adds a payee's name to the list each time you write a check or enter a transaction for a new payee.

5. Press Tab to move to the $ (Amount) field and enter the check amount. You can use up to 10 characters to enter the amount. Characters can consist of only numbers, commas, and decimal points. Quicken enters commas if you don't and if room is available for them.

The largest value you can enter in the Amount field is 9999999.99. Because this number is difficult to read without commas (the number is $9,999,999.99), you probably will want Quicken to have enough room to insert commas. If you use some of the 10 characters for commas, the largest value you can enter is 999,999.99.

> ### Note
>
> If you need to add several amounts together for a check, Quicken 3's new pop-up calculator can help. Click the down arrow in the $ (Amount) field to display a calculator you can use to compute the check amount. Chapter 7, "Using Quicken Shortcuts," explains how to use this feature.

When you complete the $ (Amount) field and press Tab, Quicken writes out the amount on the next line of the check just as you do when writing a check manually. To save space, Quicken may abbreviate hundred as Hndrd, thousand as Thsnd, and million as Mill.

6. (Optional) Press Tab to move to the first line of the address block. The optional Address field provides five 30-character lines. If you use envelopes with windows and enter the payee's address in this field, the address shows in the envelope window. This field saves time that otherwise is spent addressing envelopes.

When using the Address field, you need to type the payee's name on the first line. Quicken provides a shortcut for you. If you type ' (apostrophe) or " (quotation marks) and then press Enter, Quicken copies the name from the Pay to the Order Of field. (Because the Pay to the Order Of field has space for 40 characters and the address lines have only 30 characters, this shortcut may cut off up to the last 10 characters of the payee's name.)

Press Tab to move to the second line of the address block. Type the street address or post office box and press Tab. Then type the city, state, and ZIP code. Press Tab to type any additional address information on the fifth address line.

7. (Optional) Press Tab to move to the Memo field, which you can use to describe the check further (such as **April rent**) or to tell the payee your account or loan number.

8. Press Tab to move to the Category field, in which you can assign a category or subcategory to a check so that you know what the check covers, such as utilities expense, interest expense, or entertainment. You also can use the Category field to describe the class into which a check falls. (Chapter 4, "Organizing Your Finances," describes categories and classes.) To learn about the Category field, refer to the later section "Assigning Categories and Classes to Checks."

You can use the Category field to enter another Quicken account if the check that you are writing represents a transfer of funds between your checking account and another account. (Chapter 6, "Using the Register," explains transfer transactions.) Quicken provides a listing of the most typical categories for home or business use to enable you to categorize your most frequent transactions quickly.

9. After the check is complete, record the check by choosing Record at the bottom of the Write Checks window, or press Enter if the cursor is positioned in the last field in the Write Checks window.

After Quicken records the check, your computer beeps, and the recorded check scrolls off screen. A new, blank check hidden by the preceding check is left on-screen, ready to be completed.

> **Note**
>
> You can turn off the beep through the **B**eep When Recording and Memorizing general preference. Turning off the beep is particularly attractive if you are entering several checks at a time and become annoyed with the constant beeping. Chapter 21, "Customizing Quicken," explains how to select general preferences and turn off the beep.

Quicken enables you to add an additional message to checks. If you select the Allow Entry of Extra Message on Check preference, Quicken displays the Message field, as shown in figure 5.2, on the check. (See "Setting Check Preferences" later in this chapter.) To enter a message, press Tab after you have assigned a category to the check in the Category field to move to the Message field.

Fig. 5.2

The Write Checks window displays a Message field if you select the check preference that enables you to enter an extra message on checks.

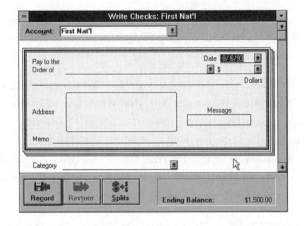

The message field gives you another 24 characters for additional information you want printed on the check, such as an account number for a credit card or a loan number for a mortgage. Because this information doesn't show through an envelope window, don't use the line for address information.

Assigning Categories and Classes to Checks

To help you track how you spend your money, Quicken uses categories, sub-categories, classes, subclasses, and accounts to classify your expenses. In the Write Checks window, Quicken has designated the Category field for this purpose.

When you press Tab to move to the Category field in the Write Checks window and then click the down arrow, Quicken displays the list of categories, classes, and accounts from the Category & Transfer list. From this list, highlight the category that you want to assign to the check. Then choose the category name (or subcategory, class, or account name) or press Enter. Quicken inserts the category name in the Category field in the Write Checks window.

The QuickFill feature in Quicken also works from the Category field in the Write Checks window. When you type the first characters in a category name, Quicken searches the Category & Transfer list to find the first category that begins with the characters you type. Suppose that you have a category named Entertainment, and that it's the only category name that starts with the letters Ent. If you type **Ent**, Quicken searches the Category & Transfer list until it finds a category that begins with Ent. When Quicken finds Entertainment, the QuickFill feature fills in the remaining letters of the category name.

You also can use QuickFill to enter an account name in the Category field when transferring money to another account. You learn more about using QuickFill to write checks in Chapter 7, "Using Quicken Shortcuts."

You also assign subcategories, classes, and subclasses to checks in the Category field. Subcategories, classes, and subclasses were explained in Chapter 4, "Organizing Your Finances."

To assign a subcategory, click the down arrow to display the Category & Transfer list and select the subcategory from the list. Quicken enters the parent category name and the subcategory name in the Category field. You also can use the QuickFill feature to enter a subcategory in the Category field. Type or enter the category first; then type a : (colon) and begin typing the subcategory name. QuickFill enters the rest of the subcategory when it finds the matching subcategory name in the Category & Transfer list.

To assign a class to a check transaction, type a / (slash) after the category or subcategory name in the Category field. Then type the class name or press Ctrl+L to display the Class list and select a class from the list. To assign a subclass to a check transaction, type a : (colon) after the class name. Then type the class that you want to function as a subclass, or press Ctrl+L to display the Class list and select the class from the list.

> **Tip**
> The QuickFill feature also works for entering classes. After you type a few characters after the slash, QuickFill enters the rest of the class when it finds the matching class name in the Class list.

> **Note**
>
> You can add categories, subcategories, and classes to the Category & Transfer list and the Class list (respectively) as you enter checks, or *on the fly*. Just type the new category, subcategory, or class, and Quicken displays the appropriate dialog box to enter information about the new subcategory or class.

Quicken doesn't require that you assign categories to transactions. If you want to track your income and expenses so that you know where your money comes from and where it goes, however, you should assign a category to each transaction that you enter in Quicken. To ensure that you do assign a category to each transaction, you can select the **W**arn If a Transaction Has No Category option from the list of **G**eneral preferences. When you select this preference, Quicken displays a warning message each time you record a transaction without an assigned category. Chapter 21, "Customizing Quicken," explains how to select this preference.

> **Note**
>
> Quicken provides defined Home, Business, or Home and Business categories, which you select when you create your Quicken data file. The Home category list provides categories for most general household expenses, and the Business category list includes general business income and expense categories. Home and Business categories combine both sets of categories into the category list. To access these categories, click the drop-down list box in the Category field, choose the Cat List button on the Iconbar, or press Ctrl+C.

Changing the Date Field Display

You can change the way dates are entered and displayed in the Write Checks window by setting the preference that controls how dates are entered. By default, Quicken displays dates as *mm/dd/yy*; however, you can change the way dates are displayed (to *dd/mm/yy*) by changing the date preference. If you change the date preference, dates are entered and displayed with the day first, followed by the month. August 18, 1994, for example, is entered and displayed as 18/08/94 instead of 08/18/94. See Chapter 21, "Customizing Quicken," to learn how to set the date preference.

The way dates are entered has no impact on the way dates are printed on checks. To change the date format on printed checks, see the section "Setting Check Preferences" later in this chapter.

> **CPA TIP: Paying Early To Receive Discounts**
>
> Businesses and individuals often receive discounts for paying bills early, so consider early payment when writing checks. In effect, not taking early payment discounts is an extremely expensive way to borrow money from the vendor. Suppose that a vendor normally requires payment within 30 days but gives a 2 percent discount for payments received within 10 days. If you pay within 30 rather than 10 days, you pay the vendor a 2 percent interest charge for paying 20 days later. Because one year contains roughly 18 20-day periods, the 2 percent for 20 days equals approximately 36 percent annually.
>
> Although you may need to borrow this money, you probably can find a much cheaper lender. As a rule of thumb, if a vendor gives you a 1 percent discount for paying 20 days early, you are borrowing money from him at about an 18 percent annual interest rate if you don't pay early. A 3 percent discount works out to a whopping 54 percent per year.

Reviewing and Editing Checks

From the Write Checks window, you can return to, review, and edit the checks you write. You can correct errors in a payee's name, for example, change the check amount, or change the category or subcategory assigned to the check. Suppose that you write a check to pay several bills to the same person or business, such as the bank where you have your mortgage, your car loan, and a personal line of credit. If you receive another bill from the bank, you may need to change the check amount.

Note

When you write and record a check in the Write Checks window, Quicken enters the check transaction in the Check Register; however, the check remains accessible from the Write Checks window until you print the check. Quicken doesn't store checks in the Write Checks window after they are printed. To review checks that have been printed, you must access the Check Register and then locate the checks by using the Find window. Chapter 7, "Using Quicken Shortcuts," explains how to locate checks and transactions.

You can use the scroll bar on the right side of the Write Checks window to move through the checks that you have written but not yet printed. Click the up arrow on the scroll bar to display the preceding check; click the down arrow to display the next check. You also can press PgUp to display the preceding check, press PgDn to display the next check, press Home three times to display the first check, or press End three times to display the last check.

Quicken arranges by date the checks you have written at the Write Checks window but haven't printed. Those checks with the earliest dates are listed first, followed chronologically by later checks. Checks with the same date are arranged in the order you entered them. To edit a check you already have recorded, display the check you want to change, and then edit the appropriate fields.

Deleting and Voiding Checks

You can delete at any time checks that you have written but not yet printed. Checks that you already have printed, however, must be voided so that you have a complete record of every check number in your Check Register. The following sections explain how to delete and void checks in Quicken.

Caution

You shouldn't delete a check that you have written and printed with Quicken. When you delete a check, Quicken removes all record of the transaction. Deleting the check removes the check information and leaves a gap in your check-numbering sequence. Instead, you need to void a check transaction that you want to remove because of a lost check, a check that you have stopped payment on, or an improperly printed check, but don't delete such checks. Information for voided transactions remains in the Check Register so that you can track each prenumbered check.

Deleting Checks

You can delete a check that you have written at the Write Checks window as long as you haven't printed the check. You may want to delete a check that you have written if, for example, you discover that you have already paid the bill or if you decide against making the payment at all.

Note

After checks are printed, Quicken no longer stores them in the Write Checks window. Printed check information is saved in the Check Register. Chapter 6, "Using the Register," teaches you how to use the Check Register.

To delete a check from the Write Checks window, follow these steps:

1. Use the scroll bar or the PgUp or PgDn keys to display the check that you want to delete.

2. Choose Delete Transaction from the Edit menu or press Ctrl+D.

3. Quicken displays the message OK to Delete transaction? (see fig. 5.3). Choose OK to delete the check.

Fig. 5.3
Quicken confirms whether you want to delete a check.

When you delete a check, Quicken removes all check information from the Write Checks window and the Check Register.

Voiding Checks

You may need to void a check when you want to stop payment, when you lose a check and write another one to replace it, or when a check prints incorrectly and you must print another. To void a check, go to the Check Register, highlight the transaction, and then choose Void Transaction from the Edit menu (or press Ctrl+V). You learn more about voiding transactions in the Check Register in Chapter 6, "Using the Register."

> **Note**
>
> Because you never would need to void a check that you haven't yet printed, you don't void checks from the Write Checks window.

Postdating Checks

Postdating means that you enter a future date for a check transaction. Traditionally, people use postdated checks as a way to delay a payment. The payee can't or shouldn't cash the check before the date printed on the check. With Quicken, you can use postdated transactions to delay checks being cashed. Perhaps more importantly, you can forecast your cash flows and balances by entering those checks that you know are in the future.

The steps for entering postdated checks mirror those for entering regular checks. The only difference, of course, is that the check date is in the future. When you enter postdated checks, Quicken calculates two account balances: the current balance, which is the account balance for the current date, and the ending balance, which is the account balance after the last postdated check. Quicken determines the current date by looking at the system date.

> **Note**
>
> If your computer's system date is incorrect, refer to your Windows user manual to learn how to set or reset the date in your system.

Postdating checks takes on an added feature in Quicken because you can review postdated checks for those that you should print. To do this, Quicken uses a built-in program called Billminder, which looks for postdated checks that it thinks you should print. You are reminded that checks are due every time you start your computer with Quicken Billminder messages and every time you start Quicken with Quicken Reminders messages (see fig. 5.4).

Fig. 5.4
A Reminders
message tells you
that your post-
dated checks are
due.

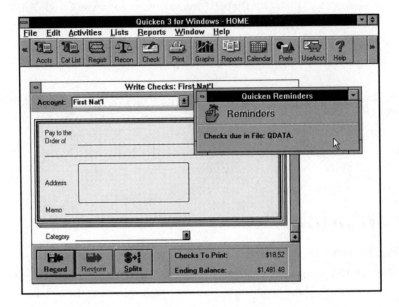

Splitting Check Transactions

The Write Checks window provides a field for assigning a category or subcategory to the check transaction. You can assign a check written to the power company, for example, to the Utilities category. You can assign a check written to pay for office supplies to the Supplies category. Many transactions, however, fit into more than one category, like the payment to your credit card company or payment to a department store. When you need to assign a check to more than one category, use the Splits command button at the bottom of the Write Checks window. When you choose Splits, Quicken displays the Splits window, which provides additional category fields and more space to assign categories and subcategories to a check (see fig. 5.5).

To split a check transaction, follow these steps:

1. Enter the date, payee, check amount, address (if applicable), and memo (if applicable) for the check, as explained earlier in this chapter.

2. Choose Splits (or press Ctrl+S). Quicken displays the Splits window (refer to fig. 5.5).

CPA TIP: Tracking Income and Expenses with Split Transactions

When you want to track your income and expenses closely, enter split transactions for payments to department stores and discount stores where you buy different types of items. If you don't split the transaction to record a check to pay your Sears charge for tools, clothing, and cosmetics purchases, for example, and lump the total check transaction into one category, your expenses aren't accurately reflected.

3. In the first Category field, type the category name or click the down arrow to select a category from the Category & Transfer list.

Note

Quicken includes the **D**rop Down Lists Automatically preference that automatically displays drop-down lists for some fields when you move to those fields. If this preference is selected, the drop-down list in the Category field in the Splits window automatically appears. If this feature annoys you because the list covers the command buttons in the Splits window, you can change the Drop Down List Automatically preference. To change the preference, click the Prefs button on the Iconbar, choose the **Q**uickFill preference button, and then click the **D**rop Down Lists Automatically check box to remove the check mark. Choose OK and then choose **D**one to save the preference setting.

Use the Category field in the Splits window in the same way that you use the Category field in the Write Checks window. You also can use the Category field to record transfers to other accounts. Up to 30 lines are available in the Splits window to assign categories, subcategories, or transfer accounts.

4. (Optional) Press Tab to move to the Memo field. Type a description of the category or the amount. The Memo field provides a 27-character space that you can use to describe a transaction, to explain why you selected a category, or to detail how you calculated the amount.

5. Press Tab to move to the Amount field. You can use the Amount field in two ways, depending on whether you accessed **Splits** before or after you enter the amount on the Write Checks window.

If you chose the **Splits** button *before* you make an entry in the Amount field on the Write Checks window, Quicken adds each amount you enter in the Splits window's Amount field and then enters this total in the $ (Amount) field in the Write Checks window.

If you chose the **Splits** button *after* entering a check amount in the Write Checks window, Quicken shows this amount in the first Amount field in the Splits window and in the Splits Total at the bottom of the Splits window. If you then enter a number in the first Amount field in the Splits window, Quicken calculates the difference between the check amount in the Write Checks window and the new amount you entered, and then places this difference in the second Amount field in the Splits window and in the Remainder field at the bottom of the Splits window.

Quicken keeps track of the amounts that you have assigned to transactions in the Splits window. Notice the Transaction Total field, which shows the difference between the Splits Total and the Remainder amount (refer to fig. 5.5).

> **Note**
>
> You can enter percents in the Splits window's Amount fields. If you enter a check for $1,200 and 25 percent of this amount is to be entered in the first Splits field, move to the Amount field, type **25%**, and press Tab. When you press Tab to move to the next field, Quicken calculates the number that equals 25 percent of $1,200 and enters this value in the Amount field.

6. Press Tab to move to the next line of the Splits window. Repeat steps 3 through 5 for each category and amount combination you want to record. You can record up to 30 category and amount combinations. Figure 5.6 shows a completed Splits window.

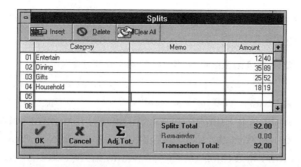

Fig. 5.6
Use the Splits window for a check transaction to assign more than one category.

If you use all 30 split transaction Amount fields, Quicken has nowhere to make the Write Checks window amount equal to the total Splits Total amount. You manually must adjust the Write Checks window amount or one of the Splits window amounts. You also can choose Adj. Tot. (Adjust Total) to total the Amount fields in the Splits window and insert the total into the $ (Amount) field in the Write Checks window.

7. To record the categories and amounts in the Splits window, choose OK. Quicken returns to the Write Checks window and indicates the split transaction with the word --SPLITS-- in the Category field (see fig. 5.7).

8. Choose Record to record the check with the split transaction amounts.

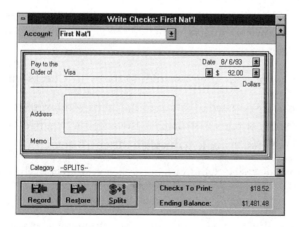

Fig. 5.7
Quicken enters the word --SPLITS-- in the Category field of the Write Checks window when you assign more than one category or sub-category to a check.

If you use check forms with vouchers and enter individual invoices and invoice amounts in the Splits window, Quicken prints this information on the voucher. Vendors then can record your payments correctly, and you no longer have to spend time trying to explain which invoice a check pays. Remember that room is available on the voucher only for the first 15 lines in the Splits window. If you use all 30 lines in the Splits window, only half of the split transaction detail appears.

Calculating Check Amounts in Split Transactions

You can calculate the amount that you want to write a check for by using the Splits window. Perhaps you have several invoices from the same vendor, but each invoice represents a different type of expense that you want to assign to different categories. You can use the Splits window to assign the categories, enter the amounts, and calculate the total amount to enter as the check amount in the Write Checks window.

To have Quicken calculate the check amount in a split transaction, follow these steps:

1. Fill out the Write Checks window as usual, except for the amount.

2. Choose Splits (or press Ctrl+S) to display the Splits window (refer to fig. 5.5).

3. Enter the information in the Splits window. As you enter amounts, Quicken keeps track of the split transaction amounts in the Transaction Total field at the bottom of the window.

4. After you finish entering lines in the Splits window, choose Adj. Tot. (Adjust Total). Quicken adds the entries in the Amount fields in the Splits window and enters the total in the $ (Amount) field in the Write Checks window.

5. Choose OK or press Enter to return to the Write Checks window.

6. (Optional) If you need to return to the Splits window to make a change, choose Splits or press Ctrl+S, make the necessary changes, and then choose Adj. Tot. again to recalculate the check amount.

7. At the Write Checks window, choose Record to record the check.

Editing Split Transactions

You can change the information in the Splits window just as you can change any other transaction. To edit a split transaction, follow these steps:

1. Display the check whose split transaction information you want to edit.

2. Choose Splits (or press Ctrl+S) to display the Splits window.

3. Press Tab to move to the field in the Splits window that you want to edit and select a new category, type a new memo, or enter a new amount.

You also can use the following Splits buttons from the top of the Splits window to edit information:

Insert	Inserts a line between two other lines in the Splits window
Delete (Ctrl+D)	Deletes the highlighted line in the Splits window
Clear All	Clears all lines in the Splits window

> **Note**
>
> If you change an amount in a split transaction, the Splits window may not balance (the Splits Total won't equal the Transaction Total). If necessary, you can choose Adj. Tot. to recalculate the transaction amount. Don't choose Adj. Tot. to recalculate if the amount in the $ (Amount) field in the Write Checks window is the correct amount and you're just reallocating amounts to categories or subcategories in the Splits window.

4. After making changes in the Splits window, choose OK to save the changes and return to the Write Checks window.

5. Choose Record to record the changed split transaction.

Deleting Split Transactions

Just as you can delete checks with only one category or subcategory assigned to them, you also can delete split transactions. Use the same discretion when deleting a split transaction that you use for deleting a check assigned to only one category or subcategory, as explained earlier in this chapter.

You delete split-transaction checks the same way you delete single-category checks, as explained earlier.

Undoing Split Transactions

After you split a check transaction, you can go back, undo the split, and assign only one category or subcategory to the transaction. Follow these steps to undo a split transaction:

1. Display the check whose split transaction you want to undo.

2. Click the Cat List button on the Iconbar or press Ctrl+C to display the Category & Transfer list.

3. Click the scroll bar or press the up- and down-arrow keys to highlight the single category or subcategory that you want to assign to the check.

4. Choose Use. Quicken moves to the transaction line in the Check Register where the check was recorded and displays the Replace Splits with Single Category? dialog box.

5. Choose Yes to assign the category or subcategory to the check.

6. Choose Record to record the check transaction with only one category or subcategory.

7. To return to the Write Checks window, click the Checks button on the Iconbar or press Ctrl-W.

Setting Check Preferences

Tip
You can change any of the check preference settings at any time.

Quicken enables you to set check preferences so that you can determine the way Quicken prints the date on checks, whether the message line prints, and whether split category information prints on voucher-style checks. You also can tell Quicken to change the date on your checks to the date you print them and to warn you if you're going to use the same check number twice.

To set check preferences, follow these steps:

1. Choose Preferences from the Edit menu or click the Prefs button on the Iconbar. Quicken displays the Quicken for Windows Preferences dialog box, shown in figure 5.8.

Fig. 5.8
The Quicken for Windows Preferences dialog box includes the areas in which you can set preferences.

2. Choose the Checks preference button. Quicken displays the Check Preferences dialog box, shown in figure 5.9.

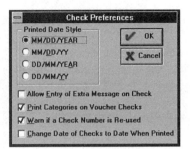

Fig. 5.9
Quicken enables you to set check preferences so that checks print the way you want them.

3. In the Printed Date Style section, select the date format that you want Quicken to use to print dates on checks.

4. To display a message field on checks and print the message on checks, select Allow **E**ntry of Extra Message on Check.

5. If you want to print split categories on voucher-style checks, select **P**rint Categories on Voucher Checks.

6. To have Quicken warn you if the check number that you print already appears in the Check Register, select **W**arn if a Check Number is Re-used.

7. If you want Quicken to print the current system date as the check date, select **C**hange Date of Checks to Date When Printed.

8. Choose OK to save the check preference settings and return to the Quicken for Windows Preferences window.

9. Choose Done.

Printing Checks

Before you can begin to print checks, you must choose the proper printer settings so that Quicken knows the printer that you are using, the check format, and so forth. After you have the correct printer settings to print checks, you need to position them in your printer properly before you start printing.

Before you begin to print checks with Quicken, make sure that your printer is set up in Windows to print in Windows applications. Refer to Chapter 1,

Tip
Aligning checks in your printer is easy with Intuit's on-screen alignment feature.

"Preparing To Use Quicken for Windows," to learn how to set up Windows to use your printer.

CPA TIP: Reviewing Checks for Errors

After you receive your checks from Intuit, review them carefully to ensure that they are free of printing errors. Most importantly, examine the bank account number to make sure that it is correct. If you find an error, return the checks immediately and have them reprinted. Unless the printing error was caused by wrong information you submitted, your checks will be reprinted at no charge.

Setting Up Quicken to Print Checks

Tip
You can print a logo on your checks if the logo comes from a Windows bit-map (.BMP) file. See the section "Printing a Logo on Checks" to learn how to import a logo to Quicken and print it on checks.

Before you can begin printing checks, you must enter information about your printer and the style of checks you are using.

Note

Don't try to print checks with Quicken until you have entered the information about your printer. Checks won't print properly unless Quicken knows the type of printer you are using, the paper feed your printer uses, the style of checks you use, and the printing style (print left, print centered, or print portrait style).

To set up Quicken to print checks, follow these steps:

1. Choose Printer Setup from the File menu.

2. From the Printer Setup submenu, choose Check Printer Setup. Quicken displays the Check Printer Setup dialog box (see fig. 5.10).

Fig. 5.10
Use the Check Printer Setup dialog box to tell Quicken about your printer and the check style that you are using.

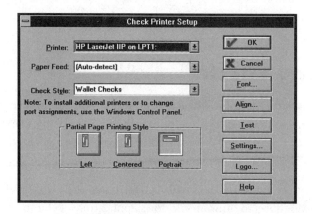

3. If your installed printer doesn't appear in the Printer drop-down list, select the correct printer from the list.

4. Quicken uses Auto-detect to determine whether your printer is continuous-feed or page-oriented. If the paper feed isn't correct, select the appropriate paper feed for your installed printer from the Paper Feed drop-down list.

5. Choose the Check Style drop-down list box to display a list of check styles. Select the check style that matches the checks you ordered to use with Quicken.

> **Note**
>
> Entering the correct check style is extremely important when you set up Quicken to print checks. The information on checks doesn't print the same for different check styles. If you don't enter the correct check style when you set up Quicken to print checks, you can change the check style when go to print checks.

6. In the Partial Page Printing Style section, choose the position that matches the way you load a partial page of checks in your printer.

> **Note**
>
> The partial page printing style applies only to page-oriented printers.

7. (Optional) Select the Font command button to display the Check Printing Font dialog box (see fig. 5.11). Here, you can change the font, font style, and size that Quicken uses to print information on checks. In the Font list box, select the font you want to use. In the Font Style list box, select the style. In the Size list box, select the size print you want to use. Quicken shows a sample of the font, style, and size in the Sample area. If you don't see a sample, choose Regular from the Font Style list box.

Choose OK to save your font selections. Quicken returns to the Check Printer Setup dialog box.

Learning Quicken

Fig. 5.11
The Check
Printing Font
dialog box to set
the font, font
style, and size that
Quicken uses to
print information
on checks.

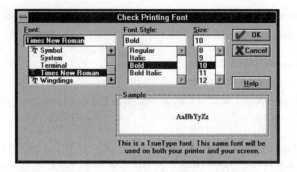

8. You can change other print settings, such as the paper tray, paper size, orientation, and number of copies by choosing Settings. Quicken displays a dialog box for your installed printer. Figure 5.12 shows the dialog box for a Hewlett-Packard LaserJet IIP printer.

Fig. 5.12
The HP LaserJet IIP
dialog box shows
the default settings
for the Hewlett
Packard LaserJet
IIP printer. You
can change any of
the default
settings.

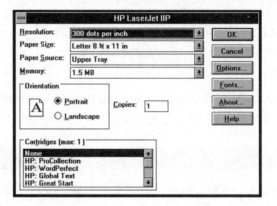

Set the correct resolution, paper size, and source. If you are using a printer that supports different memory configurations, specify how much memory is available for your printer. (Notice that the **Memory** text box isn't available if your printer doesn't support different memory configurations.) Choose the appropriate paper position for printing: Portrait or Landscape. Leave the Copies setting at 1 for check printing. If your printer supports cartridge fonts (built into the printer drive for your printer), choose a cartridge from the Cartridges list box.

When the settings in the printer dialog box are the way you want them, choose OK to return to the Check Printer Setup dialog box.

> **Note**
>
> From the printer dialog box (refer to fig. 5.12), you can choose **O**ptions to change the dithering and intensity control options. *Dithering* determines how detailed the graphic images appear in printed documents. Choosing coarse dithering, for example, produces graphic images at 300 dpi (dots per inch). *Intensity control* increases or decreases the darkness of graphics. You shouldn't need to change these options, as they aren't relevant to check printing.
>
> You also can install fonts for your printer by choosing **F**onts from the printer dialog box shown in figure 5.12. Installing fonts is beyond the scope of this book. If you want to venture out and install new fonts to use in Quicken, refer to your Windows and printer manuals to learn how to install new fonts.

9. Choose OK to save the printer settings in the Check Printer Setup dialog box.

From the Check Printer Setup dialog box, you can print a test check and align your pre-printed checks. These activities are covered in the next few sections.

Aligning Checks

Before you start printing checks, you should print a test check to ensure that your checks are properly positioned and aligned in your printer and that the vertical and horizontal print settings are correct. If you're using continuous-feed checks, use the sample checks that were enclosed in your Quicken software package to print a sample check. If you're using a page-oriented printer (like a laser, inkjet, or PostScript printer), print a test check on plain paper so that you don't waste any of your checks. You learn how to print both types of test checks in the following sections.

After you go through the process of aligning checks by entering the vertical and horizontal print settings, the alignment settings in Quicken will remain and you won't need to repeat this process each time you print checks.

Printing a Test Check on Continuous-Feed Printers. To print a test check on a continuous-feed printer, follow these steps:

1. Insert the continuous-form checks into the printer as you would insert continuous-form paper.

2. Choose Printer Setup from the File menu.

3. Choose Check Printer Setup from the Printer Setup submenu. Quicken displays the Check Printer Setup dialog box.

4. Choose Test. Quicken prints a test check to Jane Doe.

Review the test check to make sure that Quicken printed the information in the proper positions on the check. If the check information was printed in the correct positions, you don't need to change the alignment settings and you're ready to print checks in Quicken.

If the check information isn't printed in the correct positions, you need to enter alignment settings so that Quicken knows where to print the information on your checks.

Aligning Continuous-Feed Checks. After you determine that the information on the test check wasn't correctly positioned, you need to enter alignment settings. To enter alignment settings for continuous-feed checks, follow these steps:

1. From the Check Printer Setup dialog box, choose Align to display the Check Printer Alignment window (see fig. 5.13).

Note

For continuous-feed checks, disregard the Checks on Page section of this dialog box.

Fig. 5.13
The Check Printer Alignment window enables you to show Quicken how the information on your test check printed.

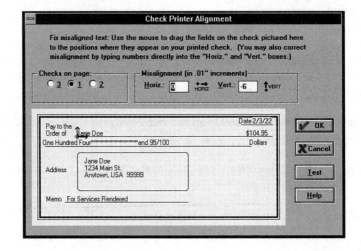

2. You can enter the approximate values, measured in .01-inch increments, that the printed information was off from the correct positioning on the check. For information that is printed too far to the left or
right on the check, enter the approximate distance in the Horiz text
box. For information that is printed up or down too far, enter the approximate distance in the Vert text box.

Using the alignment cursor, however, to move the text on the check
in the Check Printer Alignment window is much easier. Just hold down
the left mouse button as you move (drag) the text around the on-screen
check until it looks the same as the printed test check. Then, release the
left mouse button to leave the text where you placed it. Quicken automatically enters the appropriate values in the Horiz and Vert text boxes.

> **Note**
>
> If the printing needs only a small adjustment vertically or horizontally, increase
> or decrease the values in the **Horiz** or **Vert** text boxes by one or two. Reposi-
> tioning the text by extremely small increments is difficult when using the
> mouse.

3. When the text in the on-screen check in the Check Printer Alignment
dialog box matches the positioning on the test check, choose Test to
print another test check. Quicken uses the alignment of the text in the
on-screen check to adjust the text on the printed check.

4. Review the test check for proper positioning. If the information on the
test check is printed in the correct positions, choose OK to return to the
Check Printer Setup dialog box. Choose OK again to save your check
alignment settings.

If the text on the test check didn't print in the correct positions, repeat
steps 3 and 4.

Printing a Test Check on Page-Oriented Printers. If you're using a laser,
inkjet, PostScript, or other page-oriented printer, you also need to print a test
check to determine the proper alignment settings. To print a test check on a
page-oriented printer, follow these steps:

Tip
Use plain paper when printing a test check on page-oriented printers so that you don't waste any checks. You can overlay the test check on your preprinted checks to see how the text lines up.

1. Load regular paper into your page-oriented printer.

2. Choose Printer Setup from the File menu.

3. Choose Check Printer Setup from the Printer Setup submenu. Quicken displays the Check Printer Setup dialog box.

4. Choose Test. Quicken prints a test check to Jane Doe. Figure 5.14 shows the test check (on plain paper) printed by Quicken on a page-oriented printer.

Review the test check to make sure that Quicken printed the information in the proper positions on the check. If the check information was printed in the correct positions, you don't need to change the alignment settings, and you're ready to print checks in Quicken.

Fig. 5.14
A test check printed on plain paper. Match the printed text to a blank check.

If the check information isn't printed in the correct positions, you need to enter alignment settings so that Quicken knows where to print the information on your checks.

Aligning Page-Oriented Checks. After you determine that the information on the test check wasn't correctly positioned, you need to enter alignment settings. To do so, follow these steps:

1. From the Check Printer Setup dialog box, choose Align to display the Check Printer Alignment window (refer to fig. 5.13).

2. In the Checks on Page section, choose the number of checks on the preprinted check form page that you are aligning.

> **Note**
>
> You must enter alignment settings for partial pages of checks. Therefore, you must enter alignment settings for a page with 2 checks and enter alignment settings for a page with 1 check.

3. In the Horiz and Vert text boxes, you can enter the approximate values, measured in .01-inch increments, that the printed information was off from the correct positioning on the check. For information printed too far to the left or right on the check, enter the approximate distance in the Horiz text box. For information that is printed up or down too far, enter the approximate distance in the Vert text box.

Using the alignment cursor to move the text on the check in the Check Printer Alignment window is much easier, however. Just hold down the left mouse button as you move (drag) the text around the on-screen check until it looks the same as the printed test check. Then, release the left mouse button to leave the text where you placed it. Quicken automatically enters the appropriate values in the Horiz and Vert text boxes.

> **Note**
>
> If the printing needs only a small adjustment vertically or horizontally, increase or decrease the values by one or two in the Horiz or Vert text boxes. Repositioning the text by extremely small increments is difficult when using the mouse.

4. When the text in the on-screen check in the Check Printer Alignment dialog box matches the positioning on the test check, choose Test to print another test check. Quicken uses the alignment of the text in the on-screen check to adjust the text on the printed check.

5. Review the test check for proper positioning. If the information on the test check is printed in the correct positions, choose OK to return to the Check Printer Setup dialog box. Choose OK again to save your check alignment settings.

If the information on the test check didn't print in the correct positions, repeat steps 3 and 4.

Printing Your Checks

After your checks are aligned properly, you're ready to print a check. Printing checks with Quicken is fast, easy, and even fun. Just don't forget to sign your checks after they are printed. Signing checks is the one task that Quicken can't perform for you.

To print checks, follow these steps:

1. Load the blank checks into your printer.

   If you are using a page-oriented printer, place the check form sheets in the printer paper tray, as you would place regular sheets of paper. If your printer prints on the face-down side of the paper, for example, make sure that your checks are inserted face down. Also make sure that your checks are positioned in the proper order according to check number (the sheet with check number 3456 comes before the sheet with check number 3459).

2. With the Write Checks window on-screen, choose Print Checks from the File menu to display the Select Checks to Print dialog box (see

Fig. 5.15
The Select Checks to Print dialog box shows you how many checks you need to print.

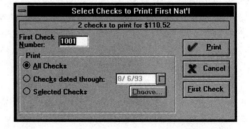

   fig. 5.15). At the top of the dialog box, Quicken tells you how many checks you need to print and the total dollar amount of the checks to be printed.

3. Quicken displays the number of the next check in the First Check Number text box. If the number Quicken displays isn't the same as the number in the upper right corner of the next check, type the correct check number. You also can press the + (plus) and − (minus) keys to change the number.

4. In the Print section, select which checks you want to print, as follows:

- To print all checks, choose All Checks.

- Choose Checks Dated Through if you have postdated checks that you want to print. (Unless you specify a date through which to print checks, Quicken prints only those checks dated on or before the current date.) In the date text box, type the date through which you want Quicken to print postdated checks.

- To select the checks that you want to print, choose Selected Checks, and then select Choose. Quicken displays a second Select Checks to Print dialog box (see fig. 5.16).

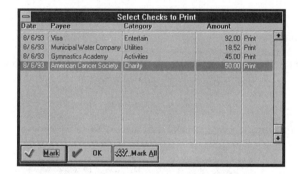

Fig. 5.16
Quicken lists all checks written, but not yet printed, in the second Select Checks to Print dialog box.

To select a check to print, use the scroll bar or the up and down arrow keys to highlight the check. Then choose Mark or press the space bar. Quicken puts the word Print next to the check amount for the check that you select to print.

To deselect a check previously marked for printing, highlight the check and choose Mark or press the space bar. To select all checks for printing or to deselect all checks for printing, choose Mark All.

After you finish selecting checks to print, choose OK to return to the first Select Checks to Print dialog box (refer to fig. 5.15).

5. If you're printing continuous-feed checks, choose the First Check button to print only the first check out of the group of checks selected.

> ### Note
>
> If you want to print a test check before you begin printing on your preprinted checks, choose the **Test** button in the Print Checks dialog box (see fig. 5.17). Quicken prints the test check and displays the message Is the alignment OK? If so, choose Yes; otherwise, choose No and Quicken displays the Check Printer Alignment dialog box (refer to fig. 5.13). Follow the steps in the earlier section "Aligning Checks" to complete the Check Printer Alignment dialog box.
>
> If you want to change the alignment of text on printed checks before you begin printing, choose the **Align** button in the Print Checks dialog box (see fig. 5.17). Quicken displays the Check Printer Alignment dialog box. Follow the steps in the section "Aligning Checks" to complete this dialog box.

6. Choose **Print**. Quicken displays the Print Checks dialog box, shown in figure 5.17.

7. If the check style that appears in the Check Style drop-down list box isn't correct, select the correct one from the drop-down list.

8. For page-oriented printers, choose the Three, Two, or One check icon to match the number of checks that are on the first page of checks.

Fig. 5.17
After you select which checks you want to print, Quicken displays the Print Checks dialog box.

9. For voucher-check styles, an extra text box—Additional Copies—appears in the Print Checks dialog box. Type the number of additional check copies that you want to print.

> **Note**
>
> If you're using Quicken in your small business and have temporary checks that don't have your company's name or address, you can print this information on checks. To do so, select the Print Your Company Name and Address check box in the Print Checks dialog box (refer to fig. 5.17). Then proceed to print checks as usual.

10. Choose **Print** to begin printing checks. Quicken displays a message that checks are printing.

If you are printing on a partial page of checks and selected to print partial pages in landscape printing style (checks are inserted vertically in your printer), Quicken displays the message Do the Checks Have a Tear-Off Strip? If the partial page of checks you are printing still have the tear-off strip attached, choose Yes. Otherwise choose No. Quicken begins printing checks on the partial page.

11. After the checks are printed, Quicken displays the Did check(s) print OK? message. Review the printed checks carefully.

If your checks printed correctly, choose OK. Quicken returns to the Write Checks window.

If one or more of your checks printed incorrectly, perhaps the alignment wasn't right or the check forms jammed in the printer. Type the number of the first check that printed incorrectly and then choose OK. Quicken returns to the Select Checks to Print dialog box. Repeat steps 3 through 11 to reprint the checks that printed incorrectly.

> **CPA TIP: Voiding Misprinted Checks**
>
> Write **VOID** in large letters across the face of checks that Quicken incorrectly prints. This precaution prevents anyone from later signing and cashing the checks.

Reprinting a Check

If you decide later, even after leaving the Print Checks dialog box, that you want to reprint a check, you can. Suppose that the original check somehow gets lost or destroyed. Because you still must pay the person, you need to reprint the check. Rather than re-enter all the same information, you can reprint the original information. (If you lose a check, consider placing a stop-payment order with your bank.)

When you enter checks you plan to print using the Write Checks window, Quicken records the checks in the Check Register. Because Quicken hasn't assigned check numbers, however, the word Print is entered in the Num (Check Number) field in the Check Register to indicate that the check is one that you have set up to print using the Write Checks window. When Quicken prints the checks, it replaces the word Print with the actual check number.

By itself, this bit of information isn't all that exciting, but it does enable you to trick Quicken into reprinting a check. All you need to do is change a check's number to the word Print. Quicken then assumes that the check is one you want to print. To print the check after you change the number to the word Print, follow the steps earlier in the section "Printing Checks."

After you reprint a check, Quicken enters the new check number in the Num (Check Number) field for the check transaction in the Check Register. You then must enter a voided transaction for the original check number so that each check is accounted for in the Check Register. Chapter 6, "Using the Register," explains how to enter transactions in the Register and how to void transactions.

Printing a Logo on Checks

With Quicken 3 for Windows, you can print a logo on your checks. Using logos in Quicken has two requirements, however:

■ The logo must come from artwork from a Windows bit-map (.BMP) file.

■ The logo artwork must not be larger than one-inch square.

To print a logo on your checks, follow these steps:

1. Choose Printer Setup from the File menu.

2. Choose Check Printer Setup from the Printer Setup submenu. Quicken displays the Check Printer Setup dialog box (refer to fig. 5.10).

3. Choose Logo to display the Check Logo Artwork dialog box, shown in figure 5.18.

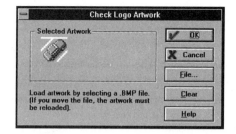

Fig. 5.18
The Check Logo Artwork dialog box displays the logo that prints on checks.

4. Choose File to display the Open Artwork File dialog box (see fig. 5.19). Change the directory to the directory where your bit-map files are stored by double-clicking and scrolling to the correct path within the Directories list box. Then select the bit-map file from the File Name list box. (Bit-map files have the extension BMP.) Choose OK to paste the artwork in the Selected Artwork area of the Check Logo Artwork dialog box.

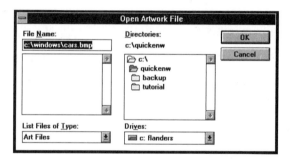

Fig. 5.19
Select your artwork bit-map file from the Open Artwork File dialog box.

5. If this logo is the one you want to print on checks, choose OK. If it isn't, choose File again and select another bit-map file.

6. When you're ready to print checks, follow steps 1 through 6 in the earlier section "Printing Checks" to display the Print Checks dialog box (refer to fig. 5.17).

7. From the Print Checks dialog box, select the Print Check Artwork check box to put a check mark in the box.

> **Note**
>
> This check box isn't available if you print wallet-style checks. This check box also isn't available unless you have previously selected a bit-map file, as explained in steps 1 through 5.

8. Print the checks as usual.

Summary

This chapter described the basics of writing and printing checks with Quicken. You learned how to do the following:

- Use the Write Checks window

- Write and record a check

- Review, edit, and delete checks in the Write Checks window

- Assign more than one category to a check by splitting the check transaction

- Set up Quicken to print checks correctly

- Print checks

- Print logos on checks

The next chapter shows you how to use the Register to enter checks, deposits, and other withdrawals. You will see the transactions that Quicken enters for the checks that you write and learn how to review and edit transactions, and delete, insert, and void transactions in the Register.

Chapter 6

Using the Register

Your checkbook, or check register, is your most fundamental financial tool. You probably agree that your check register largely summarizes your financial life. Money flows into your checking account in the form of wages for a household or sales collections for a business. Money flows out of the checking account to pay expenses.

Moving your check register to Quicken provides two major benefits. First, Quicken does the arithmetic of deducting checks and withdrawals and adding deposits—a trivial contribution until you remember the last time an error in your arithmetic caused you to bounce a check. Second, Quicken records each checking account transaction in the Register so that you can use Quicken's Reports feature to summarize and extract information from the Register—information that helps you plan and control your finances more effectively.

Quicken's Register is the program's major component. Every other program feature that writes checks, reconciles accounts, and prints reports depends on the Register. Every user works with Quicken's Register directly by entering transactions into the Register and indirectly by using the information stored in the Register. In fact, you can enter any of the financial transactions you record directly into the Quicken Register.

Chapter 7, "Using Quicken Shortcuts," describes Quicken features that you can use to speed up your work in the Register. Chapters 9, 10, and 11 describe how you can use the Register to track assets, credit card purchases, loans, and other liabilities. Chapter 15, "Monitoring Your Investments," describes a special set of tools that Quicken provides for managing your investments. To track and monitor your investments, Quicken provides the Investment Register.

This chapter describes the basics of using Quicken's Register, including the following:

- Displaying the Register

- Recording checks, deposits, withdrawals, and other transactions in the Register

- Assigning more than one category to a transaction

- Postdating transactions

- Using Quick-Report for instant transaction reports

- Printing the Register

> **Note**
>
> If you don't print checks using Quicken, you probably will enter all your checking account transactions in the Register. If you do print checks with Quicken, you should enter check information in the Write Checks window (although you also can print checks from information entered in the Register). When you enter and record a check in the Write Checks window, Quicken records the transaction in the Register and updates the account balance. The steps for entering check information in the Write Checks window are outlined in Chapter 5, "Writing and Printing Checks." The steps you take to record a transaction in the Register screen are described in this chapter.

> **Note**
>
> This chapter focuses on the Register for a checking account. Although all Quicken Registers work basically the same, a few slight differences exist. You learn about Credit Card, Cash, Asset, Liability, and Investment Registers in later chapters.

Displaying the Register

Display the Register when you want to do the following:

- Enter checks that you write manually

- Enter deposits and ATM withdrawals

- Enter other types of transactions, such as interest earned from your bank account and service charges

- Postdate transactions

- Review transactions

- Edit or delete transactions

- Void a transaction

- Locate a specific transaction

- Print the Register

Note

Each account that you set up in Quicken has its own Register. You must select the account that you want to work with to display its Register.

To display the Register (shown in fig. 6.1), follow these steps:

1. Choose Account from the Lists menu, press Ctrl+A, or click Accts on the Iconbar to display the Account list.

2. Scroll the Account list to highlight the account whose Register you want to use, and then choose Use. If you want to enter transactions for your checking account, for example, highlight your checking account in the Account list and choose Use.

Quicken displays the Register for the account that you selected.

Tip

If you're working in the Write Checks window, you can display the Register for your account by pressing Ctrl+R. To return to the Write Checks window, press Ctrl+W.

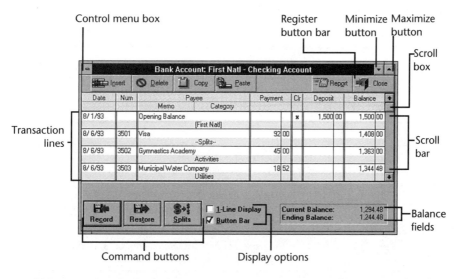

Fig. 6.1

The Register appears when you select an account to use from the Account list.

Note

You also can click Registr on the Iconbar to display the Register; however, you already must be working in the account that you want to use for Quicken to display the proper Register. If you're reconciling your credit card account and click Registr on the Iconbar, for example, Quicken displays the Register for the credit card account. Similarly, if you're writing checks in the Write Checks window and click Registr, Quicken displays the Register for the checking account from which you are writing checks.

Reviewing the Register

The displayed Register looks similar to the manual check register that you use (refer to fig. 6.1). The Register window includes the following:

- *Register button bar.* This new Quicken 3 for Windows feature includes buttons at the top of the Register that you can use to perform the following activities:

Button	Description
Insert	Inserts a blank transaction line in the Register
Delete	Deletes the selected transaction from the Register
Copy	Copies the selected transaction to the Windows Clipboard
Paste	Pastes a transaction from the Windows Clipboard to the selected transaction line
Report	Generates a QuickReport that lists all transactions that contain the same payee as the selected transaction
Close	Closes the Register window

- *The transaction lines of the Register.* Transaction lines include fields to enter the following information:

Field	Records
Date	The date of the transaction.
Num	The check number. You also can use this field to enter **ATM** (for automatic teller machine transaction) or any other descriptive term for transactions that don't involve checks.
Payee	The person or firm you are paying, or, in the case of a deposit, the source of the deposit.
Memo	An optional field to enter a check memo or description of the transaction.
Category	The category or subcategory assigned to the transaction. You also use the Category field to assign a class and subclass to a transaction. (Refer to Chapter 4, "Organizing Your Finances," for more on categories and classes.)
Payment	The amount of the check or withdrawal.

Learning Quicken

Field	Records
Clr (Cleared)	Indicates whether the transaction has cleared the bank. You learn more about cleared transactions in Chapter 8, "Reconciling Your Bank Account."
Deposit	The amount of the deposit or bank credit.
Balance	Quicken calculates the balance in your account after the current transaction and enters the result here. You can't make an entry in the Balance field.

■ *Command buttons.* The buttons at the bottom of the Register perform the following activities:

Button	Description
Record	Records the selected transaction. Choose Record when you are finished entering a transaction in the Register.
Restore	Reverts the transaction you are editing to the way it was before you started editing.
Splits	Opens the Splits window so that you can assign more than one category, subcategory, class, or subclass to a transaction. (You learn more about splitting transactions later in this chapter.)

■ *Display options.* These two check boxes are included in the Register so that you can change the way the Register appears on-screen. If you want to display more transactions at a time, select the 1-Line Display check box to condense the Register to one line for each transaction. Removing the check mark from the **Button Bar** check box hides the Register's button bar from the display. Hiding the button bar also enables you to display more transactions at a time.

■ *Balance fields.* If you enter postdated transactions in the Register (transactions whose dates are later than the current system date), Quicken displays two balance fields: the Current Balance field and the Ending Balance field. If displayed, the Current Balance field shows the balance in the account based on all transactions entered with dates through the current date. The Ending Balance field shows the balance of all entered transactions. If no postdated transactions are in the Register, Quicken displays only the Ending Balance field.

Tip
Before recording transactions, use the balance fields to gauge the effect of the transactions you want to record (is there money to cover the checks you need to write?).

> **Note**
>
> You can't make entries to or edit the Current Balance or the Ending Balance fields. Quicken calculates these fields based on the transactions entered in the Register.

Moving Around the Register

As you get up to speed with Quicken, you will want to move through the Register quickly so that you can enter transactions as fast as possible or review prior transactions without having to move through the Register line by line.

You easily can move from transaction to transaction in the Register window by using the scroll bar on the right side of the window. Just click the down arrow to move to the next transaction, or click the up arrow to move to the preceding transaction.

You also can use the scroll box to move quickly through transactions in the Register window. To move through the Register window using the scroll box, follow these steps:

1. Put the mouse pointer on the scroll box.

2. Press and hold down the left mouse button as you drag (move) the scroll box up or down the scroll bar.

As you drag the scroll box, Quicken displays a date and check number in a box to the left of the scroll box. This information represents the date and check number of the transaction that will be at the top of the Register window when you release the scroll box.

You also can use the keyboard to move from transaction to transaction and from field to field in the Register window. The following keys help you move around the Register window quickly and easily:

Press	To Move
↑	To the same field in the preceding transaction
↓	To the same field in the next transaction
Tab	To the next field in the same transaction
Shift+Tab	To the preceding field in the same transaction

Press	To Move
Home	To the beginning of the current field
End	To the end of the current field
Home Home	To the first field in the current transaction
End End	To the last field in the current transaction
Ctrl+Home	To the first transaction in the Register
Ctrl+End	To the first blank transaction line in the Register
PgUp	Up one window of transactions
PgDn	Down one window of transactions
Ctrl+PgUp	To the first transaction in the current month
Ctrl+PgDn	To the last transaction in the current month

Note

If you want to find a specific transaction, such as a check written to a particular payee or a check written on a certain date, you can use the Find window to locate the transaction. Finding transactions in the Register is explained in Chapter 7, "Using Quicken Shortcuts."

Changing the Register Display

When you start using Quicken, the Register is displayed using two lines of text for each transaction (other than the highlighted transaction). Figure 6.1 shows the Register in normal, or two-line, view. You can change the Register display so that each transaction takes up only one line in the Register; that way, Quicken compresses each transaction line into one line and increases the number of transactions shown in the window. Don't worry, your data is safe—some of it is just hidden from view.

To change the Register display to one-line, select the **1-Line Display** check box at the bottom of the Register. Quicken enters a check mark in the check box and condenses the Register, as shown in figure 6.2.

To change the Register display back to two-line, select the **1-Line** option check box again. The Register now appears with two lines for each transaction.

Fig. 6.2
Quicken increases
the number of
transactions
displayed in the
Register window
when you select
the 1-Line Display
option.

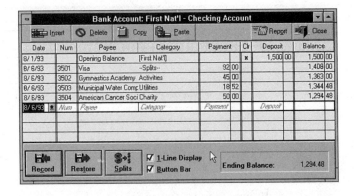

> **Note**
>
> Quicken doesn't provide the one-line display in the Investment Register. A transaction line in an Investment Register contains more information than can be condensed into one line.

You also can change the Register display by hiding the Register button bar. The button bar is included on the Register so that you quickly can select commands to perform activities; however, you also can choose these commands from the menu bar. On the Register button bar, for example, Quicken includes the Insert button, which you can use to insert a blank transaction line in the Register. You can choose Insert from the Edit menu to perform the same function.

To hide the Register button bar, select the **B**utton Bar check box at the bottom of the Register window to remove the check mark. Quicken removes the button bar from the Register display, as shown in figure 6.3.

To display the Register button bar, select the **B**utton Bar check box again.

Fig. 6.3
Quicken hides the
Register button bar
when you select
the Button Bar
check box.

Resizing the Register

With Quicken 3 for Windows, you can resize, maximize, or minimize the Register just as you do in other Windows applications. When you maximize the Register window, Quicken enlarges the window to fill the screen. When you minimize the Register window, Quicken reduces the Register to an icon at the bottom of the Quicken application window.

To resize the Register window, follow these steps:

1. Point to any corner of the Register window. The mouse pointer changes to a two-headed arrow, which indicates that the window can be sized.

2. Press and hold the left mouse button and drag the corner of the Register window to enlarge it or reduce its size.

3. Release the mouse button when the Register window is sized the way you want it.

To maximize the Register window, click the upward-pointing triangle (the Maximize button) in the upper right corner of the window. Figure 6.4 shows the Register window after it's maximized. To restore the Register window to its original size, click the Restore button (with the two triangles) in the upper right corner of the window.

Restore button

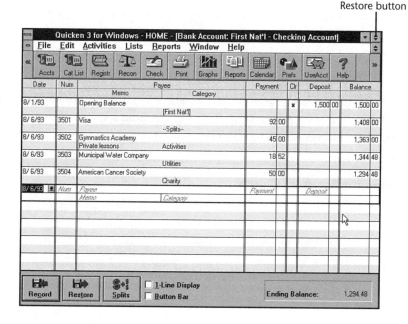

Fig. 6.4
You can enlarge the Register to fill the screen by clicking the Maximize button in the upper right corner of the Register window. Return the window to its default size by clicking the Restore button.

To minimize the Register window, select the downward-pointing triangle (the Minimize button) in the upper right corner of the window. Figure 6.5 shows the Register as an icon after the Register window is minimized. To restore the Register window to its original size, double-click the Register icon.

Fig. 6.5

The Register icon appears at the bottom of the Quicken application window when you minimize the Register. Restore the Register window to its original size by double-clicking the Register icon.

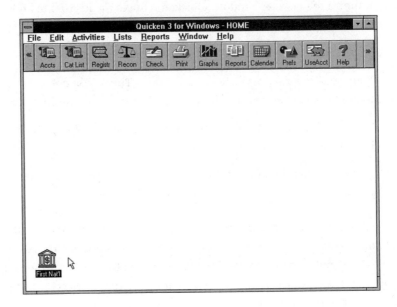

Using the Register Button Bar

Quicken 3 for Windows displays a button bar at the top of the Register so that you quickly can select a few of the more common Quicken commands. The Register button bar includes the Insert, Delete, Copy, Paste, Report, and Close buttons.

To use the button bar to perform operations, select the appropriate button by clicking it. You also can press the Alt key in combination with the underlined letter in the button name. To select the Insert button, for example, press Alt+N.

Closing the Register Window

If you don't need to use the Register window any longer, you can close the Register so that it's removed from the Quicken application window. You can reopen the Register window at any time.

To close the Register window, choose Close on the Register button bar or double-click the Control menu box in the upper left corner of the window.

Recording a Check in the Register

Recording a check in the Quicken Register closely parallels recording a check by hand in a paper checkbook register. The Register screen, however, makes the whole process easier. You can record any check in the Register, including checks you want to print. Typically, however, you record checks you wrote previously by hand directly into the Register. You record checks you want to print in the Write Checks window, which is described in Chapter 5.

To record a check, follow these steps:

1. Choose Account from the Lists menu, press Ctrl+A, or click the Accts button on the Iconbar to display the Account list.

2. Scroll the Account list to highlight the checking account you want to use, and then select Use. Quicken displays the Register for your checking account.

3. Enter the check date in the Date field in the *mm/dd/yy* format.

The first time you enter a transaction in the Register in the current Quicken session, the program fills the Date field with the system date (the current date according to your computer's internal memory). After you enter your first transaction in the Register, Quicken fills the Date field with the last date used.

To edit the date, you can move the cursor to the part of the date month, day, or year that you want to change and type over the date already on-screen. Alternatively, you can use the + (plus) and – (minus) keys to change the date one day at a time. To change the existing date of 5/11/94 to 5/13/94, for example, press the plus key twice. To change the date of 5/11/94 to 5/9/94, press the minus key twice.

Tip

You can use the new pop-up calendar to enter dates in the Date field. Click the Date field's down arrow to display the calendar. See Chapter 7, "Using Quicken Short-cuts," for more details.

Note

You can change the way dates are entered and displayed by setting the preference that controls how dates are entered. By default, Quicken displays dates as *mm/dd/yy*; however, you can change the way dates are displayed (to *dd/mm/yy*) by changing the date preference. If you change the date preference, for example, dates are entered and displayed with the day first, followed by the month. August 18, 1994, for example, is entered and displayed as 18/08/94 instead of 8/18/94. See Chapter 21, "Customizing Quicken," to learn how to set the date preference.

Tip
The Write Checks window provides a more convenient method of writing and printing checks. Chapter 5 explains how to write checks in the Write Checks window.

4. Press Tab to move to the Num field. Enter the number of the check in this field. You can use the + (plus) key to enter the next check number or the – (minus) key to enter the check number before the last check number used. If the check number from the preceding transaction was 1892, for example, press the plus key to enter 1893 as the check number in the next transaction line or press the minus key to enter 1891 as the check number.

Checks you recorded in the Write Checks window but haven't printed show the word Print in the Num field. If you want to enter a check that you want to print later, you can type **Print** in the Num field.

> **Note**
>
> QuickFill works from the Num field in the Register. When you Tab to the Num field, Quicken displays a list of references (ATM, Deposit, Next Chk #, and so forth). Select a reference from the list or begin typing the reference in the Num field. Quicken enters the selected reference or completes the reference that you begin to type.
>
> You can customize the list that's displayed from the Num field by defining your own reference item (up to 5 characters). You learn more about QuickFill and customizing the Num field list in Chapter 7, "Using Quicken Shortcuts."

5. Press Tab to move to the Payee field. Type the name of the person or business that you wrote the check to. You have space for up to 31 characters.

6. Press Tab to move to the Payment field. Enter the check amount, using up to 10 characters for the amount. You can enter a check as large as $9,999,999.99. The decimal point counts as one of the 10 characters but the commas don't.

> **Note**
>
> If you need to add several amounts together for a check you're entering in the Register, Quicken 3's new pop-up calculator can help. Just click the down arrow in the Payment (or Deposit) field to display a mini-calculator that you can use to compute the transaction amount. Refer to Chapter 7, "Using Quicken Shortcuts," to learn how to use the new pop-up calculator to enter amounts.

7. Press Tab to reach the Clr (Cleared) field, which shows whether a transaction has been recorded by the bank. Use this field as part of *reconciling*, or explaining the difference between your check register account balance and the balance the bank shows on your monthly statement. To mark a transaction as cleared, enter an asterisk (*), the only character Quicken accepts here in the Clr field. During reconciliation, Quicken changes the asterisk to an X (see Chapter 8, "Reconciling Your Bank Account").

8. (Optional) Press Tab twice to move through the Deposit field and to the Memo field, where you can use up to 31 characters to describe a transaction. If you are making several payments a month to the bank, the Memo field enables you to specify the house payment, the school loan, the hot tub, the boat, and so on.

9. Press Tab to move to the Category field, which you can use to assign a category, subcategory, transfer account, or class to a transaction. You use the Category field to classify expenses and income.

When you move to the Category field, Quicken displays a drop-down list with the list of categories, subcategories, and accounts from the Category & Transfer list. (If the drop-down list doesn't appear automatically, click the arrow in the Category field to display the list.) From the list, select the category, subcategory, or transfer account that you want to assign to the check transaction and press Enter. Quicken inserts the category, subcategory, or account name in the Category field in the Register.

> ### Note
>
> You can assign more than one category to a single transaction. This procedure is called *splitting a transaction*. You may need to split a transaction if, for example, you are writing one check to a department store to pay for clothing, computer supplies, and cosmetics. Obviously, no one category describes these different expenses. By splitting the transaction, you can assign three categories to the check transaction so that each expense is properly classified in your records. You learn how to split a transaction later in this chapter.

Tip
You also can use QuickFill to enter an account name in the Category field when transferring money to another account.

Quicken's QuickFill feature also works from the Category field in the Register. When you type the first characters in a category name, Quicken searches the Category & Transfer list to find the first category that begins with the characters you type. Suppose that you have a category named Utilities, and it's the only category name that starts with the letter *U*. If you type a **U** in the Category field, Quicken searches the Category & Transfer list until it finds a category that begins with *U*. When Quicken finds Utilities, the QuickFill feature fills in the remaining letters of the category name for you: *tilities*. You learn about using QuickFill to fill in the Category field in Chapter 7, "Using Quicken Shortcuts."

To use the QuickFill feature to enter a subcategory in the Category field, type or enter the category name, type a : (colon), and then begin typing the subcategory name. QuickFill enters the rest of the subcategory when it finds the matching subcategory name in the Category & Transfer list.

> **Note**
>
> If the category or subcategory that you want to assign to a check transaction isn't included in the drop-down list, you can add it *on the fly* as you enter a transaction in the Register. Just type the new category name in the Category field. When Quicken doesn't find the category in the Category & Transfer list, the Set Up Category dialog box appears so that you can enter the information about the new category. Choose OK when the Set Up Category dialog box is complete; Quicken returns to the Register window with the new category name in the Category field. You learn more about adding categories and subcategories in Chapter 4, "Organizing Your Finances."

Tip
You can add classes to the Class list as you enter transactions. Type the new class; then enter information about the new class in the dialog box that appears.

To assign a class to a check transaction, type a / (slash) after the category or subcategory name in the Category field. Then type the class name or press Ctrl+L to display the Class list and select a class from the list. The QuickFill feature also works for entering classes. When you type a few characters after the slash, QuickFill enters the rest of the class when it finds the matching class name in the Class list.

To assign a subclass to a check transaction, type a : (colon) after the class name. Then type the class that you want to function as a subclass, or press Ctrl+L to display the Class list and select the class from the list.

> **Note**
>
> Quicken doesn't require that you assign categories, subcategories, or classes to transactions. If you want to track your income and expense so that you know where your money comes from and where it goes, however, you should assign a category to each transaction that you enter in Quicken. To ensure that you do assign a category to each transaction, you can select the **Warn Before Recording Uncategorized Transactions** preference from the list of **G**eneral preferences. To learn how to select this preference, refer to Chapter 21, "Customizing Quicken."

10. Record the transaction by choosing Record. Figure 6.6 shows check transactions recorded in the Register.

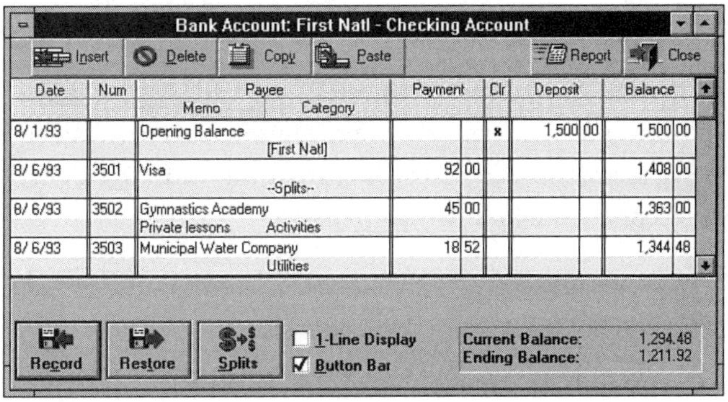

Fig. 6.6

Use the Register to record checks that you write manually. Quicken saves all the check information and updates your account balance.

Quicken calculates the new balance in the account each time you record a transaction and enters the amount in the Balance field for each transaction. If the balance is too large for a positive or negative number to display, Quicken displays asterisks in the Balance field. Quicken uses negative numbers to indicate that you have overdrawn your account. If you have a color monitor, Quicken displays negative amounts in a different color.

After you enter a few transactions in the Register, you can use Quicken's QuickFill feature. QuickFill makes entering payees and transactions fast and easy. When you Tab to the Payee field, Quicken displays a drop-down list with previously entered transactions plus the transactions from the Memorized Transaction list. (You learn about the Memorized Transaction list in Chapter 7, "Using Quicken Shortcuts.") If you begin typing a few characters of the payee name, Quicken moves through the list and highlights the first transaction that matches what you type.

If you want to use the information for that transaction, just press Tab; QuickFill fills in the rest of the payee name for you, plus the other information for the selected transaction (amount, memo, category, and so forth). If you don't want to use the information for the transaction that Quicken highlights from the list, you can type a few more characters in the Payee field or select the transaction from the drop-down list that you do want to use to enter your new transaction. Refer to Chapter 7, "Using Quicken Shortcuts," for more detailed information on QuickFill.

If the check transaction that QuickFill completes for you is the way you want it, you're ready to record the check. If the amount is different, you can edit the transaction before choosing Record.

Recording a Deposit in the Register

As you may expect, recording a deposit in the Quicken Register is like recording a deposit in your checkbook's paper register. To record a deposit in the Quicken Register, follow the preceding steps for recording a check in the Register, except for the following differences:

1. Press Tab to move to the Num field. Select Deposit from the reference list displayed in the Num field. Quicken enters DEP in the Num field.

Tip
You also can select a deposit transaction from the drop-down list displayed from the Payee field.

2. In the Payee field, enter a description of the deposit transaction. A business recording a deposit from a customer, for example, can describe the deposit by using the customer name, such as **Acme Manufacturing**. A home user recording a payroll deposit can describe the deposit as **Payroll Check**. You could describe interest as **October Interest Income**.

3. Press Tab to move past the Payment and Clr fields to the Deposit field. As with the Payment field, Quicken enables you to enter only numbers, with amounts under $9,999,999.99.

4. Record the deposit transaction by choosing the Record button (see fig. 6.7).

Recording Other Withdrawals

The steps for recording other withdrawals such as automated teller machine transactions, electronic fund transfers, and automatic payments parallel the steps for recording a check. (Quicken includes several references for other types of transactions, such as ATM, EFT, and XMIT.) You enter the date, reference, payee, payment amount, and (optionally) a memo description and a category. Record the withdrawal by choosing Record after the transaction is complete.

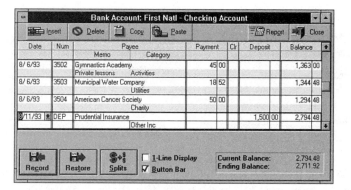

Fig. 6.7
A deposit transaction is recorded in the Register just like you record checks and other transactions. Use the Deposit (DEP) reference in the Num field to identify deposit transactions.

CPA TIP: Reviewing Bank Fees

Consider the monthly service fees a bank charges when choosing a bank and in keeping minimum balances. Most banks charge monthly service fees of about $5. Some banks waive the $5 fee if you keep an average balance of $200 at all times in your account. The $5 a month translates into $60 a year. Because $60 in fee savings equals $60 in interest, the interest rate the bank pays people who keep their minimum balance at $200 is $60 divided by $200, or 30 percent. The return is even better than that for most people because the interest income gets taxed, but the fee savings don't. Probably no other $200 investment in the world is risk-free and pays 30 percent "interest."

Recording Transfers Between Accounts

You can use the Category field to record transfers from one account to another. Suppose that you are recording a check drawn on your checking account for deposit to your account with the Acme Credit Union. The check isn't an expense, so it shouldn't be categorized as utilities, medical, insurance, or something else. It's a transfer of funds from one account to another. You can identify such transfers by selecting the account name from the dropdown list from the Category field.

Tip
Select Transfer from the Num field reference list so that each transfer transaction is marked as such. When you select Transfer, Quicken enters TXFR in the Num field.

The drop-down list includes all categories, subcategories, and accounts. When you select an account (instead of a category or subcategory) in the Category field, Quicken enters brackets around the category name to indicate that the transaction is a transfer from the current account to the account in the Category field.

> **Note**
>
> The drop-down list from the Category field lists categories first (income categories, then expense categories), followed by accounts. Because the accounts are located at the end of the drop-down list, you can access them more quickly by pressing the End key to reach the end of the list.

If you record a transfer transaction, Quicken records the transaction in the Registers for both accounts. In the transaction shown in figure 6.8, a payment of $500 is recorded in the checking account and, at the same time, a deposit of $500 is recorded in the First Savings account. Figure 6.9 shows the Register for the First Savings account with the $500 deposit.

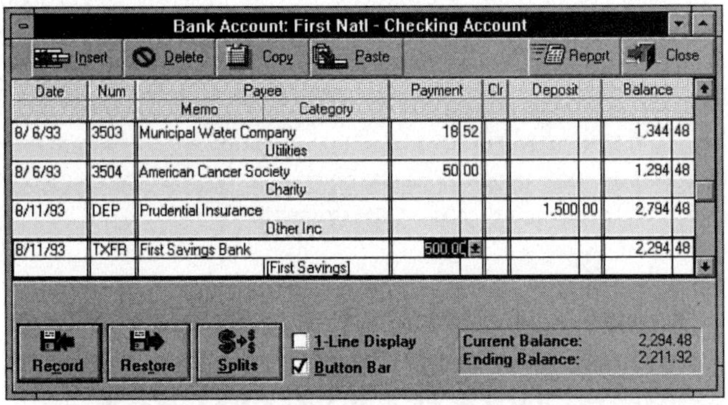

Fig. 6.8
Quicken encloses brackets around the account name in the Category field when you record a transfer transaction.

Fig. 6.9
Press Ctrl+X to go to the corresponding transfer transaction.

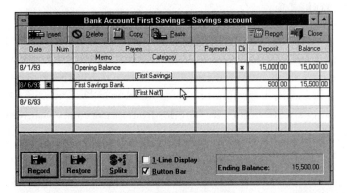

> **Note**
>
> You quickly can move to the corresponding transfer transaction in the other account Register if you want to review the transaction to make sure that it was recorded correctly. To go to the corresponding transaction, highlight the transfer transaction in the account Register where you recorded the transfer transaction and then choose **G**o To Transfer from the **E**dit menu (or press Ctrl+X).

Entering Uncleared Transactions

You learned in Chapters 1 and 3 that you should enter the ending balance from your last bank statement as the starting balance in your Quicken bank account. This makes reconciling easy the next time you receive your bank statement and start to reconcile your bank account with Quicken.

Using the balance from your last bank statement, however, doesn't account for transactions that occurred before you started using Quicken but haven't cleared through your bank. To reflect your account balance accurately in Quicken, you must enter all uncleared transactions from the date of your last bank statement to the date that you start using Quicken. If your last bank statement was dated 2/15/94, for example, and you started using Quicken on 3/01/94, then you must enter all transactions that occurred between 2/15/94 and 3/01/94 in addition to those transactions that occurred before 2/15/94 but didn't show up on your last statement.

This chapter shows you how to enter check, deposit, and other withdrawal transactions in the Register, which is all you need to know to enter uncleared transactions. Just move to a blank transaction line in the Register and begin entering uncleared transactions like you enter any other transaction.

Make sure that you enter the correct date and check number for each transaction. After you record the transaction by choosing Record, Quicken sorts your transactions in the Register and places the transactions that you just entered in order by date.

Splitting Transactions

Earlier in this chapter you learned how to enter transactions in the Register and how to assign a category to a single transaction. But what happens when you write a check for an expense that covers more than one category, such as the check you write to the bank to pay a mortgage payment that pays principal, interest, insurance, and property taxes? In this case, you need to split the transaction, or assign more than one category or subcategory to the transaction. (Subcategories further divide a category into second-, third-, fourth-, and so on levels.) You may want to divide the Utilities category so that you can track expenses for electricity, gas, and water, for example. Subcategories are explained in more detail in Chapter 4, "Organizing Your Finances."

> **Note**
>
> You can split transactions when you write a check from the Write Checks window or enter a manual check in the Register. Quicken enables you to assign up to 30 categories or subcategories to a single transaction.

A transaction line in the Register window provides one field to assign a category or subcategory. Occasionally, however, you need to be able to break down a transaction into multiple categories, such as in the mortgage payment example. By splitting the transaction, Quicken provides additional Category fields so that you can assign more than one category to a transaction or further describe a transaction.

To split a transaction, follow these steps:

1. Display the Register and enter the transaction as usual (except for the Category field).

2. Choose the Splits button (or press Ctrl+S). Quicken displays the Splits window, as shown in figure 6.10.

3. In the Category field, type the category name or click the down arrow to select a category from the Category & Transfer list. Use the Category field in the Splits window in the same way that you use the Category field in the Register. You also can use the Category field to record transfers to other accounts. Up to 30 lines are available on the Splits window to assign categories, subcategories, or transfer accounts.

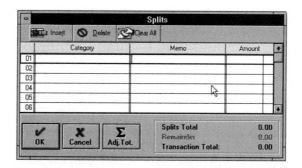

Fig. 6.10
The Splits window provides additional category fields so that you can assign more than one category to a transaction in the Register.

4. (Optional) Press Tab to move to the Memo field. Type a description of the category or the amount. The Memo field provides a 27-character space you can use to describe a transaction, to explain why you selected a category, or to detail how you calculated the transaction amount.

5. Press Tab to move to the Amount field. You can use the Amount field in two ways, depending on whether you choose Splits before or after you enter the amount on the Register.

If you choose Splits before you make an entry in the Payment or Deposit fields in the Register, Quicken adds each amount you enter in the Amount field in the Splits window. Quicken then asks how you want the amount recorded: as a payment or as a deposit. See the section "Calculating Transaction in Split Transactions" later in this chapter.

If you choose Splits after entering a payment or deposit amount in the Register, Quicken shows this amount in the first Amount field in the Splits window and in the Splits Total at the bottom of the Splits window. If you then enter a number in the first Amount field in the Splits window, Quicken calculates the difference between the transaction amount in the Register and the new amount you entered and then places this difference in the second Amount field in the Splits window and in the Remainder field at the bottom of the Splits window. Quicken keeps track of the amounts that you have assigned to transactions in the Splits window. Notice the Remainder field, which shows the difference between the Splits Total and the Transaction Total.

> **Note**
>
> You can enter percents in the Splits window's Amount fields. If you enter a deposit for $1,600 and 25 percent of this amount is to be entered in the first Splits field, move to the Amount field, type **25%**, and press Tab. When you press Tab to move to the next field, Quicken calculates the number that equals 25 percent of $1,600 and enters this value in the Amount field.

6. Press Tab to move to the next line of the Splits window. Repeat steps 3 through 5 for each category and amount combination you want to record. You can record up to 30 category and amount combinations.

Figure 6.11 shows a completed Splits window.

Fig. 6.11
Use the Splits window to assign more than one category or subcategory to a transaction.

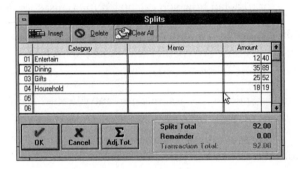

If you use all 30 split transaction Amount fields, Quicken has nowhere to make the Register amount equal to the total Splits Total amount. You must manually adjust the Register amount or one of the Splits window amounts. You also can choose Ad**j**. Tot. (Adjust Total) at the bottom of the Splits window to total the Amount fields in the Splits window and insert the total into the Payment or Deposit field in the Register.

7. To record the categories and amounts in the Splits window, choose OK. Quicken returns to the Register and indicates a split transaction by entering the word --Splits-- in the Category field (see fig. 6.12).

8. Choose Record to record the check with the split transaction amounts.

Entering Negative Amounts in Split Transactions

You can enter negative amounts in split transactions to represent withholdings for payroll checks, for example, or amounts deducted from a deposit. To enter a negative amount in the Splits window, just press the – (minus) key before you enter the amount. Figure 6.13 shows the Splits window with negative amounts for a payroll check.

Fig. 6.12
Quicken enters the word --Splits-- in the Category field for a split transaction in the Register.

Fig. 6.13
When you want to enter withholdings or other deductions from a split deposit transaction, enter a negative sign before the amount.

Calculating Transaction Amounts in Split Transactions

When entering a split transaction, you can have Quicken calculate the transaction amount as you enter lines in the Splits window. To have Quicken calculate the transaction amount, follow these steps:

1. Enter the transaction information into the Register as usual, except for the amount.

2. Choose Splits (or press Ctrl+S). Quicken displays the Splits window (refer to fig. 6.10).

3. Enter the information in the Splits window. As you enter amounts, Quicken keeps track of the split transaction amounts in the Transaction Total field at the bottom of the window.

4. After you finish entering lines in the Splits window, choose Ad**j**. Tot. at the bottom of the window. Quicken sums the entries in the Amount fields in the Splits window.

5. Choose OK. Quicken displays the Payment or Deposit dialog box, as shown in figure 6.14.

Fig. 6.14
When Quicken calculates the transaction amount from the Splits window, select whether you're entering a payment or deposit.

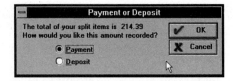

6. Tell Quicken how to record the total of the Amount fields in the Splits window. Select the **P**ayment option button to enter the amount in the Payment field in the Register. Select the **D**eposit option button to enter the amount in the Deposit field in the Register.

7. Choose OK to return to the Register. Quicken enters the Splits window amount in the Payment or Deposit field as you specified.

8. If you need to return to the Splits window to make a change, choose **S**plits (or press Ctrl+S), make the necessary changes, and then choose Adj. Tot. again to recalculate the payment or deposit amount.

9. At the Register, choose Re**c**ord to record the transaction.

CPA TIP: Tracking Income & Expenses with Split Transactions

When you want to track your income and expenses closely, enter split transactions for payments to department stores, discount stores, and so on where you buy different types of items. If you don't split the transaction to record a check to Wal-Mart where you buy hardware, cleaning supplies, office supplies, and so on, for example, and lump the total check transaction into one category, your expenses aren't reflected accurately.

Editing Split Transactions

You can change the information in the Splits window just as you can change any other transaction. To edit a split transaction, follow these steps:

1. Highlight the split transaction in the Register.

2. Choose **S**plits (or press Ctrl+S) to display the Splits window.

3. Make any necessary changes to categories, memos, or amounts in the Splits window.

> **Note**
>
> If you change an amount, the Splits window may not balance (the total amount in the Splits window won't equal the transaction amount in the Register). If necessary, choose Adj. Tot. to recalculate the transaction amount. *Don't* choose Adj. Tot. to recalculate if the amount in the Payment or Deposit field in the Register is the correct amount and you're just reallocating amounts to categories or subcategories in the Splits window.

To delete a line in the Splits window, click the **Delete** button or press Ctrl+D. To delete all lines, click the Delete button or press Ctrl+D at each line.

4. After making changes in the Splits window, choose OK to save the changes and to return to the split transaction in the Register.

5. Choose Record to record the changed split transaction.

Deleting Split Transactions

Just as you can delete transactions with only one category or subcategory assigned to it, you also can delete split transactions. Use the same discretion when deleting a split transaction that you use for deleting a transaction assigned to only one category or subcategory, as explained later in the section "Deleting a Transaction from the Register."

You delete split transactions the same way you delete single-category transactions. To delete a split transaction, follow these steps:

1. Highlight the split transaction that you want to delete.

2. Choose Delete Transaction from the Edit menu, click the Delete button from the register button bar, or press Ctrl+D. Quicken displays the message Delete the Current Transaction?

3. Choose Yes to delete the split transaction or No if you decide that you don't want to delete the split transaction.

> **Note**
>
> If you try to delete a transaction that is part of a split transfer transaction (where one part of the split transaction transfers funds from one Quicken account to another), you must delete the transaction from the account where the transaction originated; in other words, the account that you entered the split transfer transaction in. Press Ctrl+X to locate the split transfer transaction. After you find the split transfer transaction, highlight the transfer transaction and choose the **Delete** button on the Register button bar (or press Ctrl+D) to delete the transaction. Quicken then deletes the corresponding transaction in the other account.

Undoing Split Transactions

After you split a transaction, you can go back, undo the split, and assign only one category or subcategory to the transaction. Follow these steps to undo a split transaction:

1. Highlight the split transaction that you want to undo.

2. Click the Cat List button on the Iconbar (or press Ctrl+C) to display the Category & Transfer list.

3. Use the scroll bar or the up- and down-arrow keys to highlight the single category or subcategory that you want to assign to the transaction.

4. Choose Use. Quicken displays the Replace Splits with Single Category? dialog box.

5. Choose Yes to assign the category or subcategory to the transaction.

6. Choose Record to record the transaction with only one category or subcategory.

Reviewing and Editing Register Transactions

You can review and edit transactions by accessing the Register at any time. You may want to review a transaction to make sure that you recorded the transaction correctly. You also may want to review a transaction to see whether you received a deposit or remembered to pay a particular bill.

You can move from transaction to transaction in the Register window by using the scroll bar on the right side of the window or by using the keyboard. (You learned about moving around the Register earlier in this chapter.)

To edit a transaction in the Register, follow these steps:

1. Highlight the transaction in the Register that you want to change.

2. Click the field that you want to edit or press Tab to move to the field.

3. Type over the existing information or select a new item from the drop-down list.

   If you decide that you want to cancel changes that you have made to a transaction, choose Restore. Quicken restores the transaction to the way it was before you began editing.

4. Choose Record to save the changes to the transaction.

Tip
To correct a mistake made while editing a field in a transaction, choose Undo from the Edit menu or press Alt+Backspace.

By default, Quicken selects the general preference that requests confirmation when changing a transaction in the Register. The confirmation message appears when you go to another transaction or a new window without first recording the changes in the transaction. Therefore, if you don't choose Record after editing a transaction, Quicken displays a message asking you to confirm the change to the transaction. Choose Yes to change the transaction. If the transaction that you are editing is a reconciled transaction (the transaction has cleared the bank and has been marked as cleared against your bank statement), Quicken asks you to confirm that you want to change a reconciled transaction. Choose Yes to change the reconciled transaction.

Deleting a Transaction from the Register

Quicken enables you to delete a transaction that you inadvertently entered twice, entered in the wrong account Register, and so on. When you delete a transaction, it's removed permanently from the Register.

CPA TIP: Voiding Checks versus Deleting Checks

You shouldn't delete transactions for manual checks or for checks you have written with Quicken. When you delete a transaction, Quicken removes all record of the transaction. If the transaction involves a check, deleting the transaction removes the check information and leaves a gap in your check-numbering sequence. Void a check transaction that you want to remove because of a lost check, a check that you have stopped payment on, or an improperly printed check, but *don't delete* such checks. Information for voided transactions remains in the Register so that you can track each prenumbered check. You learn how to void a transaction later in this chapter.

You should delete a recorded transaction only under the following conditions:

- *You inadvertently enter a transaction that shouldn't be entered at all.* If you enter a deposit transaction in the Register and subsequently don't make the deposit, for example, you should delete the transaction. Or if you enter a transaction for a bank fee in the Register that the bank later rescinds, delete the bank fee transaction.

- *You duplicate transaction information.* If you withdraw funds from an automatic teller machine and enter the transaction twice in the Register, for example, you should delete one of the two transactions.

- *You enter a transaction in the wrong Quicken Register* (Quicken provides a Register for each account that you set up). If you enter a credit card payment (that you make manually) in the Register for your checking account but want to track your credit card purchases in the Credit Card Register, you should copy the transaction to the Credit Card Register and then delete the transaction from the Checking Account Register. You learn how to copy transactions in Chapter 7, "Using Quicken Shortcuts."

In all other cases, you should void or reverse transactions in the Register so that you have complete records of all your check numbers and have established a proper audit trail (a history of each and every transaction) in the Register.

If you need to delete a transaction, follow these steps:

1. Display the Register for the account from which you need to delete the transaction.

2. Highlight the transaction that you want to delete.

3. Choose Delete from the Register button bar, choose Delete Transaction from the Edit menu, or press Ctrl+D.

4. Quicken displays the Delete the Current Transaction? dialog box, shown in figure 6.15. Choose Yes to delete the current transaction. If the transaction you are editing is a reconciled transaction (the transaction has cleared the bank and has been marked as cleared against your bank statement), Quicken asks you to confirm that you want to delete a reconciled transaction. Choose Yes to delete the reconciled transaction.

Fig. 6.15
Quicken confirms that you want to delete a transaction before it is removed from the Register.

When you delete a transaction, Quicken removes all transaction information from the Register.

If you delete a transaction from one Quicken account that is part of a transfer transaction (where you transferred funds from one Quicken account to another), the corresponding transaction in the other account also is deleted. To quickly find the corresponding transfer transaction, press Ctrl+X.

If you try to delete a transaction that is part of a split transfer transaction, you must delete the transaction from the account where the transaction originated—in other words, the account in which you entered the transfer transaction.

Voiding a Transaction

You may need to void a check when you want to stop payment, when you lose a check and write another one to replace it, or when a check prints incorrectly and you must print another.

> **Note**
>
> If you void a transaction that is part of a transfer from one account to another, voiding any part of the transaction also voids the other parts of the transaction that are recorded in the other Registers.

To void a check from the Checking Account Register, follow these steps:

1. Display the Register for your checking account.

2. Highlight the transaction for the check that you want to void. If you are voiding a manual check that you haven't yet entered in the Register, enter the date and check number in a blank transaction line. Keep this transaction highlighted as you move to the next step.

3. Choose Void Transaction from the Edit menu (or press Ctrl+V). Quicken enters **VOID** in the Payee field before the payee name and marks the transaction with an X in the Clear column so that the transaction isn't considered an uncleared item when you perform your account reconciliation.

4. Choose Record.

Figure 6.16 shows the Register with a voided check transaction. When you void a check, Quicken erases the amount of the transaction and adjusts your checking account balance. Quicken also subtracts the amount of the voided check from the category originally assigned to the check transaction.

Fig, 6.16
Quicken inserts
VOID in the
Payee field of a
transaction that
you void in the
Register.

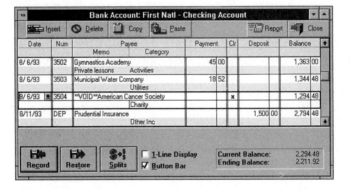

Inserting a Transaction in the Register

You can insert a blank transaction line anywhere in the Register. When you insert a line, Quicken inserts the transaction line above the currently highlighted transaction line. You can use this blank transaction line to record another transaction. Usually, transactions are recorded in the blank transaction line at the end of the Register, however.

To insert a transaction into the Register, follow these steps:

1. Display the Register.

2. Highlight the transaction line just below the place where you want to insert a blank transaction line.

3. Choose Insert from the Register button bar, choose Insert Transaction from the Edit menu, or press Ctrl+I. Quicken inserts a blank transaction line just above the highlighted line.

> **Note**
>
> When you enter and record a transaction in an inserted transaction line, Quicken sorts the transactions and moves the inserted transaction, if necessary, in proper date order. You therefore shouldn't bother inserting transactions unless you insert them in the proper date order in the Register.

Postdating Transactions

Postdating transactions means that you enter a future date for a check or deposit transaction. Traditionally, people use postdated checks as a way to delay a payment. The payee can't or shouldn't cash the check before the future date. With Quicken, you can use postdated transactions to delay checks being cashed. Perhaps more importantly, you can forecast your cash flows and balances by entering those checks and deposits that you know are in the future.

The steps for entering postdated transactions mirror those for entering regular transactions. The only difference, of course, is that the check or deposit date is in the future. When you enter postdated transactions, Quicken calculates two account balances: the current balance, which is the account balance for the current date, and the ending balance, which is the account balance after the last postdated transaction. Quicken determines the current date by looking at the system date.

Learning Quicken

Figure 6.17 shows the First Nat'l Account Register with a postdated transaction. The ending balance incorporates all the transactions for the account, including postdated transactions. The current balance is the account balance at the current date.

Fig. 6.17

Quicken enters a boldfaced line to separate transactions whose dates are on or before the current date and postdated transactions (those with future dates).

Quicken identifies postdated transactions by inserting a boldfaced line between the current and previous transactions and the postdated transactions. In figure 6.17, notice the boldfaced line between the last two transactions.

CPA TIP: Receiving Discounts for Early Payment

Businesses and individuals often receive discounts for paying bills early. Consider early payment in setting the check date. Not taking early payment discounts is an extremely expensive way to borrow money from the vendor. Suppose that a vendor normally requires payment within 30 days but offers a 2 percent discount for payments received within 10 days. If you pay within 30 rather than 10 days, you essentially pay the vendor a 2 percent interest charge for paying 20 days later. Because one year contains roughly 18 20-day periods, the 2 percent for 20 days equals approximately 36 percent annually.

Although you may need to "borrow" this money, you probably can find a much cheaper lender. As a rule of thumb, if a vendor gives you a 1 percent discount for paying 20 days early, you are borrowing the vendor's money at about an 18 percent annual interest rate if you don't pay early. A 3 percent discount works out to a whopping 54 percent a year.

Using QuickReport for Instant Transaction Reports

If you want a quick report of all transactions that contain the same payee, you can use Quicken 3 for Windows' new QuickReport feature. When you select QuickReport from the Register, Quicken lists all transactions (in the current account) that contain the same payee as the selected transaction through the current date. Quicken shows the date, check number (or other reference), description, memo, category or subcategory name, cleared status, and amount for each transaction in the list.

To see a QuickReport for a selected transaction in the Register, follow these steps:

1. Display the Register and highlight the transaction containing the payee for which you want a list of transactions.

2. Choose Report on the Register button bar.

Quicken quickly filters all transactions and displays only those that contain the same payee as the transaction you selected. Figure 6.18 shows the QuickReport for the payee PSI.

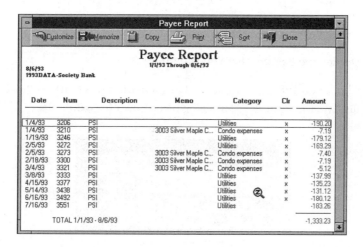

Fig. 6.18
The QuickReport feature displays a report of all tran-sactions that contain the same payee.

3. To remove the QuickReport from your screen, choose Close at the top of the report.

You can change the report settings using the buttons at the top of the Quick-Report. You also can print a QuickReport by choosing Print; however, first make sure that the report settings in Quicken are set for your printer. Changing report settings and entering printer settings are explained in Chapter 18, "Creating and Printing Reports."

Printing the Register

You should print a paper register each time you enter a group (perhaps more than five) of check and deposit transactions. A printed copy of the Register enables you to review checking account transactions without turning on your computer. It also can provide a way to recover your financial records if no backup files exist. (Chapter 20, "Managing Your Quicken Files," describes the steps for backing up your Quicken data files.)

> **Caution**
>
> Before you print the Register, make sure that Quicken is set up to print reports and lists. Refer to Chapter 4, "Organizing Your Finances," to learn how to set up Quicken to print reports and lists.

To print the Register, follow these steps:

1. Display the Register that you want to print.

2. Choose Print Register from the File menu (or press Ctrl+P). Quicken displays the Print Register dialog box, shown in figure 6.19.

Fig. 6.19
The Print Register dialog box appears when you press Ctrl+P from the Register.

3. Quicken automatically enters the year-to-date date range in the Print Transactions From and To text boxes. Change the dates using the + (plus) and – (minus) keys, or click the arrow to display the drop-down list boxes and select a date range. If, for example, you are printing only the transactions for the day's batch of transactions, enter the current date as the Print Transactions From date. If you are printing a copy of

the month's transactions, enter the first day of the month as the Print Transactions From date.

Select the date of the last check or deposit transaction that you want included in the printed Register in the To text box. If you are printing only the transactions for the day's batch of transactions, enter the current date as the To date. If you are printing a copy of the month's transactions, enter the last day of the month as the To date.

4. (Optional) If you want, you can press Tab to move to the Title text box and type a title for the Register Report.

5. To specify how Quicken prints the Register Report, select the Print One Transaction Per Line check box if you want to abbreviate each transaction to fit on one line in the printed Register. (Quicken normally prints three lines for each transaction.)

   Select the Print Transaction Splits check box if you want to see the extra category names, memos, and amounts on the printed version of the Register.

   Select the Sort By Number check box if you want to print the Register in check number order instead of chronological order. When you select to print the Register in check order, Quicken doesn't print a running account balance.

6. Choose Print. Quicken displays the Print Report dialog box.

7. In the Print To section, select where you want the Register printed. To print to your printer, select the Printer option button. You also can save the Register to an ASCII Disk File, a Tab-delimited Disk File, or a 123 (.PRN) disk file. You also can preview the Register Report on your Screen.

8. Select the Print in Color check box to print the Register in color. You must have an installed color printer to print the Register in color.

   Select the Print in Draft Mode check box, if desired, and if your installed printer supports draft mode printing.

9. Next, select the print range. Select the All option button to print all pages of the Register. Otherwise, select the Pages option button and specify which pages you want to print.

10. Choose Print or press Enter to begin printing the Register.

> ## CPA TIP: Printing the Register
>
> At the end of each month, print a copy of the Register for the transactions you entered in that month. Store the Register with the bank statement for the month. That way, if you ever have questions about a previous month or have the bad luck of losing your Quicken data file, you can reconstruct transactions from previous months. You can discard the now redundant individual Registers that show each group of transactions for the month. You don't need these with a copy of the entire month.

Summary

This chapter introduced you to Quicken's Register, the central repository of all your checking account information. In this chapter, you learned the following:

- How to display the Register

- About the basic parts of the Register and how to move around the Register

- How to change the appearance of the Register

- How to use the Register button bar to perform basic operations

- How to record check, deposit, and withdrawal transactions in the Register

- How to record transfer transactions between accounts

- About splitting transactions so that you can assign more than one category to a transaction

- How to edit, delete, and void a transaction in the Register

- How to insert a blank transaction line in the Register

- About postdating transactions

- How to generate a QuickReport that lists all transactions containing the same payee as the selected transaction

- How to print the Register

The next chapter describes Quicken shortcuts that you can use to make check writing and working in the Register more efficient and easier.

Chapter 7

Using Quicken Shortcuts

You learned how to write a check at the Write Checks window in Chapter 5, "Writing and Printing Checks." In Chapter 6, "Using the Register," you learned how to use the Register to record transactions. This chapter describes how you can use Quicken shortcuts to make check writing and using the Register faster and easier. These features can help you write checks and enter transactions quickly, save and reuse information you record repeatedly in transactions, or search through the Register for specific transactions.

Using the Mini-Calendar To Enter Dates

Quicken 3 for Windows includes a new pop-up calendar, or mini-calendar, that you can display from the Date field in the Write Checks window or the Register. When the calendar is displayed, you quickly can select the date that you want to enter for a transaction.

To use the mini-calendar to enter dates, follow these steps:

1. Click Check on the Iconbar (or press Ctrl+W) to display the Write Checks window. Alternatively, click Registr on the Iconbar or press Ctrl+R to display the Register.

2. Press Tab, if necessary, to move to the Date field.

3. Click the down arrow next to the Date field. Quicken displays the mini-calendar. Figure 7.1 shows the mini-calendar displayed from the Date field in the Register.

4. Click the date you want to enter in the Date field.

In this chapter, you learn how to use the following shortcuts:

- The new pop-up calendar to enter dates

- The new pop-up field calculator to calculate amount fields

- Quicken's on-screen calculator

- QuickFill

- The Cut, Copy, and Paste commands

- Memorized transactions to save checks and other transactions that you frequently record

- The Find command to locate a specific transaction

Fig. 7.1

Quicken displays a mini-calendar when you click the arrow next to the Date field of the Register. Use the calendar to enter a date in the Date field.

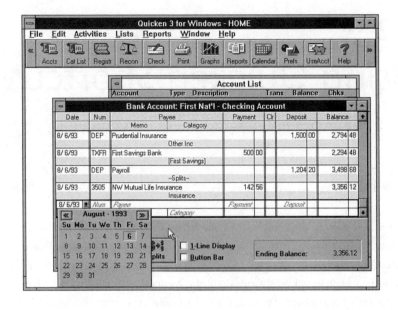

Tip

To move quickly from month to month in the calendar, click the left-arrow button to move to the previous month and the right-arrow button to move to the next month.

To select a date using the keyboard, press the right- or left-arrow key to move a day at a time within the displayed month. Press the up- or down-arrow key to move a week at a time. Notice that when a day is highlighted in the first or last week in a month, pressing the up- or down-arrow keys moves to the preceding or next month. When the date that you want to select is highlighted, press Enter.

You also can enter dates quickly using the following keys from the keyboard:

Key	Function
+ (plus)	Adds one day to the current date shown or one month to the current *mm/yy* shown
– (minus)	Subtracts one day from the current date or one month from the current *mm/yy* shown
T	Enters the current system date
M	Enters the first day of the current month
H	Enters the last day of the current month
Y	Enters the first day of the current year
R	Enters the last day of the current year

To remove the mini-calendar from the Write Checks window without selecting a date, click outside the calendar or press Esc.

Using the Mini-Calculator in Amount Fields

The new mini-calculator that pops up from the $ (Amount) field in the Write Checks window, in the Payment and Deposit fields in the Register, and in the Amount fields in the Splits window is very handy for adding several amounts that you want to include in one check, deposit, or other transaction. The mini-calculator is used just like a regular calculator. When you're finished with a calculation, Quicken enters the result in the amount field where the calculator was displayed.

To use the mini-calculator to enter amounts, follow these steps:

1. Click the Check button on the Iconbar (or press Ctrl+W) to display the Write Checks window. Alternatively, click Registr on the Iconbar (or press Ctrl+R) to display the Register.

2. Fill in the fields of the check or transaction as usual.

3. Click the arrow in the $ (Amount) field in the Write Checks window or the Payment or Deposit field in the Register. If you're splitting a transaction, click the arrow in the Amount field in the Splits window. Quicken displays the mini-calculator, shown in figure 7.2.

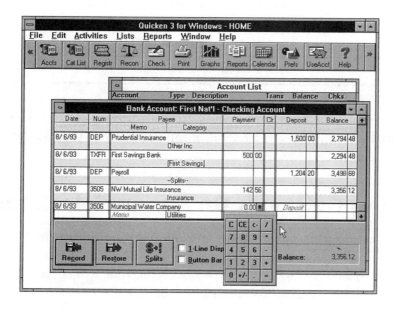

Fig. 7.2
Quicken displays a mini-calculator that you can use to calculate entries in amount fields.

4. Perform your calculation. As you enter a number in the calculator, Quicken displays the number in the amount field.

To perform calculations, use the calculator keys listed in table 7.1. You can use the keys on your keyboard to enter numbers and mathematical operators in the calculator, or you can click the numbers and operators on the calculator.

Table 7.1 Available Calculator Keys

Operator	Function
+	To add
–	To subtract
/	To divide
*	To multiply
<-	To erase the first number to the left as displayed in the Amount field
.	To add a decimal point
+/-	To change the sign of a number; for example, to change 44 to −44 and vice versa
=	To total the calculation
C	To clear all numbers from the calculation
CE	To clear the last number entered

After you perform the calculation, click = on the calculator, press the = key on the keyboard, or press Enter. Quicken enters the result of your calculation in the amount field.

Using Quicken's On-Screen Calculator

A convenient tool that Quicken offers is its on-screen calculator (see fig. 7.3). Quicken's calculator is accessible from any Register, the Write Checks window, or from reports. You can access the calculator during bank account reconciliation as well. The calculator operates like most other regular calculators.

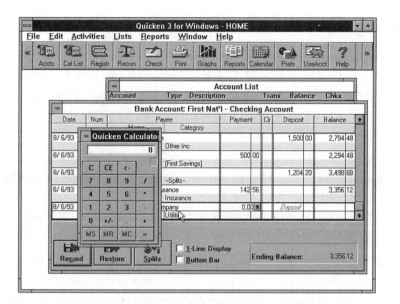

Fig. 7.3
The on-screen calculator is always accessible and handy as you work in Quicken.

Note

Quicken includes both an on-screen calculator and a mini-calculator. Quicken's on-screen calculator can be accessed from anywhere in Quicken. On the other hand, Quicken's mini-calendar is displayed from amount fields only.

To use the on-screen calculator, follow these steps:

1. From the Activities menu, choose Use Calculator to access the calculator.

2. Use the mouse or the keyboard to operate the calculator. The calculator uses the same keys as the mini-calendar (refer to table 7.1), except that the following additional keys are available:

MC	Clears a value from memory
MR	Recalls the value in memory (the value remains in memory)
MS	Stores the displayed value in memory

3. After you perform your calculation, remove the calculator from the screen by double-clicking the Control menu box (in the top-left corner of the calculator) or by pressing Esc.

Using QuickFill

Writing checks in the Write Checks window and entering transactions in the Register is faster and easier with Quicken's improved QuickFill feature. Quick-Fill is now available when editing existing checks and transactions. And you now will see more transaction information displayed as you fill in fields that use QuickFill.

When you type a few characters in a field, Quicken searches previous transactions in the Register and the Memorized Transaction list to find a matching entry in that particular field. (You learn about the Memorized Transaction list later in this chapter.) When Quicken finds a match, the QuickFill feature fills in the rest of the check or transaction with the information that it found.

QuickFill works when you make an entry in the Pay to the Order of field or the Category field in the Write Checks window and in the Num, Payee, and Category fields in the Register. QuickFill also works when you edit an existing check or transaction.

When you install Quicken 3 for Windows, QuickFill is set to do the following:

- Automatically complete the field in a transaction as you type

- Recall a memorized or previously entered transaction when you press Tab to leave the Payee field

- Open the drop-down list automatically when you press Tab to move to a field in which QuickFill can be used

- Place down-arrow buttons beside fields in which you can use QuickFill (click a button to display a drop-down list)

You can change the way QuickFill works by setting the QuickFill preferences. You also can set a QuickFill preference to have Quicken automatically memorize each transaction you enter for a new payee. (This preference isn't selected when you install Quicken 3 for Windows.) See the later section "Setting Quick-Fill Preferences" to learn how to change the way QuickFill works.

Using QuickFill at the Num Field in the Register

When you press Tab to move to the Num field, Quicken displays a list of references that you can use to describe a transaction (ATM, Deposit, Next Chk #, and so forth). Select a reference from the list or begin typing the reference in the Num field. Quicken enters the selected reference or completes the reference that you begin to type. If you select the Next Chk # reference, Quicken adds 1 to the previously entered check number.

You can customize the reference list that's displayed from the Num field in the Register by defining your own reference or editing a reference that you previously entered. Quicken includes the following references in the Num field list:

ATM	Automatic teller machine transactions
Deposit	Deposits to the account
EFT	Electronic funds transfer transactions
Next Chk #	Adds 1 to the previous check number used
Print	Indicates a check is recorded but not yet printed
Transfer	A transfer from one account to another account
XMIT	A transaction transmitted to CheckFree (electronic bill paying service)

Note

You can't edit any of the references that Quicken includes in the Num field list. You can edit only those references that you previously defined using the <New> option from the NUM field list.

To define your own reference in the Num field list, follow these steps:

1. From the Register, press Tab to move to the Num field. Quicken displays the Num field list, shown in figure 7.4.

2. To add a new reference to the list, select <New>. Quicken displays the Add New Num/Ref dialog box, shown in figure 7.5.

3. Type the new reference, using up to five characters.

4. Choose OK to add the reference to the Num field list.

Fig. 7.4

Quicken displays a list of references you can use in the Register's Num field. Define your own reference by selecting <New>.

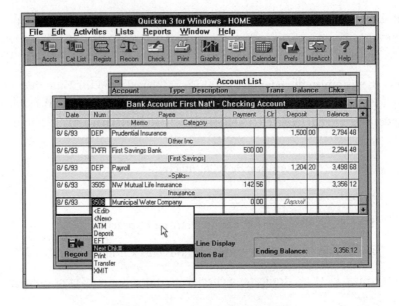

Fig. 7.5

Define a Num field reference in the Add New Num/Ref dialog box.

To delete a previously defined reference, follow these steps:

1. From the Register, press Tab to move to the Num field. Quicken displays the Num field list.

2. Select <Edit> from the reference list. Quicken displays the Edit Num List dialog box.

3. Highlight the reference that you want to delete and choose Delete. To define a new reference, choose New.

4. Choose Done when you are finished deleting or adding references.

Using QuickFill in the Pay to the Order of Field in the Write Checks Window

Quicken searches the Memorized Transaction list and the last three months of transactions in the Register when you type a few characters in the Pay to the Order of field of the Write Checks window. When Quicken finds a transaction with the same payee name, QuickFill fills in the rest of the payee name from the transaction it found in the Memorized Transaction list or the previous transactions in the Register.

Follow these steps to use QuickFill at the Payee field:

1. At the Write Checks window, enter the check date as usual.

2. Type a few characters in the Pay to the Order of field, such as **Ca**. Quicken searches the Memorized Transaction list and the last three months of transactions in the Register for a payee name that starts with *Ca*. When Quicken finds the first transaction with the payee *Carmel Boy Scouts*, for example, QuickFill fills in the rest of the payee name and shows you the rest of the available transactions beginning with *Ca* above the payee name.

3. If the payee name (or in this example, *Carmel Boy Scouts*), is indeed the payee that you want to enter in the transaction, press Tab. QuickFill fills in the rest of the transaction information for that payee—the transaction amount, the memo field (if used), and the category or subcategory—exactly like the transaction that Quicken found.

   If Quicken finds the matching transaction in the Memorized Transaction list, it displays <MEM> at the end of the transaction detail shown above the payee name. If Quicken finds the matching transaction in the Register, it displays <REG> at the end of the transaction detail shown above the payee name.

   If QuickFill doesn't fill in the payee information that you want, keep typing characters in the Pay to the Order of field until QuickFill finds the payee that you want. You also can select the payee that you want from the Pay to the Order of field's drop-down list box.

> **Note**
>
> If more than one payee name exists in the Memorized Transaction list or more than one previous transaction exist in the Register that begins with the characters you type, QuickFill enters the transaction information for the first payee name found.

Figure 7.6 shows the payee name filled in by QuickFill from the Memorized Transaction list; figure 7.7 shows a check payee from a transaction in the Register.

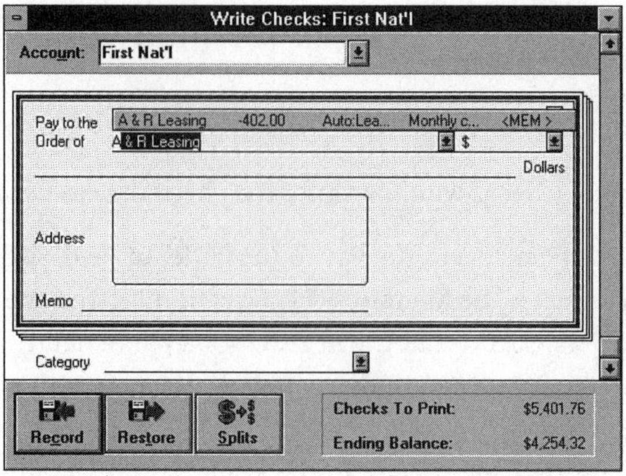

Fig. 7.6
QuickFill fills in the payee name from a matching transaction from the Memorized Transaction list.

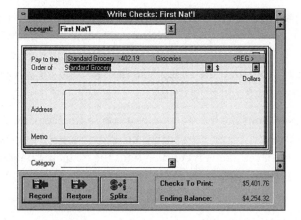

Fig. 7.7
QuickFill fills in the payee name from a matching transaction from the Register.

After QuickFill fills in the check, you can edit any of the check fields as necessary. When the correct entries are made to all the check fields, record the check by choosing Record.

Using QuickFill at the Payee Field in the Register

You also can use QuickFill to help enter payees in the Payee field in the Register. To use QuickFill at the Payee field in the Register, follow these steps:

1. In the Register, enter the transaction date and reference (in the Num field) as usual.

2. Press Tab to move to the Payee field. Quicken displays a drop-down list with previously entered transactions, plus the transactions from the Memorized Transaction list. (You learn about the Memorized Transaction list later in this chapter.) The drop-down list includes the payee, amount, category, and memo for each transaction in the list.

If you begin typing a few characters of the payee name, Quicken moves through the list and highlights the first transaction that matches what you type. Type **In**, for example. Quicken searches the drop-down list for a payee name that starts with *In*. When Quicken finds the first transaction with the payee Indianapolis Power & Light, for example, Quick-Fill highlights the transaction and fills in the rest of the payee name in the Payee field.

If you want to use the information for that transaction, press Tab. QuickFill fills in the rest of the information for the selected transaction (amount, memo, category, and so forth). If you don't want to use the information for the transaction that Quicken highlights from the list, you can type a few more characters in the Payee field or scroll the drop-down list to highlight the transaction that you do want to use to enter your new transaction.

3. After QuickFill fills in the transaction in the Register, you can edit any of the transaction fields as necessary. When the correct entries are made to all the transaction fields, record the transaction by choosing Record.

Using QuickFill To Fill in Category Fields

QuickFill also works when you type a few characters in the Category field of a check or transaction in the Register. QuickFill searches the Category & Transfer list and searches for the first category or transfer account that begins with the characters you type.

If you want to enter a subcategory, you can type a colon (:) after the category name is filled in. Quicken searches the subcategories under that particular category and enters the first one that it finds. If you want to enter a class, you can type a slash (/), and a few characters after the category or subcategory name is filled in. Quicken then searches the Class list and enters the first class it finds that begins with the characters you type. (Refer to Chapter 4, "Organizing Your Finances," for more information on classes.)

To use QuickFill to fill in the Category field, follow these steps:

1. At the Category field for a new or existing check or new or existing transaction in the Register, type a few characters of the category name that you want to assign to the transaction. Quicken searches the Category & Transfer list for the first category or transfer account that matches the characters you type.

When Quicken finds a matching category or transfer account, QuickFill fills in the rest of the category or transfer account name.

2. If this category or transfer account is the one you want to assign to the transaction, press Tab to accept it.

   If the category or transfer account name filled in by QuickFill isn't the one that you want, type a few more characters or press Ctrl+down arrow or Ctrl+up arrow until Quicken finds the right name.

3. To enter a subcategory after QuickFill fills in the category name, press End to go to the end of the category name and type a colon (:). Quick-Fill fills in the first subcategory for the category that it just filled in. If the subcategory isn't the one that you want, type a few more characters or press Ctrl+down arrow or Ctrl+up arrow to find the next or preceding subcategory under the category. Press Tab to accept the subcategory.

4. To enter class information, type a slash (/) after the category or subcategory name that QuickFill fills in and then type a few characters of the class name. Quicken searches the Class list for the first class that begins with the characters that you type. When a match is found, QuickFill fills in the class name. To accept the class, press Tab. If the class isn't the one you want, type a few more characters or press Ctrl+down arrow or Ctrl+up arrow to find the next or preceding class.

   To enter a subclass, type a colon after the class name, and then enter the subclass name. QuickFill suggests a class, but after a colon, will do nothing with characters entered. Press Tab to accept a subclass.

Note

If the category or class that you want to assign to a check or transaction in the Register isn't in the Category & Transfer list or the Class list (because they're new), you can add a new category or class by typing the new name in the Category field. When you press Tab after you enter a new category or class name in the Write Checks window or the Register, Quicken displays the appropriate dialog box for you to enter information to set up the new category or class. Follow the usual steps for adding categories and classes. Refer to Chapter 4, "Organizing Your Finances," for information on how to add a category and class.

Setting QuickFill Preferences

If you don't want to use the QuickFill feature in the way that Quicken sets up
at installation, you can change the preferences so that QuickFill works the
way you want.

To change QuickFill preferences, follow these steps:

1. From the Edit menu, choose Preferences or click the Prefs button on the
   Iconbar to display the Quicken for Windows Preferences dialog box.

2. Choose the QuickFill preferences button to display the QuickFill Preferences dialog box, shown in figure 7.8.

3. Choose the check box for any or all of the QuickFill preferences listed
   in table 7.2.

4. When the QuickFill preferences are set as you want them, choose OK to
   save the settings.

Tip
You can change
QuickFill prefer-
ences at any time.
QuickFill prefer-
ences don't change
the way Quicken
processes your
data.

Learning Quicken

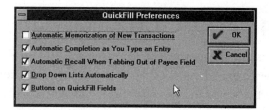

Fig. 7.8
To change the way
QuickFill works,
select preferences
in the QuickFill
Preferences dialog
box.

Table 7.2 QuickFill Preference Settings	
Setting	**Description**
Automatic Memorization of New Transactions	When you select this setting, Quicken auto-matically memorizes each new transaction that you enter for a new payee. (Investment transactions, however, aren't memorized.) Memorized transactions are added to the Memorized Transaction list (see the later section "Using Memorized Transactions").
Automatic Completion as You Type an Entry	Quicken automatically fills in each field in a transaction as you type characters in a field if you select this setting. This pref-erence works with check number, payee, category, subcategory, class, subclass, security names, investment action, and transfer account names that you type in a field. Quicken selects this preference by default.

(continues)

Table 7.2 Continued	
Setting	**Description**
Automatic Recall When Tabbing Out of Payee Field	This setting, selected by default, causes Quicken to recall automatically the matching memorized transaction, or previously entered transaction from the Register, when you press Tab to leave the payee field.
Drop Down Lists Automatically	This setting, selected by default, causes Quicken to display the drop-down list automatically for fields that use QuickFill. Deselect this setting if you don't want to see the drop-down list each time you move to a QuickFill field.
Buttons on QuickFill Fields	This setting, selected by default, puts a button beside each field that uses Quick-Fill. To see the drop-down list, click the button.

Copying Part of a Transaction

Quicken provides fast and easy ways to copy information between transactions. If you want to add the same memo to several transactions, you can copy the text in the Memo field and paste it to the Memo field in another transaction.

To copy transaction information, follow these steps:

1. In the Register, highlight the transaction that you want to copy.

2. Drag the mouse pointer to highlight the information you want to copy, or press Shift+left arrow or Shift+right arrow to highlight the information to the left or right of the cursor, respectively (see fig. 7.9).

3. From the Edit menu, choose Copy (or press Ctrl+Ins). Quicken copies the highlighted text to the Windows Clipboard.

4. Highlight the transaction to which you want to copy the information. Press Tab to move to the field to which you want to copy the transaction information.

5. From the Edit menu, choose Paste (or press Shift+Ins) to copy the information to the field in the other transaction.

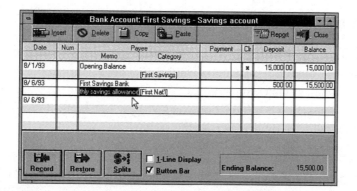

Fig. 7.9
Highlight information in a transaction that you want to copy to another transaction.

Copying Entire Transactions

If you enter a transaction in the wrong account Register, you can copy the information to the correct account and then delete the transaction from the wrong account. If you enter a transaction for a deposit in your Check Register, for example, but the deposit was actually made in your savings account, you can copy the deposit transaction to the savings account Register and then delete the transaction from the checking account Register.

You also can copy transactions within the same account. If you have a transaction that mirrors another transaction, simply copy the transaction to a blank transaction line in the Register.

To copy a transaction, follow these steps:

1. In the Register, highlight the transaction that you want to copy.

2. Choose Copy on the button bar or choose Copy Transaction from the Edit menu. Quicken copies the entire transaction in the Windows Clipboard.

3. Move to a new transaction line within the same Register, or access another account Register and move to a new transaction line. (Moving around the Register is explained in Chapter 6, "Using the Register.")

4. Choose Paste on the button bar or choose Paste Transaction from the Edit menu. Quicken enters the copied transaction information from the Windows Clipboard to the new transaction line.

Using Memorized Transactions

To speed the check-writing process, you can have Quicken memorize recurring checks from the Write Checks window. For quick entry in the Register, you also can have Quicken memorize recurring transactions. A memorized check or transaction is information you save from one transaction so that you can recall it for other checks or transactions.

Tip
Memorizing checks is valuable if you address checks, because you don't have to re-enter the payee's address every time you write a check.

Many transactions you enter probably are similar from week to week and month to month. For a household, you may write a mortgage check, a car loan check, a utility bill check, and so on. For a business, you may write weekly payroll checks to employees and monthly checks to major vendors. Because transactions often are similar, Quicken enables you to store transaction information in a special list known as the *Memorized Transaction list*. Rather than re-enter the same information, you can reuse transaction information.

You can recall a memorized transaction from the Memorized Transaction list. Quicken enters the transaction information in the Write Checks window or the Register. You can edit or delete a memorized transaction directly from the memorized lists.

CPA TIP: Memorizing Transactions To Save Time

Memorized transactions provide a quick way to enter lengthy, split transactions that you always assign to the same categories or subcategories. A transaction to record your paycheck, for example, involves several split lines because you must assign categories for federal withholding, state withholding, FICA withholding, Medicare withholding, and so on, to each paycheck transaction. If you have Quicken memorize a paycheck transaction and then recall the transaction, Quicken enters the categories for you. Then, if necessary, you just change the amounts assigned to the categories.

Memorizing a Check

When you have Quicken memorize a check, Quicken stores the payee name, amount, address (if applicable), memo, and category for the check in the Memorized Transaction list. Later, you can recall the memorized check to a blank check, and Quicken automatically fills in the check information with the same information as the memorized check.

To memorize a check, follow these steps:

1. Display the check you want to memorize in the Write Checks window.

2. From the Edit menu, choose **M**emorize Transaction (or press Ctrl+M).

3. If you have Quicken memorize a split check transaction, Quicken displays a message window that asks whether you want to memorize the split amounts as percentages of the check amount. Choose Yes to memorize the percentages, or choose No if you want the actual amounts memorized. This feature is handy if a memorized check amount varies, but the split is always based on the same percentages.

4. Quicken displays a message that it is about to memorize the transaction. Choose OK to save the check information in the Memorized Transaction list.

Memorizing a Transaction in the Register

Because so many Register transactions are largely the same every month, Quicken enables you to store transaction information in a Memorized Transaction list. Rather than enter the information over and over, you can recall it from the list of memorized transactions.

Quicken can memorize any transaction that you enter into your system. You can memorize a transaction from any Quicken account Register, including investment account Registers.

> **Note**
>
> Quicken stores memorized investment transactions in a separate Memorized Transaction list. (Refer to Chapter 15, "Monitoring Your Investments," to learn about memorized investment transactions.) In this section, you learn how to memorize and recall transactions in the Checking Account Register; you can use the same steps to memorize and recall transactions in any other non-investment account Register.

Quicken saves the memorized transactions to the Memorized Transaction list when you have Quicken memorize the following types of transactions:

- Checks

- Deposits

- Banking fees

- Interest earned

- Automatic teller machine transactions

- Any other transaction recorded in the following account Registers: Bank, Credit Card, Cash, Asset, and Liability

To memorize a transaction in a Register, follow these steps:

1. In the Register, enter the transaction you want Quicken to memorize. You can enter as little or as much of the transaction that you want Quicken to memorize. If you want Quicken to memorize only the payee and the category, for example, enter only that information and continue with steps 2 through 4.

2. With the transaction still highlighted, choose Memorize Transaction from the Edit menu (or press Ctrl+M).

3. If you have Quicken memorize a split transaction, Quicken displays a message that asks whether you want to memorize the split amounts as percentages of the transaction amount. Choose Yes to have Quicken memorize the percentages; choose No if you want the actual amounts memorized. This feature is handy if a memorized transaction amount varies, but the split is always based on the same percentages.

4. Quicken displays a message that it is about to memorize the transaction. Choose OK to save the transaction information in the Memorized Transaction list.

5. After Quicken memorizes the transaction information, you can complete the transaction, if necessary, and choose Record.

> **Note**
>
> Quicken doesn't memorize the date of a transaction or the check or transaction number. When you recall a memorized transaction, Quicken enters the current date. You assign the check number when you enter or print a check transaction.

Recalling a Check or Transaction

When you want to enter information in the Write Checks window or the Register from a memorized transaction, you must recall the transaction from the Memorized Transaction list. Suppose that you have Quicken memorize a check for the monthly cleaning payment. When you need to pay Susan Alexander Cleaning Services again, you recall the memorized check from the Memorized Transaction list, shown in figure 7.10.

Fig. 7.10

The Memorized Transaction list includes transactions that you have had Quicken memorize.

The Memorized Transaction list shows all memorized transactions (except memorized investment transactions). For checks, you want to recall only those transactions that show Chk in the Type column. Chk indicates that the transaction was memorized from the Write Checks window. Check transactions include information that appears only in the Write Checks window, such as the address data and the extra message line.

Figure 7.10 shows some of the information saved as part of the Memorize Transaction operation. The address information and message also are saved, but the address and message don't show in the Memorized Transaction list.

The Memorized Transaction list is sorted by payee. For each payee, Quicken shows the transaction amount, the transaction type (Chk, Pmt, Dep, and so on), whether the transaction is a split transaction, the memo (if any), the category assigned to the memorized transaction, whether the memorized transaction has cleared the bank, and to which transaction group (if any) the memorized transaction belongs. Chapter 14, "Scheduling Future Trans-actions," describes transaction groups.

To recall a memorized transaction, follow these steps:

1. Access the Write Checks window and display a blank check, or access the Register and move to a blank transaction line.

2. From the Lists menu, choose Memorized Transaction (or press Ctrl+T) to display the Memorized Transaction list (refer to fig. 7.10).

3. Use the scroll bar or press the up- and down-arrow keys to highlight the memorized transaction you want to recall.

4. Choose the Use button, double-click the transaction, or press Enter to select the memorized transaction. Quicken uses the memorized transaction to fill in the check in the Write Checks window or the transaction line in the Register.

5. Edit the transaction information, if necessary.

6. Choose Record to record the check.

Caution

If you recall a memorized transaction into a transaction line with a recorded transaction, Quicken replaces the existing transaction information with the recalled memorized transaction. Be careful not to recall a memorized transaction to a valid transaction line in the Register. You can remove the memorized transaction by choosing the Restore button before recording the transaction.

Editing a Memorized Transaction

Over time, the transaction information that Quicken has memorized may need to be updated. Updating transaction information doesn't present a problem. To edit a memorized transaction, follow these steps:

1. From the Lists menu, choose Memorized Transaction (or press Ctrl+T) to display the Memorized Transaction list (refer to fig. 7.10).

2. Use the scroll bar or press the up- and down-arrow keys to highlight the memorized transaction that you want to edit.

3. Choose Edit. Quicken displays the Edit Memorized Transaction dialog box, shown in figure 7.11.

Fig. 7.11

The Edit Memorized Transaction dialog box shows the saved information for the selected memorized transaction.

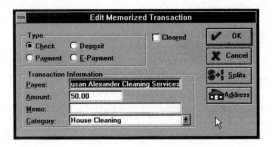

4. Change the type of transaction by choosing the appropriate option from the type box: Check, Payment, Deposit, or E-Payment (electronic mail payment).

5. To change the cleared status, choose Cleared.

6. Tab to the text box that you want to change and type over the existing information.

7. To change the information for a memorized split transaction, choose Splits to display the Splits window. Edit the information in the Splits window and choose OK to return to the Edit Memorized Transaction dialog box.

8. To change the address and message line (if applicable) for printed checks, choose Address. Quicken displays the Printed Check Information dialog box. Change or add the address, using up to five lines. Change or add a message line, if applicable. Choose OK to return to the Edit Memorized Transaction dialog box.

9. Choose OK to save the changes to the memorized transaction.

Deleting a Memorized Transaction

At some point, the original reasons you had for memorizing a transaction may no longer apply. Eventually, you may pay off the mortgage or car loan, children may outgrow the need for day care, or you may decide to stop spending money on an item, such as club dues or cable television.

At any time, you can delete memorized transactions from the Memorized Transaction list. To delete a memorized transaction from the list, follow these steps:

1. From the Lists menu, choose Memorized Transaction (or press Ctrl+T) to display the Memorized Transaction list (refer to fig. 7.10).

2. Use the scroll bar or press the up- and down-arrow keys to highlight the memorized transaction that you want to delete.

3. Choose Del.

4. Quicken displays a message that you are about to delete a memorized transaction. To delete the memorized check, choose OK. If you decide not to delete the memorized transaction, choose Cancel or press Esc.

Using QuickReport with Memorized Transactions

To get a quick report listing of all transactions containing the payee name for a specific memorized transaction in the Memorized Transaction list, use Quicken's new QuickReport feature. When you select QuickReport, Quicken lists all transactions (in all accounts) with the same payee name as the highlighted memorized transaction in the Memorized Transaction list. Quicken shows the date, account, check number (if applicable), description, memo, category or subcategory name, cleared status, and amount for each transaction in the list.

To get an instant report for a memorized transaction, follow these steps:

1. From the Lists menu, choose Memorized Transaction (or press Ctrl+T) to display the Memorized Transaction list (refer to fig. 7.10).

2. Highlight the memorized transaction for which you want a list of transactions containing the same payee.

3. Choose Report at the bottom of the Memorized Transaction list. Quicken quickly filters all transactions and displays only those that contain the same payee as the memorized transaction that you selected.

4. To remove the QuickReport from your screen, choose Close at the top of the report.

> **Note**
>
> You can change the report settings by using the buttons at the top of the Quick-Report. You also can print the QuickReport by choosing Print. First, however, you must make sure that the report settings in Quicken are set for your printer. See Chapter 18, "Creating and Printing Reports," for information on how to change the report settings and enter printing settings.

Printing the Memorized Transaction List

Quicken enables you to print lists of memorized transactions. Assuming that you entered payee addresses, a printed list of memorized transactions can act as a directory of the people and businesses to whom you write checks.

Caution

Before you print the Memorized Transaction list, make sure that Quicken is set up to print reports and lists. Refer to Chapter 4, "Organizing Your Finances," to learn how to set up Quicken to print reports and lists.

To print a list of memorized checks and other transactions, follow these steps:

1. From the Lists menu, choose Memorized Transaction (or press Ctrl+T) to display the Memorized Transaction list.

2. From the File menu, choose Print List (or press Ctrl+P). Quicken displays the Print Report dialog box, shown in figure 7.12.

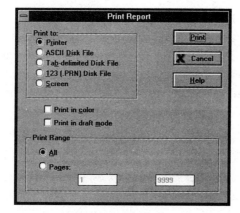

Fig. 7.12
The Print Report dialog box appears when you press Ctrl+P from the Memorized Transaction list.

3. In the Print To section, choose where you want the Memorized Transaction list printed. To print to your printer, select the Printer option button. You also can save the Memorized Transaction list to an ASCII Disk File, a Tab-delimited Disk File, a 123 (.PRN) disk file, or preview the list on your Screen.

4. Choose Print in Color to print the Memorized Transaction list in color. You must have an installed color printer to print the list in color.

   If desired, choose the Print in Draft Mode check box if your printer supports draft mode printing.

5. Choose the print range. Choose All to print all pages of the Memorized Transaction list. Otherwise, choose Pages and specify which pages you want to print.

Learning Quicken

6. Choose **Print** or press Enter to begin printing the Memorized Transaction list.

CPA TIP: Saving Time with Memorized Checks

Consider as candidates for the Memorized Transaction list each check you regularly write using Quicken: rent, house payment, utility payment, car loans, and so on. Using memorized checks saves you time you otherwise spend typing, finding addresses, and describing checks.

Finding Transactions

You may write only a handful of checks and make only one or two deposits a month. Even with such low volume, however, you soon will have several dozen transactions in a Register. As you write more checks and make additional deposits, searching through your Register for specific transactions becomes more and more difficult. You eventually may want to know whether you recorded a deposit or paid a bill, or when you last paid a vendor.

Tip
You also can use the Find window to search for a check that you have written, but not yet printed, from the Write Checks window.

You easily can locate the transaction in the Write Checks window or in the Register by using Quicken's Find window. You can look for transactions where the payee is Stouffer's Office Supplies, where the category is Utilities, or where the amount is $88.44, for example.

One way to search through transactions is to use an exact match. An *exact match* means that you look for a transaction that has a payee, an amount, a category, or another piece of transaction information exactly equal to what you want.

To search through transactions in the Register, follow these steps:

1. From the Register, choose Find from the Edit menu (or press Ctrl+F). Quicken displays the Find window, shown in figure 7.13.

2. In the Find text box, type the information you are looking for. If you are looking for a check transaction to CompuServe, for example, type **CompuServe** in the Find text box. If you are looking for a check for $100 but don't know who it was made to, type **100** in the Find text box.

Fig. 7.13
Use the Find
window to locate
a transaction.

Learning Quicken

Use match characters to search for transactions based on a field that includes or excludes certain letters, characters, or series of characters. Match characters include three special characters: the question mark (?), double periods (..), and the tilde (~). The question mark can represent any one character. Double periods represent any character at the beginning, middle, or end of what you type. The tilde identifies a word, character, or group of characters to exclude from the search.

To search for transactions whose dates are the first 9 days in July 1994, type **7/?/94** in the Find text box. To search for transactions whose dates are after July 9, 1994, type 7/??/94.

Type **..computer..** to find checks to payees with the word *Computer* in the name. Quicken finds Computer Superstore, Jones Computers, and A-1 Computer Stores.

To find transactions assigned to categories other than the *Interest* category, type **~interest** in the Find text box.

> **Note**
>
> Search characters can be used in combination. For example, you can type **~..Smith..** to find transactions to payees other than those with the name Smith in the name.

3. Next, tell Quicken where to look for the information that you entered in the Find text box. From the **S**earch drop-down list, select one of the following search options:

All Fields	Searches every field in every transaction in the Register
Amount	Searches the Payment or Deposit fields (or the Amount field in the Splits window)

Cleared Status	Searches only those transactions with the specified cleared status
Memo	Searches the Memo field only
Date	Searches only the Date field
Category/Class	Searches the Category field only
Check Number	Searches the Num (Check Number) field only
Payee	Searches the Payee field only

4. From the Match If drop-down list, select how you want Quicken to match the information you entered in the Find text box. You may want to find only transactions that match the Exact text you entered in the Find box, or you may want to find all transactions that are Greater than the amount you entered in the Find text box.

5. Begin the search by choosing Previous or Next. To look through transactions in the Register with dates earlier than the date of the selected transaction, choose Previous. To search through transactions in the Register with dates after the date of the selected transaction, choose Next.

   If Quicken finds a transaction that matches the search request that you entered in the Find window, it highlights the transaction (the Find window remains open for additional searches).

   To repeat the search, choose Previous or Next again. When Quicken reaches the first or last transaction in the Register, it displays a message asking whether you want to continue the search from the beginning or end of the account. Choose Yes to continue or No to stop the search.

   If no transactions are found that match your search request, Quicken displays a message that no matching transactions were found. Choose OK to stop the search.

6. To remove the Find window from the screen, double-click its Control menu box.

As you work in the Write Checks window or the Register, you can keep the Find window open by minimizing it or moving it to an unused portion of the screen. From the Help menu, choose Tutorials and then Introduction to Windows to learn how to work with open windows.

> **Note**
>
> Whenever you are working in the Write Checks window, you quickly can switch to the Register for the checking account that you're writing checks from by pressing Ctrl+R. To switch from the Register to the Write Checks window, press Ctrl+W.

Summary

This chapter showed you how to speed up your work in Quicken using shortcuts. You learned how to do the following:

- Use the new pop-up calendar and calculator to fill in the Date and Amount fields

- Use QuickFill to fill in the Num, Payee, and Category for a transaction

- Customize QuickFill to work the way you want it

- Copy information from one transaction to another and copy transactions to other account Registers

- Memorize and recall transactions that you frequently enter

- Edit and delete memorized transactions

- Use QuickReport to get an instant report of all transactions containing the same payee as the selected memorized transaction

- Print the Memorized Transaction list

- Use the Find window to locate a transaction in the Register

In the next chapter, Part I of *Using Quicken 3 for Windows* wraps up by showing you how to reconcile your bank account. The hours and hours you have spent performing this task in the past will turn into minutes when you reconcile your account with Quicken.

Chapter 8

Reconciling Your Bank Account

Reconciling your bank account regularly is one of the most important steps you can take to protect your cash and the accuracy and reliability of your financial records. Most people, however, probably don't reconcile their bank account—unless they feel guilty or frustrated. The work is tedious and usually aggravating as you search, often futilely, for the transaction that explains the difference between the bank's records and your personal records. Fortunately, Quicken provides a fast and easy method of reconciliation.

Understanding the Reconciliation Process

Reconciling a bank account isn't difficult. You probably already understand the mechanics of the reconciliation process. For readers who are a bit rusty with the process, however, the next few paragraphs briefly describe how reconciliation works.

To reconcile a bank account, you perform three basic steps:

1. Review the bank statement for new transactions and errors. You want to verify that you have recorded each transaction correctly.

2. Find the transactions not recorded by the bank or cleared, and total these transactions.

3. Verify that the difference between your checkbook balance and the bank balance equals the total of the uncleared transactions. If the totals don't agree, you need to repeat steps 1 and 2.

In this chapter, you learn how to do the following:

- Reconcile a bank account using Quicken

- Mark transactions as cleared

- Print and use Reconciliation Reports

- Create balance-adjustment transactions

- Correct and catch reconciliation errors

If you still find the process of reconciliation confusing, examine your monthly bank statement. The back of your current bank statement probably explains the whole process step by step.

Reviewing the Bank Statement

The first step in reconciling an account is to review the bank statement. First, find any new transactions that the bank recorded and that you now need to record. These transactions may include withdrawals from the automatic teller machine or checks that your spouse wrote and didn't tell you about. You need to record these transactions in the Register before you proceed with the reconciliation.

You can enter bank transactions such as bank service fees, overdraft charges, and interest income after you begin reconciling your account with Quicken.

For each transaction, confirm that the checking account transaction recorded in the Register and on the bank statement are the same amount. If you find a transaction that isn't recorded in both places for the same amount, review the discrepancy and identify the incorrect transaction.

CPA TIP: Reviewing Canceled Checks

Carefully review each canceled check for authenticity. If a check forger successfully draws a check on your account, you can discover the forgery by reviewing canceled checks. You need to find forgeries if you hope to recover the money.

Checking Cleared Transactions

The second step in bank account reconciliation is to calculate the total dollar value of those transactions that haven't cleared the bank. By adding up all the checks that haven't cleared (usually known as *outstanding checks*) and all the deposits that haven't cleared (usually known as *deposits in transit*), you calculate an amount that represents the logical difference between the bank's records and your records.

Usually, the mechanics of the second step work in the following way: look over the bank statement to identify the checks and deposits that have cleared; mark the cleared transactions in the Register; then add up all the transactions that haven't cleared.

Verifying that Balances Correspond

The final step is a quick one: verify that the difference between the Quicken Register balance and your bank statement balance is the total of the transactions that *haven't* cleared. If you correctly perform steps 1 and 2 during the reconciliation process, the balance in your Quicken Register and the ending bank balance should differ by the total of all transactions not yet cleared. If the two amounts don't differ by precisely this amount, you must repeat steps 1 and 2 until you locate and correct the error. Refer to the later section "Catching Common Errors" to learn some causes for differences in your checkbook balance and the bank's balance.

Reconciling Your Bank Account with Quicken

Quicken makes reconciling a bank account easier by automating the steps and doing the arithmetic for you. To reconcile an account, follow these steps:

1. Click the Accts button on the Iconbar (or press Ctrl+A) to display the Account list.

2. Highlight the bank account that you want to reconcile; then choose the Use button or press Enter. Quicken displays the Register for the account.

3. Choose Reconcile from the Activities menu, or click the Recon button on the Iconbar. Quicken displays the Reconcile Bank Statement dialog box, with the name of the account that you are reconciling on the title bar (see fig. 8.1).

Fig. 8.1

The Reconcile Bank Statement dialog box shows the name of the account that you are reconciling on the title bar.

Quicken automatically enters the bank statement's opening balance in the **Bank Statement Opening Balance** text box. Quicken uses the ending balance from the last reconciliation as the opening balance for this reconciliation. If this is the first time you have reconciled your bank account with Quicken, the opening balance that you entered when you added the account to your system is entered in the Bank Statement Opening Balance text box.

4. If the bank statement's balance at the start of the period that the bank statement covers is different than the opening balance entered by Quicken, type the correct opening balance from your statement. (Be sure to read the section "Adjusting Opening Balance Differences" later in this chapter to learn how to handle differences in the bank statement's opening balance.)

> **Note**
>
> Quicken strongly recommends that you use the ending balance from your last bank statement as the opening balance in a new bank account. Therefore, if you used the ending balance as your opening balance, the opening balance that Quicken enters in the Bank Statement Opening Balance field should be correct.

5. Move to the Bank Statement Ending Balance text box and type the bank statement balance shown at the end of the period that the bank statement covers. This amount also appears on the bank statement.

Tip
Use the Service Charge text box to enter check charges, ATM charges, or any other fees that your bank assesses.

6. Move to the Service Charge text box. If you didn't record monthly service fees, record them now by entering the appropriate amount in the Service Charge text box. Then enter the service charge transaction date in the Date text box, or click the down arrow to display the mini-calendar and select a date. (You learn how to use the mini-calendar to enter dates in Chapter 7, "Using Quicken Shortcuts.")

7. (Optional) Move to the Category drop-down list box for the service charge transaction. If you entered an amount in the Service Charge text box and want to assign the service charge to a category, select from the text list box the category or subcategory that you want to assign to the service charges.

8. Move to the Interest Earned text box. If you haven't recorded monthly interest income in this account yet, record this amount now by entering the appropriate amount. Type the date that the interest was credited to your bank account in the Date text box, or click the down arrow to display the mini-calendar and select a date. (You learn how to use the mini-calendar to enter dates in Chapter 7, "Using Quicken Short-cuts.")

> ### CPA TIP: Earning Interest in Checking Accounts
>
> If you normally keep a large account balance, you should have an interest-bearing checking account. You shouldn't keep your money in an account that doesn't earn interest.
>
> Before you close your current account and open a new one, however, review the fees that your bank charges for each type of account. Weigh the interest factor against the fee schedule to determine the most beneficial account type for your business. If your bank doesn't offer interest-bearing accounts to businesses, you may want to deposit excess cash into a savings or money market account. Remember that you can set up savings and money market accounts in your Quicken system and use the Reconcile feature to balance each account.

9. (Optional) Move to the Category drop-down list box for the interest transaction. If you entered an amount in the Interest Earned text box and want to assign the interest income to a category, select from the drop-down list the category or subcategory that you want to assign to the interest income.

10. (Optional) If you didn't print a copy of the Reconciliation Report the last time that you reconciled your bank account, you can print a copy of the report now by choosing the Report command button.

11. Choose OK when the Reconcile Bank Statement dialog box is complete. Quicken displays the Reconcile Bank Account window, shown in figure 8.2.

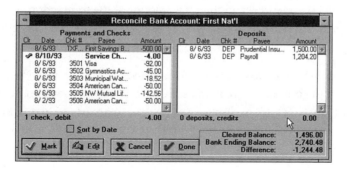

Fig. 8.2
The Reconcile Bank Account window lists all uncleared payments and checks on the left and all uncleared deposits on the right.

The Reconcile Bank Account window lists all uncleared transactions (transactions that aren't marked as cleared in the Clr field in the Register), with the Payments and Checks list on the left and the Deposits list on the right side of the window. The Reconcile Bank Account window shows the total number and total amount of payments, checks, and deposits marked as cleared during the reconciliation process. This window also shows the cleared balance in your account, the bank's ending statement balance, and the difference. When the difference is zero, you've successfully balanced your bank account.

12. (Optional) If your bank statement lists transactions in date order, you can reorganize the uncleared transactions in the Reconcile Bank Account window so that they are in date order (instead of check number order). To reorganize uncleared transactions by date, select the Sort by Date check box. To return the uncleared transaction to check number order, select the Sort by Date check box again to remove the check mark.

Tip

If you accidentally mark the wrong transaction as cleared, change its status by clicking the transaction, or by highlighting it and then choosing Mark or pressing the space bar.

13. Mark payments, checks, and deposits that have *cleared* (were recorded by) the bank. To mark a payment or check as cleared, click the payment or check that you want to mark as cleared. You can also mark an item as cleared by highlighting the payment or check and then selecting the Mark command button or pressing the space bar. (To highlight the payment or check, use the scroll bar on the side of the Payments and Checks list or the up- and down-arrow keys to move through the transaction list.) Follow the same procedure to mark a deposit as cleared in the Deposits list.

Quicken enters a check mark in the Clr column and shows the cleared transaction in darker type.

As you mark transactions as cleared, Quicken adds the total number of cleared transactions and the total amount of the transactions marked as cleared. These totals are shown below the Payments and Checks list and the Deposits list.

14. (Optional) To correct transactions entered incorrectly in the Register, select the transaction that you want to change and then choose the Edit button. Quicken displays the Register window and highlights the selected transaction. Edit the transactions in the Register in the usual manner. (Chapter 6 describes how to edit transactions in the Register.)

Then return to the Reconcile Bank Account window by clicking the Recon button on the Iconbar or by choosing Reconcile from the Activities menu.

> **Note**
>
> To mark a range of transactions as cleared, click the first transaction in the range to highlight it; then Shift-click the last uncleared transaction within the range that you want to mark as cleared (press the Shift key and simultaneously click). Quicken highlights the range of transactions and enters a check mark in the Clr column for each transaction within the range. To mark checks 3405 through 3425 as cleared, for example, click check number 3405, and then Shift-click check number 3425.
>
> You also can mark a range of transactions as cleared by dragging your mouse through the range. Just point to the first transaction in the range and then drag the pointer through the other uncleared transactions in the range that you want to mark as cleared. Release the mouse button at the last uncleared transaction within the desired range. Quicken enters a check mark in the Clr column for each transaction as you drag the mouse pointer through the range of transactions.

15. When the difference between the Cleared Balance and the Bank Ending Balance is zero, choose Done to indicate that you are finished with the reconciliation. Quicken changes each asterisk in the Clr field in the Register to an x. Then Quicken congratulates you and asks whether you want to create a Reconciliation Report, as shown in figure 8.3. (Refer to the next section, "Printing Reconciliation Reports," to learn how to print a Reconciliation Report.)

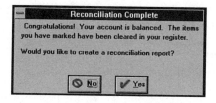

Fig. 8.3

Quicken congratulates you when your bank account balances with your bank statement.

You can leave the reconciliation process at any time by choosing Cancel or pressing Esc. When you choose Cancel, Quicken displays the Save Changes dialog box. Choose Save to leave the reconciliation process and save the work that you have done so far (such as the bank statement ending balance, service charges, interest income, and transactions marked as cleared). If you don't want to save the work you have done so far, choose **Don't Save**. Quicken returns to the Register you were in before you began reconciliation. If you save your work, when you return to the reconciliation process you can pick up where you left off.

Note

If the difference between the Cleared Balance and the Bank Ending Balance isn't zero, you may need to make a balance adjustment. The section "Creating Balance Adjustment Transactions" later in this chapter shows you how to adjust your account so that it balances with your bank statement.

CPA TIP: Understanding Debits and Credits

If you understand double-entry bookkeeping, you probably recognize that Quicken uses the labels *debit* and *credit* incorrectly from your perspective. Don't be confused by this usage. The reconciliation summary uses the terms from the bank's perspective to help people who don't understand double-entry bookkeeping.

Printing Reconciliation Reports

Many people like to keep printed records of their reconciliations. Printed copies of the Reconciliation Report show how you reconciled your records with the bank, indicate all checks and deposits still outstanding, and show all transactions that cleared the bank in a given month. This information may be helpful if you subsequently discover that the bank made an error or that you made a reconciliation error.

Printing the Report

To print a Reconciliation Report, follow these steps:

1. From the Reconciliation Complete dialog box shown in figure 8.3, choose Yes. The Reconciliation Report Setup window appears (see fig. 8.4).

2. (Optional) In the Report Title text box, enter the title that you want printed on the Reconciliation Report. You may want to use the month and year to distinguish one report from another.

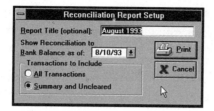

Fig. 8.4
The Reconciliation
Report Setup
dialog box appears
when you opt to
print a Reconcilia-
tion Report.

3. In the Show Reconciliation to Bank Balance As Of box, type the date that you performed the reconciliation. Alternatively, click the down arrow to select a date from the mini-calendar. (Refer to Chapter 7, "Using Quicken Shortcuts," to learn how to use the mini-calendar to enter dates.)

4. In the Transactions to Include section, select the level of detail that you want included in the Reconciliation Report. Select All Transactions if you want to print all the details of every transaction (cleared and uncleared). Select Summary and Uncleared to summarize transactions marked as cleared and to show detail of uncleared transactions.

5. Choose the Print button. Quicken displays the Print Report dialog box, shown in figure 8.5.

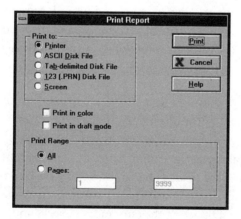

Fig. 8.5
Use the Print
Report dialog box
to tell Quicken
where you want
your report
printed.

6. In the Print To section, select where you want the Reconciliation Report printed. To print to your printer, select Printer. You also can print the Reconciliation Report to an ASCII Disk File, a Tab-delimited Disk File, or a 123 (.PRN) Disk File. Lastly, you can print the report to your Screen so that you can preview it.

7. (Optional) Select the Print in Color check box to print the Reconciliation Report in color. You must have a color printer installed to print the list in color.

   If your printer supports draft mode printing and you want to speed up printing the report, select the Print in Draft Mode check box.

8. Select the print range. By default, the All option button is selected to print all pages of the Reconciliation Report. To print certain pages of the Reconciliation Report, select the Pages option button and then specify which pages you want to print.

9. Choose the Print button or press Enter to begin printing the Reconciliation Report.

Reviewing the Reconciliation Report

The printed Reconciliation Report includes three distinct components: the Reconciliation Summary, the Cleared Transaction Detail, and the Uncleared Transaction Detail. If you select to print All Transactions in the Reconciliation Report (refer to fig. 8.4), Quicken prints all three components. If you select to print Summary and Uncleared transactions in the Reconciliation Report (refer to fig. 8.4), only the first and third parts print.

A Reconciliation Summary Report, shown in figure 8.6, essentially restates the reconciliation summary shown at the bottom of the Reconcile Bank Account window. The reconciliation summary in the Reconciliation Report has two sections:

- Bank Statement — Cleared Transactions

- Your Records — Uncleared Transactions

The first section calculates the ending balance according to the bank statement by subtracting the cleared checks and adding the cleared deposits from the beginning bank balance. The second section calculates the ending Register balance by subtracting the outstanding checks and adding the deposits in transit from the ending bank balance.

The Reconciliation Summary Report isn't a report you read; rather, the report documents how you reconciled the account. For this reason, you don't need to review this report unless, for some reason, you need to explain to the bank what the balance should be, or unless you need to see which transactions were outstanding when you reconciled.

```
                            August 1993
First Nat'l                                                    Page 1
8/10/1993
                        Reconciliation Summary


     BANK STATEMENT -- CLEARED TRANSACTIONS:

         Previous Balance:                                  1,500.00

             Checks and Payments        6   Items           -259.52
             Deposits and Oth...        1   Item           1,500.00

         Ending Balance of Bank Statement:                 2,740.48

     YOUR RECORDS -- UNCLEARED TRANSACTIONS:

         Cleared Balance:                                  2,740.48

             Checks and Payments        2   Items           -642.56
             Deposits and Oth...        1   Item           1,204.20

         Register Balance as of 8/10/1993:                 3,302.12
             Checks and Payments        0   Items               0.00
             Deposits and Oth...        0   Items               0.00

         Register Ending Balance:                          3,302.12



                            August 1993
First Nat'l                                                    Page 2
8/10/1993
                Uncleared Transaction Detail after 8/10/1993

 Date    Num      Payee           Memo       Category     ClrAmount

Uncleared Checks and Payments

 8/ 6/93TXFR First Savings...              [First Savings]   (500.00)
 8/ 6/933505 NW Mutual Lif...              Insurance         (142.56)

Total Uncleared Checks and Payments            2   Items-642.56


Uncleared Deposits and Other Credits

 8/ 6/93DEP  Payroll                       Salary          1,204.20

Total Uncleared Deposits and Other Credits     1   Item1,204.20


Total Uncleared Transactions                   3   Items561.64
```

Fig. 8.6
Print a Reconciliation Report after you reconcile your bank account. Use this report as documentation of the reconciliation process.

If you select to print All Transactions in the Reconciliation Report, the Cleared Transaction Detail section of the report shows each cleared check, payment transaction, cleared deposit, and other credit transactions you marked with a check mark as part of the most recent reconciliation. The report doesn't include the transactions that you marked as cleared in a prior reconciliation.

The Cleared Transaction Detail section includes most of the information related to a transaction, including the transaction date, the check or transaction number, the payee name or transaction description, any memo description, and the amount. Checks and payments are displayed as negative amounts because these amounts decrease the account balance. Deposits are displayed as positive amounts because these amounts increase the account balance. The total dollar amount and the total number of cleared transactions in the Cleared Transaction Detail section support the data shown in the first section of the Reconciliation Summary section.

> **Note**
>
> Because of space constraints, some Payee, Memo, and Category field entries in the Cleared Transaction Detail section are truncated on the right.

The Uncleared Transaction Detail section of the Reconciliation Report (refer to fig. 8.6) is identical to the Cleared Transaction Detail section of the report, except that the uncleared transactions for your checking account are summarized. The Uncleared Transaction Detail section is broken down into transactions dated before the reconciliation date and transactions dated after the reconciliation date.

Like the Cleared Transaction Detail section of the report, the Uncleared Transaction Detail section includes most of the information related to a transaction, including the transaction date, the check or transaction number, the payee name or transaction description, any memo description, and the amount. Checks and payments are shown as negative amounts because they decrease the account balance. Deposits are shown as positive amounts because they increase the account balance. The total dollar amount and the total number of uncleared transactions in the Uncleared Transaction Detail section support the data shown in the second section of the Reconciliation Report.

Creating Balance Adjustment Transactions

If you can't *reconcile* an account—that is, if the difference amount shown in the Reconcile Bank Account window equals any number other than zero (refer to fig. 8.2)—the difference may be due to a difference in the opening balance that Quicken shows in the Reconcile Bank Statement dialog box (refer to fig. 8.1) and the opening balance shown on your bank statement.

Quicken handles these differences by adjusting the opening balance difference. Quicken handles any other differences (not arising from an opening balance difference) by creating a balancing adjustment.

Adjusting Opening Balance Differences

If you changed the amount in the Bank Statement Opening Balance text box in the Reconcile Bank Statement dialog box to match the opening balance on your bank statement, Quicken shows the opening balance difference in the Reconcile Bank Account window.

The following three reasons can cause your Quicken opening balance to differ from your bank statement's opening balance:

■ You are reconciling your account with Quicken for the first time, so Quicken is using the opening balance you entered when you set up your checking account as the bank statement opening balance. If the opening balance that you entered when you set up your checking account didn't account for uncleared checks written before you started your Quicken system (because you didn't enter previous transactions), then your bank's opening balance differs from the opening balance in your account by the amount of uncleared checks.

Assume that you set up your checking account on January 1 and entered the opening balance shown in your manual checkbook register—$3,500. If, however, you had written three checks totaling $500 that hadn't cleared the bank by January 1, your opening bank statement balance would be $500 greater, or $4,000.

The opening balance difference remains until you enter all uncleared transactions and adjust Quicken's opening balance to agree with the amount that actually was in your checking account the day you started using Quicken (in this example, you adjust the opening balance to $4,000). You can enter uncleared transactions without leaving the reconciliation by choosing the Edit button to access the Register.

> **Note**
>
> Quicken can do an automatic opening balance adjustment at the end of the reconciliation process; however, don't let Quicken make this adjustment unless you agree with the amount. In this section, you learn how to make opening balance adjustments when you complete the reconciliation process.

■ You didn't enter previous transactions before you began using Quicken. When you later entered these previous transactions, you changed the opening balance in the Checking Account or Bank Account Register to reflect your checking account's balance on the first day of the year. The opening balance difference remains until you mark previous transactions as cleared. To do so, leave the reconciliation and go to the Register.

For each cleared transaction, type X in the Clr field. Because all previous transactions may not have cleared the bank, you should review your bank statements, beginning with the first of the year, to account for all numbered checks and deposits.

■ You aren't using the most current bank statement, or you haven't reconciled a previous month's statement. Reconcile your account first against the earliest monthly statement, and then reconcile your account against each subsequent statement.

When you choose **Done** to finish a reconciliation when an opening balance difference exists, Quicken displays the Create Opening Balance Adjustment dialog box (see fig. 8.7).

Fig. 8.7
You can adjust your opening balance if the reconciliation difference results from a difference in the opening balance.

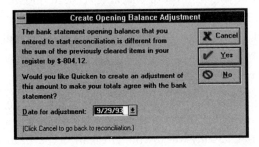

If you have exhausted all your efforts at locating the opening balance difference, you can have Quicken create an adjustment to your opening balance. Enter the date for the opening balance adjustment in the Date for Adjustment text box. Choose Yes to create the adjustment; choose No if you don't want to adjust the opening balance but want to proceed with the reconciliation. Choose Cancel if you don't want to adjust the opening balance and want to return to the Reconcile Bank Account window to review cleared transactions.

Adjusting for Other Differences

If other differences arise (other than an opening balance difference) at the completion of the reconciliation, as a last resort you may want to make a *balance adjustment*. A balance adjustment means that Quicken creates a transaction that forces the difference amount to zero.

When you finish the reconciliation (by selecting **Done**) when the difference between the Cleared Balance and the Bank Ending Balance isn't zero, Quicken displays the Adjust Balance dialog box, shown in figure 8.8.

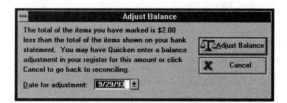

Fig. 8.8
The Adjust Balance dialog box enables you to tell Quicken whether you want to make a balance adjustment.

In the Adjust Balance dialog box, Quicken informs you of the magnitude of the reconciliation difference. To create the balance adjustment, follow these steps:

1. In the Date For Adjustment box, type or select the date that you want Quicken to use for the balance adjustment transaction.

2. Choose the Adjust Balance button. Quicken enters a balance adjustment transaction to your account and displays the Reconciliation Complete: Balance Adjusted dialog box.

3. If you want to create a Reconciliation Report, choose **Yes** and follow the steps for printing a Reconciliation Report earlier in this chapter. To finish the reconciliation process and return to the Register without printing a Reconciliation Report, choose **No**.

Figure 8.9 shows a balance adjustment transaction in the Register.

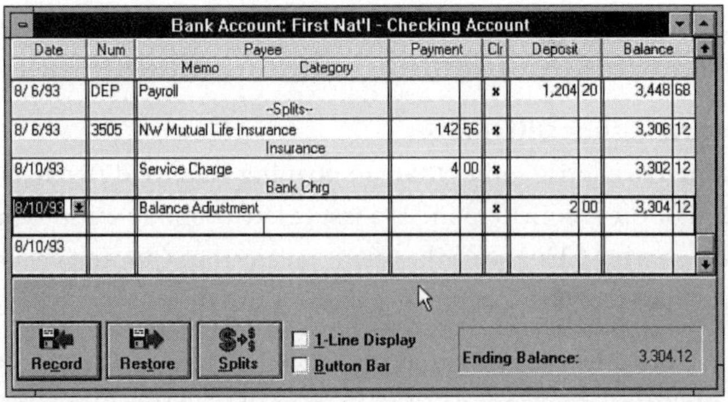

Fig. 8.9

Quicken creates a balance adjustment transaction in the Register for the account that you are reconciling.

CPA TIP: Finding Reconciliation Differences

Although Quicken provides the adjustment feature, you probably shouldn't use it because it camouflages errors in the Register. As a result, you never really can be sure where the error occurred. The difference amount equals a number other than zero because you are missing one or more transactions in the Register, you incorrectly marked a transaction as cleared, or perhaps you transposed some numbers (such as typing **$87.00** as **$78.00**).

The difference also may occur because someone forged checks or embezzled from your account. If you can't reconcile the account, make sure that the previous month's reconciliation resulted in a difference equal to zero. If the previous month's reconciliation shows a difference other than zero, you must reconcile that month (and perhaps the months before that one) before you can get the current month's difference to be displayed as zero.

Catching Common Errors

You easily can make several errors when recording transactions in a checking account. These errors can make reconciling an account difficult or even impossible. At times, a general search for errors may not be as helpful as looking for certain kinds of errors. The next few sections identify some of the more common errors and explain how to catch them.

Transposing Numbers

Transposing numbers is a frequent error in recording any financial transaction. For example, you may *write* a check for $32.67 but *record* the check as $23.67 or $32.76. This error appears obvious but is surprisingly easy to make and often difficult to catch. When you review each transaction, you see all the correct numbers. The numbers, however, are arranged in a slightly different order. If the difference is divisible by 9, a transposition error is likely.

When searching for transposed numbers, you can focus on the decimal places of the transaction where the transposition error may have occurred. Table 8.1 summarizes by amounts where the transposition error may have occurred.

Table 8.1 Possible Locations of Transposition Errors	
Error Amount	**Decimal Places of Transposition**
$.09 to $.72	In cents (for example, $.12 versus $.21 or $1.19 versus $1.91)
$.90 to $7.20	Between the dollar decimal position immediately to the left of the decimal place and the cents decimal position to right of the decimal place (for example, $32.56 versus $35.26 or $2,004.56 versus $2,005.46)
$9.00 to $72.00	Between the two positions immediately to the left of the decimal place (for example, $1,423 versus $1,432 or $281 versus $218)
$90.00 to $720.00	Between the second and third positions immediately to the left of the decimal place (for example, $1,297 versus $1,927 or $1,124 versus $1,214)

Forgetting To Record Transactions

The most common mistake is forgetting to record transactions. In a personal checking account, these omissions often include decreases in the account (for example, automated teller machine withdrawals) and increases in the account, such as interest income. In a business checking account, manual checks seem to be a common culprit; you tear out a blank check for a purchasing trip and subsequently forget to record the check.

If the amounts differ because of one transaction, identifying the missing transaction can be as easy as finding a transaction on the bank statement that equals the difference. Also, examine the sequence of checks to see whether any are missing.

Entering Payments as Deposits or Deposits as Payments

Another error is to enter a payment transaction as a deposit transaction or a deposit transaction as a payment transaction. This error, until found, can be particularly frustrating. If you look at the Register, you see that every transaction is recorded and every number is correct.

Tip
The new Missing Checks Report can help you identify missing checks. Chapter 18, "Creating and Printing Reports," explains how to create this new report.

An easy way to find such an error is to divide the error in half and see whether the result equals another transaction amount. If the result does match another transaction amount, you may have incorrectly recorded the transaction. Suppose that you now have a difference of $1,234.56 between the Register and the bank statement balances. If you divide $1,234.56 by 2, you get $617.28. If you see a $617.28 transaction in the Register, verify that you recorded this transaction in the correct column. If you recorded a $617.28 payment as a deposit or recorded a $617.28 deposit as a payment, the difference will equal twice the transaction amount, or $1,234.56.

Offsetting Errors

You may have more than one error in your account, and these errors may partially offset each other. Suppose that you forgot to record an automatic teller machine withdrawal of $40, and then made a transposition error in which you recorded a deposit as $216 rather than the correct amount of $261. The difference equals $5, which is the combined effect of both transactions. This difference is calculated as

$$-40 + (261 - 216) = \$5$$

Although the difference seems small, you actually have two large errors in the account.

With offsetting errors, remember that when you find one of the errors, you may feel that you are moving further away from the goal of a zero difference. Don't get discouraged if one minute you are $5 away from completing the reconciliation, and the next minute you are $50 away from completing the reconciliation. Finding errors is still progress—even if the difference grows larger.

Summary

This chapter explained how to reconcile your account with Quicken. You learned how to do the following:

- Reconcile a bank account
- Enter information from your bank statement
- Mark transactions that have cleared

■ Print and read a Reconciliation Report

■ Adjust for reconciliation differences and detect common errors

The next chapter begins Part II of *Using Quicken 3 for Windows*, "Getting the Most from Quicken for Windows." In Part II, you learn how to manage your credit card transactions, track loans, use accounts to track your assets and other liabilities, use Quicken to prepare for income taxes, and pay bills electronically with CheckFree.

I

Learning Quicken

Part II

Getting the Most from Quicken for Windows

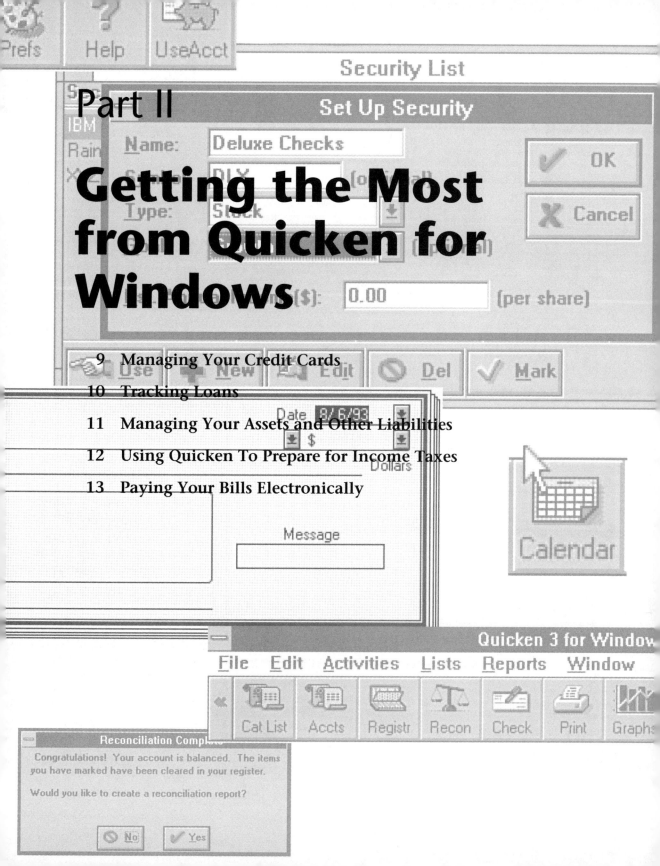

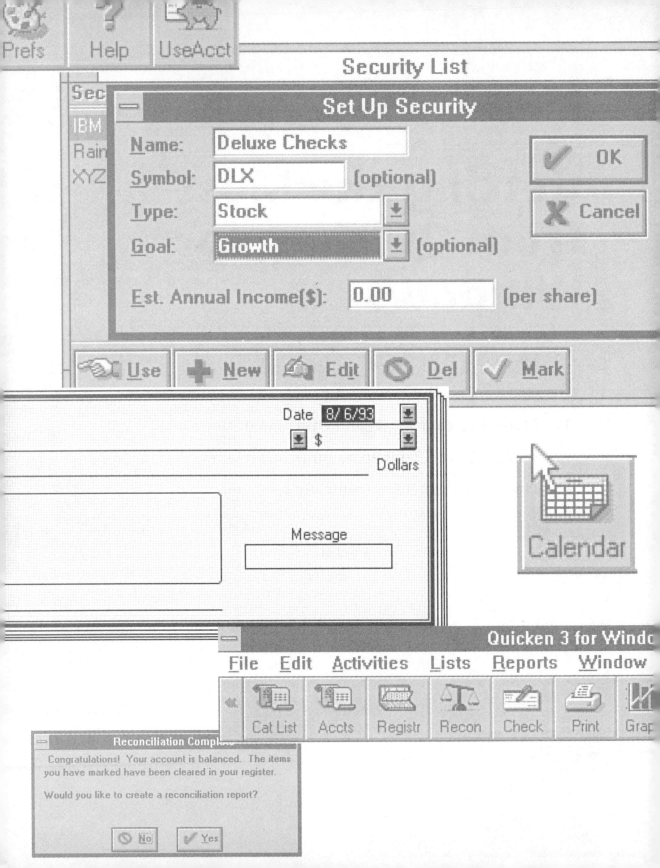

Prefs   **Help**   **UseAcct**

Security List

Sec

IBM

Rain

XYZ

Set Up Security

_N_ame: **Deluxe Checks**

S_y_mbol: **DLX**   (optional)

_T_ype: **Stock**   ▼

_G_oal: **Growth**   ▼   (optional)

_E_st. Annual Income($): **0.00**   (per share)

✔ OK

✘ Cancel

☞ _U_se   ➕ _N_ew   ✎ E_d_it   ⊘ _D_el   ✔ _M_ark

Date **8/ 6/93** ▼

▼ $ ▼

Dollars

Message

Calendar

Quicken 3 for Windo

_F_ile   _E_dit   _A_ctivities   _L_ists   _R_eports   _W_indow

Cat List   Accts   Registr   Recon   Check   Print   Gra

Reconciliation Complete

Congratulations! Your account is balanced. The items
you have marked have been cleared in your register.

Would you like to create a reconciliation report?

⊘ _N_o   ✔ _Y_es

Chapter 9

Managing Your Credit Cards

If you're like most people, you use several credit cards to buy merchandise. Now that many service providers such as doctors, lawyers, and dentists are accepting credit cards as payment, you may be making even more credit purchases.

The more you buy on credit and the more credit cards you use, the more important managing your credit becomes. With Quicken, you can set up individual Credit Card accounts that help you record and keep track of purchases, payments, and finance charges. Credit Card accounts also can help you track a line of credit (such as a line of credit for working capital to set up your new business) from your bank.

You can use an IntelliCharge account with your Quicken VISA card. The Quicken VISA card is like any other credit card, except that the name *Quicken* appears on the card and the card is issued to Quicken users only. *IntelliCharge* is an Intuit-provided service that updates your Credit Card Register automatically by disk or modem.

This chapter shows you how to set up an IntelliCharge account and how to receive your statement on disk or by modem. It also offers ways for you to review and categorize your credit transactions. You must have a Quicken VISA card to utilize the IntelliCharge feature in Quicken.

If you don't pay your credit card balance each month, setting up a Credit Card account will help you manage your credit transactions.

This chapter shows you how to do the following:

- Set up a Credit Card account

- Track credit card activity in a Credit Card account

- Reconcile your Credit Card account

- Pay your credit card bills

- Set up an IntelliCharge account

- Update your IntelliCharge account with statements received on disk or by modem

II

Getting the Most

If you do pay the balance on your credit card bills each month, you probably don't need to set up a Credit Card account. Instead, enter the payment transaction in the Register for the account that you use to pay your credit card bill and split the transaction to assign multiple categories to it (Chapters 5 and 6 discuss how to split transactions). The categories that you assign to a credit card transaction classify the purchases that you make.

CPA TIP: Show Credit Card Liabilities on a Balance Sheet

The balance carried on your credit cards is a liability. If you want all liabilities reflected in your net worth, set up a Credit Card account so that these liabilities appear in your Net Worth Reports or balance sheet statements.

Using a Credit Card Account

If you pay your credit card bill in full every month (good for you!), you don't need to set up a Credit Card account, unless you want to track exactly where and when charges are made. Your credit card spending is recorded in your checking account when you write your check to pay the credit card company. And because your credit card balance is reduced to zero each month, you don't need to keep track of that balance.

But for those of you who might carry a credit card balance, set up and use the Register of a Credit Card account to keep records of your credit card spending. Follow the same steps you would for using any other Register: set up an account, enter transactions, and then reconcile the account.

Setting Up a Credit Card Account

First, you need to set up the account and record the beginning balance. (Because you are working with a liability, the beginning balance is what you owe.) To set up a Credit Card account, follow these steps:

Tip
You also can choose the New button from the Account list (press Ctrl+A) to display the Select Account Type dialog box.

1. Choose Create New Account from the Activities menu. The Select Account Type dialog box appears (see fig. 9.1).

2. Select the Credit Card Account option button.

3. Choose OK or press Enter. The New Account Information dialog box appears (see fig. 9.2).

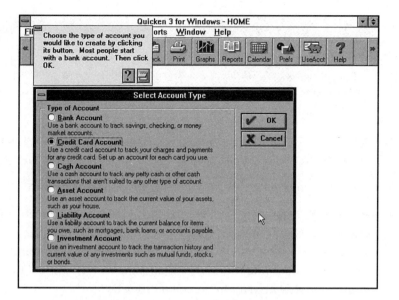

II

Getting the Most

Fig. 9.1
In the Select
Account Type
dialog box, select
the Credit Card
Account option
button to set up a
Credit Card
account.

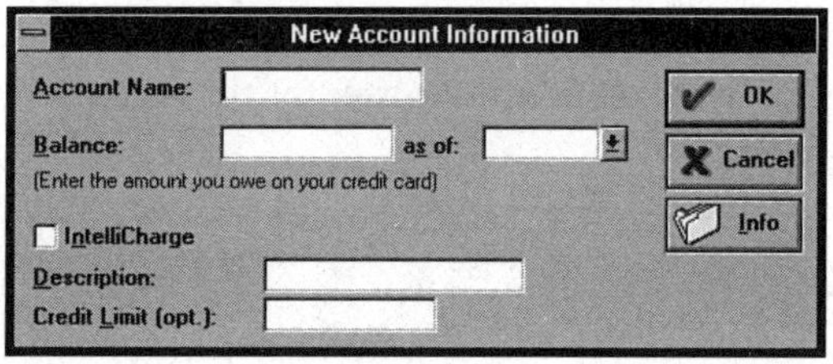

Fig. 9.2
Use the New
Account Informa-
tion dialog box to
enter information
about the Credit
Card account you
are creating.

4. In the Account Name text box, type the Credit Card account name
(**MasterCard**, **VISA**, or **Discover**, for example). You can use up to 15
letters, spaces, and any symbols in the account name except the
following:

     :] [/ | ^

5. Type your outstanding credit card balance in the Balance text box. If
the credit card balance is zero, you must enter **0** in the Balance text box
(you can't leave it blank).

6. In the As Of text box, type the date (in *mm/dd/yy* format) that corresponds with the balance you entered.

Note

The IntelliCharge check box is used to designate a Credit Card account as an IntelliCharge account. See the section "Using the IntelliCharge Account" later in this chapter for instructions for setting up an IntelliCharge account.

---

7. (Optional) In the Description text box, type a description of the Credit Card account, using up to 21 characters.

8. (Optional) Type your credit limit in the Credit Limit text box.

9. (Optional) To enter more detail for the Credit Card account, such as the bank name, account number, contact person, telephone number, and interest rate, click the Info button. The Additional Account Information dialog box appears. Add the desired details, and then choose OK to return to the New Account Information dialog box.

10. After entering the necessary information in the New Account Information dialog box, choose OK to add the Credit Card account to the Account list. The Credit Card Register for the account that you just created appears.

Note

If you choose the New button from the Account list to set up a new account, Quicken displays the Account list—not the Register—after you add account information to the New Account Information dialog box.

Figure 9.3 shows the Register for the account named MasterCard.

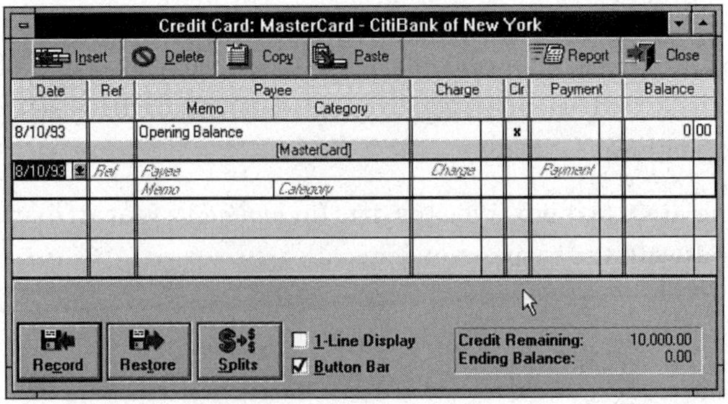

Fig. 9.3
Use the Credit Card Register to enter credit card purchases.

Tracking Credit Card Activity

To track your credit card activity, enter all your credit card transactions into the Credit Card Register. Credit card purchases are entered directly into your Credit Card account; payments are entered into the Bank Account Register that you use to pay bills when you reconcile your credit card statement.

Although the process of entering transactions is the same in all Quicken Registers, some minor differences exist between the Bank Account Register and the Credit Card Register. You record each use of your credit card in the Charge field in the Credit Card Register. Payments to the credit card company appear in the Payment field. If you filled in the Credit Limit text box when you set up the Credit Card account, Quicken shows the credit remaining in the lower right corner of the Register window (above the Ending Balance field). Figure 9.4 shows a Credit Card Register containing several credit card purchase transactions.

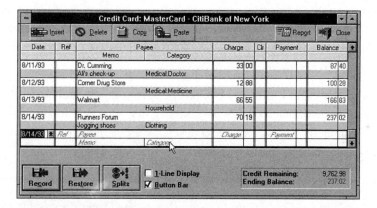

Fig. 9.4
Enter credit card purchases in the Charge field in the Credit Card Register. Payments and credits are entered in the Payment field.

II

Getting the Most

Note

You can enter, edit, and delete credit card transactions the same way that you enter transactions in the Bank Account Register. Refer to Chapter 6, "Using the Register," to review the techniques for entering, editing, and deleting transactions in the Bank Account Register.

If you receive a cash advance from your credit card, record it in the Charge field. If you also use a Cash account to track your cash expenditures, enter the name of that account in the Category field for the transaction. This step enters the cash advance in your Cash account. Chapter 11, "Managing Your Assets and Other Liabilities," gives you some instructions for using a Cash account.

CPA TIP: Paying Back Cash Advances

If you can get cash advances with your credit card, don't make the mistake of assuming that the cash you receive is interest-free for 30 days. Cash advances begin accruing interest on the day the cash is advanced to you. Also, on each cash advance, banks usually charge an additional fee of as much as 1.5 percent. If you are in a bind for cash, get that cash advance—but pay it back as soon as possible to avoid excessive interest charges.

Reconciling Your Credit Card Account

When you receive your credit card statement each month, review it carefully to make sure that you have entered all credit purchases in the Credit Card Register. Reviewing your statement also can help you uncover unauthorized uses of your credit card. You may find that the statement contains credit purchases that you or your spouse didn't make.

Before you pay your credit card bill, reconcile your statement balance with the balance in your Quicken Credit Card Register. After you successfully reconcile your credit card statement, Quicken gives you the option of paying the entire Credit Card account balance or making a partial payment.

To reconcile your Credit Card account, follow these steps:

1. While in the Credit Card Register, choose Pay Credit Card Bill from the Activities menu or click the Recon button on the Iconbar. The Credit Card Statement Information dialog box appears, with the name of the Credit Card account in the title bar (see fig. 9.5).

2. Type the sum of the charges and cash advances shown on your statement in the Charges, Cash Advances text box.

3. In the Payments, Credits text box, enter the sum of the payments and credits shown on your credit card statement.

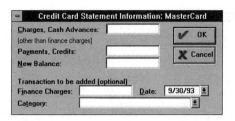

Fig. 9.5
The Credit Card
Statement Infor-
mation dialog box
appears when you
choose Pay Credit
Card Bill from the
Activities menu.

4. In the New Balance text box, type the balance due as shown on your
   credit card statement.

5. (Optional) Enter any finance charges that appear on your credit card
   statement in the Finance Charges text box (in the Transaction To Be
   Added section). Quicken enters a credit card transaction in your Credit
   Card Register for finance charges.

6. Enter the date on which the finance charges were assessed in the Date
   text box, or click the down arrow and select the date from the mini-
   calendar.

7. Move to the Category text box. If you entered an amount in the
   Finance Charges text box and want to assign the finance charge to a
   category, from the drop-down list select the category or subcategory
   that you want to assign to the finance charge transaction that Quicken
   enters (you may enter Int Exp for interest expense, for example).

CPA TIP: Avoid Credit Card Interest

Avoid credit card interest and finance charges. The Tax Reform Act of 1986
disallowed deductions for consumer or personal interest on federal and most
state income tax returns. More importantly, credit card annual interest rates
are usually 18 percent to 21 percent (if you are considered a high risk, even
more). Consequently, with the lost tax deduction and high interest costs,
carrying credit card balances that accrue interest just doesn't make sense.

8. Choose OK after entering all the necessary information in the Credit
   Card Statement Information dialog box. The Pay Credit Card Bill window appears (see fig. 9.6).

II

Getting the Most

Fig. 9.6

The Pay Credit Card Bill window lists all uncleared charges on the left and all uncleared payments on the right.

The Pay Credit Card Bill window shows the total number and total dollar amount of charges and payments marked as cleared during the reconciliation process. All uncleared transactions also are listed in the Pay Credit Card Bill window. The Charges list appears on the left side and the Payments list appears on the right side of the window.

The Pay Credit Card Bill also shows the cleared balance in your Credit Card account, the credit card statement's balance, and the difference. When the difference is zero, you've successfully balanced your Credit Card account.

9. Mark as cleared the charges and payments that appear on your credit card statement. (Refer to Chapter 8, "Reconciling Your Bank Account," to learn how to mark transactions as cleared.)

To change the cleared status of a transaction, simply repeat the marking process.

As you mark transactions as cleared, Quicken adds the total number of cleared transactions and the total amount of the transactions marked as cleared. These totals are shown below the Charges list and the Payments list.

10. (Optional) To correct transactions entered incorrectly in the Credit Card Register, highlight the transaction that you want to change, and then choose Edit. The Credit Card Register appears, with the transaction that you selected in the Pay Credit Card Bill window highlighted. Edit the transactions in the Register in the usual manner (see Chapter 6 for details), and then click the Recon button on the Iconbar or choose Pay Credit Card Bill from the Activities menu to return to the Pay Credit Card Bill window.

11. When the difference between the Cleared Balance and the Statement Balance is zero, choose Done to indicate that you are finished with the reconciliation. The Make Credit Card Payment dialog box appears. The next section of this chapter explains how to pay your credit card bill.

If the difference between the Cleared Balance and the Statement Balance in the Pay Credit Card window doesn't equal zero when you choose Done to complete the reconciliation, an Adjusting Register to Agree with Statement window appears. To accept Quicken's opening balance or missing charges adjustments, select categories to assign to the adjustment transactions in the appropriate Category text boxes. Then choose the Adjust Balance button. Quicken enters a Balance Adjustment Transaction in the Credit Card register. If you don't want to make the adjustments, choose Cancel. Quicken returns to the Pay Credit Card Bill window.

To leave the reconciliation process at any time, choose Cancel. The Save Changes? dialog box appears. Choose Save to save the work that you have done so far (bank statement ending balance, service charges, interest income, and transactions marked as cleared) before leaving the reconciliation. If you prefer not saving the work you have done so far, choose Don't Save to return to the Register you were in before you began the reconciliation. If you save your work, you can proceed from that point when you return to the reconciliation. Otherwise, you must start over.

Tip
Chapter 8 gives tips on finding and correcting reconciliation errors for a bank account. These tips also apply to reconciling a credit card statement.

CPA TIP: Monitoring Your Credit Card Statements

Balancing your Credit Card account helps you avoid unauthorized credit transactions. Because you don't need to give your signature when you use your credit card number for purchases made by telephone, all that an unauthorized user needs is your account number, expiration date, and current address to make a credit purchase by telephone.

If you don't monitor your credit card statements on a timely basis, you may not be aware of fraudulent usage until several thousand dollars have been charged. Most credit card companies protect you against unauthorized credit transactions, but you must inform them within a certain time period for their safeguards to take effect.

Paying Your Credit Card Bill
Now that you have reconciled your Credit Card account with your credit card statement, you're ready to pay your credit card bill. You can write a check in Quicken that pays the entire balance or makes a partial payment, or you can

choose to pay nothing at all at this time. If you don't use Quicken to write checks, a transaction is entered in the Bank Account Register from which you write manual checks for the credit card payment.

To pay your credit card bill, follow these steps:

1. In the Make Credit Card Payment dialog box (see fig. 9.7), select the bank account to use for paying your credit card bill from the **Bank Acct** drop-down list.

Fig. 9.7
The Make Credit Card Payment dialog box appears when you successfully reconcile your Credit Card account.

Note

If you don't want to pay your credit card bill at this time, choose Cancel in the Make Credit Card Payment dialog box. Quicken returns you to the Credit Card Register.

2. In the Payment Will Be section, select **Printed** if you want to write and print a check using Quicken. Select **Hand Written** if you want to write a manual check and have Quicken enter the check transaction in the Register.

3. Choose OK.

If you chose to write a computer check, the Write Checks window appears. The check is initially filled in with the outstanding balance amount in the $ (Amount) field. To make a partial payment rather than pay the outstanding balance, move to the $ (Amount) field and change the amount to whatever you want to pay. Choose the Record button to record the check in the Write Checks window, the Credit Card Register, and the Bank Account Register.

If you chose to write a manual check, Quicken displays the Register and fills in the transaction with the outstanding balance amount in the Payment field. If you plan to make a partial payment rather than pay the full balance, change the dollar amount in the Payment field to the amount you want to pay. Then choose the Record button to record the transaction in the Register. Quicken also records the payment in the Credit Card Register.

Using the IntelliCharge Account

IntelliCharge is a service that you can use in Quicken to track your Quicken VISA card activity. With IntelliCharge, you receive your monthly credit card statements on disk or by modem, thus enabling you to record your credit card activity in your IntelliCharge account instantly. Your credit transactions not only are recorded but are assigned automatically to categories (according to Intuit's standard list).

If you want to receive your statements by modem, you must use the local access number for CompuServe where Quicken downloads statement information. You don't need a CompuServe membership to use IntelliCharge, however.

Tip
To obtain a Quicken VISA card, complete the application form enclosed in your Quicken 3 for Windows package.

Note

If you don't have a Quicken VISA card, don't set up an IntelliCharge account; IntelliCharge accounts work only with Quicken credit cards.

Setting Up an IntelliCharge Account

Before you can begin using IntelliCharge to record your credit card transactions, you must set up a Credit Card account as an IntelliCharge account. Setting up an IntelliCharge account is much like setting up a regular Credit Card account.

To set up an IntelliCharge account, follow these steps:

1. Refer to the steps for setting up a regular Credit Card account explained earlier in this chapter. In the New Account Information dialog box (refer to fig. 9.2), select the IntelliCharge check box to designate that the Credit Card account is an IntelliCharge account. The Description

text box changes to the Credit Card Number text box. In that text box, enter the 13- or 16-digit account number of your Quicken VISA card. Make sure that you enter the correct account number from your card or your latest Quicken VISA statement.

2. After completing the New Account Information dialog box for an IntelliCharge account, choose OK or press Enter. The IntelliCharge Account Information dialog box appears (see fig. 9.8).

Fig. 9.8
The IntelliCharge Account Informa-tion dialog box appears when you choose to set up an IntelliCharge account.

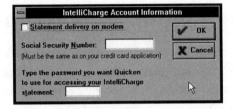

3. If you want to download your Quicken VISA statements by modem, select the Statement Delivery on Modem check box. Leave the check box blank if you want to receive your statements on disk.

4. Type your Social Security number in the Social Security Number text box. Make sure that this is the same number that you entered when you filled out your Quicken VISA application.

5. If you chose to receive your statements on disk, skip to step 6. If you chose to receive your statements by modem, you must supply a pass-word for Quicken to use when accessing your IntelliCharge statement. In the last text box in the IntelliCharge Account Information dialog box, type a password to prevent unauthorized access to your Quicken VISA statement file. Passwords can be up to eight characters long but must include at least four non-blank characters.

> **Note**
>
> You don't have to have a CompuServe membership to use IntelliCharge. Call CompuServe at (800) 848-8980 to get the local access number where Quicken downloads statement information.

6. Choose OK to complete the setup of your IntelliCharge Credit Card account.

Quicken adds your IntelliCharge account to the Account list (see fig. 9.9). A lightning bolt character appears in the Type column to designate that this Credit Card account is an IntelliCharge account.

Fig. 9.9
Your IntelliCharge account is added to the Account list with a lightning bolt character in the Type column.

If you chose to receive your statement by modem, you now must set the modem preferences so that you can download IntelliCharge information by modem.

Setting Modem Preferences

If you chose to receive your IntelliCharge statements by modem when you set up the account, you first must set the modem preferences in Quicken. The program must have information about the type of phone you use, the access telephone number, the modem speed and port, and any initialization strings that your modem uses.

To set modem preferences in Quicken, follow these steps:

1. Choose Preferences from the Edit menu or click the Prefs button on the Iconbar. The Quicken for Windows Preferences dialog box appears.

2. Choose the Modem preference button. The Modem Preferences dialog box appears (see fig. 9.10).

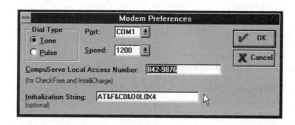

Fig. 9.10
Enter the information about your telephone and modem in the Modem Preferences dialog box.

II

Getting the Most

3. In the Dial Type section, select the Tone option button if the telephone line your modem uses supports Touch-Tone dialing. Select the Pulse option button if your phone line supports only pulse dialing.

4. In the Port drop-down list box, select the communications port of your computer (such as COM1 or COM2) that your modem uses.

5. In the Speed drop-down list box, select the speed at which your modem operates. If you're unsure about which speed to select, refer to your modem manual.

6. In the CompuServe Local Access Number text box, type the local access number for the CompuServe network through which IntelliCharge downloads your statements. If you don't have this number, call (800) 848-8980 and press 2 at the prompt. The system asks for the speed of your modem and the telephone number from which you are calling, and then gives you the CompuServe network number nearest you.

> **Note**
>
> If your telephone line needs a special prefix to obtain an outside line, include the prefix in the local access number that you enter in the CompuServe Local Access Number text box. If your telephone line needs a pause after a prefix, add a comma before you type the telephone number.

7. (Optional) In the Initialization String text box, type any special letters, digits, and other characters to be sent to your modem to begin transmission. Most initialization strings begin with the letters AT. Refer to your modem manual for this information.

8. Choose OK to save your modem preference settings and return to the Quicken for Windows Preferences dialog box.

9. Select Done to close the Quicken for Windows Preferences dialog box.

Converting a Credit Card Account to IntelliCharge

If you already have set up a Credit Card account for your Quicken VISA card, you need to convert the account to an IntelliCharge account if you want to receive your statements on disk or by modem. To convert a regular Quicken VISA Credit Card account to an IntelliCharge account, follow these steps:

1. From the Account list, highlight the Quicken VISA Credit Card account that you want to convert to an IntelliCharge account.

2. Choose the Edit button to display the Edit Account Information dialog box.

3. Select the IntelliCharge check box to change the regular Credit Card account to an IntelliCharge account.

4. When you select the IntelliCharge check box, the Description text box changes to the Credit Card Number text box. In this text box, enter the 13- or 16-digit account number of your Quicken VISA card. Make sure that you enter the correct account number from your card or your latest Quicken VISA statement.

5. Choose OK; the IntelliCharge Account Information dialog box appears (refer to fig. 9.8). Follow steps 3 through 6 earlier in the section "Setting Up an IntelliCharge Account" to complete the IntelliCharge Account Information dialog box.

II

Getting the Most

Note

If you have used previous versions of Quicken, notice that the term you're used to seeing, IntelliCard, is changed to Intelli*Charge*. Also, when you imported IntelliCard transactions into the Register, asterisks (*) were entered in the Clr (Cleared) column. Then, when you reconciled your IntelliCard account, Quicken changed each asterisk to an X when you marked the transaction as cleared. Now, IntelliCharge imports transactions into the Register and enters an X in the Clr column instead of an asterisk.

Updating Your IntelliCharge Credit Card Account

Updating your IntelliCharge Credit Card account is the same as entering credit card transactions in a regular Credit Card account, except that Intelli-Charge enters the transactions for you (by way of disk file or modem transmission). Every month, Intuit sends you your Quicken VISA card statement.

If you choose to receive your statements on disk, Intuit mails you a file that contains your credit card activity (purchases, cash advances, finance charges, credit, and payments) during the current statement period.

If you choose to download your statement information by modem, Intuit makes an electronic statement available each month for you to download to your Quicken system. After Quicken reads credit card transactions from the IntelliCharge statement, the transactions are displayed in the IntelliCharge Statement window so that you can review and mark any transactions for edit or further review in the Register. After your review, transactions are recorded in the Credit Card Register.

The following sections explain how to receive your Quicken VISA card statements on disk and by modem, review transactions in the IntelliCharge Statement window, and record credit card transactions in the Register.

Receiving Your Statement on Disk. When you receive your statement on disk, you quickly can import the credit card transactions into your IntelliCharge Credit Card account.

To receive your statement on disk and update your IntelliCharge account, follow these steps:

1. Display the Register for your IntelliCharge Credit Card account.

2. Choose Get IntelliCharge Data from the Activities menu. The Get IntelliCharge Data dialog box appears, showing your IntelliCharge account number (see fig. 9.11).

Fig. 9.11
Specify the drive in which your IntelliCharge statement disk is located in the Get IntelliCharge Data dialog box.

3. Insert the disk that contains your Quicken VISA card statement file into drive A or B.

4. Type the appropriate drive letter (**A** or **B**) in the Statement Disk Drive field, and then choose OK.

   Quicken copies each credit card transaction to the IntelliCharge Statement window as it reads them from the disk. You can't change any of these transactions as they are being read from the disk. After the transactions are entered in the IntelliCharge Statement window, however, you can review them and mark transactions that you want to edit (in the Credit Card Register).

5. IntelliCharge assigns categories to your credit card transactions (see the later section "Assigning Categories to IntelliCharge Transactions" for details). If IntelliCharge determines that a category that hasn't been set up in the Category & Transfer list should be assigned to a transaction, you are given a choice of setting up a category or selecting a category from the Category & Transfer list.

   If you want to set up a category, choose the Set Up button. The Set Up Category dialog box appears; enter the information for the new category.

   If you want to select a category from the Category & Transfer list, choose the Select button to select a category. The Category & Transfer list appears; select a category from the list.

After all credit card transactions are read from the disk file, the IntelliCharge Statement window appears and shows the date, payee, amount, and category for each credit card transaction.

The next step in updating your IntelliCharge account is to review all the transactions in the IntelliCharge Statement window to make sure that they match your records and that the category assigned to each transaction is appropriate. See the later section "Reviewing Credit Card Transactions" for more information on reviewing the transactions.

Receiving Your Statement by Modem. Receiving your Quicken VISA card statement by modem is similar to receiving your statement on disk, except that you download the statement file rather than insert a disk file into your computer's disk drive.

To receive your statement by modem and update your IntelliCharge account, follow these steps:

1. Display the Register for your IntelliCharge Credit Card account.

II

Getting the Most

2. Choose Get IntelliCharge Data from the Activities menu. The Get IntelliCharge Data dialog box appears (see fig. 9.12).

Fig. 9.12

Prepare your modem for transmission; then choose OK in the Get IntelliCharge Data dialog box.

3. Turn on your modem and make sure that your telephone line is plugged in.

4. Choose OK in the Get IntelliCharge Data dialog box to initialize your modem and download your IntelliCharge statement file. Quicken copies each credit card transaction to the IntelliCharge Statement window as it reads them from the downloaded statement file.

   You can't make changes to any of these transactions as they are being read from the file. After the transactions are entered in the IntelliCharge Statement window, however, you can review them and mark transactions that you want to edit (in the Credit Card Register).

5. IntelliCharge assigns categories to your credit card transactions (see the later section "Assigning Categories to IntelliCharge Transactions" for details). If IntelliCharge determines that a category that hasn't been set up in the Category & Transfer list should be assigned to a transaction, you are given a choice of setting up a category or selecting a category from the Category & Transfer list.

   If you want to set up a category, choose the Set Up button to set up a new category. The Set Up Category dialog box appears; enter the information for the new category.

   If you want to select a category from the Category & Transfer list, choose the Select button. The Category & Transfer list appears; select a category from the list.

After all credit card transactions are read from the downloaded file, the IntelliCharge Statement window appears and shows the date, payee, amount, and category for each credit card transaction.

The next step in updating your IntelliCharge account is to review all the transactions in the IntelliCharge Statement window to make sure that they match your records and that the category assigned to each transaction is appropriate. See the next section for more information on reviewing the transactions in the IntelliCharge Statement window.

Reviewing Credit Card Transactions

After you receive your IntelliCharge statement (on disk or by modem), you need to review your credit card transactions to make sure that they match your records and that the categories assigned by IntelliCharge are appropriate. You can review credit card transactions in the IntelliCharge Statement window, which appears after transactions are read from the disk file or the downloaded file.

You can mark items for further review in the IntelliCharge Statement window. When you do so, Quicken places five question marks (?????) in the Ref field of the transaction in the Credit Card Register. To mark a transaction for further review, highlight the transaction that you want to mark and then choose the Mark button or press the space bar. Repeat the procedure to unmark the transaction.

IntelliCharge assigns categories to your credit card transactions according to Intuit's standard category list (see the later section "Assigning Categories to IntelliCharge Transactions" for more details on how IntelliCharge assigns categories). To change the category that IntelliCharge assigns to a transaction, highlight the transaction you want to change in the IntelliCharge Statement window and then choose the Categorize button. When the Category & Transfer list appears, select the appropriate category for the credit card transaction.

To delete a category assigned to a transaction, highlight the transaction with the category you want to delete and then choose the Delete Cat button.

Recording IntelliCharge Transactions in the Register

After you finish reviewing the credit card transactions in the IntelliCharge Statement window, you're ready to record the transactions in the Credit Card Register.

To record the credit card transactions, choose the Record All button in the IntelliCharge Statement window. Quicken records the transactions in the Credit Card Register and displays the Make Credit Card Payment dialog box.

II

Getting the Most

To complete this dialog box and pay your Quicken credit card bill, follow the steps provided earlier in the section "Reconciling Your Credit Card Account." If you don't want to make a credit card payment at this time, choose Cancel.

> **Note**
>
> If a transaction appears in your IntelliCharge statement that doesn't match your records, you can dispute the item by contacting Primerica Bank immediately at (800) 772-2221. You also must notify the bank, in writing, of any disputed item.

Mark any disputed items in the IntelliCharge Statement window for further review. After you record the credit card transactions from the IntelliCharge Statement window to your Credit Card Register, use the Find window (press Ctrl+F) to locate the disputed transaction(s) in the IntelliCharge account Register. Because Quicken inserts five question marks (?????) in the Ref field of marked transactions, you can search for ????? in the Num field (this field corresponds to the Ref field in a Credit Card Register).

Assigning Categories to IntelliCharge Transactions

This section explains how IntelliCharge assigns categories to your credit card transactions. Because you don't assign the categories yourself, you should understand how IntelliCharge assigns categories.

The first time that you use IntelliCharge to update your Credit Card account, IntelliCharge categorizes transactions according to Intuit's standard category list. (The standard category list is contained in the file INTELLIC.CAT on your Quicken 3 for Windows program disks and copied to your hard disk when you install Quicken.) If you later change any of the assigned categories, IntelliCharge picks up the changes in subsequent updates by scanning the Credit Card Register.

IntelliCharge looks for a payee that matches the payee in the transaction in the current statement. When it finds a matching payee, it assigns the category assigned to the previous transaction—the one you changed—to the current transaction. IntelliCharge copies the category from the most recent transaction with a matching payee.

If IntelliCharge finds a matching payee in a split transaction, it copies the category information from the first line in the Splits window.

If IntelliCharge doesn't find a matching payee in the Credit Card Register, it assigns a category to the new credit card transaction from its own list of standard categories.

> **Note**
>
> Remember that you can change the category that IntelliCharge assigns to a credit card transaction by highlighting the transaction in the IntelliCharge Statement window and choosing the **C**ategorize button.

Summary

This chapter showed you how to use Quicken's Credit Card accounts to manage your credit card activity. It discussed the following issues:

- How to set up and use a Credit Card account

- How to reconcile your Credit Card account and pay your credit card bill

- How to set up and use Quicken's IntelliCharge service with your Quicken VISA card

- How to receive your IntelliCharge statements on disk or by modem

- How to review and categorize IntelliCharge transactions

The next chapter shows you how to track your outstanding loans using Quicken 3 for Windows' new loan features.

II

Getting the Most

Chapter 10

Tracking Loans

With Quicken 3 for Windows, setting up and tracking your outstanding loans is easy. With Quicken's new loan features, you can keep accurate records of your amortized loans, outstanding loan balances, and loan payments. An *amortized loan* is a loan where a specified rate of interest is charged to the outstanding principal portion of the loan.

Your home mortgage, car loan, and student loan are examples of amortized loans that you can set up accounts for in Quicken. Part of a payment on an amortized loan reduces the principal balance; the other part is the interest charge. Quicken keeps track of the principal and interest portion of loan payments and even can alert you when loan payments are due.

Quicken can handle many different types of loans, including variable interest-rate loans, loans with balloon payments, negative-amortization loans, and even loans based on Canadian compounding methods. For each of these types of loans, you can generate a payment schedule that shows each payment, the portion of the payment that reduces the principal balance, the interest portion of the payment, and the outstanding principal balance.

You can use Quicken's Loan Planner at any time to compare loan alternatives. If you are thinking about buying a new home, for example, you can use the Loan Planner to calculate your new monthly payment based on different interest rate scenarios. You also can use the Loan Planner to determine what your monthly mortgage payments would be if you extended the loan period, and to generate a payment schedule to learn how much you will owe on a loan in 5 years, 10 years, and so on.

In this chapter, you learn how to do the following:

- Set up a fixed-rate loan, a variable interest-rate loan, a loan with a balloon payment due, and other types of loans in Quicken

- Make loan payments

- Make principal prepayments on a loan

- Edit loan information, delete a loan, or pay off a loan

- Refinance a loan, using the Refinance Planner

- Use the Loan Planner

- Summarize year-to-date interest paid on a loan

II

Getting the Most

Quicken enables you to create liability accounts to record your other liabilities (other than amortized loans). Examples of other liabilities for which you may want to set up a liability account include personal loans, taxes payable, accounts payable, insurance premiums, and so forth. You can set up a separate liability account for each liability, or you can group related liabilities into one account. Quicken also helps you remember to make timely payments on your loans. Chapter 11, "Managing Your Assets and Other Liabilities," shows you how to set up accounts to track other liabilities.

Setting Up Loans

For each outstanding amortized loan, you should set up a separate loan account in Quicken. Be sure to have your loan documents handy before you begin setting up loan accounts. You need the following information:

- *Original balance of loan.* The amount you borrow at the time you take out a loan. If you borrow $20,000 to buy a new automobile, for example, $20,000 is the principal portion of the loan.

> ### Note
>
> You can use the Loan Planner to calculate any one loan variable. If you know the principal balance, loan term, and payment on a loan, for example, you can use the Loan Planner to calculate the interest rate. If you know the interest rate, loan term, and payment, you can use the Loan Planner to calculate the original principal balance.

- *Current interest rate.* The amount you pay to use the principal. The longer you use the money, the more interest you pay the lender.

> ### CPA TIP: Computing Interest on a Loan
>
> Interest is computed periodically (monthly, quarterly, or annually, for example) as a percentage of the outstanding principal balance of the loan. In the automobile loan example, you will pay back the $20,000 plus the interest computed during the loan term. The interest portion of a loan is a future cost and isn't considered a liability for purposes of your net worth. In other words, a liability listed on your statement of net worth represents the outstanding principal portion of the loan and doesn't include the interest portion.

- *Original length of loan.* The period or length of the loan (usually 30 years—or 360 months—for home mortgages).

- *Principal and interest payment.* The payment required by the terms of the loan agreement. Make sure that the payment amount you use is only for principal and interest and doesn't include amounts for real estate or insurance escrow.

- *Escrow amounts.* Portions of your loan payment may be for real estate taxes, insurance, and so forth. The bank *escrows* (holds) these funds for you until payment is due and then makes the payment for you.

> **Note**
>
> You also can set up a loan in Quicken for a *receivable*—a loan that *you* make to another individual or company. To set up a loan receivable, be sure to select the Lend Money option when you begin to set up the loan. For details, see "Setting Up Loans You Make" later in this chapter.

Quicken handles several types of loans, including fixed-rate loans, variable-rate loans, loans with a balloon payment due, negative amortization loans, zero-interest loans, and Canadian amortization loans. The next several sections explain how to set up each of these loan types in Quicken.

Setting Up a Fixed-Rate Loan

A *fixed-rate loan* charges the same interest rate throughout the loan period. If you have a fixed-rate 30-year mortgage at 8.5 percent, for example, your interest rate through the 30-year term of the loan remains constant at 8.5 percent.

To set up a fixed-rate loan in Quicken, follow these steps:

1. Choose Set Up Loans from the Activities menu (or press Ctrl+H). Quicken displays the View Loans window, shown in figure 10.1.

   The View Loans window is the main information window for all loans set up in Quicken. You can view a payment history and projected payments for the loan by selecting the loan in the Loan drop-down list. You learn more about the View Loans window later in this chapter.

2. To set up a new loan, choose the New button in the upper left corner of the View Loans window. Quicken displays the Set Up Loan Account dialog box, shown in figure 10.2.

II

Getting the Most

Fig. 10.1

The View Loans window appears when you choose Set Up Loans from the Activities menu.

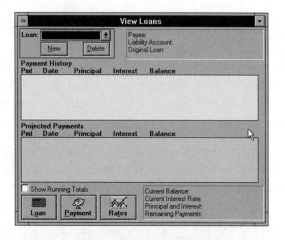

Fig. 10.2

The Set Up Loan Account dialog box appears when you choose to set up a new loan.

3. In the Loan Type section of the dialog box, indicate the type of loan you are setting up. Select Borrow Money for a loan made to you, or Lend Money for a loan made by you to someone else.

4. In the Liability Account area, do one of the following:

   ■ Select New Account if you want to define a new liability account for the loan you are setting up. Then press Tab to move to the New Account text box and type a name for the new account—for example, **Mortgage** or **Car Loan**.

   ■ Select Existing Account if you have manually tracked a loan in Quicken and therefore already have a liability account established. From the drop-down list, select the existing liability account.

5. Choose OK to close the dialog box and set up the loan account.

Quicken adds the loan account as a liability account in the Account list and displays the Set Up Loan dialog box so that you can enter information about the loan, such as the loan's length, original loan balance, interest rate, and so forth (see fig. 10.3). Note that the account name you entered or selected in the Set Up Loan Account dialog box now appears in the Loan/Account Name field of the Set Up Loan dialog box.

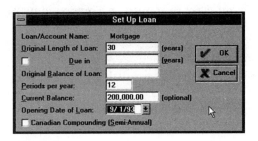

Fig. 10.3
In the Set Up Loan dialog box, you enter specific information about an outstanding loan.

To enter information about the loan, follow these steps:

1. In the Original Length of Loan text box, specify the original loan term, in years. Type **5** for a five-year loan, **30** for a 30-year loan, and so forth.

2. If you are setting up a loan with a balloon payment, use the **Due In** text box to specify the number of years until the balloon payment is due. For all other types of loans, leave this text box blank. (You learn about loans with balloon payments later in this chapter.)

3. For existing loans, type the original principal balance of the loan in the Original **B**alance of Loan text box. If you are setting up a new loan (one for which you haven't made previous payments), leave this text box blank.

4. In the Periods per Year text box, type the number of payments you make each year. For monthly payments, type **12**. For semiannual payments, type **2**.

5. In the Current Balance text box, type the principal balance of the loan as of today. For a new loan, enter the total amount of the loan.

6. For the Opening Date of Loan option, specify the date from the drop-down list. Select today's date or the date that you want to use to start tracking the loan.

> **Note**
>
> The system date on your computer must be correct for today's date to be correct.

7. Canadian users who need to calculate interest based on semiannual compounding can select the Canadian Compounding (**S**emi-Annual) check box.

8. When the Set Up Loan dialog box is complete, choose OK. Quicken displays the Set Up Loan Payment dialog box.

Next, you must enter information about the loan payments that you will be making, such as the escrow amounts included in a loan payment (if any), whether you write checks with Quicken or manually, the payee's name, and so forth. Follow these steps to enter loan payment information in the Set Up Loan Payment dialog box (see fig. 10.4):

Tip
For variable-rate loans, type the interest rate that is now being charged. You learn more about variable-rate loans later in this chapter.

1. In the Current Interest Rate text box, type the interest rate that applies to the loan as of today's date. If your loan rate today is 7 percent, for example, type **7** (Quicken enters the percent sign automatically).

2. In the Principal and Interest text box, Quicken calculates the regular payment amount (principal plus interest), based on the interest rate, the principal balance, and the term information entered earlier. You can change the regular payment amount in the Principal and Interest text box; however, Quicken then recalculates the length of the loan in the Set Up Loan dialog box (refer to fig. 10.3).

Fig. 10.4
Enter details about loan payments in the Set Up Loan Payment dialog box.

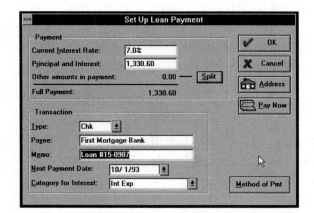

3. If other amounts or fees are included in your loan payment—real estate taxes, home insurance premiums, and so on—choose the Split button to display the Splits window, shown in figure 10.5.

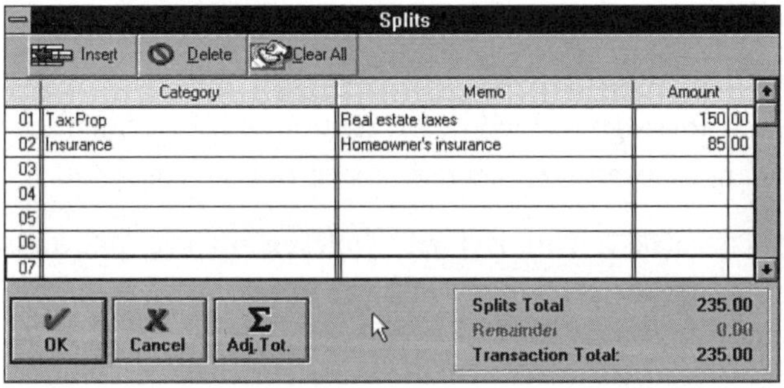

Fig. 10.5
Use the Splits window to enter other amounts or fees included in your loan payment and assign a category to each.

4. In the Splits window, enter the category, a description (optional), and the amount for each fee included in the loan payment. If insurance premiums and real estate taxes are included in the loan payment, for example, enter a separate line for each in the Splits window and assign the appropriate categories.

   Choose OK when the Splits window is complete. Quicken returns to the Set Up Loan Payment dialog box (refer to fig. 10.4).

5. In the Type drop-down list, indicate the type of transaction you want to enter when you make a loan payment. If you plan to use Quicken to write checks for the loan payments, for example, select Chk.

Note

If you write checks with Quicken for your loan payment, you can print the payee's address on the check automatically. Choose the Address command button in the Set Up Loan Payment dialog box, enter the payee's address, and then choose OK. Quicken saves the payee's address and prints it on each loan payment check.

6. In the Payee text box, type the name of the payee to whom you make the loan payment. The payee is normally the creditor who granted the loan.

7. (Optional) If you want, you can type a memo for the loan payment transaction in the Memo text box. If you print checks with Quicken,

including the loan account number in the Memo field of the check helps the lender match your check with the loan file.

8. In the Next Payment Date drop-down list, specify the date that the next loan payment is due.

9. In the Category for Interest drop-down list, indicate the category that you want to assign to the interest portion of the payment. For a mortgage loan, for example, you may assign the category Mort Int.

   When you make a loan payment, Quicken enters a split transaction and separates the principal portion of the payment from the interest portion.

10. Now that you have entered the information about your loan, you need to indicate the payment method that you want to use. Select the Method of Pmt button from the Set Up Loan Payment dialog box. Quicken displays the Select Payment Method dialog box, shown in figure 10.6.

Fig. 10.6
Select the payment method that you want to use to make loan payments.

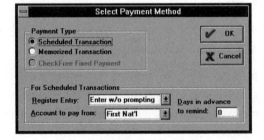

11. Select the appropriate payment type. You can choose from the following three methods for making loan payments:

   ■ *Scheduled Transaction.* Select this option if you want Quicken to enter the loan payment in your Register (or in the Write Checks window, if you choose to write the loan payment check with Quicken).

   Quicken knows when loan payments are due (from the Next Payment Date setting in the Set Up Loan Payment dialog box) and how often to make loan payments (from the Periods per Year setting in the Set Up Loan dialog box). You learn more about scheduled transactions in Chapter 14, "Scheduling Future Transactions."

- *Memorized Transaction.* Select this option if you want to memorize the loan payment transaction and then recall the transaction in the Write Checks window or the Register each time a loan payment is due. Refer to Chapter 7, "Using Quicken Shortcuts," to learn how to memorize a transaction.

- *CheckFree Fixed Payment.* When you select this option, you can set up the loan payment as a fixed (recurring) payment if you use CheckFree to make your payments. See Chapter 13, "Paying Your Bills Electronically," to learn how to use CheckFree services with Quicken.

12. If you selected the Scheduled Transaction option, fill in the For Scheduled Transactions section at the bottom of the Select Payment Method dialog box. The options are described as follows:

   - In the **Register** Entry drop-down list, indicate whether you want Quicken to enter the loan payment in your Register with or without asking you to confirm the transaction.

   - In the Account to Pay From drop-down list, specify the checking account into which the loan payment should be entered.

   - In the **Days** in Advance to Remind text box, type the number of days ahead of time that you want Quicken to enter loan payments in your Register.

13. When the Select Payment Method dialog box is complete, choose OK to return to the Set Up Loan Payment dialog box (refer to fig. 10.4).

14. If you want to make a loan payment now, choose the **Pay** Now button; otherwise, go to step 15.

   Quicken displays the Choose Account To Pay FROM dialog box. Select the checking account that you want to use to make the loan payment and choose OK.

   Quicken displays the Register for the checking account and enters the loan payment transaction. Choose Record to record the loan payment transaction in the Register. If you use Quicken to write checks, from the Register select Print in the Num field and then choose Record to enter the loan payment in the Write Checks window. Click the View Loans window title bar (which appears behind the Write Checks window or the Register) or press Ctrl+H to return to the View Loans window.

15. Choose OK in the Set Up Loan Payment dialog box to return to the View Loans window and display the new loan (see fig. 10.7). If all the scheduled payments don't appear in the Projected Payments list, you can use the scroll bar to display the rest of the payments.

Fig. 10.7
The View Loans window displays the new loan and its scheduled payments.

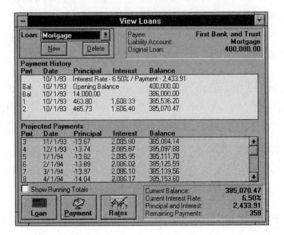

16. Close the View Loans window by double-clicking the Control menu box.

Setting Up a Variable-Rate Loan

A *variable-rate loan* charges a different, or *variable*, interest rate throughout the loan period. If you have a six-month variable-rate loan, for example, your rate is adjusted every six months throughout the loan period.

To set up a variable-rate loan in Quicken, follow the steps for setting up a fixed-rate loan as described in the preceding section. In the Set Up Loan Payment dialog box (refer to fig. 10.4), type the rate that you now are being charged for the Current Interest Rate.

When the interest rate changes on your loan, change the current interest rate that Quicken uses to amortize the loan, using one of the following two methods:

■ Change the interest rate, effective today, by entering the new interest rate in the Current Interest Rate option in the Set Up Loan Payment dialog box.

- If you know in advance when the interest rate changes take effect, you can program rate changes in Quicken, as discussed later in this section.

> **Note**
>
> If your loan agreement expressly states the effective dates for interest rate changes and the new rates, you can enter those changes as you set up your loan. For most variable-rate loans where the rate is adjusted on a periodic basis (semiannually, annually, biannually, and so forth), you probably won't know the new interest rate until you are notified by your lender.

To access the Set Up Loan Payment dialog box so that you can enter the new interest rate, use one of these three methods:

- Choose the Payment button in the View Loans window when the loan name is displayed in the Loan list box.

- Press Ctrl+T to display the Memorized Transaction list, highlight the loan payment in the list, and choose the Edit button.

- Press Ctrl+J to display the Scheduled Transaction list, highlight the loan payment in the list, and choose the Edit button. You learn about the Scheduled Transaction list in Chapter 14, "Scheduling Future Transactions."

To program a rate change, follow these steps:

1. Choose Set Up Loans from the Activities menu to display the View Loans window. Make sure that the loan for which you want to change the interest rate appears in the Loan drop-down list box.

2. Choose the Rates button. Quicken displays the Loan Rate Changes dialog box, as shown in figure 10.8.

3. Choose the New button to display the Insert an Interest Rate Change dialog box.

4. Enter the interest rate and the date that the new rate is effective. Quicken calculates the new regular payment amount. You can increase or decrease the regular payment amount.

Fig. 10.8
The Loan Rate
Changes dialog
box shows a
history of rate
changes for the
selected loan.

> **Note**
>
> When you change the interest rate, Quicken calculates the regular payment
> based on the original length of the loan. If you increase the regular payment
> amount, however, Quicken reduces the loan term. When you decrease the
> regular payment amount, Quicken doesn't change the loan term, but adds
> the unpaid amount of the loan to the last payment amount.

Tip
To edit and delete
interest rate
changes in the
Loan Rate Changes
dialog box, choose
the Edit and Del
buttons.

5. Choose OK to add the new interest rate and date to the Loan Rate
   Changes dialog box.

6. Choose Done to save the interest rate change.

Setting Up Loans with Balloon Payments

A *balloon-payment loan* requires that the unpaid principal balance of a loan be
paid at the end of the payment period. The balance payment (*balloon payment*) is due when specified by the loan contract. If the provisions of your
loan are "30 due in 5," for example, the loan is amortized over 30 years. The
unpaid principal balance, however, is payable at the end of the fifth year.

To set up a loan with a balloon payment, follow these steps:

1. Follow the steps for setting up a fixed-rate loan, as described earlier in
   the section "Setting Up a Fixed-Rate Loan."

2. In the Original Length of Loan text box in the Set Up Loan dialog box
   (refer to fig. 10.3), type the period over which the loan is amortized. If
   the loan is amortized over 30 years, for example, type **30**.

3. In the same dialog box, select the Due In check box and type the number of years in which the balloon payment is due. Type **5**, for example,
   if the loan calls for the balloon payment in five years.

4. Fill in the rest of the Set Up Loan dialog box and then choose OK.

> **Note**
>
> If payments on your balloon-payment loan don't reduce the principal balance of the loan (payments cover only interest), don't set up the loan in Quicken to track payments. Instead, memorize a regular transaction for the loan payment and assign the entire amount of the transaction to interest expense. See Chapter 7, "Using Quicken Shortcuts," to learn how to memorize transactions.

Setting Up Loans You Make

As noted earlier in this chapter, you can set up a loan in Quicken for which you receive payments (you make the loan). To set up a loan that you make, select the Lend Money option in the Set Up Loan Account dialog box (refer to fig. 10.2). In the Set Up Loan Payment dialog box (refer to fig. 10.4), enter the name of the borrower in the Payee text box and select an income category to assign to deposit transactions in the Category for Interest text box.

When you set up a loan for which you are receiving payments, Quicken creates a memorized loan deposit transaction and also creates an asset account as the account it uses to track the outstanding balance of the loan.

Setting Up Other Types of Loans

You can use Quicken's new loan feature for other types of loans: negative-amortization loans and zero-interest loans. The following sections describe how to set up these types of loans.

Setting Up Negative-Amortization Loans. A *negative-amortization* loan is one in which the payment required on the loan is less than the accrued interest. As you make payments on the loan, no reduction of the principal takes place, and the amount by which the interest exceeds the payment is treated as an increase to the principal balance. Usually, negative-amortization loans are a temporary arrangement between the lender and the loan holder.

Obviously, loan payments that don't cover the accrued interest can't continue for the length of the loan. Setting up a negative-amortization loan in Quicken therefore entails making a few changes to the way that the loan is amortized for the periods that the negative-amortization loan is in effect.

To handle negative-amortization loans, follow the steps for setting up a fixed-rate loan explained earlier in this chapter, except for the following steps:

1. In the Original Length of Loan text box in the Set Up Loan dialog box (refer to fig. 10.3), specify the period over which you are making reduced payments.

2. In the Set Up Loan Payment dialog box (refer to fig. 10.4), specify the current interest rate in the Current Interest Rate text box. Then change the amount that Quicken enters in the Principal and Interest text box to the amount you are actually paying.

   Because the payment is less than the interest on the loan for the period, the payment schedule in the View Loans window shows the principal balance at the end of the loan term to be greater than the original amount of the loan.

3. When your payment is due to increase (to at least cover the accrued interest each period), change the regular payment amount and the effective date in the Loan Rate Changes dialog box (refer to fig. 10.8).

When you increase the regular payment amount on a negative-amortization loan, the payment schedule in the View Loans window shows a reduced or zero balance at the end of the loan term.

Setting Up Zero-Interest Loans. Loans that don't accrue interest over the loan term are called *zero-interest loans*. The entire loan payment that you make reduces the principal balance (except for any other charges and fees included in the payment amount).

To set up a zero-interest loan, type **0** (zero) for the Current Interest Rate in the Set Up Loan Payment dialog box (refer to fig. 10.4). The Category for Interest list box should be left blank so that zero amounts don't show up on reports.

Making Loan Payments

After your loan is set up in Quicken, you are ready to enter or make loan payments when they are due. The method used to make loan payments depends on the method you chose in the Select Payment Method dialog box (refer to fig. 10.6). If you selected the Scheduled Transaction or the CheckFree Fixed Payment option, your loan payment transactions are entered automatically. If you chose to memorize loan payments, however, you must recall the memorized loan payment in the Write Checks window or the Register, as described in the following section.

When you make a loan payment, Quicken enters the principal and interest portion of the payment—and any other charges and fees—in the Splits window, and assigns the appropriate category to each part of the payment.

Quicken uses the payment schedule (or amortization schedule) in the View Loans window to enter the appropriate principal and interest amounts for each payment. Each time you make a payment, Quicken updates the loan balance.

You can make regular loan payments or make an additional principal payment and add it to a regular payment. Later sections of this chapter describe how to make prepayments and how to undo loan payments made in error.

Recalling a Memorized Loan Payment

When you set up a loan in Quicken and select the Memorized Transaction option as the payment method, Quicken memorizes the loan payment information and adds it to the Memorized Transaction List. (You learn about the Memorized Transaction List in Chapter 7, "Using Quicken Shortcuts.")

When the time comes to make a loan payment, follow these steps to recall the memorized loan payment:

1. If you're writing a check for the loan payment with Quicken, display the Write Checks window. If you're writing a manual check, display the Register for the checking account that you use to write checks.

2. In the Payee field in the Register or the Pay to the Order Of field in the Write Checks window, begin typing the payee name. QuickFill completes the full name of the payee. Press Tab to accept the payee when it is correct. Quicken displays the Confirm Principal and Interest dialog box, as shown in figure 10.9.

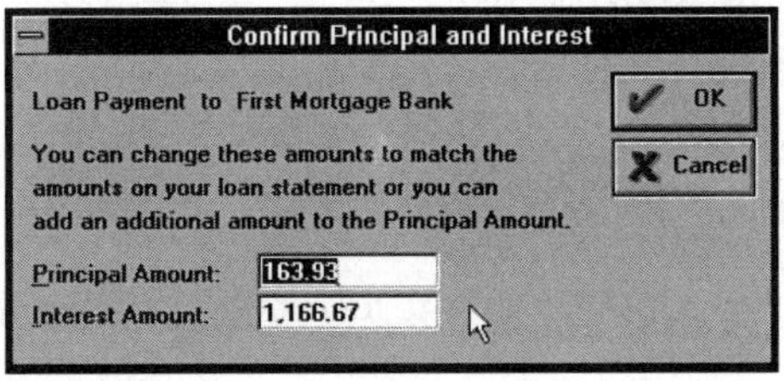

Tip
You also can recall a memorized loan payment by pressing Ctrl+T to display the Memorized Transaction list. Then highlight the loan payment transaction in the list and choose the Use button.

Fig. 10.9
Review the principal and interest of a loan payment in the Confirm Principal and Interest dialog box.

3. If you want to change the principal or interest amount, type the new amount over the existing amount.

   Note that any changes affect only this payment. All future loan payments are separated into principal and interest based on the payment schedule in the View Loans window.

4. When the principal and interest amounts are correct, choose OK.

> **Note**
>
> If you *increase* the principal amount of a loan payment, you are making an additional principal payment. When you prepay the principal of a loan, Quicken recalculates the payment schedule in the View Loans window. The adjustment to the payment schedule may shorten the term of the loan.
>
> If you *decrease* the principal amount of a loan payment, Quicken recalculates the payment schedule in the View Loans window. The adjustment to the payment schedule doesn't change the loan term; however, an extra balance may be shown at the end of the repayment period.

5. Choose OK to return to the Write Checks window or the Register.

6. (Optional) Remember that if your loan payment includes any charges or fees, Quicken enters those amounts and categories in the Splits window, following the principal and interest amounts. If you want to review the amounts, choose the Splits button to open the Splits window. Then choose OK to return to the Write Checks window or the Register.

7. Choose Record to record the loan payment.

Undoing Loan Payments

If you accidentally record a loan payment you didn't actually make, you can delete the loan payment transaction from the Register. Follow these steps to undo a loan payment transaction:

1. Highlight the loan payment transaction in the Register for the bank account that you use to make loan payments.

2. Choose the Delete button on the Register button bar (or press Ctrl+D).

3. Quicken asks you to confirm that you want to delete the transaction. Choose Yes.

Quicken removes the transaction from the Bank Account and Liability Account Registers, and from the payment schedule in the View Loans window.

Making Principal Prepayments

By making additional principal payments during the term of your loan, you reduce the loan term and pay less total interest on the loan.

To make a principal prepayment, follow these steps:

1. Recall the loan payment in the Write Checks window or the Register, as explained earlier in the section "Recalling a Memorized Loan Payment."

2. When Quicken displays the Confirm Principal and Interest dialog box (refer to fig. 10.9), type the increased amount in the **P**rincipal Amount text box. This action tells Quicken that you are making an additional principal payment.

3. Choose OK to return to the Write Checks window or the Register. Quicken recalculates the loan payment amount to include the additional principal payment.

4. Choose Re**c**ord to record the loan payment.

> **Note**
>
> If you make a separate principal payment (not with your loan payment), don't recall the loan payment. Just enter a transaction for the principal payment in the Write Checks window or the Register and enter the liability account in the Category field.

> **CPA TIP: Cutting Your Mortgage Loan Term**
>
> By making one extra mortgage payment each year, you can cut some years off your loan term. If your regular payment amount each month is $1,000, for example, just make one extra payment of $1,000 and apply it to the principal of your loan. (Be sure to indicate when you submit the extra payment that you want the total amount applied to the principal balance.)

Editing a Loan

At any time, you can change any of the loan details from the View Loans window, except for the loan name. The loan name is the name Quicken assigns to the principal account that it uses to track your loan balance. The principal account is set up as a liability account. You can change the name of an account from the Account list, however. Refer to Chapter 3, "Defining Your Accounts," to learn how to change account names.

To change loan details, follow these steps:

1. Choose Set Up Loans from the Activities menu (or press Ctrl+H). Quicken displays the View Loans window.

2. From the Loan drop-down list, select the loan that you want to change.

3. To change the details of the loan, choose from the following options (in any order):

   ■ To change the length of the loan, balloon-payment date (if applicable), original and current balances, periods per year, or opening date of the loan, choose the Loan button. Quicken displays the Set Up Loan dialog box.

   ■ To change the loan payment details, choose the Payment button. Quicken displays the Set Up Loan Payment dialog box.

   ■ To change the future interest rates that Quicken uses to amortize the loan, choose the Rates button. Quicken displays the Loan Rate Changes dialog box.

4. Make the necessary changes in the dialog box or window and then choose OK or Done to return to the View Loans window. Then repeat step 3 as necessary until all changes are complete.

Note

If you need to change only the payment information for a loan, select the loan in the Memorized Transaction list and choose the Edit button. Quicken displays the payment information for the memorized loan payment. Make the necessary changes and choose OK.

Deleting a Loan

If you have paid off a loan, you need to delete the loan from Quicken. If you have mistakenly set up a loan in Quicken, you also must delete it. When you delete a loan, Quicken removes all loan information from the View Loans window, the Memorized Transaction list, the Scheduled Transaction list (if applicable), and the Electronic Payee list (if applicable).

To delete a loan, follow these steps:

1. Choose Set Up Loans from the Activities menu (or press Ctrl+H). Quicken displays the View Loans window.

2. From the Loan drop-down list, select the loan that you want to delete.

3. Choose the Delete button.

4. Quicken asks you to confirm that you want to delete the amortized loan. Choose OK.

> **Note**
>
> When you delete a loan, Quicken deletes the loan from the View Loans window but doesn't delete the liability account from the Account list. Refer to Chapter 3, "Defining Your Accounts," to learn how to delete accounts.

Paying Off a Loan

It's a happy day when you finally pay off a loan—especially a home mortgage that you may have been paying for 30 years!

> **CPA TIP: Paying Off a Loan**
>
> When paying off a loan, check with your lending institution for the exact payoff for the loan on the date that you will be making the payment. Make sure that you are specific about the date for which you want payoff information. Just one or two days makes a difference in the amount of interest that has accrued on your loan.

To pay off a loan, follow these steps:

1. Record the last payment on the loan, as usual. This should reduce the principal balance on the loan to zero (see the payment schedule in the View Loans window).

2. Choose Set Up Loans from the Activities menu or press Ctrl+H. Quicken displays the View Loans window.

3. In the Loan drop-down list, select the loan that you paid off.

4. Choose the Delete button.

5. Quicken asks you to confirm that you want to delete the amortized loan. Choose OK. Quicken removes the loan from the View Loans window; however, the liability account remains in the Account list. Refer to Chapter 3, "Defining Your Accounts," to learn how to delete the liability account.

Refinancing a Loan

With fluctuating mortgage rates, many homeowners refinance home mortgages to take advantage of lower interest rates. If you refinance a loan that you have set up in Quicken, you first must set up a new loan and then pay off—or delete—the old loan.

Follow the steps in the earlier sections of this chapter for setting up a loan. Be sure to make these specific changes:

1. Specify a new name for the refinanced loan—for example, type **Refinance**.

2. In the Set Up Loan dialog box (refer to fig. 10.3), enter the total term of the new loan in the Original Length of Loan text box. Enter the amount that you are refinancing in the Original Balance of Loan text box.

   Quicken sets up your loan and creates a new liability account for the new loan.

3. Display the Register for the new liability account. If your new loan account is called Refinance, for example, display the Register for the Refinance account.

4. Highlight the Opening Balance transaction.

5. Change the description in the Payee field in the Register from Opening Balance to the name of the new lender who is refinancing your loan.

6. Choose the Splits button to display the Splits window.

7. In the first line of the Splits window, type the name of the old loan in the Payee field. Then, type the outstanding balance on the old loan in the Amount field. This transaction pays off the balance in the old loan and transfers the balance to the new loan.

8. If the new loan includes any closing costs, enter those in the next line of the Splits window.

9. If the new loan amount is greater than the outstanding balance of the old loan, you may receive cash from the new lender. If so, enter the account in which you want to deposit the money (checking, savings, and so forth) in the Category field and enter the amount of cash received in the Amount field.

10. When the Splits window is complete, choose OK to return to the Register.

11. Choose Record to record the edited opening balance transaction. Quicken enters a corresponding transaction in the old loan account Register that wipes out the balance.

12. Now that the old loan account balance is zero, you can delete the loan from Quicken. To delete the loan, select the loan in the View Loans window and choose the Delete button.

13. Choose OK to confirm that you want to delete an amortized loan.

> **Note**
>
> When you delete the loan that you have refinanced, Quicken doesn't delete the liability account. The liability account, with a zero balance, remains in the Account list. Refer to Chapter 3, "Defining Your Accounts," to learn how to delete the liability account.

Using the Refinance Planner

Although refinancing your mortgage may save on your monthly payment, refinancing is rarely achieved without incurring additional costs (closing costs and mortgage points). Don't be fooled into thinking that refinancing is the answer just because you can secure a lower interest rate. Mortgage lenders usually charge closing costs and points to refinance a mortgage. If your existing mortgage isn't very old and you incurred closing costs to obtain your mortgage, refinancing may not be prudent unless the refinance rate is significantly less than your current rate. You may find, though, that refinancing makes a great deal of sense and results in significant savings.

Quicken's Refinance Planner can help you determine whether refinancing your current mortgage is cost-effective. The Refinance Planner shows your new monthly payment amount (based on the refinance rate), how much you save per month by refinancing, the total closing costs you will incur if you refinance, and the amount of time necessary to recoup those closing costs with monthly savings from refinancing.

> ### CPA TIP: Refinancing Your Mortgage
>
> Many mortgage lenders will refinance only 80 percent of your home's current market value—or less. If the value of your home hasn't appreciated and your current mortgage balance is greater than 80 percent of the market value of your home, you may not be able to find a lender to refinance your mortgage.

To use the Refinance Planner, follow these steps:

1. Choose Financial Planners from the Activities menu. Quicken displays the Financial Planners submenu.

2. Choose Refinance. Quicken displays the Refinance Planner, as shown in figure 10.10.

Fig. 10.10
The Refinance Planner can calculate how much you will save if you refinance your mortgage at a lower interest rate.

3. In the Existing Mortgage section, type your current payment amount in the Current Payment text box; type the escrow amount for insurance, property taxes, and so on in the Impound/Escrow Amount text box.

Quicken subtracts the escrow amount from your current payment and enters the result as the Monthly Principal/Int. This amount is the portion of your monthly payment that relates to the principal balance of your mortgage loan and the mortgage interest due.

4. In the Proposed Mortgage section, type the data for the new mortgage. In the Principal Amount text box, type the amount that you are planning to refinance. Remember that this amount isn't the same amount as your original mortgage because you have paid down some principal since the beginning of the mortgage.

In the Years text box, type the number of years that you plan to extend the refinanced mortgage loan—usually 30 or 15 years.

In the Interest rate text box, type the refinancing rate. Type 8.75% as **8.75**, for example; don't type a percent sign.

Quicken calculates the new monthly principal and interest payment and your monthly savings (your old monthly principal and interest payment minus the new monthly principal and interest payment).

5. In the Break Even Analysis section, type any costs you will incur by refinancing. In the Mortgage Closing Costs text box, type the amount that the mortgage bank is charging to refinance your mortgage. In the Mortgage Points text box, type the percentage point(s) that you are being charged. Usually, this amount is from 1 percent to 4 percent, but can vary from lender to lender and also is based on the size of the loan.

Quicken calculates the total closing costs to refinance and determines how many months you will need to break even (how many months to recover the closing costs, using the monthly savings from refinancing).

Figure 10.10 shows a monthly savings of $118.37 when refinancing a mortgage of $125,000 at 7 percent. With closing costs of $2,250, it will take 19 months to break even, or recover the closing costs using the monthly savings.

6. Choose the Close button to remove the Refinance Planner from the screen.

Getting the Most

II

CPA TIP: Weighing Income Tax Implications of Refinancing

When you refinance your mortgage, in essence, you're giving up deductible interest by refinancing at a lower interest rate. Now, mortgage interest on up to two residences is generally fully deductible (subject to the 3 percent reduction for itemized deductions if your adjusted gross income is greater than $100,000, or $50,000 if filing separately). You may end up paying more in taxes a few years down the road than you would if you hadn't refinanced. Consider the income tax implications before you make the decision to refinance.

Tips on Refinancing

Use the Refinance Planner to help you determine whether refinancing is a viable option for you. Also consider the following:

■ Even if the Refinance Planner shows that you will save on your monthly payment by refinancing your mortgage, in the long run refinancing could cost you more. If you extend your current mortgage over a longer time period than it's originally set to come due, you may end up paying more in interest than you would have had you stayed with the original mortgage at the higher rate.

If you now have a 30-year mortgage at 10.5 percent, for example, but have made payments for 6 years, your mortgage comes due in 24 years. If you refinance for another 30 years, even though the refinance interest rate is lower, you have in effect created a 36-year loan with an interest rate change in year 6.

Many times, this scenario results in lower monthly payments, but more interest paid over the term of the loan. You can prevent this result, however, by refinancing at a lower rate and shortening the mortgage term. Just continue to make your old payment and apply the excess (the amount of the old payment that exceeds the new payment) to the principal. Your loan will be paid off more quickly and you will avoid paying more in interest.

■ When you're shopping for mortgage interest rates, be sure to lock in the rate or have the rate guaranteed by the mortgage company or bank. Just one half-point rise in interest rates can make a difference in your decision to refinance. Most lenders require that you file an application, however, before they will give you a locked-in rate.

■ Mortgage points charged to refinance aren't fully tax-deductible in the year you refinance. Deductions for points paid to refinance a mortgage (unlike points paid up front when you buy a home) must be spread over the life of the loan. If you paid $2,400 in mortgage refinancing points for a 30-year loan, for example, you can deduct only $80 each year.

Two exceptions exist for deducting points on refinancing. If part of the loan is used for renovations, the points attributable to that part of the loan are fully deductible. Also, if you refinanced previously and didn't fully deduct the points incurred to refinance, you can deduct them in the year that you pay off the loan (you pay off the existing loan when you refinance a loan).

■ Carefully scrutinize mailings that you receive from mortgage brokers. On the surface, the deal that the brokers are offering may sound great, but what you don't know is how much they charge in *up-front fees* (fees that are charged even though the loan never closes). Be suspicious if you read or hear about up-front money for appraisals, credit checks, and application fees that are greater than $500. Also make sure that your money is refundable if the loan doesn't close—and that this provision is stated clearly in writing.

Using the Loan Planner

If you want to calculate "what-if" scenarios to determine how much a loan payment would be if you borrowed *x* amount at *x* interest rate over *x* period of time, you can use Quicken's Loan Planner to calculate the loan. The Loan Planner also can produce a payment (amortization) schedule. An amortization schedule shows what portion of your payments goes to paying interest and what portion goes to reducing the principal balance of the loan.

You can select the type of calculation to make with the Loan Planner. You can calculate the payment per period when you know the loan amount, the annual interest rate, the number of years the loan will be outstanding, and the number of payments made each year. You can calculate the loan amount when you know the annual interest rate, the number of years the loan will be outstanding, the number of payments made annually, and the payment per period amount.

To calculate loan amounts or payments per period of a loan and produce a payment schedule, follow these steps:

1. Choose the Financial Planners option from the Activities menu. Quicken displays the Financial Planners submenu.

2. Choose Loan. Quicken displays the Loan Planner dialog box, as shown in figure 10.11.

Fig. 10.11

The Loan Planner can help you determine the payment amount of a loan or the principal amount of a loan.

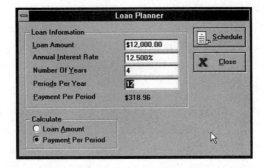

3. Specify the type of calculation that you want to make. To have Quicken calculate the loan amount, select the Loan Amount option button. Quicken enters the word CALCULATED in the Loan Amount text box.

   To have Quicken calculate the payment amount, select the Payment Per Period option button. Quicken enters the word CALCULATED in the Payment Per Period text box.

4. If you're calculating the payment per period, type the amount of the loan in the Loan Amount text box. Otherwise, go to step 5.

5. In the Annual Interest Rate text box, type the annual interest rate. If the annual loan interest rate is 12.5 percent, for example, type **12.5**.

> **Caution**
>
> Don't mistake the annual *percentage* rate (APR) for the annual *interest* rate. The APR encompasses all the costs of obtaining credit and includes not only interest charges but loan fees and other borrowing costs. The APR, required by truth-in-lending laws, provides a way to compare the overall costs of obtaining loans. The APR, however, shouldn't be used to calculate the loan payment.

6. In the Number of Years text box, type the number of years you must make payments. If the loan is a 5-year car loan, for example, type **5**. If the loan is a 30-year mortgage, type **30**.

7. In the Periods per Year text box, type the number of payments you must make each year. Typically, because most payments must be made monthly, this number is **12** and appears by default.

8. If you are calculating the loan amount, enter the payment amount in the Payment per Period text box.

9. Press Tab after you enter the value for the last text box in the Loan Planner. Quicken calculates the payment per period amount and enters the result in the Payment per Period text box, or calculates the loan amount and enters the result in the Loan Amount text box.

Earlier, figure 10.11 showed the payment per period on a $12,000 loan at 12.5 percent interest with 4 years of monthly payments to be $318.96.

10. (Optional) To produce a payment schedule for the loan, choose the Schedule button after you finish calculating the loan amount or the payment per period.

Quicken displays the Approximate Payment Schedule dialog box, shown in figure 10.12. The Approximate Payment Schedule dialog box shows the approximate interest and principal portions of each loan payment and the loan balance after the payment. To move up and down in the payment schedule, use the scroll bar or the PgUp and PgDn keys. You can use the Home and End keys also; Home displays the first page of the payment schedule, and End displays the last page of the payment schedule. Choose OK or Cancel to return to the Loan Planner.

Note

To print a copy of the payment schedule, choose the Print button from the Approximate Payment Schedule dialog box. Quicken displays the Print Report dialog box. Indicate where you want to print the Approximate Payment Schedule and the pages that you want to print. Choose OK to print the report.

II

Getting the Most

Fig. 10.12
The Approximate Payment Schedule window shows the approximate interest and principal portions of each loan payment.

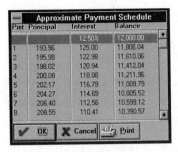

11. Choose the Close button when you are finished using the Loan Planner.

CPA TIP: Calculating the Affordable Mortgage

If you are uncertain how big a mortgage you can afford when buying a home, use the Loan Planner to help you determine what amount you can afford. To calculate the principal amount, enter in the appropriate Loan Planner text boxes the amount you decide that you can spend for housing from your monthly income (Payment per Period) and the current Annual Interest Rate.

If you want to pay less interest over the life of the mortgage and pay off the mortgage balance sooner, use 15 years as the total years to pay. If you can't afford the monthly mortgage payments for a 15-year loan, use 30 years. With this information, you can calculate the total loan amount, which gives you a better idea of what to look for in a mortgage.

CPA TIP: Converting to Payment-in-Advance

Quicken normally calculates an arrangement known as a *payment in arrears*, or an *ordinary annuity*. These terms mean that the payment is made at the end of the payment period, as is the case with loan payments. With some loans, however, payments are made at the beginning of the period. This beginning-of-the-month arrangement is known as a *payment in advance*, or an *annuity due*. To convert a payment in arrears to a payment in advance, divide the payment amount Quicken calculates by the following factor:

(1 + (annual interest rate/periods in a year))

To convert the $318.96 payment in arrears from the earlier example to a payment in advance on a 12.5 percent loan (.125), make the following calculation:

$318.96/(1 + (.125/12))

This calculation produces a result of $315.67.

Summarizing Year-to-Date Interest

Normally, your lending institution sends a reporting form to you in January that shows the amount of interest you paid during the prior year. A copy of this form also is sent to the IRS to ensure that you report the proper amount on your income tax return, if applicable.

If you don't receive this form, or want to check your records against the records of your lending institution, you can create a report that summarizes the year-to-date interest paid on a loan.

To summarize year-to-date interest on a loan, create an itemized category report and select only the Int Exp category (or the category that you use for the interest expense portion of loan payments). See Chapter 18, "Creating and Printing Reports," to learn how to create an itemized category report.

> **Note**
>
> To see how much interest you will pay on a loan in a future year, choose the Show Running Totals check box in the View Loans window. Quicken changes the payment history and projected payments schedules to show the cumulative principal and interest amounts.

Summary

This chapter explained how to use Quicken to track your outstanding loans. You learned the following:

- How to set up the various loan types in Quicken
- How to make and undo loan payments, including principal prepayments
- How to edit loan details, delete a loan, and pay off a loan
- How to handle the refinancing of a loan
- How to use the Refinance Planner
- How to use the Loan Planner

The next chapter shows you how to complete your financial picture by adding other asset accounts and liability accounts to your Quicken system. After you establish these accounts, Quicken easily can determine your *net worth* (assets minus liabilities).

Chapter 11

Managing Your Assets and Other Liabilities

Quicken originally was designed as an electronic check register for writing and recording checks. The newer releases of Quicken, however, can do much more than keep track of your checking account. You can maintain financial records for any asset or liability by using Quicken's familiar register format.

Assets are personal or business resources that have lasting value. For individuals, assets include such items as a house, cars, furniture, and investments. For businesses, assets include money owed by customers (accounts receivable), inventory held for resale, and any fixtures or equipment used in the business.

Liabilities are debts—any money you owe others. For individuals, liabilities include mortgages, car loans, credit card debts, and income taxes. For businesses, liabilities include amounts owed to suppliers (accounts payable), wages payable to employees, and loans from banks and leasing companies.

The benefits of using Quicken to track your other assets (in addition to bank accounts) and your liabilities are similar to the benefits derived from tracking bank accounts. By carefully tracking your other assets, you know what those assets now are worth and why they may have changed in value. By carefully tracking your liabilities, you maintain a firmer control over your debts, which helps you make regular payments, and you have concrete records showing why the amounts of your debts have changed. With your assets and your liabilities carefully documented this way, you can use Quicken to generate a report that states your personal or business financial net worth.

This chapter teaches you how to do the following:

- Set up accounts for other assets and liabilities

- Record assets and liabilities and track their values

- Record assets and liabilities using transfer transactions

- Use a Cash account to keep track of your cash expenditures

- Update account balances

- Measure your net worth by creating a Net Worth Report, or balance sheet

The only drawback to tracking your other assets and liabilities is the additional effort you expend keeping track. In many cases, however, the benefits you realize more than merit this effort.

In essence, using Quicken to track all your assets, as well as your liabilities, gives you a complete picture of your entire financial state in one place. You not only have a powerful record-keeping tool for your cash inflows and outflows, but also all the information you need to determine your overall financial health, or *net worth*, within easy access.

This chapter describes generally how to use Quicken to keep records of your other assets and your liabilities. You learn why and how to use Quicken to generate Net Worth Reports, or *balance sheets*. If Quicken's record-keeping possibilities intrigue you, read Chapters 22 and 23 for more information.

Setting Up Accounts for Other Assets and Liabilities

You must set up a Quicken account for each asset or liability for which you want to keep computer records. You can track any asset or liability you want. Only one limit or restriction exists: you can keep a maximum of only 255 accounts in a single Quicken file. You must remember, however, that any accounts you want grouped on a single balance sheet must be set up in the same file. Typically, this restriction means that all your business accounts must be kept in one file and all your personal accounts in another file.

After you create a Quicken file, take the following steps to set up your accounts:

1. Choose Create New Account from the Activities menu. Quicken displays the Select Account Type dialog box.

2. The Select Account Type dialog box lists four asset account types: Bank Account, Cash Account, Asset Account, and Investment Account. If the asset is a bank account, select the Bank Account option button (you learned about bank accounts in Chapter 3). If the asset is cash, such as that in your wallet or in the petty cash box, select the Cash Account option button. If the account is an investment, select the Investment Account option button. (Refer to Chapter 15 for specifics on defining an investment account.) For any other assets—accounts receivable, real estate, and so on—select the Asset Account option button.

The Select Account Type dialog box also lists two liability account types: Credit Card and Liability. If the liability is the balance on your VISA or MasterCard account, select the Credit Card Account option button (Chapter 9 explains credit card accounts). If the liability is an unamortized debt, select the Liability Account option button.

Tip

For amortized loans, set up a loan in Quicken as explained in Chapter 10, "Tracking Loans." When you set up a loan, Quicken automatically creates a Liability account to track the principal balance of the loan.

3. Choose OK or press Enter. The New Account Information dialog box appears (see fig. 11.1).

4. In the Account Name text box, type the new account name. You can use up to 15 letters, spaces, and any symbols in the account name except the following:

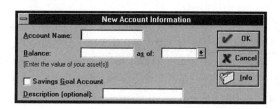

Fig. 11.1
Use the New Account Information dialog box to enter information about the new account you're creating.

5. In the Balance text box, type the starting account balance (as discussed for a Bank account in Chapter 3). You can list assets at their original costs or their current market values. Liabilities are listed at their current balances. If the starting balance is zero, you must enter **0** in the Balance text box; you can't leave the Balance text box blank.

6. In the As Of text box, type the date on which the balance you entered is correct, using the *mm/dd/yy* format, or click the down arrow to select a date from the mini-calendar. (Refer to Chapter 7, "Using Quicken Shortcuts," to learn how to use the mini-calendar to enter dates.)

Tip
Use the + (plus) and – (minus) keys to move the date ahead and back one day.

7. (Optional) When you create an asset account, the Savings Goal Account check box appears in the New Account Information dialog box (refer to fig. 11.1). You can select the Savings Goal Account check box if you want to set up the asset account to earmark savings for some future goal. Refer to Chapter 17, "Saving for the Future with Quicken," to learn how to use a Savings Goal account.

Getting the Most

8. (Optional) In the Description text box, type a description of the account, using up to 21 characters.

9. (Optional) If you want to enter additional information about an asset or liability account that you are defining (such as a bank name, account number, contact person's name, and telephone number), choose the Info button. Quicken displays the Additional Account Information dialog box. Enter the other information that you want to add to your account and then choose OK to return to the New Account Information dialog box.

10. When the information in the New Account Information dialog box is complete, choose OK or press Enter to add the account. Quicken displays the Register for the account that you just created.

Quicken also adds the new account in the Account list and organizes all accounts alphabetically within each account type. Account types are listed in the Account list in the same order as in the Select Account Type dialog box. Thus, the first accounts listed are Bank accounts, followed by Credit Card, Cash, Asset, and Liability accounts. Investment accounts are listed last.

Recording Assets and Liabilities

After you initially set up an account—whether an asset account or a liability account—you can maintain it in one of two ways: by recording transactions directly in the Register, or by using transfer transactions.

Recording Transactions in the Register

Before recording transactions in a Register, you must select the account that you want to use from the Account list (press Ctrl+A). Highlight the account you want to update or revise and then choose the Use button. After you select an account from the Account list, you can use that account's Register to enter transactions that increase or decrease your balance, just as you do in your Quicken Bank account.

Figure 11.2 shows how the Register may look for a major real-estate asset (a personal residence). This Asset Register is almost identical to the regular Bank Account Register and is used the same way. Transaction amounts that decrease the asset account balance are recorded in the Decrease field of the Register (the Payment field on the Bank account version of the Register window). Transaction amounts that increase the asset account are recorded in the Increase field of the Register (the Deposit field on the Bank account version). The total real-estate account balance appears in the bottom right corner of the Register window. If you have *postdated transactions*—transactions with dates in the future—the current balance also is shown.

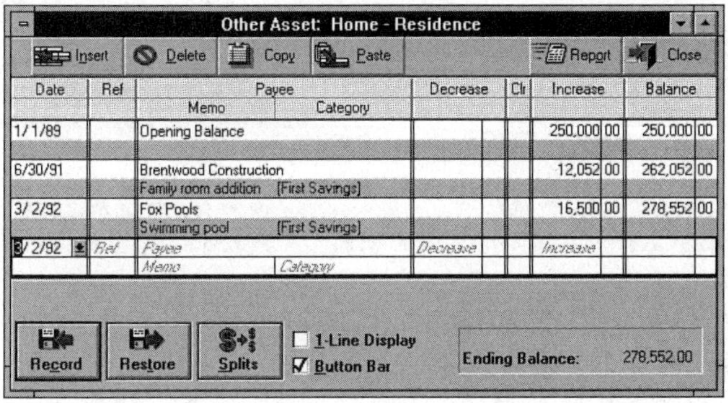

Fig. 11.2
Use an Asset account called Real Estate or Home to record the value of your personal residence.

In figure 11.2, the opening balance of $250,000 shows what you may have paid originally for your home. The two subsequent transactions—one for the addition of a new family room and the other for a new backyard swimming pool—show what changed the value of your home. By keeping these records, you can keep better track of the value of your home and any reasons for changes in its value.

The Register for a Liability account, as shown in figure 11.3, also mirrors the Bank Account Register in appearance and operation. Transaction amounts that increase the amount owed are recorded in the Increase field of the Register. (On the Bank account version of the Register window, this field is labeled Payment.) Transaction amounts that decrease the amount owed are recorded in the Decrease field of the Register. (On the Bank account version of the Register, this field is labeled Deposit.) The total liability balance is shown in the bottom right corner of the Register window. If you have postdated transactions, the current balance also is shown. You don't use the Clr field when tracking a Liability account.

Tip
To record the liability on your home, set up a loan in Quicken (see Chapter 10). Then Quicken automatically creates a Liability account to track the principal balance of the loan.

II

Getting the Most

Fig. 11.3

The Liability
Account Register
is similar to the
Bank Account
Register.

> **Note**
>
> Quicken automatically creates a Liability account when you set up an amortized loan (see Chapter 10). When loan payments are made, only the principal reductions are recorded in the Register for a loan or mortgage. The interest portion is reported as interest expense and should be assigned to a category set up for mortgage interest (Mort Int).

Using Transfer Transactions

Entering transactions directly into a Register is one way to maintain correct account balances for another asset or liability account. You can choose a second way to maintain correct account balances for other assets and liabilities, however. Quicken enables you to enter an account name in the Category field in the Write Checks and Register windows. Quicken then uses the information from the checking-account transaction to record the appropriate transaction in one of the asset or liability accounts.

If you write a check to the remodeling company that makes improvements to your home and enter the account name for your home (for example, **House**, **Home**, or **Real Estate**) in the Category field (in the Write Checks window or the Checking Account Register), Quicken records a corresponding increase in the Asset account set up to track the value of your home. This increase is equal to the payment made from your checking account. When you enter an account name in the Category field for a transaction, Quicken places that account name in brackets ([Home]) to show that the transaction is a transfer transaction.

Figure 11.4 shows the transfer transaction that Quicken enters when you write a $5,000 check for a remodeling job. When you record the check, Quicken records a corresponding $5,000 increase in the account that you use to track the value of your home.

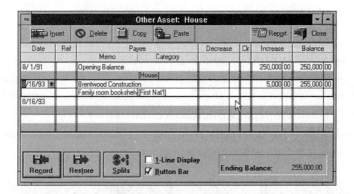

Fig. 11.4

When you pay for improvements, Quicken records a corresponding transaction in the account you use to track the value of your home.

> **Note**
>
> A convenient way to move between different parts of the same transfer transaction is to choose **G**o to Transfer from the **E**dit menu (or press Ctrl+X). After you record a payment in the Check Register, you may want to look at the asset or liability account to see how the account balance was affected.

Tracking Cash Expenditures with Cash Accounts

Cash accounts work well when you want to keep complete, detailed records of miscellaneous cash outlays. (*Miscellaneous cash outlays* are all those paid out of pocket with actual currency rather than with a check, such as $5.80 for stamps, $12 for lunch, or $7.50 for parking.) Often, you don't really need this level of control or detail. But when you do want such detailed records, a Cash account gives you just the tool you need for the job.

II

Getting the Most

> ### CPA TIP: Keeping Track of Petty Cash
>
> The Quicken Cash account is a convenient way for businesses to keep track of petty-cash expenditures and reimbursements. Even very large businesses can benefit by using Quicken for petty-cash accounting.

Figure 11.5 shows a Cash Account Register (called Petty Cash), which is almost identical to the Bank Account Register. Money flowing in and out of the account is recorded in the Spend and Receive fields. (In the Bank Account Register, money flowing out of the account is recorded in the Payment field and money flowing into the account is recorded in the Deposit field. In the Asset and Liability Account Registers, money flowing into and out of the account is recorded in the Increase and Decrease fields.)

Fig. 11.5
Set up a Petty Cash account to track the cash expenditures that your business makes.

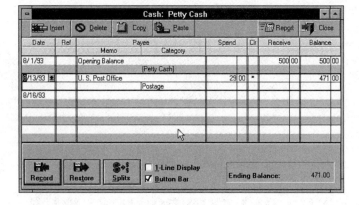

As with the Asset and Liability Account Registers, the Clr field usually isn't used. You can use this column, however, to match receipts against entries to indicate that you have backup records. Press C in this field to show that you have entered a cash transaction from an actual receipt. Quicken enters an asterisk (*) in the Clr field.

Updating Account Balances

If you need to change the account balances in an Asset, Liability, or Cash account, you can reconcile the account, or update the balance. When you update an account's balance, Quicken enters a balance adjustment transaction in the Register.

Suppose that the Register you use to keep track of your petty or pocket cash shows $68.50 as the on-hand cash balance, but the actual balance is $61.88. To reflect the correct cash balance, you must enter a transaction for the difference or update the account balance.

Updating account balances works the same for Cash, Asset, and Liability accounts. To update your account balance, follow these steps:

1. Display the Register for the account whose balance you want to update.

2. Choose Update Balances from the Activities menu, and then choose Update Cash Balances. Quicken displays the Update Account Balance dialog box (see fig. 11.6).

3. In the Update This Account's Balance To text box, enter the amount to which the account balance should be adjusted. In the example, you would enter **61.88**.

4. (Optional) From the Category for Adjustment drop-down list box, select the category to which you want to assign the difference between the old and new account balances. You can use a miscellaneous category or, if you know exactly what the difference stems from, use that category.

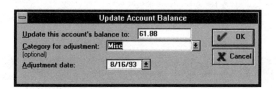

5. In the Adjustment Date text box, enter the date that you want Quicken to use for the balance adjustment transaction in the Register.

6. Choose OK. Quicken makes the adjustment transaction to update the account balance. Figure 11.7 shows the adjustment transaction created by the Update Account Balance transaction so that the account balance is now $61.88.

Tip
You also can display the Update Account Balance dialog box by clicking the Recon button on the Iconbar.

Fig. 11.6
Enter the amount that you want as an ending balance in the Update Account Balance dialog box.

II

Getting the Most

Fig. 11.7
Quicken enters an adjustment transaction in the Register when you update your account balance.

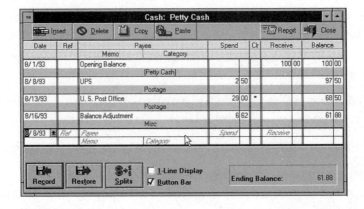

CPA TIP: Assigning Categories To Balance Adjustments

Often you don't really know which category explains the difference between the old and new account balances. Transactions you forgot to record or recorded incorrectly may cause the discrepancy. Essentially, what you are trying to do when you update your account balance is to correct or record erroneous or missing transactions. If you can't decide which category to assign to the balance adjustment transaction, enter the category that you use most frequently with the Register that you are balancing. If most of your petty-cash transactions involve postage payments, for example, enter **Postage** in the **C**ategory for Adjustment text box.

Caution

You can't guess or estimate tax-deduction amounts. *Don't*, therefore, use the method described in the preceding CPA tip to increase your tax deductions. The Internal Revenue Service may disallow deductions that you can't support with evidence as to the exact type and amount of the deduction.

Measuring Your Net Worth

A balance sheet is one traditional tool individuals and businesses use to measure net worth. The balance sheet lists all your assets and liabilities. The difference between assets and liabilities is called *owner's equity*, or *net worth*. A balance sheet differs from reports such as income statements and cash-flow reports, which summarize financial activity occurring over a certain period of time. A balance sheet provides a "snapshot" of your personal or business finances at a particular moment in time.

> ### Note
>
> Before you create a balance sheet, make certain that all your asset and liability accounts are located in the same Quicken file.

Creating a balance sheet with Quicken is a two-step process. First, you must set up an account for each asset, with a beginning balance amount for each asset that is equal to the asset's cost or value. Generally, *assets* are items you have paid for that have lasting value. *Personal assets* include such items as the cash in your wallet, the surrender value of a life insurance policy, any investments, your home, and durable personal items such as your car and furniture. *Business assets* usually include cash, accounts receivable, inventory, and other property and equipment.

The second step in creating a balance sheet is to set up accounts for all your liabilities, recording the balance owed on each liability. *Liabilities* are amounts you now owe other people, banks, or businesses. *Personal liabilities* encompass such items as credit card balances, income taxes, car loans, and mortgages. *Business liabilities* usually include accounts payable, wages and salaries owed employees, income and payroll taxes, and bank credit lines and loans.

> ### CPA TIP: Use Consistent Dates To Determine Market Value
>
> The cost or market value information must be accurate for your net worth calculation also to be accurate. Use only one method for appraising your assets or liabilities: original cost or fair market value. Mixing the different methods can yield inaccurate results. Note also on your opening balances whether you used original cost or fair market value to determine these appraisals. If you use fair market value, be sure to document the source you used to make your estimate of fair market value.

After you enter the costs or market values of all your assets and liabilities, you can generate a report that calculates your net worth by subtracting your liabilities from your assets. The desired result, of course, is for the difference to be a positive one. Whether you are determining your net worth as a business or an individual, you want the net worth amount to grow larger in time, because this amount acts as a financial cushion should you ever experience fiscal difficulties.

Figure 11.8 shows an example of a personal balance sheet, or Net Worth Report, created by Quicken. At the top of the page, Quicken lists each asset account and its balance as of a specific date. Below the asset accounts, Quicken lists each liability account and its balance as of a specific date. The difference between assets and liabilities is *total net worth*. In figure 11.8, the net-worth amount is $19,773.57.

Fig. 11.8

A personal Net Worth Report lists your assets and your liabilities. The difference between the two is your net worth.

```
                          Net Worth Report
                     (Includes unrealized gains)
                          As of 8/16/93
8/16/93                                                        Page 1
 SAMPLE-All Accounts
                                              8/16/1993
                       Acct                    Balance

         ASSETS
         Cash and Bank Accounts
            Cash                                   36.55
            Checking                            3,873.77
            Savings                             4,500.00

            Total Cash and Bank Accounts        8,410.32

         Other Assets
            Home                              153,375.17

            Total Other Assets                153,375.17

         Investments
            Chandler                           50,138.54
            Marmona Fund                        14,633.57
            Steve's IRA                         13,961.31

            Total Investments                   78,733.42

         TOTAL ASSETS                          240,518.91

         LIABILITIES
            Credit Cards
              Visa                                495.67

            Total Credit Cards                    495.67

            Other Liabilities
              Margin Loan                       18,637.50
              Mortgage                         201,612.17

            Total Other Liabilities            220,249.67

         TOTAL LIABILITIES                     220,745.34

         OVERALL TOTAL                          19,773.57
```

A business balance sheet looks essentially the same, although the assets and liabilities listed usually are different.

Chapter 18, "Creating and Printing Reports," describes how to print a personal Net Worth Report and a business balance sheet, as well as each of Quicken's other reports.

Summary

In this chapter, you learned how easy using Quicken is for nearly all your personal or small-business accounting needs. The chapter described how Quicken can help you keep records on such assets as real estate or accounts receivable and on liabilities such as mortgage loans. You learned the following:

- How to set up Asset, Liability, and Cash accounts

- How to record the value of your assets in an Asset account, and how to record your liabilities in a Liability account

- How to use transfer transactions to record changes to Asset and Liability accounts

- How to use a Cash account to track cash expenditures

- How to update the balance in an Asset, Liability, or Cash account

- How to measure your net worth

Chapter 12 describes how to make tax time less hectic by using Quicken to accumulate tax data in reports that you easily can use to prepare your return. You also learn how to export tax data to tax preparation programs, such as TurboTax.

II

Getting the Most

Chapter 12

Using Quicken To Prepare for Income Taxes

A basic accounting requirement for businesses and individuals is to complete the required federal income-tax forms at the end of the year to report income and expenses. Although everyone knows that taxes are inevitable, not everyone organizes financial activities so that tax time isn't a surprise. With Quicken, you can designate categories and subcategories as tax-related and accumulate your tax information in seconds. Whether you prepare your own income-tax return or hand your tax information to a paid tax accountant, Quicken alleviates the burden of gathering tax data.

The beginning of this chapter explains how to use categories for income-tax purposes. Some Quicken users also want to know how to export the income-tax deduction data inside Quicken to external income-tax preparation packages, such as TurboTax. The mechanics of exporting income-tax data also are covered in this chapter.

Using Tax-Related Categories

The basic rule for using categories (and subcategories) to accumulate your tax data is to set up a category or subcategory for each taxable income item or tax deduction that you have. The best way to do so is by reviewing your last two income-tax returns to determine which items you have. If you make charitable contributions each year and itemize your deductions, you will want to make sure that you have a category set up (and designated as tax-related) to

II

Getting the Most

In this chapter, you learn how to do the following:

■ Set up a category or subcategory as tax-related

■ Set the tax schedule preference so that you can assign a tax form or schedule to each tax-related category

■ Assign a tax-related category to a transaction

■ Create reports that summarize your tax-related transactions

■ Export data to a tax preparation program

assign to charitable contribution transactions. If you want to track a taxable income item or tax-deduction item in more detail, you can use subcategories and designate the subcategories as tax-related.

> ## CPA TIP: Designating Categories as Tax-Related
>
> If you don't itemize your deductions (because the total of your itemized deductions doesn't exceed the standard deduction amount), designating the categories for charitable contributions, interest expense, real estate taxes, investment fees, and so on as tax-related isn't necessary.

The following examples may help you better understand how to use categories and subcategories. Real estate investors complete the Schedule E tax form; farmers complete the Schedule F tax form; sole proprietors complete the Schedule C tax form; partnerships complete the Schedule 1065 tax form; and corporations complete one of the three corporate income-tax forms: 1120A for small corporations, 1120S for S Corporations, and 1120 for all other corporations.

> ## CPA TIP: Taxing S Corporation Income
>
> *S Corporations* are corporations that have elected to be treated as partnerships for income-tax purposes. The income from the S Corporation isn't taxed to the S Corporation, but rather to its shareholders.

You also will need to complete an equivalent state income-tax form. Make sure that you or an accountant easily can prepare the tax return with the information Quicken produces. (The more time the accountant takes, the more money you pay to have the accountant prepare the return.)

If you are using Quicken for a sole proprietorship and you hold and resell inventory, you need Part III of the Schedule C form to calculate the cost of goods sold and the inventory balances. You can use the periodic inventory approach described in Chapter 23 to produce the information for Part III of the Schedule C form.

If you are using Quicken for a partnership or a corporation, you must report asset and liability amounts on the tax return. You also want to verify that Quicken provides the data necessary to complete these lines of the tax return.

The easiest approach probably is to set up accounts to track each asset and liability that appears on the tax return. Another approach is to use accounts that you can combine to calculate the total asset or liability figure that needs to be entered on the tax return.

Sole proprietors also must consider one other thing: you may need to complete more than one Schedule C form. You can't aggregate a series of dissimilar businesses and report the consolidated results on one Schedule C. If you own a tavern, practice law, and run a small manufacturing business, you must complete three Schedule C forms: one for the tavern, one for the law practice, and still another for the manufacturing firm. Quicken can handle this situation, but you need to account for each business that needs a separate Schedule C in a separate Quicken file. (Chapter 20, "Managing Your Quicken Files," explains how to set up and select different Quicken files.)

You also can work with categories that you need to combine with other categories to calculate an entry on a tax form. Suppose that you are a sole proprietor of a restaurant. Although total wages go on one line of the Schedule C tax form, you may want to track several categories of wages (subcategories), including waitresses, dishwashers, cooks, bartenders, and so on. Here, you have several wage subcategories that must be added to calculate the wages amount that goes on the tax form. The Tax Schedule Report can help you accumulate data from more than one subcategory.

After you understand how to use categories to classify your tax-related items, you must set up categories and subcategories in your Quicken file as tax-related.

For tax-related categories and subcategories, you also can designate the tax form or schedule to which the category or subcategory relates. If, for example, you set up a category for business entertainment expenses (Bus Enter) as tax-related, you also can specify the form or schedule that business expenses should be reported on. Because business expenses are reported on Form 2106, you would select this form when setting up the category. To assign a tax form or schedule to a tax-related category or subcategory, you must set the tax schedule preference in Quicken so that the Form text box appears when you set up a new category. The next section shows you how to set this preference.

Setting the Tax Schedule Preference

If you want to assign a tax form or schedule to a category or subcategory that you're setting up as tax-related, you first must set the tax schedule preference so that the appropriate text box appears.

To set the tax schedule preference, follow these steps:

1. Choose Preferences from the Edit menu or click the Prefs button on the Iconbar. Quicken displays the Quicken for Windows Preferences dialog box.

2. Choose the General preference button. Quicken displays the General Preferences dialog box, shown in figure 12.1.

Fig. 12.1

Set the tax schedule preference so that Quicken displays the Form option when you set up a tax-related category.

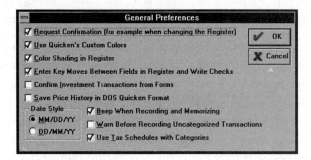

3. Select the Use Tax Schedules with Categories preference check box at the bottom of the General Preferences dialog box.

4. Choose OK to save the tax schedule preference setting and return to the Quicken for Windows Preferences dialog box.

5. Choose Done to close the Quicken for Windows Preferences dialog box.

Setting Up a Tax-Related Category

In Chapter 4, "Organizing Your Finances," you learned how to set up categories and subcategories. If you want to track taxable income items and tax deductions, however, you must set up categories and subcategories as tax-related.

To set up a tax-related category or subcategory, follow these steps:

1. Choose Category & Transfer from the Lists menu, press Ctrl+C, or click the Cat List button on the Iconbar to display the Category & Transfer list.

2. If you're setting up a new category in Quicken that you want to designate as tax-related, choose the New button. Quicken displays the Set Up Category dialog box, shown in figure 12.2.

If you want to designate an existing category or subcategory as tax-related, highlight the category or subcategory and choose the Edit button. Quicken displays the Edit Category dialog box, shown in figure 12.3.

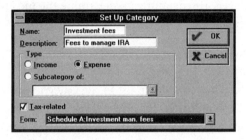

Fig. 12.2

Use the Set Up Category dialog box to enter information for a new category or subcategory.

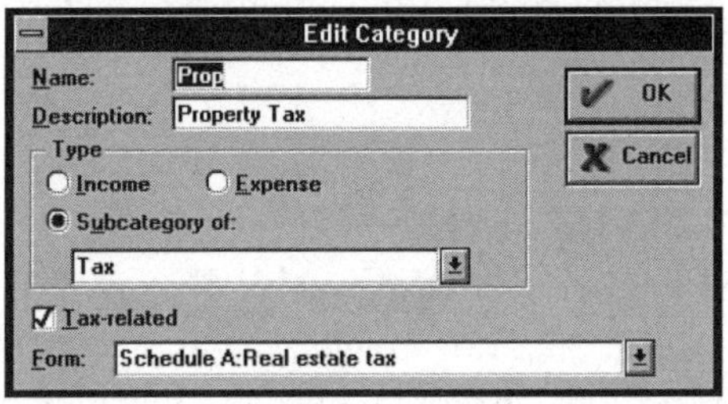

Fig. 12.3

Use the Edit Category dialog box to designate an existing category or subcategory as tax-related.

3. For new categories or subcategories, complete the Set Up Category dialog box, as described in Chapter 4. Select the Tax-related check box. From the Form drop-down list, select a form or schedule (if the category you are setting up is for real estate taxes, for example, select Schedule A: Real Estate Tax).

For existing categories or subcategories, select the Tax-related check box in the Edit Category dialog box. From the Form drop-down list, select a form or schedule.

4. Choose OK to set up the category or subcategory as tax-related.

Assigning Tax-Related Categories to Transactions

After your categories and subcategories are set up as tax-related, you can start tracking your taxable income items and your tax deductions. Each time that you assign a tax-related category or subcategory to a transaction, Quicken accumulates the amounts as taxable income or a tax deduction. At any time, you can generate a Tax Schedule Report that summarizes your tax-related transactions for whatever period necessary. If, for example, you pay estimated federal income taxes on a quarterly basis, you may need to generate a Tax Schedule Report every three months to determine the income you have received for the period.

Assign a tax-related category or subcategory to a transaction in the same manner that you assign any category or subcategory: select the category or subcategory from the drop-down list in the Category field of the Write Checks window or the Register. Just make sure that the transaction to which you are assigning a tax-related category or subcategory is truly taxable income or a tax-deductible item. Don't, for example, assign a tax-related category to a personal entertainment expense or the purchase of furniture for your home, neither of which are tax-deductible.

Summarizing Tax-Related Transactions at Year's End

During the year, you should assign tax-related categories and subcategories to each transaction for taxable income or for a tax-deductible expense (as explained in the preceding section). When you use Quicken's tax-related categories and subcategories, extracting the information you need to complete a tax form is simple. You just print the report that summarizes the categories and subcategories that track taxable income and income-tax deductions. This report is called the Tax Summary Report.

To create a Tax Summary Report, follow these steps:

1. Choose Home from the Reports menu and then select Tax Summary from the submenu.

    Quicken searches all accounts from the beginning of the year to the current date and displays the Tax Summary Report window (see fig. 12.4).

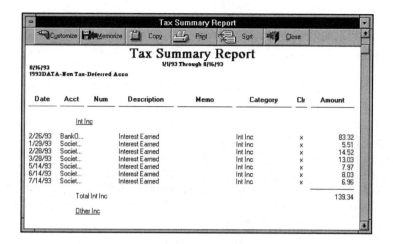

Fig. 12.4

The Tax Summary Report groups and subtotals your tax-related transactions by income categories (listed first) and expense categories (listed next).

2. (Optional) To change the date that the report covers, choose Customize from the report button bar. Quicken displays the Customize Tax Summary Report dialog box. In the Report Dates section, select the reporting period from the Report Dates drop-down list box or customize the reporting period by selecting the dates that you want the report to cover from the From and To drop-down list boxes. Choose OK to return to the Tax Summary Report window.

3. Choose Print on the report button bar to print the Tax Summary Report.

Tip

Refer to Chapter 18, "Creating and Printing Reports," for more information on customizing and printing reports.

II

Getting the Most

CPA TIP: Gathering Tax Information

Although tax forms give most of the general information about the kinds of expenses, IRS instructions and regulations may require that you gather additional information. One example is that the business usage of a vehicle owned by a business is subject to different limitations, which aren't necessarily found in Quicken. Consult a tax advisor when you encounter questionable areas.

Another report, the Tax Schedule Report, not only subtotals your tax-related categories and subcategories by taxable income and tax-deductible expenses, but groups and subtotals the transactions by line item, by form, or by schedule. When you choose to create the Tax Schedule Report, Quicken searches all your accounts for transactions assigned to tax-related categories and subcategories. The Tax Schedule Report groups and subtotals the tax-related transactions first by line item, and then by tax form or schedule. Taxable income transactions, by form or schedule, are listed first, followed by tax-deductible transactions.

If you manually prepare your tax return, you can use the Tax Schedule Report to complete tax forms and schedules. If you pay a CPA or tax attorney to prepare your return, you can give them a copy of the Tax Schedule Report and save that person time (and yourself tax preparation fees) because the tax information needed already is subtotaled.

If you use a tax preparation software program, like TurboTax, to prepare your return, you can transfer the data in the Tax Schedule Report directly to that program.

To create a Tax Schedule Report, follow these steps:

1. Choose **H**ome from the **R**eports menu and then select Tax Schedule from the submenu. Quicken searches all accounts from the beginning of the year to the current date and displays the Tax Schedule Report window (see fig. 12.5).

Fig. 12.5

The Tax Schedule Report groups and subtotals your tax-related transactions by line item and by tax form or schedule.

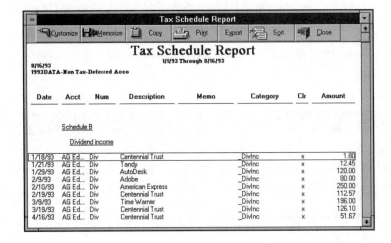

2. (Optional) To change the date that the report covers, choose **C**ustomize from the report button bar. Quicken displays the Customize Tax Schedule Report dialog box. In the Report Dates section, select the reporting period from the Report Dates drop-down list box or customize the reporting period by selecting the dates that you want the report to cover in the From and To drop-down list boxes. Choose OK to return to the Tax Schedule Report window.

3. Choose Print on the report button bar to print the Tax Schedule Report.

Refer to Chapter 18, "Creating and Printing Reports," for more information on customizing and printing reports. Refer to the next section to learn how to export the report data to a tax preparation program.

Exporting Quicken Data into Tax Preparation Programs

You can transfer the tax data you collect and store in Quicken directly into several popular income-tax preparation packages. TurboTax, for example, imports Quicken data if you follow general steps. Even if you don't have TurboTax, you still may be able to apply the same general steps discussed in this section to export Quicken data to other tax preparation packages.

When you export Quicken data, you first must export the data to a tax export file with the TXF (Tax Exchange Format) file extension. After your data is exported to a TXF file, you can start your tax preparation program and import the TXF file to that program.

To export your Quicken data to a tax export file, follow these steps:

1. Create the Tax Schedule Report, as explained in the preceding section. Make sure that the report dates are from January 1 of the prior year to December 31.

2. Choose Export on the report button bar. Quicken displays the Create Tax Export File dialog box, shown in figure 12.6. Notice that the Tax export files (*.TXF) format type already is selected in the Save File as Type drop-down list box.

3. In the File Name text box, type the file name that you want Quicken to use to name the tax export file. Make sure that your file name meets the criteria for file names.

4. The Directories list box displays the current directory. You can select a different directory. You should probably export the file to the directory where your tax program is located.

5. The Drives drop-down list box displays the current drive. Select the drive to which you are exporting the Tax Schedule Report.

Getting the Most

II

Fig. 12.6

To export your Quicken tax data to another tax preparation program, use the Create Tax Export File dialog box.

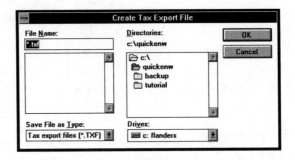

6. When the Create Tax Export File dialog box is complete, choose OK.

Quicken creates a TXF file with your Tax Schedule Report information ready to be imported to your tax preparation program. Refer to the documentation for your tax preparation program to learn how to import the TXF file to the program.

Summary

This chapter described the basic steps to take to ensure that Quicken produces the data necessary to complete federal and state income-tax returns. You learned how to do the following:

■ Set the tax schedule preference so that you can select a tax form or schedule for tax-related categories and subcategories

■ Set up a tax-related category or subcategory

■ Assign tax-related categories and subcategories to transactions for taxable income or tax-deductible expenses

■ Summarize your tax-related transactions by creating a Tax Summary Report and a Tax Schedule Report

■ Export the data in the Tax Schedule Report to a TXF file that you can import to your tax preparation program

In the next chapter, you learn how to pay your bills electronically through CheckFree. If you have a modem and are ready to give up the process of handwriting or printing checks, you will benefit by Quicken's electronic bill-payment feature and CheckFree.

Chapter 13

Paying Your Bills Electronically

With Quicken, you can use CheckFree, an electronic bill payment service, to pay your bills. By using Quicken and a modem, you can send payment instructions to CheckFree Corporation (located in Ohio). Your payment instructions include all the information CheckFree needs to actually pay the bill: who you owe the money to, when the bill needs to be paid, how much you owe, and so on. CheckFree Corporation then draws a check or electronically transfers funds from your bank account to whomever you owe the money.

Paying bills electronically isn't for everyone. By getting one more party involved in the bill-paying process, you may make this process more complicated. For Quicken users who have a modem and who want to stop printing checks, however, electronic payment is appealing.

If you have been using CheckFree (Version 3.0 or higher) but now want to use Quicken to transmit electronic payment information to the CheckFree Processing Center, you need to import your CheckFree register data into Quicken. (You can't import data from earlier versions of CheckFree.) This way, you update your Register in Quicken with any CheckFree transactions

This chapter explains how to perform the following tasks:

- Set up your Quicken system for electronic payments

- Pay bills electronically

- Transmit payment information to CheckFree

- Issue stop-payment requests

- Make payment inquiries

- Send and receive electronic mail to or from CheckFree

II

Getting the Most

that Quicken doesn't include. Refer to your CheckFree manual to learn how to export your CheckFree register to Quicken.

Setting Up Your System for Electronic Payment

To begin paying your bills electronically, you need to complete four steps:

1. Complete the CheckFree paperwork.

2. Configure your modem by setting the modem preferences in Quicken.

3. Designate the bank account(s) you want to use to make electronic payments from.

4. Set up the payees (the persons or companies that you will pay electronically).

Performing these steps is easy. Completing this part of the work should take no more than a few minutes.

Completing the CheckFree Paperwork

Before you begin using the CheckFree service, you need to complete the CheckFree Service Form. The form is self-explanatory. You need to tell CheckFree Corporation how much memory your computer has, and give the company some personal information, including your Social Security number, name, and address. You also need to provide CheckFree with a credit card account number so that CheckFree can charge your account if your payment instructions cause an overdraw to your bank account.

Tip
For security reasons, choose a security code—similar to what you use for automated teller machines—to gain access to your account.

After you provide this basic information, you also need to tell CheckFree which phone lines you are using, specify which account number/security code you plan to use to gain access to the CheckFree system, and sign an authorization so that CheckFree can deduct funds from your bank account. (If you don't choose an account number or security code, CheckFree creates one for you.)

After you complete the CheckFree Service Form, attach a voided check to the form and mail the form to Intuit. To mail the form, use the business reply envelope included for returning the CheckFree service form. Intuit forwards the service form to CheckFree Corporation. In a few days, CheckFree sends you a confirmation letter that confirms or assigns the account number/

personal security code, gives you the telephone number to use for CheckFree transmissions, and the fastest *baud rate*—the transmission speed—you can use for sending payment information.

Setting Modem Preferences

Before you can begin paying bills electronically with CheckFree, you must set the modem preferences in Quicken so that the program knows the type of phone you are using, modem information (like the port your modem uses and the speed at which your modem operates), the access telephone number, and any initialization strings that your modem uses. Make sure that you have received the confirmation letter from CheckFree before you set modem preferences because you will need to enter the CheckFree access number.

Tip
If you don't have a modem, you can buy one from CheckFree Corporation for about $99 (plus $4 shipping). Call Check-Free for more information at (800) 882-5280.

To set modem preferences, follow these steps:

1. From the Edit menu, choose Preferences, or click the Prefs button on the Iconbar. Quicken displays the Quicken for Windows Preferences dialog box.

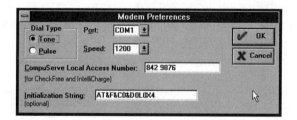

Fig. 13.1
Enter the information about your telephone and modem in the Modem Preferences dialog box.

2. Choose Modem. Quicken displays the Modem Preferences dialog box, shown in figure 13.1.

3. In the Dial Type section, choose Tone if the telephone line your modem uses supports Touch-Tone dialing. Choose Pulse if your phone line supports pulse dialing.

4. From the Port drop-down list box, select the port your modem uses in your computer, such as COM1 or COM2.

5. From the Speed drop-down list box, select the speed at which your modem operates. If you're unsure about which speed to select, refer to your modem manual for this information.

6. In the CompuServe Local Access Number text box, type the telephone number you received from CheckFree. (You don't need a CompuServe membership to use CheckFree for electronic payments.)

Getting the Most

If you use the IntelliCharge feature in Quicken to receive your Quicken VISA credit card statements by modem, use the same CompuServe local access number used when downloading your statement file. You don't need to change the number (if CheckFree provides a different number).

Note

If your telephone line needs a special prefix to obtain an outside line (many businesses require a 9 to gain access to an outside line), include the prefix in the local access number that you enter in the CompuServe Local Access Number text box. If your telephone line needs a pause after a prefix, add a comma before you type the telephone number.

If the telephone line that you use supports Call Waiting, you should disable the service before transmitting to CheckFree. Contact your local telephone company for the code you need to disable Call Waiting, and then enter that code, followed by a comma, before typing the access number for CheckFree.

7. In the Initialization String text box, type any special letters, digits, and other characters to be sent to your modem to begin transmission. Most initialization strings begin with the letters AT. Refer to your modem manual for this information.

8. Choose OK to save the modem preferences and return to the Quicken for Windows Preferences dialog box.

9. Choose Done to close the Quicken for Windows Preferences dialog box.

Setting Up Bank Accounts for Electronic Payment

After you set the preferences for your modem, you are ready to set up the bank account(s) that you will use to make electronic payments. Your bank accounts must already be set up in Quicken. Now you must identify which bank accounts you want to use for electronic payment. You can't use a credit card, asset, liability, or investment account for electronic payment—only bank accounts.

If you haven't set up the bank account in your Quicken file, create it now (see Chapter 3). Then set up a bank account for electronic payment by following these steps:

1. From the Activities menu, choose CheckFree.

2. From the CheckFree submenu, choose Setup. Quicken displays the Electronic Payment Setup dialog box, shown in figure 13.2. Because you can set up only bank accounts for electronic payment, Quicken lists only bank accounts in the Electronic Payment Setup dialog box.

Fig. 13.2
The Electronic Payment Setup dialog box lists all bank accounts in your Quicken file.

3. Highlight the bank account that you want to use to pay bills electronically and then choose Setup. Quicken displays the Electronic Payment Account Settings dialog box, shown in figure 13.3.

Fig. 13.3
Quicken displays the Electronic Payment Account Settings dialog box when you select a bank account to set up for electronic payment.

4. Make sure that a check mark appears in the Enable Electronic Payments for Account check box. If a check mark doesn't appear, select the option.

5. In the Your First Name text box, type your first name.

6. Type your middle initial in the MI text box.

7. Move to the Last text box and type your last name.

8. In the Street Address text boxes, type the appropriate information.

9. Type the name of the city or town in which you live in the City text box.

10. Enter your state's abbreviation or select your state from the list of two-character abbreviations in the State drop-down list box.

11. Move to the Zip text box and type your ZIP code. Quicken validates the entry against a list of valid ZIP codes. If Quicken doesn't recognize what you enter, Quicken presents a window to inform you that it isn't a valid ZIP code for your state and asks, Use anyway? Choose OK to accept anyway, or Cancel to return and try again.

    If Quicken still doesn't recognize the ZIP code that you enter, but you know the code is correct anyway, press Ctrl+Z to force Quicken to accept the ZIP code.

12. In the Home Phone text box, enter your home phone number, including the area code. You don't have to include the punctuation characters, such as hyphens and parentheses; Quicken adds these characters after you press Tab to move to the next text box.

13. Type the account number that CheckFree assigned to you. If you previously set up more than one bank account for electronic bill paying (which means that you filled out more than one CheckFree Service Agreement form), CheckFree gives you identifying numbers based on your Social Security number for each account. Enter this identifying number here.

14. In the CheckFree Security Code text box, enter the account number/security number or PIN number from the CheckFree confirmation letter.

15. After you complete the Electronic Payment Account Settings dialog box, choose OK. Quicken returns to the Electronic Payment Setup dialog box. The account you set up now is marked as *enabled* (designated with a lightning bolt character) for electronic payment. When you subsequently select the enabled account to use, Quicken adds several more menu options that you can use for processing electronic payments.

16. Choose Close to remove the Electronic Payment Setup dialog box.

Setting Up Payees for Electronic Payment

To pay a bill electronically, you need to collect and store information about each person or company you plan to pay so that CheckFree Corporation can process payments to the appropriate person or business. To set up a payee, just add the payee to the Electronic Payee list. From the Electronic Payee list, you can edit a payee or delete a payee to whom you no longer make payments.

Quicken enables you to make payments to payees in one of two ways: by variable payments or by fixed payments. Each month, for example, your telephone bill probably isn't the same. To pay the telephone company, you need to write a check for a varying amount each month. Quicken calls this a *normal payment*. Payees that you make ordinary payments to, like your telephone company or your utility company, are called *normal payees*. When you set up a payee to receive a normal payment, you must enter the check in Quicken each time you make payment to the payee.

On the other hand, your check to your landlord for rent is usually the same each month. In this case, you can tell Quicken to pay the same amount each month to the specified payee until you tell Quicken to no longer make the payment. Quicken calls these types of payments *fixed payments*. Payees that receive recurring payments for the same amount at a fixed interval are called *fixed, recurring payees*. When you set up a payee to receive a fixed payment, CheckFree makes the payment for you, based on the intervals that you specify.

> **Caution**
>
> Because many individuals or businesses aren't set up to handle electronic fund transfers, CheckFree mails these kinds of payments from Ohio. If the payee's location is your home town, the payment may take an extra day or two to reach the payee from Ohio. Schedule all CheckFree payments early enough to allow for delays in the mail system.

Setting Up Payees for Normal Payments. To set up an electronic payee to receive normal payments, follow these steps:

1. From the Activities menu, choose CheckFree.

2. From the CheckFree submenu, choose Electronic Payee List. Quicken displays the Electronic Payee list window, shown in figure 13.4.

3. Choose New. Quicken displays the Choose Type of Electronic Payee dialog box, shown in figure 13.5.

II

Getting the Most

Fig. 13.4
You can add
normal payees or
fixed, recurring
payees in the
Electronic Payee
list window.

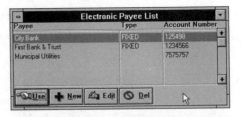

Fig. 13.5
Choose the type
of payee you are
setting up in the
Choose Type of
Electronic Payee
dialog box.

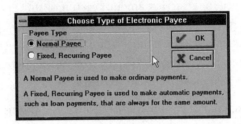

4. By default, Quicken selects the Normal Payee option. Choose OK to
   accept the selection. Quicken displays the Set Up Electronic Payee dialog box, shown in figure 13.6.

5. Enter the payee's name, street address, city, state, and ZIP code.

> **Note**
>
> Entering the payee name, address, phone number, and account number accurately is
> important because CheckFree uses this information to make payments to the payee.

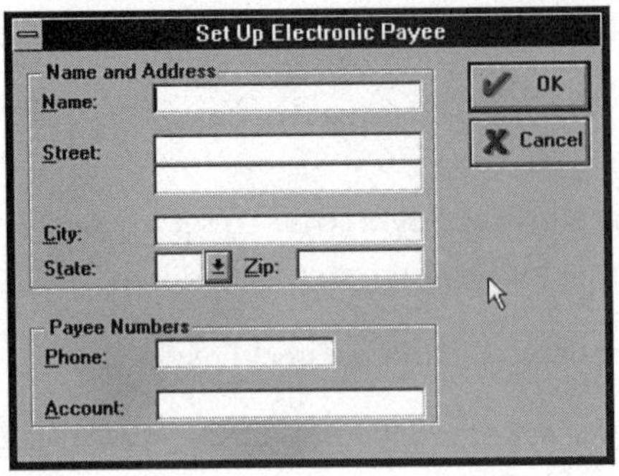

Fig. 13.6
Enter information
about a normal
payee in the Set
Up Electronic
Payee dialog box.

6. In the Phone text box, type the payee's telephone number (the number that you normally call for billing inquiries), including the area code. CheckFree must have the payee's telephone number to route payments correctly.

7. In the Account text box, type the account number that the person or business uses to identify you.

8. When the Set Up Electronic Payee dialog box is complete, choose OK. Quicken returns to the Electronic Payee list window.

To set up additional normal payees, repeat steps 3 through 8.

Setting Up Payees To Receive Fixed, Recurring Payments. If you have certain monthly payments that don't vary in amount (your rent check or a car loan payment), you can set up the payee as a fixed, recurring payee. You establish a fixed payment schedule, which tells CheckFree to pay the same amount each month to the specified payee until you instruct CheckFree to stop making the payments.

With fixed, recurring payees, you don't have to enter a check each time you make a payment—CheckFree automatically transmits a payment to the fixed, recurring payee.

To set up an electronic payee to receive fixed, recurring payments, follow these steps:

1. From the Activities menu, choose CheckFree.

2. From the CheckFree submenu, choose Electronic Payee List. Quicken displays the Electronic Payee List window (refer to fig. 13.4).

3. Choose New. Quicken displays the Choose Type of Electronic Payee dialog box (refer to fig. 13.5).

4. Choose Fixed, Recurring Payee.

5. Choose OK. Quicken displays the Set Up Electronic Payee dialog box, shown in figure 13.7.

6. Enter the name, street address, city, state, and ZIP code for the payee.

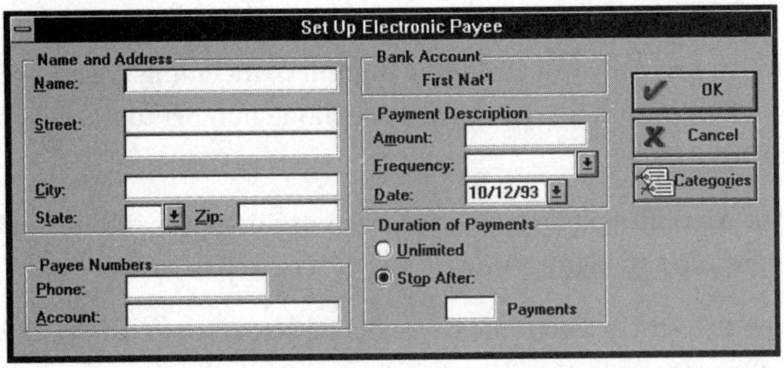

Fig. 13.7
Use the Set Up
Electronic Payee
dialog box to enter
information about
a payee to receive
fixed, recurring
payments.

7. In the **Phone** text box, type the payee's telephone number (the number that you normally call for billing inquiries), including the area code. CheckFree must have the payee's telephone number to route payments correctly.

8. In the **Account** text box, type the account number that the person or business uses to identify you.

9. In the **Bank Account** area, Quicken displays the name of the bank account that you selected to use for electronic payments. If you set up more than one bank account for electronic payments, a drop-down list is displayed. Select the appropriate account from this list.

10. Type the amount of the fixed payment in the **Amount** text box.

11. From the **Frequency** drop-down list box, select the frequency of payments (weekly, biweekly, monthly, and so forth).

12. In the **Date** text box, type the due date of the next payment.

Tip
Select a date in the
Date drop-down
list box by clicking
the down arrow to
display the mini-
calendar. Chapter
7, "Using Quicken
Shortcuts," ex-
plains how to use
the mini-calendar.

13. In the **Duration of Payments** section, choose the Unlimited option button if you want CheckFree to make regular payments until you give instructions otherwise. Choose Stop After to make fixed payments for a specified period of time, and then enter the number of payments to stop after in the Payments text box. For a rent payment, you can choose to have CheckFree make unlimited payments by selecting Unlimited. Alternatively, if you make a purchase, and the terms are that you make 12 monthly payments, choose Stop After and type **12** in the Payments box.

14. Next, choose Categories to assign category and memo information to fixed payments. Quicken displays the CheckFree Fixed Payment Categories dialog box, shown in figure 13.8.

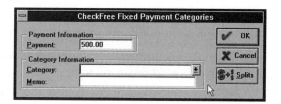

Fig. 13.8
Assign categories
to fixed payment
transactions in the
CheckFree Fixed
Payment Catego-
ries dialog box.

15. Assign the appropriate category and memo to the fixed payment. To assign more than one category to the fixed payment, choose Splits to open the Splits window. Then assign the categories and amounts to the fixed payment and choose OK to return to the CheckFree Fixed Payment Categories dialog box.

16. Choose OK to return to the Electronic Payee list window. Quicken enters the word FIXED in the Type column for a payee that you set up as fixed and recurring.

To set up additional fixed, recurring payees, repeat steps 3 through 16.

Editing and Deleting Electronic Payees

You can edit or delete a payee from the Electronic Payee list. You can change, for example, the payee's address or even the account number that the payee uses to identify you. Or you can delete a payee to whom you no longer do business with or make payments to.

> **Note**
>
> You can't edit or delete an electronic payee if an untransmitted transaction exists for the payee. You learn more about untransmitted transactions later in this chapter.

To edit or delete an electronic payee, follow these steps:

1. Choose CheckFree from the Activities menu and then choose Electronic Payee List. Quicken displays the Electronic Payee list window (refer to fig. 13.4).

2. Highlight the electronic payee that you want to edit or delete.

3. To edit an electronic payee, choose Edit. Quicken displays the Edit Electronic Payee dialog box, which resembles the Set Up Electronic Payee dialog box (refer to fig. 13.6 or 13.7). Make the necessary changes to the electronic payee information and choose OK.

II

Getting the Most

To delete an electronic payee, choose **Del**. Quicken asks you to confirm that you want to delete the payee. Choose OK. If untransmitted payments or scheduled transactions exist for this payee, Quicken displays a warning message and asks whether you want to stop payments. If so, choose OK. Quicken displays another message telling you that CheckFree will continue making payments until the next time you connect to the CheckFree processing center. Choose OK to stop payments.

Paying Bills

Paying bills electronically closely resembles the process of writing and printing checks with Quicken. For this reason, this chapter doesn't repeat the discussions of Chapter 5, "Writing and Printing Checks," which cover how to write and print checks with Quicken. Instead, this section concentrates on different parts of the process. (If you haven't used the Quicken's Write Checks window, you may want to review Chapter 5 before continuing in this chapter.)

You pay bills that aren't set up as fixed and recurring by writing a check in the Write Checks window, recording the check, and transmitting the payment information to CheckFree. For fixed, recurring payments, you don't have to write a check each time a payment is due. After you set up a fixed, recurring payee, enter all the payment information, and transmit to Check-Free, CheckFree makes payments automatically based on the payment schedule that you enter. You receive payment confirmations from CheckFree when fixed payments are made.

Making Regular Payments
After you set up the payees who you will pay electronically in the Electronic Payee list, you can begin paying bills electronically. For each bill you want to pay, follow these steps:

1. Display the Write Checks window by clicking Check on the Iconbar or pressing Ctrl+W.

2. From the Account drop-down list box, select the bank account from which you pay bills electronically. Quicken displays the electronic version of the Write Checks window, as shown in figure 13.9.

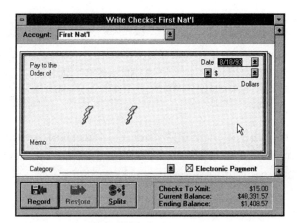

Fig. 13.9
The electronic
version of the
Write Checks
window appears
when you select a
bank account that
you have set up to
make electronic
payments.

3. If an X doesn't appear in the Electronic Payment check box in the lower right portion of the Write Checks window, select the option to activate the electronic payment feature.

4. Complete the electronic payment version of the Write Checks window in the same way you would complete the regular version of the window.

In the Date field, you can't enter a date that is less than five business days after the current date. CheckFree needs at least five business days to process payment information and make payments to your payees.

In the Pay to the Order of field, make sure that you type or select an electronic payee from the drop-down list. Quicken indicates electronic payees with the word <ELEC> next to the payee name in the list.

Tip
Use Quicken's new mini-calendar at the Date field to determine the five-business-day advance date to use for electronic payments.

> **Note**
>
> Rather than track unprinted checks, Quicken shows the total dollar amount of the checks to transmit in the lower right corner of the Write Checks window.

5. After the Write Checks window is complete, choose Record.

The check that contains the electronic payment scrolls off the screen, leaving behind an *empty* check that you can use to complete another electronic payment. Until you begin transmitting the electronic payments, you can edit these payments just as you do any other check you write at the Write Checks window.

II

Getting the Most

Tip
You also can enter and edit electronic payments by using the Quicken Register. Quicken identifies electronic payment transactions in the Quicken Register by displaying XMIT in the Num field.

> **Note**
>
> If you prefer to pay an electronic payee with a manual check or a Quicken check, make sure that an X doesn't appear in the Electronic Payment box in the lower right portion of the Write Checks window.

6. Transmit the payment information to CheckFree. See the section "Transmitting to CheckFree" later in this chapter to learn how to transmit payment information to CheckFree.

Making Fixed, Recurring Payments

After you set up a payee to receive fixed, recurring payments and transmit the payee information to CheckFree, you don't need to do anything when payments are due. CheckFree automatically makes the payments based on the intervals that you enter. If you add your apartment landlord as an electronic payee to receive monthly rent checks in the amount of $750, CheckFree automatically makes those payments on the same day each month.

Editing a Fixed, Recurring Payment. If you want to change the payment information for a fixed, recurring payment, you can do so from the Electronic Payee list.

To edit fixed, recurring payment information, follow these steps:

1. From the Activities menu, choose CheckFree. Then choose Electronic Payee List from the submenu. Quicken displays the Electronic Payee list (refer to fig. 13.4).

2. Highlight the fixed payee that you want to change.

3. Choose Edit. Quicken displays the Edit Electronic Payee dialog box, which resembles the Set Up Electronic Payee dialog box in figure 13.7.

4. Make the appropriate changes in the Edit Electronic Payee dialog box. If you need to change the fixed payment amount, for example, move to the Amount text box and type the new amount.

5. After the changes are complete, choose OK.

6. Transmit the changes to the electronic payee to CheckFree (see the later section "Transmitting to CheckFree").

Discontinuing a Fixed, Recurring Payment. If you no longer want to make fixed, recurring payments to a payee, you can discontinue fixed payments in one of two ways: issue a stop payment for the most recent fixed payment, or delete the electronic payee to whom you make fixed payments from the Electronic Payee list. When you stop payment on the most recent fixed, recurring payment and transmit to CheckFree, any future payments are stopped for this payee; however, the payee information is retained in the Electronic Payee list.

If you choose to delete the payee from the Electronic Payee list, after you transmit the deletion to CheckFree, no future payments are made to the payee. You can't delete an electronic payee, however, that has a payment that already has been made and confirmed (XMIT appears in the Register for these transactions).

To discontinue a fixed, recurring payment by issuing a stop payment on the most recent payment, follow these steps:

1. Make sure that your modem is turned on and properly connected.

2. Display the Check Register for the account that you use to make electronic payments.

3. Highlight the most recent fixed, recurring payment in the Register.

4. From the Activities menu, choose CheckFree, and then choose Stop Payment from the CheckFree submenu.

5. Quicken asks you to confirm the stop payment request. Choose OK. Quicken immediately transmits the stop payment request to CheckFree. If the transmission is successful, CheckFree discontinues any future fixed payments. If an error message appears, repeat these steps.

Quicken retains the payee information in the Electronic Payee list, but changes the type from FIXED to INACTIVE.

To discontinue a fixed, recurring payment by deleting the payee, follow these steps:

1. From the Check Register for the account that you use to make electronic payments, choose CheckFree from the Activities menu. Then choose Electronic Payee List. Quicken displays the Electronic Payee list (refer to fig. 13.4).

II

Getting the Most

2. Highlight the payee for the fixed, recurring payment that you want to discontinue or delete.

3. Choose Del.

4. Quicken asks you to confirm that you want to delete the electronic payee. Choose OK.

5. Transmit the deletion of the payee to CheckFree (as explained later in the section "Transmitting to CheckFree").

Making Loan Payments Electronically

For any amortized loan that you set up in Quicken, you can select CheckFree as the payment method to use to make loan payments. (Chapter 10, "Tracking Loans," shows you how to set up a loan in Quicken.) Before selecting CheckFree as the payment method for an amortized loan, you first must set up the lender as a fixed, recurring payee and then transmit the addition to the Electronic Payee list to CheckFree.

After your lender is set up as an electronic payee to receive fixed, recurring payments (see the earlier section "Setting Up Payees To Receive Fixed, Recurring Payments"), follow these steps to select CheckFree as the payment method for a loan:

1. From the Activities menu, choose Set Up Loans. Quicken displays the View Loans window.

2. From the Loan drop-down list box, select the loan for which you want to make loan payments electronically. Quicken displays the payment schedule and payment history for the loan in the View Loans window.

3. Choose Payments. Quicken displays the Set Up Loan Payment dialog box.

4. Choose Method of Pmt. Quicken displays the Select Payment Method dialog box. Choose CheckFree Fixed Payment.

5. Select the lender's name from the Fixed Payee drop-down list.

6. Choose OK.

Each time a loan payment is made by CheckFree and confirmed in Quicken, the payment schedule for the loan is updated to reflect the most recent payment.

Transmitting to CheckFree

After you enter the electronic payments, you need to transmit them so that CheckFree Corporation can pay them. When you transmit to CheckFree, any new payees that you have added to, or deleted from, the Electronic Payee list since the last transmission also are transmitted to CheckFree. Any changes to fixed payments are transmitted at this time.

To transmit electronic payments, electronic payee information, and changes to fixed payments, follow these steps:

1. Turn on your modem.

Quicken first tries to initialize the modem and then retries the modem twice. If a problem is encountered, a message appears that says Quicken couldn't initialize the modem. Make sure that your modem is connected properly and turned on. If Quicken continues to have a problem initializing your modem, refer to the user's manual for your modem or call Intuit's technical support staff.

2. From the Activities menu, choose CheckFree. Then choose Transmit from the submenu. Quicken displays the Transmit Payments dialog box, which tells you how many payments you must transmit (see fig. 13.10).

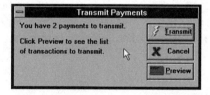

Fig. 13.10
The Transmit Payments dialog box tells you how many payments there are to transmit to CheckFree.

3. If you want to go ahead and transmit payments and payee information (if any), choose Transmit. If you want to review the payments and any other information that can be transmitted, choose Preview. Quicken displays the Preview Transmission to CheckFree dialog box, shown in figure 13.11.

In the top of the dialog box, Quicken lists the payments to be transmitted. In the lower part of the window, Quicken lists any additions or changes to electronic payees to be transmitted to CheckFree.

II

Getting the Most

Fig. 13.11

The Preview Transmission to CheckFree dialog box lists all payments and any changes to the payee list that are ready to be transmitted to CheckFree.

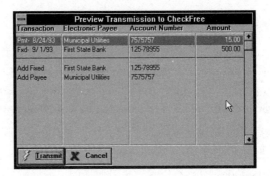

4. If you need to make changes to any of the information in the Preview Transmission to CheckFree dialog box, choose Cancel and make the appropriate changes. If the information in the Preview Transmission to CheckFree dialog box is correct, choose Transmit.

After you transmit payments, CheckFree sends confirmation numbers back to Quicken for each transmitted payment. Confirmation numbers are stored in the Memo field of each transaction.

> **Note**
>
> If you want to review information about an electronic payment, select the transaction in the Check Register, choose CheckFree from the Activities menu, and then choose Electronic Payment Info. Quicken displays the transmission date, payment date, transmission status, and the confirmation date of each electronic payment. Choose OK after you finish reviewing electronic payment information.

Issuing a Stop Payment

You can use Quicken to issue stop payment requests on electronic payments you transmitted previously. You can stop an electronic payment if the payment date is at least five business days after the current date. Obviously, as with stop payment requests issued directly to the bank, you need to make the request before the transaction is processed.

To issue a stop payment request, follow these steps:

1. Turn on your modem.

2. Display the Register for the account that you use to make electronic payments.

3. Highlight the transaction in the Register on which you want to stop payment.

4. From the Activities menu, choose CheckFree. Then choose Stop Payment.

5. Quicken asks you to confirm the stop payment. Choose OK.

Quicken immediately transmits the request to CheckFree. If the transmission is successful, Quicken enters VOID in the transaction line in the Register.

Making Electronic Payment Inquiries

You can ask CheckFree about a payment you transmitted previously. Suppose that you receive a telephone call from someone who wants to know whether you have sent them a check yet. You can make an electronic payment inquiry to check the status of this particular payment.

To make an electronic payment inquiry, follow these steps:

1. Turn on the modem.

2. Access the Register for the account that you use to make electronic payments.

3. Highlight the transaction in the Register that you want to inquire about. Electronic payments are marked with XMIT in the Num field.

4. From the Activities menu, choose CheckFree, and then choose Inquiry. Quicken displays the Electronic Payment Inquiry dialog box, which shows the details of the transmitted payment, including the date the transaction was transmitted to CheckFree, the scheduled payment date, the account number, and the confirmation number you received from CheckFree. Quicken asks whether you want to send an inquiry message to CheckFree regarding the transaction.

> **Note**
>
> This dialog box also indicates whether you can stop payment (if at least five business days still remain between the current date and the payment date).

5. Choose OK to send a payment inquiry. Quicken displays the Transmit Payment Inquiry to CheckFree dialog box, which contains the information about the transmitted payment and provides three lines on which you can make your inquiry.

6. Choose Transmit to send the payment inquiry to CheckFree.

Communicating with CheckFree

You can send messages to CheckFree at any time through your modem. This way, you easily and quickly can make general inquiries about the status of your account or to respond to inquiries from CheckFree. CheckFree also can communicate directly with you by electronic mail.

> **Note**
>
> If you want to issue a stop payment or inquire about a payment that you previously transmitted, you must use the Stop Payment and Inquiry commands from the Activities CheckFree menu. Don't use the E-Mail command to perform these activities. (Refer to the earlier sections "Making Electronic Payment Inquiries" and "Issuing a Stop Payment.")

Sending Electronic Mail to CheckFree

You can send an electronic message to CheckFree to inquire about your CheckFree account or to respond to an inquiry from CheckFree. To send an electronic mail message to CheckFree, follow these steps:

1. Turn on your modem.

2. From the Activities menu, choose CheckFree, and then choose E-Mail. The Read E-Mail window appears (see fig. 13.12).

3. Choose Create. Quicken displays the Transmit Message to CheckFree dialog box, shown in figure 13.13.

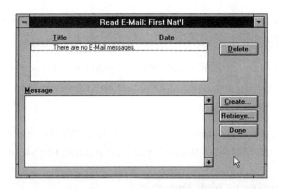

Fig. 13.12
Quicken displays
the Read E-Mail
window when you
select the E-Mail
option from
the Activities
CheckFree menu.

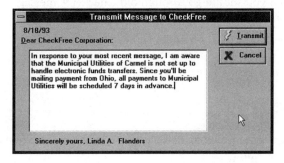

Fig. 13.13
The Transmit
Message to
CheckFree dialog
box shows your
typed message.

4. Type the message to CheckFree just as you type a message with a word processor. CheckFree wraps the end of the line to the following line so that you don't need to press Enter at the end of each line.

5. After you type the message, choose Transmit. Quicken initializes the modem and transmits the message to CheckFree.

Receiving Electronic Mail from CheckFree

CheckFree also can communicate with you by electronic mail. Each message you retrieve from CheckFree is entered, by title and date, in the Read E-Mail window (refer to fig. 13.12). You can read messages from CheckFree that you already have received at any time from the Read E-Mail window. Quicken saves all messages, in chronological order, until you delete them.

To receive electronic mail messages from CheckFree, follow these steps:

1. Turn on your modem.

2. From the Activities menu, choose CheckFree, and then choose E-Mail. The Read E-Mail window appears (refer to fig. 13.12).

3. To read an existing message, select the message title from the Title list box. The message appears in the Message area below.

4. To check for new messages from CheckFree, choose Retrieve. Quicken initializes the modem and retrieves any new messages from your electronic mailbox.

5. Quicken enters any new messages in the Title list box. Choose the title of the new message to display the message in the Message box.

Deleting Electronic Mail Messages

Occasionally, you should go through old CheckFree messages in the Read E-Mail window and delete those that are no longer important or relevant. To delete an electronic mail message, highlight the message in the Title list box and choose Delete.

Summary

This chapter described Quicken's electronic payment capability. You learned how to do the following:

- Complete the CheckFree paperwork to register for electronic bill-paying services

- Set modem preferences

- Set up a bank account for electronic payment

- Set up a normal payee to receive electronic payments

- Set up a fixed, recurring payee

- Edit and delete electronic payees

- Pay bills electronically

- Issue stop payment requests

- Make payment inquiries

- Communicate with CheckFree electronically

The next chapter begins Part III of *Using Quicken 3 for Windows*, "Planning for the Future with Quicken for Windows." In this part, you learn how to use Quicken as a financial planning tool to ensure that your future is financially sound. In the next chapter, you learn how to use Quicken's new financial calendar to schedule transactions and forecast your account balances.

II

Getting the Most

Part III

Planning for the Future with Quicken for Windows

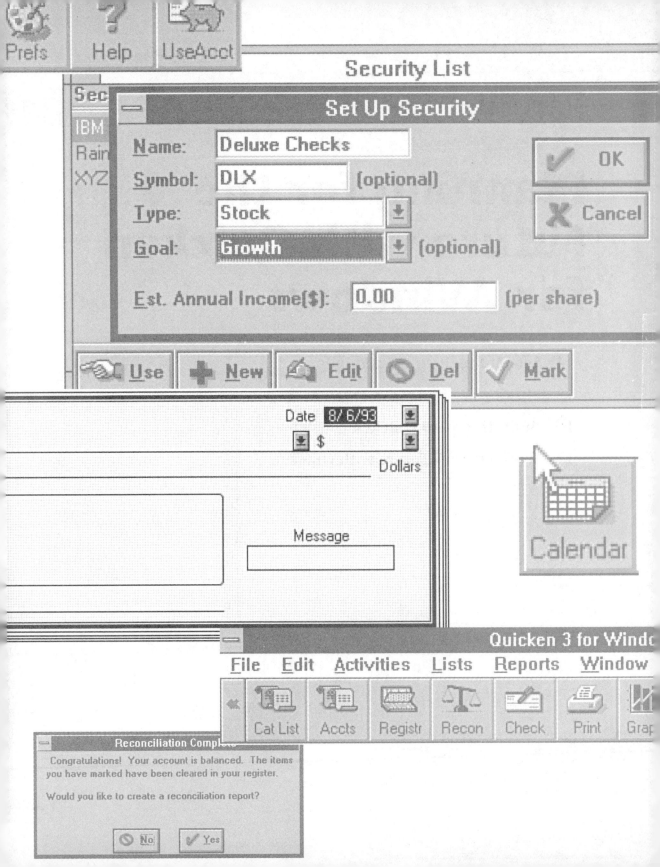

Chapter 14

Scheduling Future Transactions

With Quicken 3 for Windows, you may never again forget to pay the light bill, make a rent payment, or send a card on your mother-in-law's birthday. With Quicken's new feature to schedule transactions, you can set up bills that you know are coming due, and Quicken not only reminds you to pay them but enters the transactions for you. All you need to do is print the checks and mail them.

You also can schedule regular deposits (such as your paycheck) so that Quicken enters the deposit transaction in your Bank Account Register at regular intervals. For groups of recurring transactions that come due at the same time each period, you can set up a transaction group so that Quicken enters all transactions from the group at the same time.

> **Note**
>
> If you are a previous user of Quicken, you're probably familiar with transaction groups; however, in Quicken 3 for Windows, transaction groups combine scheduled transactions that have been previously memorized in Quicken.

Quicken provides two ways to schedule future transactions: through the Scheduled Transaction list or the new Financial Calendar. When you use the Financial Calendar, you "drag and drop" the transaction into its due date in the calendar. The calendar resembles any wall calendar you may have at home. To make the calendar even more helpful, you can add notes to the

In this chapter, you learn how to do the following:

- Pay bills by scheduling transactions

- Work with transactions in groups

- Use the Financial Calendar to schedule transactions

- Project cash flows

- Use Billminder to remind you to pay bills

III

Financial Calendar to remind you of special events such as birthdays, meetings, and so forth.

After you schedule your future transactions in Quicken, you can use the Financial Calendar's planning graph to project the balances of your accounts in the days and months ahead. The planning graph uses data from the Financial Planning Worksheet (which you provide) plus the scheduled transactions that you have entered in the Financial Calendar to show a projection of the state of your accounts each day of the selected month or period.

Scheduling Transactions

You can use Quicken to remind you about upcoming bills and deposits and to schedule those transactions ahead of time. You can schedule transactions that occur only once (such as a car repair bill) or recurring transactions that occur at regular intervals (such as your rent payment).

This chapter shows you how to schedule future transactions for payments other than amortized loan payments. You must set up loan or mortgage payments through the View Loans window. When you set up a loan, you are setting up the loan payment as a recurring transaction in Quicken. Refer to Chapter 10, "Tracking Loans," to learn how to set up a loan.

When you schedule a transaction in Quicken, you can choose to have Quicken enter and record the scheduled transaction when it's due. You also can select to have Quicken prompt you before entering the transaction so that you can change the details of the transaction, if necessary, before it's recorded. And, if you prefer not to have Quicken enter scheduled transactions for you, you can use the Scheduled Transactions feature for planning purposes only so that you can see the effect of upcoming bills and deposits on your finances through the Financial Planning Graph. (You learn about the Financial Planning Graph later in this chapter.) When Quicken enters scheduled transactions in the Register, you can then go into the Register and edit transactions as necessary.

You can schedule transactions in Quicken in two ways: through the Scheduled Transaction list or in the Financial Calendar. The next section explains how to set up a scheduled transaction through the Scheduled Transaction list. Later in this chapter, you learn how to schedule transactions in the Financial Calendar.

CPA TIP: Scheduling Recurring Transactions

To use Quicken most efficiently, set up a scheduled transaction for each recurring bill or deposit. Recurring *non-business* transactions may include mortgage payments, car payments, insurance premiums, health club dues, and preschool or day-care fees. (Note that you should set up loan payments, such as your mortgage and car payments, in the View Loans window, as discussed in Chapter 10.) Recurring *business* transactions may include bank loan payments, workers compensation insurance premiums, payroll taxes, and maintenance contracts.

The amount of a recurring transaction doesn't have to be the same for each period. Your monthly payroll taxes, for example, most likely are different each month because your total payroll isn't the same each month. You can schedule a transaction for payroll taxes, however, and select to have Quicken prompt you before entering the transaction each period. Then you can change the payment amount before the transaction is entered. You still save time because the payee, memo, category, and subcategory are entered for you, and Quicken reminded you (with plenty of advance notice) to make the payment.

Setting Up a Scheduled Transaction

You can set up a scheduled transaction for a transaction that occurs only once or for a recurring transaction. When you set up the scheduled transaction, you specify the frequency of payments or deposits. To set up a scheduled transaction in the Scheduled Transaction list, follow these steps:

1. Choose Scheduled Transaction from the Lists menu, or press Ctrl+J. Quicken displays the Scheduled Transaction list, shown in figure 14.1.

2. Choose the New button. Quicken displays the Set Up Scheduled Transaction dialog box, shown in figure 14.2.

3. From the Type drop-down list, select how you want the transaction recorded: as a payment in the Register (Pmt), as a deposit in the Register (Dep), as a check in the Write Checks window (Chk), or as an electronic payment to be transmitted to CheckFree (Epmt). (Refer to Chapter 13, "Paying Your Bills Electronically," for more on electronic payments.)

III

Planning for the Future

Fig. 14.1
The Scheduled
Transaction list
includes relative
information for
each scheduled
transaction.

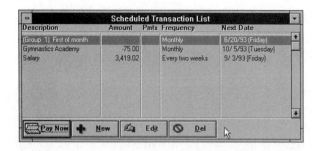

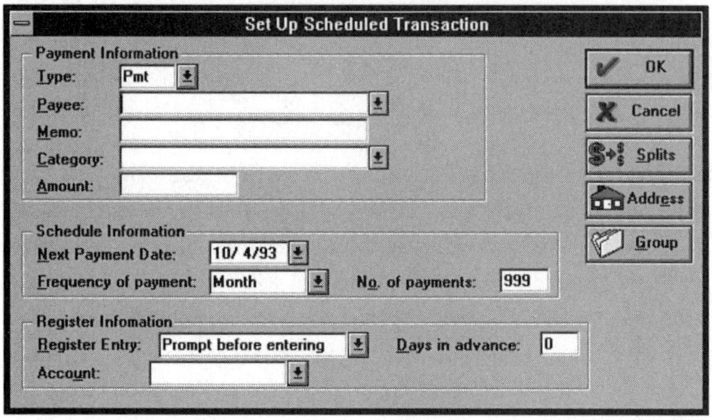

Fig. 14.2
Enter the informa-
tion about a trans-
action that you
want to schedule
in the Set Up
Scheduled Trans-
action dialog box.

For scheduled transactions that you select to record as a check in the
Write Checks window, choose the Address button to display the Printed
Check Information dialog box. Enter the address of the payee and an
optional message. Choose OK to return to the Set Up Scheduled Transaction dialog box. Quicken prints the payee's address and message on
the check when you print checks.

4. In the Payee drop-down list box, enter or select the payee to whom you
   make payment or from whom you receive a deposit.

5. (Optional) In the Memo text box, type a descriptive memo for the
   scheduled transaction, such as **Monthly rent**.

> **Note**
>
> The same memo is entered for every transaction, so be careful not to enter a
> specific date or month, such as **September rent**.

6. Select the category for the scheduled transaction from the Category drop-down list. To assign more than one category or subcategory to a scheduled transaction, choose the Splits button. In the Splits window, assign categories and amounts, and then choose OK to return to the Set Up Scheduled Transaction dialog box.

7. Enter the amount of the transaction in the Amount text box. This amount is the one Quicken enters in the Amount field when the transaction is entered each period.

8. In the Schedule Information section, select or enter the date that the next payment is due in the Next Payment Date drop-down list box. For recurring transactions, Quicken updates the next payment date each time a payment or deposit is made.

9. Select the payment frequency from the Frequency of Payment drop-down list to tell Quicken how often to enter the scheduled transaction. For transactions that occur only once, select Only Once. For recurring transactions, select Week, Two Weeks, Month, Quarter, Year, and so forth.

10. To record payments indefinitely, such as your rent payment or insurance premium, leave the No. of Payments text box at 999. Otherwise, enter the number of payments left to be made. If, for example, you originally owed 12 payments to a department store but already have made 2 payments, enter **10** in the No. of Payments text box.

11. In the Register Information section, enter the information that Quicken needs to enter the scheduled transaction. From the **Register** Entry drop-down list, select one of the following options:

    - *Enter w/o prompting.* When you start Quicken or open the Quicken file with scheduled transactions, Quicken enters scheduled transactions that are due. Quicken doesn't display a message or prompt before entering scheduled transactions.

    - *Prompt before entering.* When you start Quicken or open the Quicken file with scheduled transactions, Quicken displays the details of each scheduled transaction that is due and asks you to confirm the information and that you want the transaction entered. You can change the details of the transaction at this time or select not to enter the scheduled transaction.

■ *For planning only*. Quicken doesn't enter the scheduled transaction at any time; however, the transaction information is used in the Financial Planning Graph so that you can see the effect of future bills and deposits on your finances. (You learn about the Financial Planning Graph later in this chapter.)

12. From the Account drop-down list, select the account in which you want the scheduled transaction entered. For most bills and deposits, you probably will choose your checking account.

13. In the Days in Advance text box, tell Quicken when you want scheduled transactions entered by entering the number of days in advance that you want to be reminded of payments or deposits. If your insurance premiums are due on the 10th day of each month, for example, you may want Quicken to remind you of the payment and enter the transaction at least five days in advance so that you can write or print the check and allow enough time for the payment to arrive in the mail.

14. When the Set Up Scheduled Transaction dialog box is complete, choose OK. Quicken enters the scheduled transaction in the Scheduled Transaction list (refer to fig. 14.1).

Paying Scheduled Transactions

Quicken reminds you (through Billminder and Quicken Reminders) when scheduled transactions are due. If you entered a number in the Days in Advance text box when you set up a scheduled transaction, Quicken enters the transaction in the Register (or displays the transaction detail for confirmation) that many days before the payment's due date. Quicken enters the transaction as a postdated transaction. If, for example, the next payment date of a scheduled transaction is 12/15/93 and you entered 5 as the number of days in advance to be reminded of transactions that are due, Quicken enters the transaction in the Register on 12/10/93 but dates the transaction at 12/15/93.

You can pay scheduled transactions when they are due or in advance. You also can postpone payment of bills that are due or skip payment completely.

Paying Bills When Due. After you enter your future bills as scheduled transactions in Quicken, you won't have to worry about forgetting to pay them. Quicken will remind you through Billminder and Reminder messages that scheduled transactions are due. (You learn about Billminder and Reminder messages later in this chapter.)

If you elect to have Quicken enter scheduled transactions without prompting, you don't have to enter anything when scheduled transactions are due. When you start Quicken or open the Quicken file with scheduled transactions, Quicken enters and records the scheduled transactions that are due. If you write manual checks, the transaction is entered in the Register already. Just write the check and record the check number in the Num field in the Register. If you print checks with Quicken, scheduled transactions also are entered in the Write Checks window. Just print them and you're done.

Tip
After Quicken enters a scheduled transaction in the Register or the Write Checks window, you can make any necessary changes to the transaction.

If you select to have Quicken prompt you before entering scheduled transactions, follow these steps to pay bills when due:

1. When you start Quicken or open the Quicken file with scheduled transactions that are due, Quicken displays the Enter Schedule Transaction dialog box for each transaction (see fig. 14.3).

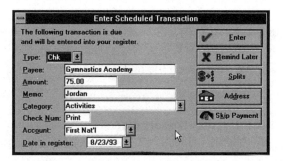

Fig. 14.3
If you select to have Quicken prompt you when scheduled transactions are due, the Enter Scheduled Transaction dialog box appears.

2. Review the transaction detail in the Enter Scheduled Transaction dialog box. If you need to change any of the transaction detail, you can do so now. To change the categories assigned to a split transaction, choose the Splits button and make the changes in the Splits window. To change the address to be printed on a check, choose the Address button.

When the information in the Enter Scheduled Transaction dialog box is correct, choose the Enter button to enter and record the transaction in the Register (and Write Checks window, if necessary). If the scheduled transaction was a one-time transaction (the frequency was set at Only Once), Quicken removes the transaction from the Scheduled Transaction list.

To postpone making payment or entering a scheduled transaction, choose Remind Later in the Enter Scheduled Transaction dialog box. The next time you start Quicken, you will be prompted again to enter the transaction.

To skip making a payment entirely, choose the Skip Payment button in the Enter Scheduled Transaction dialog box. If the scheduled transaction was a one-time transaction, Quicken removes it from the Scheduled Transaction list. If the transaction was set up as a recurring transaction, Quicken adjusts the next payment date for the following due date.

CPA TIP: Taking Early Payment Discounts

Take advantage of early payment discounts that vendors offer. Enter the transaction due dates for bills so you can pay invoices by the early payment date. If the terms of an invoice dated 1/31/94 are 2/10-net 30, you can take a 2 percent discount if you pay the invoice within 10 days of the invoice date (or by 2/10/94).

Paying Bills in Advance. You can pay bills or enter scheduled transactions at any time. If you're going on vacation, for example, you may want to pay bills early if their due date falls in the middle of your vacation.

To pay bills in advance, follow these steps:

1. From the Lists menu, choose Scheduled Transaction (or press Ctrl+J). Quicken displays the Scheduled Transaction list (refer to fig. 14.1).

2. Highlight the scheduled transaction that you want to pay in advance.

3. Choose the Pay Now button. If you select to have Quicken enter scheduled transactions without prompting, the transaction is entered in the Register. If you select to have Quicken prompt you before entering scheduled transactions, the Enter Scheduled Transaction dialog box appears for the selected transaction. Follow the steps in the preceding section for entering the scheduled transaction from the Enter Scheduled Transaction dialog box.

When you pay a scheduled transaction in advance, Quicken enters the transaction in the Register and uses the current date (unless you changed the date in the Enter Scheduled Transaction dialog box). For a scheduled transaction set up as a one-time transaction (the frequency is set at Only Once), Quicken removes the transaction from the Scheduled Transaction list after it's entered in the Register. For a recurring scheduled transaction, Quicken adjusts the next payment date for the following due date.

Reviewing Scheduled Transactions

Quicken stores all scheduled transactions in the Scheduled Transaction list, as shown earlier in figure 14.1. For each scheduled transaction in the list, Quicken shows the transaction description, the amount, the number of payments to be made, the frequency of payments, and the next payment due date.

Tip
If you want to print a copy of the Scheduled Transaction list, display the list and press Ctrl+P.

You can edit a scheduled transaction if you need to change any of the transaction details (such as the payment amount, frequency, and so forth). To edit a scheduled transaction, highlight the transaction in the Scheduled Transaction list and choose the Edit button. Quicken displays the Edit Scheduled Transaction dialog box (which resembles the Set Up Schedule Transaction dialog box shown in figure 14.2), where you can make any necessary changes.

You also can delete a scheduled transaction at any time. If, for example, you move to a house from an apartment where you were paying monthly rent, you can delete the scheduled transaction that you set up for your rent payment. To delete a scheduled transaction, highlight the transaction in the Scheduled Transaction list and choose the Del button. Quicken displays a message that you are about to delete a scheduled transaction. Choose OK to delete the scheduled transaction.

III

Planning for the Future

Note

If you want to discontinue making scheduled transactions but want to keep the scheduled transaction information in Quicken, just edit the transaction and change the value in the No. of Payments text box to **0**. You always can go back later and activate the scheduled transaction by changing the number of payments.

> ### CPA TIP: Scheduling Deposit Transactions
>
> If the company you work for uses an automatic deposit system to deposit your pay-check each pay period, you should schedule a deposit transaction for your paycheck. If you get paid on a regular basis, you can set the frequency in the **F**requency of Payment drop-down list box so that your deposit is entered in the Register each period. If you are a salaried employee and your paycheck is the same from pay period to pay period, you also can split your payroll deposit transaction so you can allocate to the correct categories federal tax withholding, state tax withholding, FICA (Social Security tax withholding), Medicare tax withholding, 401(k) deductions, medical insurance deductions, and so forth. Then each time Quicken records a deposit trans-action in the Register, the correct categories and amounts are entered.

Using Transaction Groups

A transaction group contains recurring transactions that you simultaneously pay or add to the Register. Transaction groups can consist of one or many transactions. You may, for example, want to set up a transaction group for the bills for which you don't receive invoices or statements (such as your rent or loan payments). You also may want to set up a transaction group for bills due at the same time each month (such as quarterly estimated tax payments and insurance premiums).

When you create a transaction group, you assign one or more memorized transactions to a group and then name it. You may set up, for example, a transaction group named *Monthly Bills*.

> ### Note
>
> A transaction must be memorized before it can be added to a transaction group.

Billminder and Quicken Reminder messages appear when you start your computer and again when you start Quicken or open a Quicken file with transaction groups that are due.

Quicken treats transaction groups the same as one scheduled transaction. When a transaction group is due, Quicken enters the transactions within the group in the Register (if you select to enter the transaction group without prompting), or it prompts you before entering the transactions within the group (if you select to prompt before entering transactions).

After you set up a transaction group, you can add, delete, or change transactions in the group. You also can delete an entire transaction group.

> ### Note
>
> If you used an earlier version of Quicken for Windows or Quicken for DOS and used transaction groups, you still can use those same transaction groups in Quicken 3 for Windows. When you install Quicken 3 for Windows, transaction groups from previous versions are converted automatically and saved to the Scheduled Transaction list.

Setting Up a Transaction Group

Before you can set up a transaction group, you must have Quicken memorize the transactions that you want included in the group. (Chapter 7, "Using Quicken Shortcuts," explains how to memorize transactions.) You can include one or several memorized transactions in a transaction group.

To set up a transaction group, follow these steps:

1. From the Lists menu, choose Scheduled Transaction (or press Ctrl+J). Quicken displays the Scheduled Transaction list (refer to fig. 14.1).

2. Choose the New button. Quicken displays the Set Up Scheduled Transaction dialog box (refer to fig. 14.2).

3. From the Account drop-down list box at the bottom of the dialog box, select the account into which the group transactions should be entered.

4. Choose the Group command button. Quicken displays the Set Up Transaction Group dialog box, shown in figure 14.4.

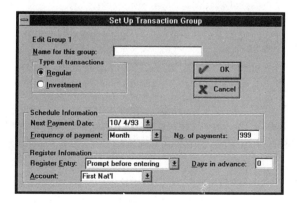

Fig. 14.4
Use the Set Up Transaction Group dialog box to enter the information for a new transaction group.

III

Planning for the Future

5. In the Name for this Group text box, enter a unique, descriptive name for the transaction group, such as **First Monthly**. You can include up to 20 characters in your transaction group names.

6. In the Type of Transactions section, select Regular for non-investment transactions or Investment to set up an investment transaction group. (Note that memorized investment transactions aren't included in the Memorized Transaction list. The Memorized Investment Transactions list contains investment transactions that you have memorized. See Chapter 15, "Monitoring Your Investments," to learn more about memorized investment transactions.)

7. Enter the scheduling and register information for the transaction group in the Schedule Information and Register Information sections. The information needed here is identical to these same sections in the Set Up Scheduled Transactions dialog box covered in "Setting Up a Scheduled Transaction" earlier in this chapter.

8. When the Set Up Transaction Group dialog box is complete, choose OK. Quicken displays the Assign Transactions to Group dialog box (shown in fig. 14.5), with the list of all memorized transactions. Now select the memorized transactions that you want to include in the transaction group.

Fig. 14.5

Select the transactions that you want to include in the transaction group from the Assign Transactions to Group dialog box.

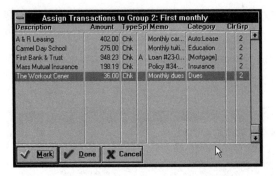

9. Highlight each transaction you want to include in the new transaction group. Choose the Mark button, press the space bar, or double-click the transaction to include it in the group. Quicken enters the group number in the Grp column next to each transaction that you select. To unmark a transaction, double-click the transaction, or highlight the transaction and choose the Mark button or press the space bar again.

You can't include a memorized transaction in more than one transaction group.

10. When you finish selecting transactions to include in the new group, choose the **D**one button. The new group is listed in the Scheduled Transaction list, as shown in figure 14.6.

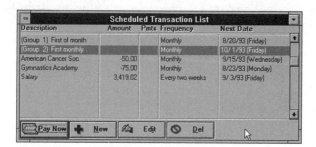

Fig. 14.6
Quicken enters transaction groups in the Scheduled Transaction list as a single item.

CPA TIP: Creating Transaction Groups for Taxes

Create transaction groups for payroll tax payments, sales tax payments, federal and state estimated tax payments, and property tax payments. These transactions seem to creep up on you without warning and involve penalties if submitted just one day late.

When a transaction group is due, Quicken displays Billminder and Reminder messages. If you select to enter a transaction group without prompting, Quicken enters all transactions within the group in the Register. If you select to have Quicken prompt you before entering a transaction group, Quicken displays the Enter Scheduled Transaction dialog box for each transaction within the group (refer to fig. 14.3).

Editing a Transaction Group

Because transaction groups segregate your checks into groups you pay together at one time, changes in payment due dates mean that you need to

III

Planning for the Future

change the transaction group. If you refinance your mortgage, for example, the due date may change from the 5th to the 15th. If you have separate transaction groups for checks you write at the beginning of the month and those you write during the middle of the month, you may need to change your transaction groups.

Note

If you need to make a change to a specific transaction within a transaction group, edit the transaction from the Memorized Transaction list. Refer to Chapter 7, "Using Quicken Shortcuts," to learn how to edit a memorized transaction.

You can change the schedule details, assign new transactions, or eliminate transactions from the group.

To edit a transaction group, follow these steps:

1. From the Lists menu, choose Scheduled Transaction (or press Ctrl+J) to display the Scheduled Transaction list.

2. Highlight the transaction group and choose the Edit button. Quicken displays the Edit Transaction Group dialog box, which mirrors the Set Up Transaction Group dialog box shown earlier in figure 14.4.

3. Change any of the information in the Edit Transaction Group dialog box. Choose OK.

4. Quicken displays the Assign Transactions to Group dialog box (refer to fig. 14.5). To add a new transaction to the group, double-click the transaction, or highlight the transaction and choose the Mark button or press the space bar. To eliminate a transaction from the transaction group, double-click the included transaction, or highlight the transaction and choose the Mark button or press the space bar.

   Quicken removes the group number from the Grp column for transactions that you eliminate from the group.

5. Choose the Done button when you are finished making changes to the transactions within the transaction group.

> **Note**
>
> If you include a memorized transaction in a transaction group and subsequently delete the transaction from the Memorized Transaction list, Quicken removes the memorized transaction from the transaction group.

Deleting a Transaction Group

You can delete transaction groups that you no longer use. When you delete a transaction group, Quicken permanently removes the transaction group from the Scheduled Transaction list, but doesn't delete the memorized transactions, which remain in the Memorized Transaction list.

To delete a transaction group, follow these steps:

1. From the Lists menu, choose Scheduled Transaction (or press Ctrl+J) to display the Scheduled Transaction list.

2. Highlight the transaction group you want to delete.

3. Choose the Del button. Quicken warns you that you are about to delete a scheduled transaction permanently.

4. Choose OK to delete the group. Choose Cancel to keep the transaction group in the list.

Using the Financial Calendar To Schedule Transactions

The second (and easiest) way to schedule transactions is directly into Quicken's new Financial Calendar (see fig. 14.7). To display the Financial Calendar, choose Financial Calendar from the Activities menu, press Ctrl+K, or click the Calendar button on the Iconbar. Not only can you schedule transactions directly into the Financial Calendar, you also can edit existing scheduled transactions, delete a scheduled transaction, or pay a scheduled transaction.

Quicken shows the current month when you display the Financial Calendar. You can change the month shown using the Prev and Next buttons on the Calendar button bar (at the top of the Financial Calendar). Choose the Prev button once to move to the preceding month; choose the Next button once to move to the next month.

III

Planning for the Future

Fig. 14.7

You easily can schedule trans- actions directly into Quicken's new Financial Calendar. You also can add notes to the Financial Calendar to remind you of birthdays, meetings, or other special events.

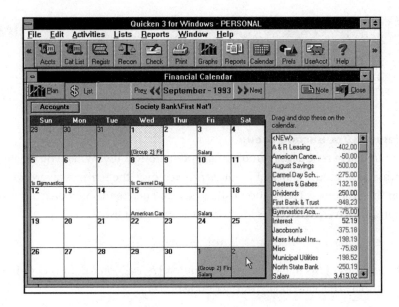

You also can change the calendar by clicking the date (September - 1993) between the Prev and Next buttons to display the Go To Date dialog box. Then enter the date that you want to change the calendar to and choose OK. This method works well for dates far into the future or past so that you don't have to click through several months.

The current date box in the calendar appears in a different color on color monitors, or is shaded on monochrome monitors. Notice that the trans- actions you entered previously in the Register are noted in the Financial Calendar. If you entered one transaction on the 5th of the month, for example, Quicken shows 1x (for one transaction) in the 5 date box.

Any scheduled transactions that you already have set up appear in the Finan- cial Calendar on the date they are scheduled to be recorded in the Register. For scheduled transactions, Quicken shows the payee's name in the date box.

You can see more detail for transactions shown in a date box by double- clicking the date box. Quicken shows the transactions in the Transactions Due window, where you can add a scheduled transaction, edit a scheduled transaction, delete a transaction, go to the Register entry for the transaction, or pay the transaction. You learn more about these activities later in this chapter.

Scheduling Transactions in the Calendar

You learned about scheduled transactions earlier in this chapter and how to set up a scheduled transaction in the Scheduled Transaction list. In this section, you learn how to schedule a future transaction directly into the Financial Calendar.

> **Note**
>
> Quicken treats scheduled transactions entered in the Financial Calendar *exactly* the same as scheduled transactions set up in the Scheduled Transaction list. Regardless of the method you use to set up a scheduled transaction, Quicken shows each scheduled transaction in the Financial Calendar in the date box for the next payment date. Future transactions scheduled in Quicken *are* shown in the Financial Calendar; however, they *aren't* entered in the Register until they become due.

To schedule a transaction in the Financial Calendar, follow these steps:

1. From the Activities menu, choose Financial Calendar, press Ctrl+K, or click the Calendar button on the Iconbar to display the Financial Calendar (refer to fig. 14.7).

2. Use the Prev and Next buttons to display the month in which you want to schedule a transaction. Or click the date between the Prev and Next buttons and enter the date in the Go To Date dialog box.

3. If the list of transactions isn't displayed on the right side of the Financial Calendar, choose the List button from the Calendar button bar. Quicken displays a list of transactions that you may want to schedule for the future. This list consists of transactions that you previously have entered in the Register, plus the memorized transactions from the Memorized Transaction list. The list shown in the Financial Calendar is the same as the drop-down list displayed from the Payee field of the Register or the Pay to the Order Of field in the Write Checks window.

4. To schedule a transaction from the list into the Calendar, point to the transaction with your mouse. The mouse pointer changes to the shape of a hand to show that the transaction can be picked up. Hold down the left mouse button as you move the mouse pointer to the date box that represents the date in which you want to schedule the transaction.

III

Planning for the Future

As you move the transaction to the Calendar, the mouse pointer changes again to a small calendar icon to show that you can drop the transaction into a day. Release the mouse button when the calendar icon is positioned in the proper date box in the Calendar. Quicken displays the Set Up Scheduled Transaction dialog box when you drop a transaction into a date box in the Calendar (see fig. 14.8).

Fig. 14.8

Drop a transaction from the list into a date box to display the Set Up Scheduled Transaction dialog box.

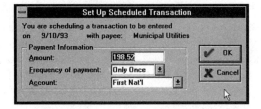

To schedule a transaction due 2/5/94, for example, point to the transaction in the list, hold the left mouse button, move the mouse pointer to the 5 date box (in the month of February - 1994), and then release the mouse button.

To schedule a new transaction in the Financial Calendar, drag the <New> item from the transaction list to the appropriate date box in the Calendar. When you release the left mouse button in the date box, Quicken displays the Set Up Scheduled Transaction dialog box that you saw earlier in figure 14.2.

5. For a previously entered transaction, confirm the information in the Set Up Scheduled Transaction dialog box (refer to fig. 14.8). You can make any necessary changes to the transaction. You can change, for example, the frequency of the transaction from Only Once to a recurring transaction (Week, Two Weeks, Month, and so forth).

   For a new scheduled transaction, complete the Set Up Scheduled Transaction dialog box as explained earlier in the section "Setting Up a Scheduled Transaction."

6. Choose OK to schedule the transaction in the Financial Calendar. Quicken shows Only Once scheduled transactions for payments with a red 1x in the date box. Deposit transactions scheduled Only Once are shown in the date box with a green 1x.

> **Note**
>
> You can schedule a transaction in the Financial Calendar into a date in the past. When you drop a transaction into a past date box, the mouse pointer changes to a register icon and Quicken displays the Edit Register Transaction dialog box with information about the transaction that Quicken is about to enter in the Register. You can change any information in the Edit Register Transaction dialog box. See the next section to learn about editing scheduled transactions in the Financial Calendar.

Editing Scheduled Transactions in the Financial Calendar

As you schedule transactions in the Financial Calendar, you can see the transactions that are due in the future. Each date box in the Financial Calendar can show only about four transactions, however. To review the details or to edit a scheduled transaction in the Financial Calendar, follow these steps:

1. Double-click the date box where the transaction that you want to see or edit is scheduled. Quicken displays the Transactions Due dialog box, with a list of transactions scheduled for that day (see fig. 14.9).

2. You can perform the following operations from the Transactions Due dialog box:

   ■ Set up a new transaction for the selected date by choosing the New button. Quicken displays the Set Up Scheduled Transaction dialog box (refer to fig. 14.2).

   ■ Change the details of the highlighted scheduled transaction for the selected date by choosing the Edit button. Quicken displays the Edit Scheduled Transaction dialog box, shown in figure 14.10. For recorded transactions in the Financial Calendar, Quicken displays the Edit Register Transaction dialog box, shown in figure 14.11. You edit a recorded transaction in the Financial Calendar just as you would in the Register.

Tip
You also can display the Transactions Due dialog box by clicking the selected date box in the Financial Calendar with the *right* mouse button.

Fig. 14.9
Double-click a date box in the Financial Calendar to see the transactions due for that date.

III

Planning for the Future

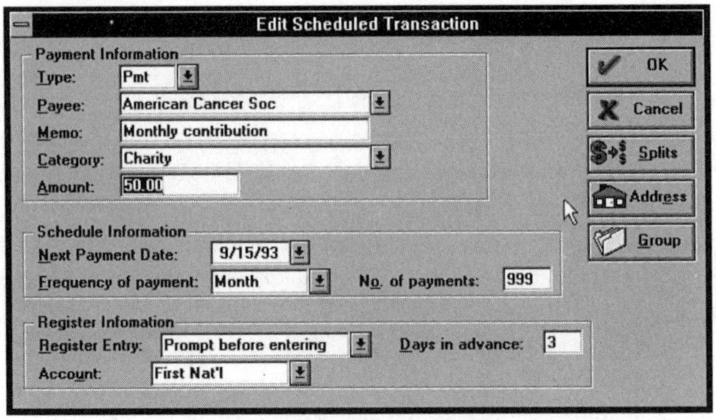

Fig. 14.10
Quicken displays the details of a scheduled transaction in the Edit Scheduled Transaction dialog box.

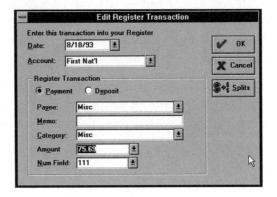

Fig. 14.11
Quicken displays the details of a past transaction entered in the Register in the Edit Register Transaction dialog box.

- Delete the highlighted scheduled transaction for the selected date by choosing the Delete button.

- For recorded transactions, the Transactions dialog box includes the Register button, which you can use to go directly to the highlighted transaction in the Register.

- Pay the highlighted scheduled transaction immediately by choosing the Pay Now button.

To remove the Transactions Due dialog box without performing an operation, click its Control menu box, click anywhere outside the dialog box, or press Esc.

Paying Scheduled Transactions from the Calendar

Quicken reminds you when scheduled transactions in the Financial Calendar are due, just like scheduled transactions that you set up in the Scheduled

Transaction list. If you choose to enter a scheduled transaction without prompting, Quicken enters the transaction in the Register when the transaction is due (or ahead of the actual scheduled date if you entered the number of days in advance to remind you when the transaction is due). If you choose to have Quicken prompt you before entering a scheduled transaction, Quicken displays the details of the transaction before entering it in the Register.

You can pay scheduled transactions in the Calendar when they are due or in advance.

Paying When Due. Follow the same steps for paying a transaction when it is due, as explained earlier in the section "Paying Bills When Due."

Paying in Advance. To pay transactions in advance from the Financial Calendar, follow these steps:

1. Double-click the date box where the transaction you want to pay in advance is scheduled. Quicken displays the Transactions Due dialog box (refer to fig. 14.9).

2. Highlight the transaction that you want to pay in advance.

3. Choose the Pay Now button. If you selected to have Quicken prompt you before entering the scheduled transaction, the Enter Scheduled Transaction dialog box appears (refer to fig. 14.3). Review the details of the transaction, make any necessary changes, and choose OK to enter the transaction in the Register or the Write Checks window now.

If you selected to enter the scheduled transaction without prompting, Quicken enters the transaction in the Register immediately.

Adding Notes to the Financial Calendar

Not only can you schedule your future transactions in the Financial Calendar, you also can use the calendar to enter reminder notes just as you would in your wall or desk calendar. Quicken doesn't display the text of a note in the Financial Calendar. Instead, a small square or note box is displayed in the date box for the date in which you enter a note.

Tip
You can color-code note boxes so that you can set up a system for spotting different kinds of notes.

III

Planning for the Future

> **Note**
>
> You can add only one note at a time in any one date in the Financial Calendar.

To add a note to the Financial Calendar, follow these steps:

1. Click the date box in the Financial Calendar in which you want to add a note (or press Alt+N).

2. Choose the Note button on the Calendar button bar. Quicken displays the Note window, shown in figure 14.12.

Fig. 14.12
Type your note or reminder in the Note window.

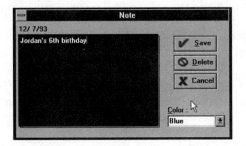

3. Type the text of your note. Press Enter to move to the next line.

4. In the Color drop-down list, select the color in which you want to display the note box in the Calendar. If you're entering a personal note (such as your spouse's birthday), for example, you could select blue. For business notes, you could use green. Develop a color scheme that is most useful to you.

5. Choose the Save button to save the note in the Calendar.

Quicken displays the note as a small square, or note box, in the upper-right corner of the date box for the date in which it was entered. The note box is the color that you selected for the note.

To review a note in the Financial Calendar, click the note box. Quicken displays the Note window with the text of the note.

To delete a note in the Financial Calendar, click the note box. At the Note window, choose the Delete button.

Projecting Future Cash Flows

After you set up your scheduled transactions in Quicken, you can use the new
Financial Planning Graph to project the balances in your accounts based on
information you enter in the Financial Planning Worksheet (which includes
your estimated cash flows) plus your scheduled transactions (which include
your known, future cash flows).

For Quicken to reflect the state of your accounts accurately, you must enter
estimated transaction data and future transaction data. You already learned
how to set up scheduled transactions so that Quicken has the future transaction data. You also must enter estimated future transaction information,
however, so that Quicken can factor this data into its projections. Estimated
transaction data is entered in the Financial Planning Worksheet.

In the following sections, you learn how to use Quicken to project your
future cash flows so that you can see the state of your accounts after future
financial obligations are met and income is received. You learn how to use
the Financial Planning Graph and how to enter estimated data in the Financial Planning Worksheet.

Reviewing the Financial Planning Graph

The Financial Planning Graph is part of the Financial Calendar. To display the graph, choose the **Plan** button from the calendar button bar.
Figure 14.13 shows the Financial Planning Graph displayed at the bottom
of the Financial Calendar.

The graph shows a projection of the state of your accounts for the month
now shown. Balances before the current date are shown in yellow or appear
lighter. Balances for future dates are shown in blue or appear darker. The
balance for the current date is shown in green or black. You can change the
date range that the graph covers by choosing the **Dates** button. Quicken displays the Graph View dialog box, where you can change the date range from
one month to two months, three months, six months, one year, or two years.
Select a date range and choose OK. (When you change the date range of the
graph, the month shown in the Financial Calendar doesn't change.)

The graph plots the dates along the horizontal axis and rounded dollar values
for the accounts along the vertical axis. To see an exact account balance for a
selected date, point to the date on the graph (the shape of the mouse pointer
changes to a hand) and then hold down the left mouse button. Quicken

III

Planning for the Future

shows the exact dollar value of the account in a small box. Release the mouse button to remove the amount box from the graph.

Fig. 14.13
The Financial Planning Graph appears in the Financial Calendar when you choose the **Plan** button from the calendar button bar.

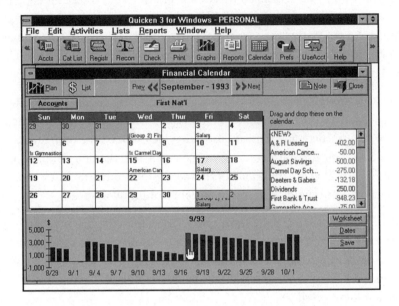

Typically, the Financial Planning Graph should show gradual rises or declines in account balances. The first time you display the graph, however, you probably will notice some sharp rises and declines. That's because Quicken doesn't yet have all the information that it needs to reflect the balances accurately in your accounts. The data that Quicken uses in the Financial Planning Graph is based on the future transactions that you have scheduled in the Calendar *and* other estimated transaction data entered in the Financial Planning Worksheet. The next section shows you how to complete the Financial Planning Worksheet so that the graph shows the appropriate account balances.

By default, Quicken includes the balances in all your cash flow accounts (bank accounts, cash accounts, and credit card accounts) in the Financial Planning Graph. You can, however, show the balance from only one account or select exactly which accounts you want to include in the graph. You learn how to select accounts later in this chapter.

Completing the Financial Planning Worksheet

As you have learned, the Financial Planning Graph uses data from your future scheduled transactions *and* estimates of all other income and expenses not scheduled in the calendar. You enter estimated future income and expenses in the Financial Planning Worksheet. To display the worksheet, choose the Worksheet button in the Financial Planning Graph. Figure 14.14 shows the Financial Planning Worksheet.

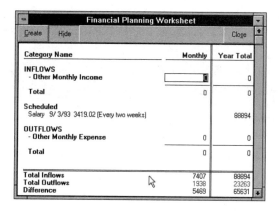

Fig. 14.14

Enter estimated income and expense projections in the Financial Planning Worksheet.

The Financial Planning Worksheet includes INFLOWS (income) and OUT-FLOWS (expenses) sections, a column for monthly data, and a Year Total column. Quicken shows one line for Other Monthly Income in the INFLOWS section and one line for Other Monthly Expenses in the OUTFLOWS section of the worksheet. The amount shown for these lines in the Monthly column is zero until you enter estimated amounts. Each scheduled transaction that you entered in the Financial Calendar or the Scheduled Transaction list is listed in the Scheduled section for INFLOWS and OUTFLOWS.

The bottom of the worksheet shows the total inflows, total outflows, and the difference between the two. A positive difference means that your estimated income more than covers your estimated expenses. A negative difference means that your estimated expenses exceed your estimated income.

Before you begin to complete the Financial Planning Worksheet, you should select the accounts that you want to include in the Financial Planning Graph (see the next section).

Selecting Accounts To Include in the Worksheet. By default, Quicken includes all your cash flow accounts (bank accounts, cash accounts, and credit card accounts) in the Financial Planning Graph. You can select the accounts that you want to include, however. If you have a credit card account set up in Quicken but don't use it, for example, you may want to select just your checking account. If you're interested in tracking your available funds, you may choose your checking account, savings account, and CD account. If funds exist in accounts that you don't intend to use for spending or for a specific savings goal, don't include that account.

CPA TIP: Excluding Retirement Plan Accounts

You shouldn't include your IRA or 401(k) accounts in cash flow projections. These accounts represent tax-deferred retirement accounts that are heavily penalized if funds are withdrawn before age 59 1/2 and not reinvested in another retirement plan.

To select accounts to include in projections, follow these steps:

1. Choose the Accounts button in the Financial Calendar. Quicken displays the Select Accounts to Include dialog box, shown in figure 14.15.

Fig. 14.15
Choose the accounts that you want to include in your cash flow projections in the Select Accounts to Include dialog box.

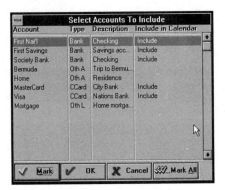

2. Highlight the account that you want to select.

3. Double-click the account, or highlight the account and then choose the Mark button or press the space bar. Quicken marks the accounts selected in the Include in Calendar column. Choose the Mark All button to include all accounts. To deselect an account, double-click the account or highlight the account, and choose the Mark button or press the space bar.

4. When you are finished selecting accounts, choose OK to return to the Financial Calendar. The Financial Planning Graph should look much different because other accounts are included.

Completing the Worksheet Manually. Now that you have selected the appropriate accounts to use in projections, you're ready to complete the Financial Planning Worksheet. Quicken provides three methods for entering estimated income and expenses in the worksheet: manually entering amounts in each category, using data from previous transactions in the Register, or using budgeted data. This section describes how to complete the Financial Planning Worksheet manually.

To enter estimates of your income and expenses in the Financial Planning Worksheet, follow these steps:

1. Display the Financial Planning Worksheet, as explained earlier.

2. Choose the Hide button to display all your income and expense categories in the worksheet.

3. Move to the monthly amount field for each income and expense category and enter a monthly estimate. As you enter amounts in categories, Quicken annualizes the amount and enters the result in the Year Total column.

> **Caution**
>
> Remember that the Financial Planning Worksheet already includes your scheduled transactions. Don't double-count income or expenses by entering amounts from scheduled transactions as estimated income or expenses. If you set up a scheduled transaction for your salary every two weeks, for example, *don't* enter an amount in the Salary category. Your salary already is accounted for in the Scheduled list of the INFLOWS section.

4. When you finish entering estimates of your income and expenses, choose the Hide button again to hide any categories with zero amounts.

5. Choose the Close button. Quicken asks whether you want to save unscheduled amounts before exiting. Choose Yes to save the worksheet and go back to the Financial Calendar. Choose No to exit without saving worksheet changes. Choose Cancel to continue working in the worksheet.

Using AutoCreate or Budget Data To Complete the Worksheet. Because entering estimated income and expenses is tedious and cumbersome, Quicken provides two other methods for completing the Financial Planning

Worksheet. Both methods are significantly faster and probably more accurate than completing the worksheet manually.

If you have been using Quicken for a while, you can estimate your future income and expenses based on past transactions in the Register. With the AutoCreate option, you select the date range for transactions that you want Quicken to use from the Register. Quicken searches the Register for transactions within the specified date range, accumulates transaction amounts by category, and enters the amounts in the appropriate category line in the Financial Planning Worksheet.

Or, if you have set up a budget in Quicken, you can enter your budgeted income and expenses in the worksheet. Quicken uses the budgeted amounts for each income and expense category in the Budget Spreadsheet to enter projected income and expenses in the Financial Planning Worksheet.

To complete the Financial Planning Worksheet from past transactions in the Register or budgeted data, follow these steps:

1. In the Financial Planning Worksheet, choose the Create button. Quicken displays the Create Unscheduled Amounts dialog box, shown in figure 14.16.

Fig. 14.16
Select the method you want to use to complete the worksheet in the Create Unscheduled Amounts dialog box.

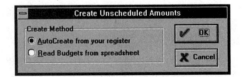

2. Select the AutoCreate from Your Register option button if you want to use past transactions from your Register to enter income and expense projections in the worksheet.

   Select the Read Budgets from Spreadsheet option button if you want to use budgeted amounts from the Budget Spreadsheet to enter income and expense projections in the worksheet.

3. Choose OK. If you selected to use budgeted data to complete the worksheet, Quicken enters the amounts from categories in the Budget Spreadsheet in the Financial Planning Worksheet. Skip to step 6.

4. If you selected to use past transactions from the Register, Quicken displays the AutoCreate Budget dialog box. In the From and To text boxes,

enter the date range for the transactions that you want Quicken to use to enter projected amounts. Then tell Quicken how you want amounts rounded: nearest $1, $10, or $100. If you want to omit certain categories from the Financial Planning Worksheet, choose the Select Categories button to display the list of categories. By default, Quicken uses any category that it finds in the date range of transactions.

5. When the AutoCreate Budget dialog box is complete, choose OK. Quicken analyzes the transactions within the specified date range in your Register and enters category amounts in the Financial Planning Worksheet.

6. Review the worksheet. The Monthly column contains unscheduled amounts from past transactions or budgeted data. The Year Total column shows scheduled and unscheduled amounts on an annual basis.

Notice that the Financial Planning Worksheet already includes your scheduled transactions. Therefore, some duplicate amounts are probably in the worksheet. When you complete the worksheet with past transaction data or budgeted data, the scheduled transaction amounts are included in their respective categories.

7. Edit the worksheet to deduct any duplicate amounts from the categories section. You learn how to edit the worksheet in the next section.

8. Choose the Close button. Quicken asks whether you want to save unscheduled amounts before exiting. Choose Yes to save the worksheet and go back to the Financial Calendar. Choose No to exit without saving worksheet changes. Choose Cancel to continue working in the worksheet.

The Financial Planning Graph should look much different now that the Financial Planning Worksheet is complete.

Editing the Worksheet. If you need to modify the Financial Planning Worksheet, you can change any of the amounts entered in the Monthly column for income and expense categories. You can't change a scheduled transaction amount (that appears in the Year Total column) from the worksheet, however.

To change an amount in the Monthly column, move to the amount field and type a new number. If you need to add an income or expense that doesn't fit into a category, enter amounts in the Other Monthly Income or Other Monthly Expense fields.

To change scheduled transaction amounts in the Year Total column, go back to the Financial Calendar and edit the scheduled transaction.

After you finish making changes to the Financial Planning Worksheet, choose the Close button. Quicken asks whether you want to save unscheduled amounts before exiting. Choose Yes to save the worksheet and go back to the Financial Calendar. Choose No to exit without saving worksheet changes. Choose Cancel to continue working in the worksheet.

Saving the Worksheet

As you now know, the Financial Planning Graph uses data from the scheduled transactions that you set up in the Financial Calendar or the Scheduled Transaction list, *plus* the data from the Financial Planning Worksheet. The graph shows the balance in your account(s) as of each day in the selected period. But what if you want to compare what has actually happened in your accounts to what you thought would happen when you first completed the worksheet?

With Quicken, you can save different projections so that you can compare actual income and expenses against projected income and expenses or so that you can perform "what-if" analyses to see the effects of hypothetical transactions. Quicken enables you to save two different projections: Scenario 1 and Scenario 2. When you save different projections, Quicken plots the previously saved projection over the actual history of your account balances in the Financial Planning Graph so that you can make a visual comparison.

To save a projection, follow these steps:

1. Choose the Save button in the Financial Planning Graph. Quicken displays the Show Saved Projection dialog box, shown in figure 14.17.

Fig. 14.17

You can save two different projections in the Show Saved Projection dialog box.

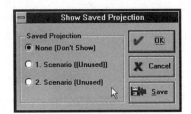

2. Select one of the Scenario option buttons. After you save a projection as Scenario 1 or 2, Quicken enters the date saved next to the Scenario option under which it was saved.

3. Choose the Save button to save the projection.

4. Choose OK to return to the Financial Calendar. Quicken plots the saved projection as a line of dots in the Financial Planning Graph (see fig. 14.18).

> **Note**
>
> To remove the saved projection line from the Financial Planning Graph, display the Show Saved Projection dialog box (shown earlier in fig. 14.17) by choosing the Save button. Then select the None (Don't Show) option button. Choose OK to return to the graph.

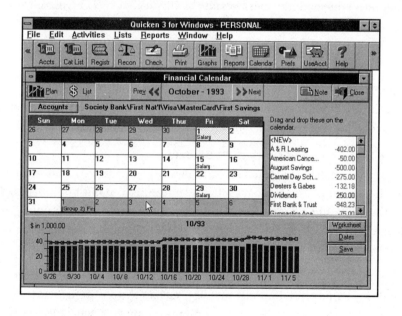

Fig. 14.18
Previously saved projections are plotted as a line of dots in the Financial Planning Graph.

To retrieve a saved projection, follow these steps:

1. Choose the Save button in the Financial Calendar. Quicken displays the Show Saved Projection dialog box (refer to fig. 14.17).

2. Select the scenario under which you saved the projection that you want to retrieve.

3. Choose OK to return to the Financial Calendar and the Financial Planning Graph. The retrieved projection is plotted in the graph as a line of dots.

> **Note**
>
> Although you can save only two projection scenarios, you can overwrite a saved projection with an updated projection. Just select one of the used scenario options in the Show Saved Projection dialog box (refer to fig. 14.17).

Getting Reminders To Pay Bills

Tip
You will find Quicken's Reminder messages great for prompting you to pay bills for which you don't receive an invoice (such as rent, payroll taxes, and loan payments).

Quicken includes two reminder features that display messages when scheduled transactions or transaction groups are due: Billminder and Reminder. Billminder and Reminder messages also alert you about other Quicken activities that are due (such as electronic payments to be transmitted if you use CheckFree).

When you start your computer or when you start Windows, a Quicken Billminder message appears if Quicken finds operations that need to be performed today. When you start Quicken or open a Quicken file, a Quicken Reminder message appears if Quicken detects activities that are due.

Using Billminder and Quicken Reminders

When you installed Quicken 3 for Windows (see Appendix A), you selected whether or not to use Quicken's Billminder feature. You must have selected to install Billminder during installation for Billminder to be active in Quicken. If you didn't, however, you can install Billminder now (see the next section).

When Billminder is active, each time you turn on your computer or start Windows, a Quicken Billminder message, such as the one in figure 14.19, appears if checks need to be printed, or if upcoming bills, scheduled transaction groups, investment reminders, or electronic payments (if you use CheckFree) are due. To remove a Quicken Billminder message from the screen, choose OK or press Enter.

Fig. 14.19
A Quicken Bill-
minder message
appears if you
have upcoming
bills or scheduled
transaction groups
due.

Note

When you installed Quicken 3 for Windows, if you selected the From **DOS** at Boot Time option, a Quicken Billminder message will appear when you start your computer. If you selected the At **W**indows start-up option, a Quicken Billminder message will appear when you start Windows. The Quicken Billminder icon opens when you select to display Billminder messages at Windows start-up.

When Quicken Reminders are active, a Quicken Reminder message appears when you start Quicken or open a Quicken file. When checks are due to print, or when scheduled transactions, investment reminders, or electronic payments are due in a Quicken file, a Quicken Reminder message appears (such as the one shown in fig. 14.20). To remove the Quicken Reminder message from the screen, click the Control menu box or press Esc.

Fig. 14.20
A Quicken Remin-
ders message
appears when you
start Quicken or
open a Quicken
file with due items.

Installing Billminder

Billminder is active after you install Quicken 3 for Windows and select to install Billminder. If you didn't select to install Billminder during install-ation, you can reinstall the program over your existing program files and select to install Billminder. When you reinstall Quicken, your data files aren't disturbed.

If you don't want to reinstall the program, you can edit your AUTOEXEC.BAT or WIN.INI files, as discussed in the Quicken user's manual.

III

Planning for the Future

> ### Caution
>
> Be careful if you decide to edit the AUTOEXEC.BAT or WIN.INI files in your system. These files contain crucial batch files that control how your system works. Making a backup copy of these files before you start to edit them is a good idea, to prevent any damage to the files that can't be remedied.

Setting Billminder and Reminder Preferences

By default, Billminder (if it was installed) and Reminders are turned on and are set up to remind you three business days in advance of postdated checks, scheduled transactions, transaction groups, and investment reminders that are due.

You can turn off Billminder and Reminders or change the number of business days in advance to be reminded of due items by setting Billminder preferences.

To set Billminder preferences, follow these steps:

1. From the Edit menu, choose Preferences, or click the Prefs button on the Iconbar. Quicken displays the Quicken for Windows Preferences dialog box.

2. Choose the Billminder preference button. Quicken displays the Billminder Preferences dialog box, shown in figure 14.21.

Fig. 14.21

You can deactivate Billminder or Reminders in the Billminder Preferences dialog box.

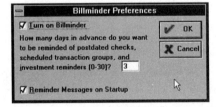

3. To turn off Billminder, choose the Turn on Billminder check box to remove the check mark.

4. To change the number of business days in advance that you are reminded of items that are due, type over the number in the next text box with a number from 0 to 30.

5. To turn off Reminder messages, click the Reminder Messages on Startup check box to remove the check mark.

6. Choose OK to save Billminder preferences and return to the Quicken for Windows Preferences dialog box.

7. Choose the Done button to close the Quicken for Windows Preferences window.

Summary

In this chapter, you learned how to use Quicken to enter future transactions that are due and to project the state of your accounts based on future cash inflows and outflows.

You learned how to do the following:

- Set up scheduled transactions

- Pay scheduled transactions

- Set up a transaction group

- Pay a transaction group

- Schedule future transactions in the Financial Calendar

- Pay scheduled transactions from the Financial Calendar

- Add notes to the Calendar

- Use the Financial Planning Graph

- Use the Financial Planning Worksheet

- Install Billminder

- Set Billminder preferences

In the next chapter, you learn about one of the more advanced features in Quicken—the Investment Register. You learn how to enter your current security positions and how to update your investment portfolio when you buy and sell securities. You also learn how to update the value of your investment portfolio to account for changing security prices.

III

Planning for the Future

Chapter 15

Monitoring Your Investments

Quicken provides a Register specifically for investments. You enter all your security holdings and transactions in the Register for each investment account you set up. The Register not only provides a way to track your investment transactions but also shows you how your investments are performing and the market value of your investments.

And now in Quicken 3 for Windows, you enter investment transactions (such as buying and selling securities, recording dividends and interest, and option trades) in new forms that prompt you for the information that Quicken needs to record the transaction. You still can enter investment transactions directly in the Register, but the new investment forms ensure that your transaction information is complete.

Another new feature in Quicken 3 for Windows deals with selling securities that were purchased at different times, or in different lots. When you sell securities, you can now specify which lots are being sold.

The Portfolio View window for investment accounts is also new in Quicken 3 for Windows. From the Investment Register, you can change to the Portfolio View to see a snapshot of your security portfolio. This snapshot shows the current market value, the return on investment, price changes, and other important data.

You now can use the QuickZoom feature in the Portfolio View of an Investment Register to edit, delete, or set up new securities. You also can use Quick-Zoom to create a QuickReport that lists the underlying transactions of the security in the Portfolio View.

In this chapter, you learn how to do the following:

- Set up investment accounts

- Set up securities

- Use the Investment Register

- Use Quick-Report to get an instant transaction listing

- Use the Portfolio View window

- Use QuickZoom to examine portfolio detail

- Update security prices

- Create a price history

- Graph security prices

- Import security prices into Quicken

III

Planning for the Future

Quicken's investment accounts show you more information about your securities. Quicken 3 for Windows includes 18 measures of investment performance and value. You now can determine, for example, a security's estimated income, investment yield, return on investment, and internal rate of return.

Quicken 3 for Windows also enables you to designate the tax status of an investment account as you set it up. You can designate an account as tax-deferred if you're setting up a 401(k) or 403(k), IRA, annuity, or Series EE and HH U.S. savings bond account. When you designate an account as tax-deferred, Quicken excludes transactions from the accounts in tax reports.

This chapter shows you how to prepare to monitor your investments with Quicken and how to track mutual funds and other investments using the Quicken Investment Register. The end of this chapter provides tips on investing and recording investment transactions.

> **Note**
>
> To save you from reviewing material you already know, this chapter doesn't explain the parts of the Investment Register that are like the other Quicken Registers you have examined in previous chapters. If you aren't well-acquainted with the basics of using Quicken, refer to Part I of this book, "Learning Quicken for Windows."

Preparing To Monitor Investments

To monitor investments with Quicken, you need to set up an investment account. When you set up an investment account, you must specify whether the account is a mutual fund account or regular investment account. The basic difference between the two accounts is difficult to grasp. If you learn the difference now, however, you will find deciding when to set up mutual fund accounts and when to set up regular investment accounts much easier.

A *mutual fund account* is a simplified investment account that keeps track of the market value and number of shares you hold of a single mutual fund. A *mutual fund* is an open-end management company that pools the money of many investors and uses it to establish a portfolio of securities. An investment advisor or a portfolio manager manages the securities of the investors.

The *regular investment account* is a more powerful investment account that you use for other investments and investment groups. The regular investment account keeps track of the market value of multiple securities, the shares, and the cash balance. (The cash balance usually represents the money with which you buy additional stocks, bonds, and so on.)

Given these differences, the easiest approach is to set up a mutual fund account for each mutual fund investment you hold, set up a regular investment account for each brokerage account you hold, and set up a regular investment account for any collection of individual investments you want to track and manage together in one Register. (If, for example, you just want to track your investment in IBM stock, set up a regular investment account named IBM.) As you work with the Quicken investment options, you will be able to fine-tune these suggestions.

CPA TIP: Investing in a Mutual Fund

A mutual fund is an excellent way to diversify your portfolio. When a single company's stock held in the fund declines, the impact on the total value of the mutual fund's portfolio is less because the fund's portfolio is made up of many securities. Also, securities appreciating in value offset security values that decline.

You also can invest in a mutual fund if you don't want to manage your own portfolio by making decisions as to which securities to buy and sell. Large mutual funds usually hire the best investment advisors available.

Another plus for mutual funds: Transaction costs when buying and selling shares in a mutual fund are often less than commission costs when buying and selling individual securities through a broker.

Working with Regular Investment Accounts

As mentioned earlier, you can set up two types of investment accounts in Quicken: a regular investment account and a mutual fund account. In this section, you learn how to set up a regular investment account. You also learn how to set up the securities that you already own and new ones you buy so that Quicken has the information it needs to track your investments accurately. This section also shows you how to enter opening share balances so that your current holdings are reflected in your new investment account.

III

Planning for the Future

Setting Up a Regular Investment Account

A regular investment account is designed to track one or more securities in the account. Regular investment accounts may have a cash balance (like a brokerage account). The Register for a regular investment account updates the cash balance after every transaction and also shows the current market value of the account. The Register, however, doesn't show the share balance (total number of shares) of securities held in the account.

To set up a regular investment account, follow these steps:

1. From the Activities menu, choose Create New Account. Quicken displays the Select Account Type dialog box.

2. Select the Investment Account option button.

3. Choose OK. Quicken displays the New Account Information dialog box, shown in figure 15.1.

Fig. 15.1

Enter the information about the investment account in the New Account Information dialog box.

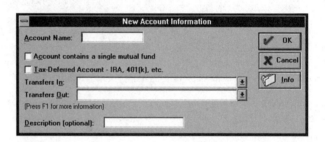

4. In the Account Name text box, enter a name for the account. The account name can be up to 15 characters long and can contain any characters except the following:

    :] [/ | ^

   You can include spaces in the account name.

5. Make sure that the Account Contains a Single Mutual Fund check box is blank so that Quicken sets up a regular investment account.

6. If the earnings from the investment account you are setting up are tax-deferred (the tax is assessed in a later time period than the earnings are received), select the Tax-Deferred Account check box. Examples of tax-deferred accounts are IRAs, 401(k) accounts, and annuities.

7. From the Transfers In drop-down list box, select the tax form or schedule to which transfers to the account should be assigned. In the Transfers Out drop-down list box, select the tax form or schedule for transfers from the account.

8. (Optional) In the Description text box, enter an investment account description, such as **Ali's College Fund**. You can use 21 characters in this description.

9. To enter additional information about the investment account, choose the Info button and enter the information in the Additional Account Information dialog box. Choose OK to save the information and return to the New Account Information dialog box.

10. Choose OK. Quicken adds the regular investment account to the Account list. If this investment account isn't the first one in your file, Quicken displays the Register for the new investment account.

   If this is the first investment account that you have set up, Quicken displays a dialog box that asks if you want to add a Portfolio View icon to the Iconbar for updating your investments. Choose Yes if you want to add the icon; otherwise, choose No. If you choose to add the icon, Quicken inserts the new Port icon at the end of the Iconbar. Use this icon to switch to the Portfolio View window. (You learn about the Portfolio View window later in this chapter.)

Note

When you set up an investment account, Quicken automatically adds investment categories to your Category & Transfer list. Investment categories all begin with an underline (_DivInc, _IntInc, and so forth). You can't delete an investment category or edit its name, but you can edit its description.

Setting Up Securities

Before you can begin entering investment transactions, you must set up securities in Quicken. When you set up a security, you define the security's symbol, type, goal, and estimated annual income. Quicken saves securities in the Security list.

To set up a security, follow these steps:

1. From the Lists menu, choose Select Security (or press Ctrl+Y). Quicken displays the Security list, shown in figure 15.2.

Fig. 15.2

Quicken saves securities in the Security list.

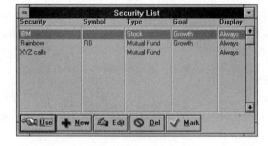

2. Choose the New button. Quicken displays the Set Up Security dialog box, shown in figure 15.3.

Fig. 15.3

Enter information about a new security in the Set Up Security dialog box.

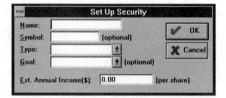

3. In the Name text box, type the name of the security. You can use up to 17 characters, including spaces.

4. In the Symbol text box, enter the symbol for the mutual fund if you plan to export or import price data from a file.

5. From the Type drop-down list, select the type of security that you are setting up (such as Stock, Bond, or CD).

> **Note**
>
> If the security type for the security you are setting up isn't included in the Type drop-down list, you can add a new security type to the Security Types list. Choose Security Type from the Lists menu and then choose the New button to enter the new security type. You also can edit or delete security types from the Security Types list.

6. (Optional) Select the goal for the security from the Goal drop-down list.

A goal enables you to record another piece of information about your investment. Quicken provides several investment goals that you may find valuable, such as Growth, Income, or College funding. You can also create your own goal. The Goal drop-down list box is optional and has no effect on the way you track or monitor an investment.

> **Note**
>
> If your goal for investing in a security isn't included in the Goal drop-down list, just add your own customized goal to the Investment Goal list. From the Lists menu, choose Investment Goal. Choose the New button to enter the new goal. You also can edit or delete existing goals from the Investment Goal list.

7. In the Est. Annual Income($) text box, enter the income that you project to earn per year from the investment in the security.

8. Choose OK to add the security to the Security list.

Repeat steps 1 through 8 to set up as many securities as you need.

> **Note**
>
> You can edit and delete securities in the Security list by highlighting the security and choosing the Edit or Del button. You also can elect to include or not include securities in the Portfolio View window. See the section "Customizing the Portfolio View" later in this chapter.

Entering Opening Share Balances for Securities

After you set up a regular investment account and add securities to the Security list, you must create the opening balance in the account. Three options are available for creating an opening balance in an investment account (regular and mutual fund), as follows:

■ *Option 1:* Enter all historical data for each security you now hold. This option entails entering the initial purchase information (date, amount invested, and number of shares) and all subsequent transactions, including acquisitions, sales and gifts, stock splits, returns of capital, dividends, interest, and capital gains distributions.

III

Planning for the Future

■ *Option 2:* Set up the opening balance as of the beginning of the current year. This option entails entering all security holdings as of the end of last year and all transactions since the beginning of the current year. For each security, you must enter the number of shares owned at the end of last year, the price per share at the end of last year, and all transactions for the current year.

■ *Option 3:* Enter current securities as held only. For each security you now hold, enter the number of shares and the current per share price.

If you want complete and accurate data for your investment accounts, you should create an opening balance using the first option. Although you will spend much time entering historical data, your reports will be more accurate, and Quicken will be able to calculate capital gains or losses for securities that you sell.

To enter the opening share balance for each security in a regular investment account by entering historical data, follow these steps:

1. Choose Account from the Lists menu, press Ctrl+A, or click the Accts button on the Iconbar to display the Account list.

2. Highlight the regular investment account for which you want to enter opening share balances, and then choose the Use button. Quicken displays the Investment Register, shown in figure 15.4. (You learn your way around the Investment Register later in the section "Using the Investment Register.")

Fig. 15.4

When you select an investment account in the Account list, Quicken displays the Investment Register.

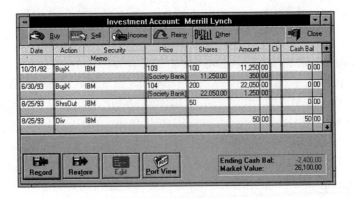

3. Press Ctrl+End, if necessary, to go to an empty transaction line in the Register.

4. To add securities purchased before you started using Quicken, choose the Other button in the button bar. Quicken displays the Other action list, shown in figure 15.5.

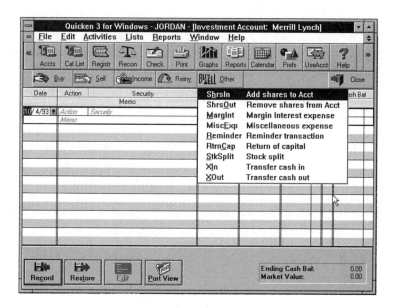

Fig. 15.5
From the Other action list, choose the action that you want to record in the Investment Register.

5. Choose the ShrsIn (Add shares to Acct) action. Quicken displays the Add Shares to Account form, shown in figure 15.6.

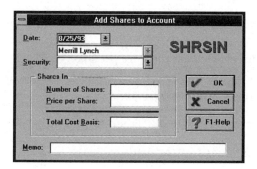

Fig. 15.6
For each security you now hold, enter the number of shares and price per share in the Add Shares to Account form.

> **Note**
>
> The Add Shares to Account form enables you to enter security holdings that you purchased before you started using Quicken or set up an investment account. When you enter security holdings in the Add Shares to Account form, you aren't required to deduct funds from the investment account or another bank account to pay for the shares.

6. In the Date drop-down list box, enter or select the date the securities were acquired. By default, Quicken enters the current system date.

   In the next drop-down list box, Quicken enters the name of the investment account that you now are working in.

7. If the investment account you are working in is set up for multiple securities (like a brokerage account), enter or select the name of the security that you own from the Security drop-down list box.

8. Enter the number of shares acquired in the Number of shares text box, according to the following rules:

   - *Stocks and mutual funds.* Enter the number of shares.

   - *Bonds.* Enter the number of bonds multiplied by 10. (If you purchased 5 bonds, for example, enter 50.)

   - *Money market funds or CDs.* Enter their total value.

   - *Collectibles (such as coins).* Enter 1.

   - *Precious metals (such as gold).* Enter the number of ounces.

Tip
To enter a share price with a fraction (for example, 5 3/8), type the whole number, a space, the numerator, a slash (/), and the denominator.

9. Enter the price per share in the Price per Share text box. Quicken calculates the total cost in the Total Cost Basis text box. Use the following rules to determine the price to enter:

   - *Stocks and mutual funds.* Enter the price per share.

   - *Bonds.* Enter 1/10 the market value.

   - *Money market funds or CDs.* Enter 1 (for one dollar).

   - *Collectibles.* Enter the total value.

   - *Precious metals.* Enter the price per ounce.

10. (Optional) Enter a description of the security transaction in the Memo text box.

11. Choose OK to record the opening balance transaction.

12. For each security opening balance that you need to add, repeat steps 3 through 11.

13. For each subsequent security transaction, such as dividends, stock splits, and reinvestments, enter a separate transaction. (You learn how to enter transactions in the Register later in the section "Entering Investment Transactions.")

14. After you finish entering security transactions, check the ending cash balance against the cash balance shown in your latest brokerage statement. If the cash balance isn't correct, go to the next section.

Updating the Cash Balance in a Regular Investment Account

After you enter your security transactions in the Investment Account Register, the ending cash balance in the Register should match the actual cash balance. If the cash balance is incorrect, you must update the balance in the account so that it reflects the actual balance.

To update the cash balance, follow these steps:

1. From the Activities menu, choose Update Balances.

2. From the Update Balances submenu, choose Update Cash Balance. Quicken displays the Update Cash Balance dialog box.

3. Enter the actual cash balance and the date for which you want to adjust the cash balance.

4. Choose OK. Quicken enters a balance adjustment transaction for the difference between the ending cash balance and the actual balance that you entered.

Working with Mutual Fund Investment Accounts

Using Quicken to monitor a mutual fund investment consists of recording your starting balance and periodically recording changes in the balance due

III

Planning for the Future

to the purchase of additional shares or the redemption of shares within the fund. You record the same information that appears on your mutual fund statements. By recording the information in the Quicken Register, however, you can use the information in several calculations that show how you are doing with your investments.

CPA TIP: Choosing No-Load Funds

If you buy mutual fund shares, you should know the difference between load funds and no-load funds. You usually purchase load funds through a broker, who charges an up-front commission that can run from 3 percent to 8.5 percent. The commission is compensation for the salesperson who placed the order and helped you select the fund. No-load funds deal directly with their customers, which means the customer pays no commission.

Research shows that on average, load funds perform no better than no-load funds. Therefore, many investors see no reason to choose a load fund over a no-load fund. To find a no-load mutual fund, flip through the *Wall Street Journal* and look for mutual fund advertisements that specify no-load.

Setting up a mutual fund investment account is similar to setting up a regular investment account. The one difference is that you don't have to set up securities before you enter the opening share balance in the account. Because mutual fund accounts aren't designed for more than one security, the fund itself is considered the one security.

To set up a mutual fund investment account, follow these steps:

1. From the Activities menu, choose Create New Account. Quicken displays the Select Account Type dialog box.

2. Select the Investment Account option button.

3. Choose OK. Quicken displays the New Account Information dialog box (refer to fig. 15.1).

4. In the Account Name text box, enter a name for the mutual fund account. The account name can be up to 15 characters long and can contain any characters except the following:

   You can include spaces in the account name.

5. Select the Account Contains a Single Mutual Fund check box.

6. If the earnings from the mutual fund account you are setting up are tax-deferred (the tax is assessed in a later time period than the earnings are received), select the Tax-Deferred Account check box. Examples of tax-deferred accounts are IRAs, 401(k) accounts, and annuities.

7. From the Transfers In drop-down list, select the tax form or schedule to which transfers to the account should be assigned. From the Transfers Out drop-down list, select the tax form or schedule for transfers from the investment account.

8. (Optional) In the Description text box, enter an investment account description of up to 21 characters.

9. To enter additional information about the mutual fund account, choose the Info button and enter the information in the Additional Account Information dialog box. Choose OK to save the information and return to the New Account Information dialog box.

10. Choose OK. Quicken displays the Set Up Mutual Fund Security dialog box, as shown in figure 15.7.

11. In the Symbol text box, enter the symbol for the mutual fund if you

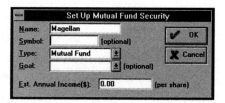

Fig. 15.7
Enter information about the mutual fund security in the Set Up Mutual Fund Security dialog box.

plan to export or import price data from a file.

12. In the Type drop-down list, select the mutual fund type.

13. (Optional) Select the goal for the mutual fund investment from the Goal drop-down list box. The goal is your purpose for investing in the mutual fund (such as growth, income, or college funding).

14. In the Est. Annual Income text box, enter the income you project to earn per year from the mutual fund.

15. Choose OK. Quicken adds the mutual fund investment account to the Account list and displays the Create Opening Share Balance dialog box, shown in figure 15.8.

III

Planning for the Future

Fig. 15.8

When you set up
a mutual fund
investment
account, Quicken
displays the Create
Opening Share
Balance dialog
box.

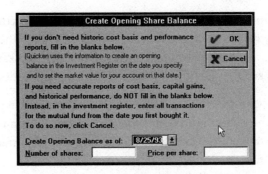

16. If you want to set up historical data for the mutual fund (Option 1 in
    the section "Entering Opening Share Balances for Securities"), choose
    Cancel to display the Investment Register for the mutual fund invest-
    ment account. Then enter the opening share balance, using the same
    steps for entering the opening share balance for each security in a regu-
    lar investment fund.

    If you choose Option 2 (from the section "Entering Opening Share
    Balances for Securities) for entering opening share balances, select or
    enter 12/31/*xx* (where *xx* is last year) in the Create Opening Balance As
    Of drop-down box. Enter the Number of shares owned on 12/31/*xx* and
    the Price per share at 12/31/*xx*.

    If you choose Option 3 (from the section "Entering Opening Share
    Balances for Securities") for entering opening share balances, select or
    enter today's date, the number of shares you now own, and the current
    price per share.

17. Choose OK when the Create Opening Share Balance dialog box is com-
    plete. Quicken displays the Investment Register and enters the opening
    balance.

If you choose Option 2 (from the section "Entering Opening Share Balances
for Securities") for entering opening share balances, you now must update
the market value of the securities in the account to reflect the current price.
See the section "Updating Security Prices" later in this chapter to learn how
to update security prices to current prices.

If you choose Option 3 (from the section "Entering Opening Share Balances
for Securities") for entering opening share balances, you don't have to enter
any other transactions. Your mutual fund investment account is set up with
the opening share balance reflected for all current security holdings.

Using the Investment Register

Now that your investment account is set up, you're ready to start using the Investment Register to track the activity in your account. For each transaction that occurs in your investment account, you will enter a transaction in the Investment Register so that all investment activity is accounted for. For example, you must record stock splits so that the number of shares in your Register reflects the number of shares you now hold, and you must enter transactions to record the receipt of dividends.

In earlier chapters, you learned about and worked with Quicken Registers. You probably use the Check Register most of all. Investment Registers work in a similar manner, but a few differences exist.

Although you can enter investment transactions directly in the Investment Register, accessing the appropriate form and entering the transaction data in the form is much easier. When you save a form (by choosing OK), Quicken enters the transaction in the proper fields in the next empty transaction line in the Register.

Because you can use forms to enter transactions, the Investment Register has an investment button bar with buttons for actions that require a transaction form (see fig. 15.9). When you sell a security, for example, you enter the security sale information in the Sell Shares form, which is accessed by choosing the Sell button.

The command buttons at the bottom of the Investment Register are used to record and restore transactions in the Register, edit an investment transaction, and change the view of the Investment Register to Portfolio View. (See the section "Using the Portfolio View of an Investment Account" later in this chapter.) The buttons on the button bar are explained in the next section.

The Action field in the Investment Register identifies the transaction. If you want to see the various actions you can enter, click the down arrow in the Action field.

Entering Investment Transactions

Each time you buy or sell a security in your investment account, receive dividends or interest, buy or redeem Treasury bills, and so forth, you should enter a transaction in the Investment Register to reflect the activity. Quicken provides new forms that make entering investment transaction information easy. To access one of the forms to enter a transaction, choose the appropriate button from the investment button bar (see table 15.1).

III

Planning for the Future

Fig. 15.9
In addition to command buttons, the Investment Register has a button bar for actions that require a transaction form.

Investment button bar

Command buttons

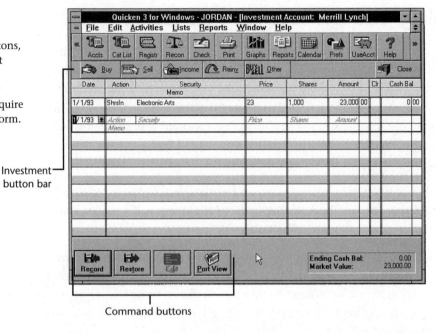

Table 15.1 Buttons on the Investment Button Bar

Form	Button	Transaction
Buy Shares	Buy	Cash purchase of securities.
Sell Shares	Sell	Cash sale of securities.
Record Income	Income	Cash received from dividends, interest income, miscellaneous income, or capital gains distributions.
Reinvest Income	Reinv	Purchase of additional shares of a security with money paid to you by the security as dividends, interest income, or capital gain distributions.
Add Shares	Other	Receive shares of a security to account without paying cash from the investment account or other bank account (for example, a gift). Use this form to enter opening share balances in a new investment account, as explained earlier in this chapter.
Remove Shares from Account	Other	Give shares to someone as a gift.
Margin Interest Expense	Other	Pay interest to your brokerage firm on a margin loan.

Form	Button	Transaction
Miscellaneous Expense	Other	Incur expenses associated with a security.
Reminder	Other	Enter a reminder message in an investment account.
Return of Capital	Other	Receive cash from an amount paid to you as total or partial payment of the money you originally invested in a security, where you aren't the one who initiated the sale.
Stock Split	Other	Receive additional shares of a security for no additional investment. Quicken recalculates the average cost per share when you enter a stock split transaction.
Transfer Cash In	Other	Transfer cash into an investment account.
Transfer Cash Out	Other	Transfer cash from an investment account.

The next sections show you how to enter each investment transaction.

> **Note**
>
> The Margin Interest Expense, Miscellaneous Income, Return of Capital, Transfer Cash In, and Transfer Cash Out forms aren't available in mutual fund investment accounts.

If you have used previous versions of Quicken and are comfortable using the Investment Register, you can enter investment transactions directly into the Register as you are accustomed to doing. Entering investment transactions is similar to entering other types of transactions in Quicken Registers. When your transaction is complete, choose the Record button to record the transaction in the Investment Register.

Buying Securities. When you purchase a security, you enter the transaction in the appropriate investment account in Quicken. If you set up an account to enter transactions through your brokerage firm, enter security purchases in this account. If you buy, sell, and manage securities yourself, you may have an investment account set up for each security you own. If this is the case, enter purchases of additional shares of a security in that security's investment account. For purchases of new securities, set up an investment account for the security and then enter the purchase in that account. (You learned how to set up an investment account earlier in this chapter.)

To enter a transaction to buy securities, follow these steps:

1. In the Investment Register, press Ctrl+End to move to the next empty transaction line.

2. Choose the **Buy** button from the button bar. Quicken displays the Buy Shares form, shown in figure 15.10.

3. Enter the date that you purchased the security in the Date text box, and then select the security in the Security drop-down list box.

4. Complete the Cost section. Enter the number of shares you bought in the Number of Shares text box, the price paid per share in the Price text box, and the commission or fees charged to you (if explicit) in the Commission/Fee text box. Quicken calculates the total amount of the purchase. If you don't know the commission or fees charged, leave the Commission/Fees text box blank and enter the total you paid for the shares in the Total of Sale text box. Quicken calculates the commissions or fees.

Fig. 15.10

Enter purchases of securities in the Buy Shares form.

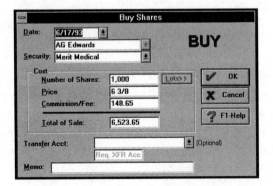

Note

When you buy a bond after its original date of issue, you pay accrued interest to the previous owner of the bond at the time of purchase. Enter the accrued interest portion of the purchase price as a separate transaction in the Miscellaneous Expense form.

5. If you are buying the security with cash in the current investment account, leave the Transfer Acct drop-down list box blank. If you are buying the security with cash from another investment account or a bank account, select the account in the Transfer Acct drop-down list box.

6. (Optional) In the Memo text box, enter a memo that describes the transaction.

7. When the Buy Shares form is complete, choose OK. Quicken removes the Buy Shares form from the screen and enters the transaction in the next empty transaction line in the Investment Register.

8. Review the information in the Register and choose Record to record the transaction.

> **Note**
>
> Use the Buy Shares form when you purchase securities. If you receive shares of a security by gift, use the Add Shares to Account form. You learn how to enter gifts of securities later in the section "Entering Gifts and Receipts of Securities."

Selling Securities. When you sell shares of a security, enter the transaction in the investment account where you recorded their purchase. With Quicken 3 for Windows, you now can identify the shares that you sell if you have purchased shares in different lots. If you bought, for example, 100 shares of IBM on 1/1/88, 200 shares on 6/30/89, and 100 shares on 5/15/90, you have three different lots of IBM stock. If you then sell 50 shares of IBM on 1/1/94, you can select which shares of the stock you are selling. Quicken keeps track of the number of shares remaining and their cost basis in each lot. If you don't specify which shares you are selling, Quicken uses the FIFO (first in, first out) rule, which assumes that the first shares purchased are the first shares sold.

To enter a transaction to sell shares of a security, follow these steps:

1. In the Investment Register, press Ctrl+End to move to the next empty transaction line.

2. Choose the Sell button from the investment button bar. Quicken displays the Sell Shares form, shown in figure 15.11.

Fig. 15.11
Enter the sale of a
security in the Sell
Shares form.

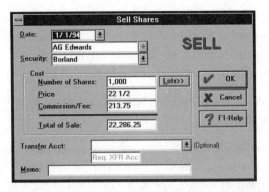

CPA TIP: Specifying Lots

To minimize the capital gain resulting from the sale of securities whose market value has increased, identify the highest per share cost basis as the shares you are selling. Suppose that you bought 100 shares of Electronic Arts at $20 and then bought another 100 shares at $25. If you later sell 100 shares for $30 per share, you should specify the second lot (or the shares purchased at $25) as the shares you are selling because the resulting capital gain is less. If you need to generate a capital loss to offset other capital gains in your portfolio, specify the shares with the highest per share cost basis.

3. To complete the Sell Shares form, follow the steps for completing the Buy Shares form as explained earlier in the section "Buying Securities."

4. To specify which lots of securities you are selling, choose the Lots button. Quicken displays the Specific Identification of Shares dialog box, shown in figure 15.12.

Fig. 15.12
Specify which
shares you are
selling in the
Specific Identifi-
cation of Shares
dialog box.

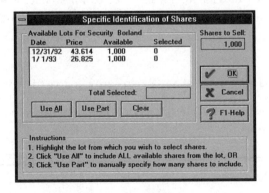

Quicken shows each security lot in the Available Lots for Security list box. Each lot is identified by the date purchased, the price per share, and the number of shares in each lot that you still own.

5. To sell all the shares in a particular lot, highlight the lot in the list box and choose the Use All button. Choose Clear to deselect lots.

   To sell part of the shares from a particular lot, highlight the lot, choose the Use Part button, and enter the number of shares you want to sell from the highlighted lot.

   Quicken keeps track of the number of shares specified as sold in the Total Selected field. When the total selected is equal to the number of shares in the Shares to Sell text box (entered by Quicken from the Sell Shares form), you have finished allocating shares to lots.

6. Choose OK. If you selected part of the shares to sell in the Specific Identification of Shares dialog box, Quicken asks whether you want to cancel lot allocations. Choose Yes to cancel; otherwise, choose No. Quicken displays the Sell Shares form.

7. When the Sell Shares form is complete, choose OK. Quicken removes the Sell Shares form from the screen and enters the sale transaction in the Investment Register.

8. Review the transaction in the Register and choose Record to record the sale transaction.

CPA TIP: Planning Security Transactions

Try to plan your security transactions to minimize the amount of net capital gain realized each year. If you are in a net capital gain position, consider selling other securities that are in a loss position. Capital losses offset capital gains dollar for dollar. You may not deduct from your taxable income more than $3,000 in capital losses against ordinary income, however. Be mindful of your net capital loss position before entering into transactions resulting in losses. Capital losses can be carried over to future years.

Recording Investment Income. If you receive dividends, interest income, miscellaneous income, or capital gains distributions from a security, enter the receipt as investment income in the Investment Register.

III

Planning for the Future

To enter a transaction to record investment income, follow these steps:

1. In the Investment Register, press Ctrl+End to move to the next empty transaction line.

2. Choose the Income button from the button bar to display the Record Income form, shown in figure 15.13.

Fig. 15.13
Enter dividends, interest income, miscellaneous income, or capital gains distributions in the Record Income form.

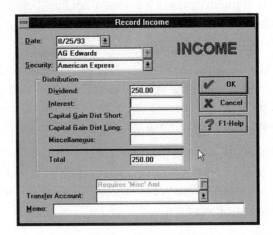

3. Enter the Date the income is received and select the security associated with the income from the Security drop-down list.

Tip
Enter reinvestment of dividends, interest income, or capital gains distributions in the Reinvest Income form, not the Record Income form.

4. In the Distribution section, enter the income received as dividends in the Dividend text box, interest in the Interest text box, short-term capital gains in the Capital Gain Dist. Short text box, long-term capital gains in the Capital Gain Dist. Long text box, or miscellaneous income in the Miscellaneous text box.

A capital gains distribution is money paid to shareholders from the sales of its underlying securities for more than the security's cost. Distributions received are a distribution of the fund's own capital gains. The mutual fund usually tells you whether the capital gains distribution is long term or short term; if it doesn't, assume that the capital gains distribution is long term.

5. If the income is retained in the current investment account, leave the Transfer Account drop-down list blank. Otherwise, select the account to which the income is to be transferred.

> **Note**
>
> If you have interest income from a tax-free bond, set up a category to assign to the tax-free interest. When you receive interest income on the bond, record the interest in the Record Income form as Miscellaneous income. Quicken displays a **C**ategory for Misc income drop-down list box when you enter miscellaneous income. Select the tax-free interest category.

6. Choose OK when the Record Income form is complete. Quicken removes the form from the screen and enters the income transaction in the Register.

7. Review the transaction in the Register and then choose Record to record the transaction.

Recording Reinvestments. When you reinvest dividends, interest income, or capital gains distributions to purchase additional shares of a security, record the reinvestment in the Investment Register.

To record a reinvestment transaction, follow these steps:

1. In the Investment Register, press Ctrl+End to move to the next empty transaction line.

2. Choose the Reinv button from the investment button bar to display the Reinvest Income form, shown in figure 15.14.

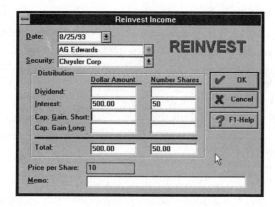

Fig. 15.14

Use the Reinvest Income form when you reinvest dividends, interest income, or capital gains distributions to purchase additional shares of a security.

3. Enter the Date that additional shares were purchased and select the security associated with the income from the Security drop-down list box.

4. In the Distribution section, enter the dollar amount of the dividends, interest income, or capital gains distributions (short or long term) used to purchase the additional shares. In the Number Shares column, enter the number of new shares you are receiving. Quicken calculates the per share price of the new shares based on the information that you enter in the Distribution section.

5. (Optional) Enter a Memo describing the reinvestment transaction.

6. Choose OK when the Reinvest Income form is complete. Quicken removes the form from the screen and enters the reinvestment transaction in the Investment Register.

7. Review the transaction in the Register and then choose Record to record the transaction.

Entering Stock Splits and Stock Dividends. You receive additional shares of stock when the company declares a stock split. Suppose that the ABC Company declares a stock split that entitles shareholders to one new share for every share they now hold. Because you own 100 shares, you are issued 100 new shares, for a total of 200.

When you receive additional shares of a security from a stock split, your total cost basis remains the same, but the per share price is adjusted downward. Suppose that you paid $10 per share for the 100 shares you purchased, which is a total investment of $1,000. With the 100 shares you receive in the stock split, your total investment is still $1,000. Your per share cost, however, is now $5.

Stock splits are entered based on the ratio of new shares issued to existing shares. In the ABC Company example, the ratio is 2:1 (two shares for every one share held).

A stock dividend occurs when a dividend is issued in the form of shares instead of cash. Most stock dividends are non-taxable. For non-taxable stock dividends, enter the transaction as a stock split for the ratio of dividend shares given per shares held. Taxable stock dividends are entered as reinvestment transactions (see the preceding section).

To enter a stock split or non-taxable stock dividend, follow these steps:

1. In the Investment Register, press Ctrl+End to move to the next empty transaction line.

2. Choose the Other button from the investment button bar to display the Other action list.

3. Choose StkSplit from the Other action list. Quicken displays the Stock Split form, shown in figure 15.15.

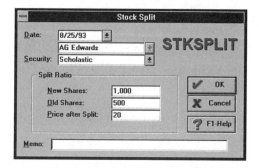

Fig. 15.15
When you receive additional shares of stock in a stock split, enter the number of new shares issued and the number of shares owned in the Stock Split form.

4. Enter the Date of the stock split and select the security to which the stock split relates from the Security drop-down list box.

5. In the Split Ratio section, enter the number of new shares received in the New Shares text box and the number of shares that you already own in the Old Shares text box. Quicken calculates the new per share price after the split.

6. (Optional) Enter a memo describing the stock split transaction.

7. Choose OK when the Stock Split form is complete. Quicken removes the form from the screen and enters the stock split transaction in the Investment Register.

8. Review the transaction in the Register and then choose Record to record the transaction.

Entering Gifts and Receipts of Securities. When you give or receive shares of stock as a gift, you must enter the activity in the Investment Register so that it reflects the correct number of shares held. Because no funds are transferred when you give shares or receive shares, you use the Remove Shares from Account and the Add Shares to Account forms to enter gift transactions.

III

Planning for the Future

You learned how to complete the Add Shares to Account form earlier in the section "Entering Opening Share Balances for Securities." Enter a gift of securities in the same way that you create an opening balance transaction in a new investment account. When you enter the receipt of shares as a gift, Quicken increases your number of shares without subtracting cash from your investment account or any other bank account.

The rules for determining the cost per share of gifted stock are complicated. For now, enter the price per share paid by the giver when the shares were originally purchased. Then consult your tax advisor to determine the cost per share that you should use.

For gifts of stock that you make, follow these steps to record the gift:

1. In the Investment Register, press Ctrl+End to move to the next empty transaction line.

2. Choose the Other button from the investment button bar to display the Other action list.

3. Choose ShrsOut from the Other action list. Quicken displays the Remove Shares from Account form, shown in figure 15.16.

Fig. 15.16

When you give shares of stock as a gift, enter the number of shares given in the Remove Shares from Account form.

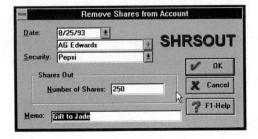

4. Enter the Date of the gift and select the security you are gifting in the Security drop-down list box.

5. In the Number of Shares text box, enter the number of shares that you are giving as a gift.

6. (Optional) Enter a memo describing the transfer of shares. You may want to enter the recipient's name or the reason for the gift.

7. Choose OK when the Remove Shares from Account form is complete. Quicken removes the form from the screen and enters the transfer of stock in the Investment Register.

8. Review the transaction in the Register and choose Record to record the transaction.

Recording Margin Loans. Brokerage firms enable their clients to borrow money to purchase securities. This type of transaction is called a *margin loan*. The brokerage firm charges interest (*margin interest*) on the loan as a bank or other lending institution would do. The cash balance in your brokerage account is negative when you borrow money on margin.

To record the interest you pay on a margin loan, choose the Other button from the investment button bar and then choose MarginInt. Quicken displays the Margin Interest Expense form (see fig. 15.17). Enter the Date, the Amount of interest charged, and an optional Memo. Then choose OK; the transaction for margin interest expense is entered in the Investment Register.

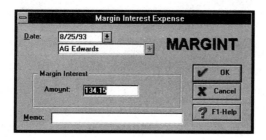

Fig. 15.17
Enter interest expense charged on a margin loan in the Margin Interest Expense form.

Alternatively, you can set up a loan in Quicken to record a margin loan. (Refer to Chapter 10, "Tracking Loans," to learn how to set up a loan.) Then transfer the proceeds of the loan to your investment account with the Transfer Cash In form, shown in figure 15.18. To access the Transfer Cash In form, choose the Other button from the investment button bar and then choose XIn. Enter the amount of the margin loan and select the liability account in Quicken in the Transfer Acct drop-down list box. Choose OK to enter the transfer transaction in the Investment Register and then choose Record to record the transaction.

When you pay the margin loan, use the Transfer Cash Out form, as shown in figure 15.19. To access the Transfer Cash Out form, choose the Other button from the investment button bar and then choose XOut. Enter the margin loan balance you are paying and select the liability account for the margin loan from the Transfer Acct drop-down list box. Choose OK to enter the transfer transaction in the Investment Register and then choose Record to record the transaction.

III

Planning for the Future

Fig. 15.18

If you set up a loan to record a margin loan, enter the loan amount and the liability account in the Transfer Cash In form.

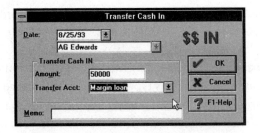

Fig. 15.19

When you pay a margin loan, enter the balance paid and the liability account for the margin loan in the Transfer Cash Out form.

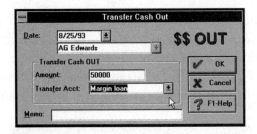

Recording Returns of Capital. A return of capital takes place when you receive money as a total or partial repayment of the money you invested in a security. A return of capital is similar to a sale, but the investor isn't the initiator of the return of capital. If you invest in mortgage-backed securities, for example, you receive a return of capital when the underlying mortgages are paid.

To record a return of capital, follow these steps:

1. In the Investment Register, press Ctrl+End to move to the next empty transaction line.

2. Choose the Other button from the button bar to display the Other action list.

3. Choose RtrnCap from the Other action list. Quicken displays the Return of Capital form, shown in figure 15.20.

4. Enter the Date you received payment and select the security to which you received a return of capital from the Security drop-down list box.

5. Enter the total or partial repayment amount in the Amount text box.

6. (Optional) Enter a Memo describing the transaction.

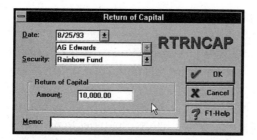

Fig. 15.20
Enter the total or partial repayment of your investment in the Return of Capital form.

7. Choose OK when the Return of Capital form is complete. Quicken removes the form from the screen and enters the transaction in the Investment Register.

8. Review the transaction and then choose Record to record the transaction in the Investment Register.

Recording Zero-Coupon Bonds. *Zero-coupon* bonds don't pay interest until the bond matures or is sold. Zero-coupon bonds are purchased at a discount and increase in value due to the accruing of interest. Unfortunately, you must report accrued interest each year as taxable interest (even though you don't receive it). Accrued interest on zero-coupon bonds is reported on Form 1099-OID.

To record accrued interest on a zero-coupon bond, enter the amount as interest in the Record Income form (refer to fig. 15.13).

To record the increase in value of a zero-coupon bond, enter the accrued interest amount as a negative amount in the Return of Capital form (refer to fig. 15.20). Negative amounts in the Return of Capital form increase your cost basis in the bond.

Recording Short Sales. A *short sale* is a sale of a security you don't actually own, but rather borrow from your broker. Quicken recognizes short sales because you enter the sale of the security before the purchase.

To record a short sale, follow these steps:

1. Access the Sell Shares form (refer to fig. 15.11), as explained earlier in the section "Selling Securities."

2. Complete the Sell Shares form for the security you are selling short. Then choose OK.

III

Planning for the Future

3. When Quicken searches the Investment Register and finds that you don't already own the security, a message is displayed that this transaction is being entered as a short sale. Choose the Confirm button, and Quicken records the short sale in the Investment Register.

Later, when you actually purchase the security (hopefully at a lower price), enter the purchase in the Buy Shares form (refer to fig. 15.10). Quicken closes the short sale and calculates the gain or loss. Gains from short sales don't appear in the Capital Gains Report but do appear in the Investment Income Report.

> ### Caution
>
> Quicken closes out a short sale before it opens a new position in a security. Therefore, if you record two short sales in the same security before buying the security, you must specify which short sale you are closing when you enter the purchase. Use the Lots button in the Buy Shares form to specify short sale lots. (You learned how to specify lots earlier in the section "Selling Securities.")

Entering Option Trades. An *option* is a contract that represents your right or obligation to buy or sell 100 shares of stock at a specified price (called the strike price) at any time during a specified period. Two types of options exist: puts and calls. A *call option* gives you the right to buy shares at a fixed price for a fixed period of time. A *put option* gives you the right to sell shares at a fixed price for a fixed period of time.

Enter the purchase or sale of options as you would any other security in the Buy Shares and Sell Shares forms. (When you set up the security for an option, use a distinctive name so that you can identify options in your Security list.) When you buy calls, use the Buy Shares form to enter the number of calls and the call price. When you exercise calls (buy the underlying shares), enter the exercise in the Sell Shares form for the original purchase price of the calls. (This transaction clears the option position from your investment account.) Next, enter the purchase of the underlying shares in the Buy Shares form. Enter the exercise price as the price per share, and enter the call price as the commission or fee paid. This adjusts the cost basis of the shares to include the price of the calls.

Recording Miscellaneous Expenses. If expenses incurred in an investment account (for example, broker fees) are paid from your investment account, enter a miscellaneous expense transaction in the account. To enter a miscellaneous expense in the Investment Register, follow these steps:

1. In the Investment Register, press Ctrl+End to move to the next empty transaction line.

2. Choose the Other button from the button bar to display the Other action list.

3. Choose MiscExp from the Other action list. Quicken displays the Miscellaneous Expense form, shown in figure 15.21.

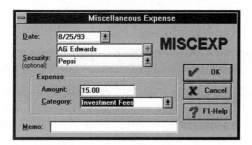

Fig. 15.21
Enter miscellaneous expenses that you pay from your investment account in the Miscellaneous Expense form.

4. Enter the Date the expense is incurred and select the security associated with the expense in the Security drop-down list box.

5. In the Expense section, enter the amount of the expense in the Amount text box and assign a category to the expense transaction in the Category drop-down list box.

6. (Optional) Enter a Memo describing the expense.

7. Choose OK when the Miscellaneous Expense form is complete. Quicken removes the form from the screen and enters the expense transaction in the Investment Register.

8. Review the transaction in the Register and then choose Record to record the miscellaneous expense transaction.

III

Planning for the Future

Editing and Deleting Investment Transactions

An investment transaction can be edited or deleted in the Investment Register as it is in other Quicken Registers. You can edit the fields in a transaction in the Investment Register or choose the Edit command button to display the transaction form and edit the information in the form. Delete a transaction by highlighting the transaction and then pressing Ctrl+D or choosing Delete Transaction from the Edit menu.

Memorizing Investment Transactions

If you enter some transactions in the Investment Register regularly, you can have Quicken memorize the transactions so that the transaction data is saved in the Memorized Investment Transaction list. Each time you need to record the transaction, simply recall it; Quicken enters the memorized transaction in the Investment Register.

> **Note**
>
> Memorizing investment transactions is similar to memorizing regular transactions in the Check Register or any other account Register. However, Quicken stores memorized investment transactions in their own list—the Memorized Investment Transaction list. Quicken stores regular memorized transactions in the Memorized Transaction list.

To have Quicken memorize an investment transaction, follow these steps:

1. In the Investment Register, highlight the investment transaction that you want Quicken to memorize.

2. From the Edit menu, choose Memorize Transaction (or press Ctrl+M).

3. Quicken displays a message that the transaction is about to be memorized. Choose OK to memorize the transaction.

When you're ready to enter a memorized investment transaction in the Investment Register, follow these steps:

1. In the Investment Register, press Ctrl+End to move to the next empty transaction line.

2. From the Lists menu, choose Memorized Investment Trans. Quicken displays the Memorized Investment Transaction list, as shown in figure 15.22.

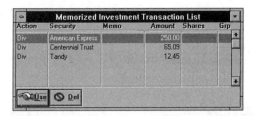

Fig. 15.22
Quicken lists the investment transactions that it has memorized in the Memorized Investment Transaction list.

3. Highlight the memorized investment transaction that you want to enter.

4. Choose the Use button. Quicken enters the memorized transaction in the Investment Register.

5. Review the transaction and then choose Record to record the memorized investment transaction in the Register.

Using Investment Reminders

You can set up investment reminders so that Quicken alerts you to actions you want to take with regard to your investment portfolio. You can use investment reminders, for example, to help you remember when a bond or CD will mature or to remind you to look at a stock's price to determine whether it's time to sell.

You can use the investment reminders in two ways: to make notes in the Investment Register and to remind yourself about certain investment transactions through the Quicken Billminder and Reminder features. Investment reminders are displayed in the Billminder window each time you start your computer and in the Quicken Reminder window each time you start Quicken. (Refer to Chapter 14, "Scheduling Future Transactions," to learn more about how Quicken Reminders work.)

> **Note**
>
> Quicken Reminders are associated with the Billminder feature. Quicken Reminders (and therefore investment reminders) don't appear if you haven't installed Billminder. See Chapter 14, "Scheduling Future Transactions," to learn how to install Billminder.

To enter an investment reminder, follow these steps:

1. In the Investment Register, press Ctrl+End to move to the next empty transaction line.

2. Choose the Other button from the investment button bar. Quicken displays the Other action list.

3. Select Reminder from the Other action list. Quicken displays the Reminder form, shown in figure 15.23.

Fig. 15.23
Enter notes or reminders about actions to be taken in your investment account in the Reminder form.

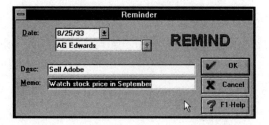

4. Enter the Date you are reminding yourself to take action on in your investment account.

> **Note**
>
> Quicken displays investment reminders every time you turn on your computer or start Quicken, regardless of the date you enter.

5. In the Desc text box, type the text of your reminder, using up to 19 characters.

6. (Optional) Enter additional information in the Memo text box.

7. Choose OK. Quicken enters the investment reminder in the transaction line in the Register.

8. Review the reminder and then choose Record to record the reminder in the Register.

Quicken displays investment reminders in the Billminder or Quicken Reminder window until you turn off the reminder. To turn off an investment reminder, double-click the Clr (Cleared) field to enter an asterisk (*) or an x.

Using the Portfolio View of an Investment Account

Quicken enables you to change the view of the Investment Register so that you can see each of your security holdings (listed alphabetically by security type), the number of shares, the current price, the market value, and the return on investment. When you change the view of the Register to the Portfolio View, you not only can see your securities listed in one place, but also update security prices, create a QuickReport listing all transactions associated with a security, and graph the price history of a security. You also can record investment transactions and edit your list of securities in the Portfolio View of the Register.

To switch to the Portfolio View of an investment account, follow these steps:

1. Display the Register for the investment account for which you want to see the Portfolio View.

2. From the Activities menu, choose Portfolio View. Alternately, choose the Port View command button at the bottom of the Investment Register (or press Ctrl+U).

Quicken displays the Portfolio View window for the investment account, as shown in figure 15.24.

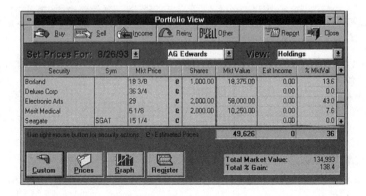

Fig. 15.24
Choose the Port View command button to display the Portfolio View of an investment account.

III

The Portfolio View window has the same buttons as those in the Register investment button bar, as well as a QuickReport (Report) button for an instant transaction listing for the selected security. (You learn about QuickReports in the next section.)

Planning for the Future

In the Portfolio View window, Quicken includes the following command buttons: Custom, Prices, Graph, and Register. All of these functions are explained later in the chapter.

Using QuickReport for Transaction Listings

Use the QuickReport button if you want an instant listing of all transactions relating to a security listed in the Portfolio View window. To create a transaction listing for a security, highlight the security and choose the Report button from the button bar.

Changing the View Date

By default, Quicken shows your securities in the Portfolio View window as of the current date. If you want to see your securities as of a different date, you can change the view date by clicking the down arrow next to the Set Prices For date field and selecting the date from the mini-calendar that Quicken displays. You also can click the Set Prices For date (click 10/4/93, for example) to display the Go to Date dialog box (see fig. 15.25), enter or select the date in which you want to view your investments, and choose OK.

Fig. 15.25

Enter the date for which you want to view your investments in the Go to Date dialog box.

> **Note**
>
> If you change the view date to a date that precedes the purchase of a security, you won't see that security in the Portfolio View window. Likewise, if you change the view date to a date after the sale of a security, you won't see the security in the Portfolio View window. The Portfolio View window shows securities held as of the date in the Set Prices For field.

Selecting Accounts To View

By default, Quicken includes securities held only in the current account in the Portfolio View window. You can select to include securities held in other investment accounts, however.

To select the accounts to view in the Portfolio View window, select an individual account or All Accounts from the accounts drop-down list box in the top portion of the window. Quicken immediately updates the Portfolio View window to include the accounts that you selected.

Changing the View of Your Investments

Quicken 3 for Windows enables you to change the view of your investments so that you can see up to six views, each containing different information about your securities. If you select to view the Portfolio View window by holdings, for example, Quicken assesses the market value of each security, its estimated income, and its market value as a percentage of the total value of all your investments in the selected account or accounts.

To change the view of your investments, select from the following options on the View drop-down list:

View Option	What You See
Holdings	The market value of each security, the estimated income, and the market value as a percentage of the total market value of all investments
Performance	The dollar amount invested in each security, the earnings in dollars for each security, and the ROI (return on investment) percentage
Valuation	The dollar amount invested in each security, the earnings in dollars for each security, and the market value of each security
Price Update	The last price of each security, the market value of each security, and the market value change
Custom 1 and 2	Custom views as determined by the Customize Portfolio View dialog box (explained in the next section)

When you select a view option, Quicken instantly changes the Portfolio View window to show the appropriate information.

Customizing the Portfolio View

If the preset views that Quicken provides for the Portfolio View window don't show the information you need to analyze your investments, you can customize the views to change the return dates, accounts, securities, and layout. You can even set up your own arrangement of column headings, such as Average Cost, Cost Basis, Gain/Loss, and Investment Yield.

III

Planning for the Future

To customize the Portfolio View window, follow these steps:

1. Choose the Custom button. Quicken displays the Customize Portfolio View dialog box.

2. In the Customize section, select the option button for the area you want to customize.

   Figure 15.26 shows the settings you can change when you select to customize return dates. Figure 15.27 shows the account list for selecting which accounts to include in the Portfolio View window. In figure 15.28, you see the security list for selecting which securities to include. Figure 15.29 shows the layout settings that you can change.

Fig. 15.26

The Dates Used for Return Calculations section appears in the Customize Portfolio View dialog box when you customize return dates.

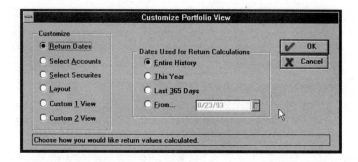

Fig. 15.27

The Select Accounts to Include list box appears in the Customize Portfolio View dialog box when you select accounts.

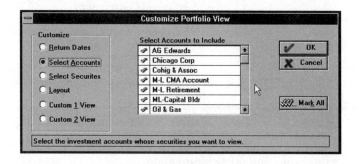

Fig. 15.28

The Select Securities to Include list box appears in the Customize Portfolio View dialog box when you select securities.

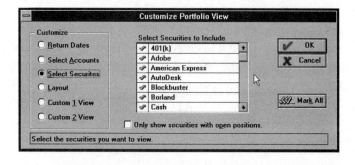

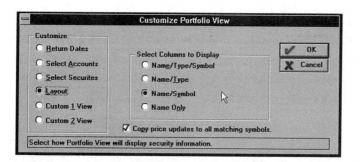

Fig. 15.29
The Select Columns to Display section appears in the Customize Portfolio View dialog box when you customize the layout.

3. Change the appropriate settings in the Customize Portfolio View dialog box or select the accounts and securities you want included in the Portfolio View window.

4. If you want to set up your own column headings, you can set up two custom views of the Portfolio View window by selecting Custom 1 View or Custom 2 View from the Customize Portfolio View dialog box. When you select the Custom 1 View option, Quicken displays the Set Custom 1 Column Views section, as shown in figure 15.30. (The same section, with a different name, appears when you select Custom 2 View.)

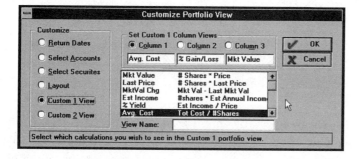

Fig. 15.30
Set up your own column headings in the Custom 1 Column Views section in the Customize Portfolio View dialog box.

Set the first column by selecting the Column 1 option button. Then select the column heading you want to use. Repeat these steps for the Column 2 and Column 3 options.

Type a name for the view in the View Name text box.

5. Choose OK to change the customize settings and return to the Portfolio View window.

If you set up custom views (see step 4) and want to change the view in the Portfolio View window to one of your custom views, select the view name you set up from the View drop-down list box.

Modifying Securities in the Portfolio View Window

Earlier in this chapter you learned how to add securities to the Security list. You can edit a security shown in the Portfolio View window, set up a new security, or delete a security. You also can display a QuickReport for a security shown in the Portfolio View window.

To add, edit, or delete a security, follow these steps:

1. In the Security column of the Portfolio View window, point to one of the securities if you are adding a new security, or point to the security you want to edit or delete. The mouse pointer changes to a magnifying glass icon.

2. Click the right mouse button to display an option menu, as shown in figure 15.31.

Fig. 15.31
Quicken displays an option menu when you click the right mouse button on a security in the Portfolio View window.

Magnifying glass pointer

Security option menu

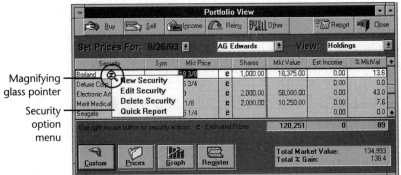

3. Select the New Security option to add a security, the Edit Security option to change information about a security, or the Delete Security option to delete a security. (You can't delete a security with trans-actions.) Quicken displays the appropriate dialog box to add a new security, edit a security, or delete a security.

To display a transaction listing for a security in the Portfolio View window, click the security using the right mouse button, and then select the QuickReport option.

Using QuickZoom To Examine Portfolio Detail

You can use QuickZoom in the Portfolio View window to see the transactions for a security. Just double-click the security. Quicken displays a Security Report, like the one in figure 15.32, with each transaction for the selected security. Choose Close to return to the Portfolio View window.

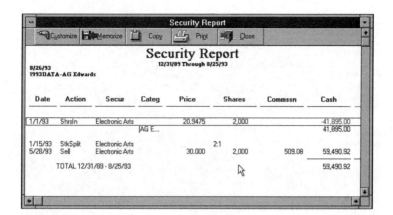

Fig. 15.32
Use QuickZoom to
display a Security
Report for the
selected security in
the Portfolio View
window.

Updating Security Prices

One of the most common investment record-keeping activities is tracking
the market value of your investments. Quicken provides several tools that
enable you to update the prices of securities in your portfolio to reflect the
current market value. You update security prices in the Portfolio View of the
Investment Register. When you enter current prices for securities, Quicken
recalculates the market value of each security and the total market value of
the investment account.

To update security prices to reflect the current market value, follow these
steps:

1. In the Register for the investment account for which you want to update prices, choose the Port View button to display the Portfolio View
   window.

2. From the View drop-down list box, select Price Update. Quicken
   changes the view of the Portfolio View window to show the security
   type, symbol, market price, number of shares, last price, market value,
   and market value change for each security (see fig. 15.33). Quicken also
   displays a column to show an estimated price or to show whether the
   security's price has increased or decreased since the previous price was
   entered.

3. Highlight the security whose price you want to update.

4. In the Mkt Price column, enter the current market price of the security.
   To record the price, move out of the Mkt Price column by pressing Tab
   or by clicking another security.

III

Planning for the Future

Tip
Use the + (plus) or
– (minus) keys to
change the secu-
rity price by 1/8
(.125).

Fig. 15.33
Quicken shows
information for
each security
when you select
the Price Update
view in the
Portfolio View
window.

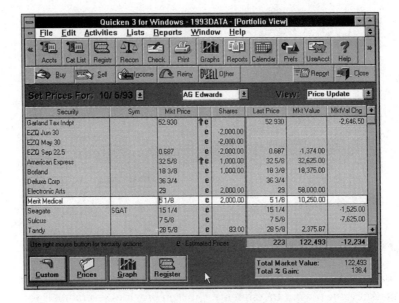

Note

If a price is unchanged from the last time you entered security prices, press the asterisk (*) key to indicate that the price remains for the current date. Quicken removes the e from the next column. (Quicken enters an e for securities that haven't been updated as of the current date.)

---

5. Repeat steps 3 and 4 for each security whose price you want to update.

6. (Optional) Choose **Print** Summary from the File menu (or press Ctrl+P) to print the contents of the Portfolio View window so that you have a paper copy of your security prices.

Note

If you want to enter security prices for other dates, change the date in the Set Prices For drop-down list box as explained earlier in the section "Changing the View Date." Then follow steps 2 through 6 to enter prices for other dates.

Creating a Price History for a Security

You can create a price history for a security so that you can evaluate its performance over time. Quicken automatically stores security prices when you update prices (as explained in the preceding section). You also can add new prices to the price history as well as change and delete prices.

To create a price history for a security, follow these steps:

1. In the Portfolio View window, highlight the security for which you want to create a price history.

2. Choose the Prices command button. Quicken displays the Price History for *xxx* dialog box (where *xxx* is the name of the selected security), as shown in figure 15.34.

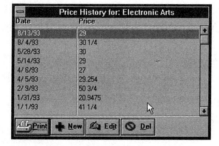

Fig. 15.34
Add, change, or delete security prices in the Price History For dialog box.

3. To add a new price, choose the New button. To edit a security price, highlight the security price and choose the Edit button. To delete a security price, highlight the security price and choose the Del button.

4. (Optional) Choose the Print button to print the price history.

5. Double-click the Control menu box or press Esc to remove the Price History for dialog box from the screen.

Graphing Security Prices

You learn about Quicken's graphs in Chapter 19, "Using Graphs To Analyze Your Finances." In the Portfolio View window, however, you can create a graph that shows a security's price history over time.

III

Planning for the Future

To graph the price history of a security, follow these steps:

1. In the Portfolio View window, highlight the security for which you want to create a price history graph.

2. Choose the Graph command button. Quicken displays the Graph Price History for the security, like the one shown in figure 15.35.

Fig. 15.35
The Graph Price History shows a security's prices over time.

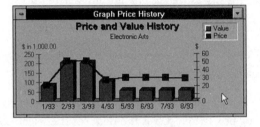

The graph plots security prices over the previous 24 months. The bars in the graph show the market value of the security at each date. The line graph shows the change in the price of the security over time.

Tip
To change the period covered by the Graph Price History, change the viewing date in the Portfolio View window and then re-create the graph.

To display a Price and Value History report, double-click the graph bar for the final month you want to include in the report.

3. Double-click the Control menu box or press Esc to remove the graph from the screen.

Importing Security Prices

You also can import price history data from an ASCII text file. The steps aren't difficult, as long as the ASCII text file looks the way Quicken expects it to. The file must contain at least two pieces of information: the security symbol and the price in decimal form. A third piece of information, the date, is optional.

The two or three pieces of information that make up a price must be together on a single line, must be separated by commas, and must not contain embedded spaces. Quicken can import the data even if one or more of the elements are enclosed in quotation marks. If the price history doesn't include a date,

Quicken uses a default date that you specify as part of the import operation. You can import all of the following, for example, as price history data:

```
DLX,36.75,8/26/93

DLX,36.75

DLX 36.75 8/26/93

"DLX",36.75."8/26/93"

"DLX","36.75""8/26/93"
```

> **Note**
>
> You can import stock prices from Prodigy's Dow Jones Service to an ASCII file in Quicken's special import format. To save stock prices to a file, refer to your Prodigy Handbook. Then perform the following steps to import stock prices from the Prodigy file.

To import prices, follow these steps:

1. Display the Register for the investment account that contains the securities to which you want to import prices.

2. Choose the Port View command button to display the Portfolio View window.

3. From the File menu, choose Import Prices. Quicken displays the Import Price Data dialog box, shown in figure 15.36.

Fig. 15.36
In the Import Price Data dialog box, enter the DOS path and file name for the file to be imported.

4. In the File text box, enter the DOS path and file name for the file that contains security prices.

5. From the Date, If Not Specified drop-down list, select the date you want to use to enter security prices. (You also can enter the date in the box.) By default, Quicken enters the current system date.

6. Choose OK to import the prices.

Reconciling Your Investment Accounts

Quicken enables you to reconcile mutual fund and regular investment accounts. The steps for reconciling these account types parallel the steps for reconciling other Quicken accounts, with a few minor differences.

In a mutual fund account, you reconcile the shares in the account, not the dollars. In a regular investment account, you reconcile cash and shares in the account.

Adjusting Investment Account Balances

If you don't want to reconcile your investment accounts, you may want to adjust their cash and share balances to agree with your brokerage or fund statements. To adjust investment account balances, follow these steps:

1. From the Activities menu, choose Update Balances.

2. To adjust the cash balance in a regular investment account, choose Update Cash Balance from the Update Balances submenu. Quicken displays the Update Cash Balance dialog box.

   To adjust the number of shares held in a regular investment account or a mutual fund investment account, choose Update Share Balance from the Update Balances submenu. Quicken displays the Update Share Balance dialog box.

3. Enter the correct cash or share balance in the appropriate dialog box. For regular investment accounts where you are adjusting the share balance, enter the security you are adjusting in the Security to Adjust text box and enter the number of shares your own in the Number of Shares text box.

4. Enter the date for which you want the cash or share balance adjusted.

5. Choose OK. Quicken enters a balance adjustment transaction in the Investment Register.

Cash balance adjustments are entered as MiscExp or MiscInc. Share balance adjustments are entered as ShrsIn or ShrsOut.

Tips on Investments and Investment Record-Keeping

Earlier parts of this book explained the procedural details of using Quicken; this section covers three additional tips.

First, you should know that unless you specify which lots of a security you are selling, Quicken applies the first in, first out (FIFO) method of record-keeping. This method means that when you sell shares of Apple Computer, for example, Quicken assumes that the shares you sell are the first shares you bought.

The FIFO assumption conforms with Internal Revenue Service regulations. The problem with FIFO is that often the first shares you bought were the least expensive. This means that when you calculate the taxable gain by subtracting the original purchase price from the sales price, you end up calculating the largest possible gain and, as a result, you incur higher income taxes.

By specifying the lots you are selling (which Quicken now enables you to do), you are using the specific identification method to record the sales and purchases of investments. Specific identification requires that you record all purchases of a particular stock as different investments, or lots. When you sell shares of Apple Computer, for example, you actually sell the shares from a specific lot. The tax-saving opportunity results from selecting the lot with the highest purchase price, because doing so minimizes your gain or maximizes your loss. (See your tax advisor for specific details.) To keep your tax-planning options open, set up each lot as a separate security.

Second, if you meticulously record the transactions that affect an investment, you can use one of Quicken's investment reports (the Performance Report) to measure the rate of return an investment produces. Although most individual investors aren't accustomed to measuring the performance of their investments, you will find doing so an invaluable exercise. Too often, individual investors don't get to measure the performance of stocks a broker recommends, a mutual fund an advertisement touts, or bonds a financial planner suggests. But with the Quicken Performance Report (described in Chapter 18), you have a convenient way to calculate precisely how well or how poorly an investment has performed. Investment performance information can help you make better investment decisions.

III

Planning for the Future

Finally, investing is more than just record-keeping. Despite the fact that Quicken provides an excellent record-keeping tool, understanding how the tool works isn't the same as understanding investments. To understand investments better, read *A Random Walk Down Wall Street* by Burton G. Malkiel, a Princeton economics professor. You should be able to find the most recent edition in any good bookstore.

Summary

This chapter described how to monitor your investments using Quicken's investment accounts. In this chapter, you learned how to do the following:

- Set up an investment account

- Set up securities in the Security list

- Use the Investment Register

- Enter investment transactions

- Memorize investment transactions

- Use QuickReport to get an instant investment transaction listing

- Use investment reminder messages

- Change the Register to Portfolio View

- Customize the Portfolio View

- Use QuickZoom to examine Portfolio detail

- Update security prices

- Create a price history for a security

- Graph security prices

- Import security prices

- Adjust investment account balances

In the next chapter, you learn how to use Quicken to set up a budget and monitor your progress toward living within the budget.

Chapter 16

Budgeting with Quicken

Budgeting has an undeserved bad reputation because people tend to think of a budget as financial handcuffs, an obstacle to enjoyment, and a drag on financial freedom. Actually, nothing is farther from the truth. Budgeting is a simple tool with astonishingly positive benefits for businesses and households. Budgets represent game plans that *calibrate*, or specify, what you need to do to succeed in business or personal financial life.

Because one of Quicken's most significant benefits is the capability of monitoring your financial success through budgeting, this chapter reviews the three steps of budgeting and describes how Quicken helps you budget more effectively.

Defining Budgeting

Budgeting consists of the following three general steps:

1. Devise a list of business or personal financial goals.

2. Use the list of goals as a guide to developing a financial game plan, or budget.

3. Use the budget to monitor your spending to determine how closely you are progressing toward your business or personal goals.

In this chapter, you learn the definition of budgeting and how to do the following:

- Set financial goals

- Enter budget amounts in Quicken's budget spreadsheet

- Automatically create a budget from actual data

- Change the spreadsheet layout

- Save and restore budget data

- Copy budget data to the Clipboard

- Print the budget spreadsheet

- Close the budget spreadsheet

III

Planning for the Future

Setting Your Goals

Budgeting begins with identifying goals in business or life. You are on your own here. When devising a list of goals, however, keep the following two things in mind:

- Keep the goals general.

- Involve other people, particularly those who must live within the budget, in setting the goals.

By stating the goals in more general terms, you don't start with built-in constraints and conflicts. Suppose that your goal is to live in an opulent fashion where the weather is warm and sunny. With this goal, you have a world of choices and an incredible range of prices. If the goal is to live in a mansion in Beverly Hills, you are limiting yourself. Living in a Beverly Hills mansion is one way but not the only way to live in an opulent fashion where the weather is warm and sunny. Keep your options open as you build a list of life goals, and you are more likely to get more of the things you want out of life and to achieve more in your business.

Also, you should involve other people in setting goals because people who work together to build a list of goals later also work together to achieve the goals. Working together also produces better goal lists.

The U.S. Air Force and many businesses play a game called *desert survival*. This game demonstrates the results of a group that works to make decisions. You pretend that a plane on which you are a passenger crashes in the desert. You are 30 miles off course and at least that far from civilization; the temperature is over 100 degrees in the shade, and you can salvage about 15 or 20 items before the plane bursts into flames. First, decide by yourself whether to stay with the wreckage or start toward civilization, and decide which items you want to keep. Next, you repeat the analysis in groups of four or five people, and this time the entire group must agree on the plan and which items to keep. An interesting point about the game and the reason that this whole issue applies to budgeting is that in almost every case, when people make the decisions together, they dramatically increase the chance of survival of all the members of the group.

Making the wrong budgeting decision may not cost you your life or your business, but the moral of the desert survival game still applies. Whether you budget personal or business finances, you build better goal lists when you involve more people. Your spouse may end up discovering an option not previously considered. A daughter may announce that she is no longer interested in piano lessons or business school. A business partner may point out a subtle flaw you overlooked.

After you finish setting your goals, write them down. Don't limit yourself to just financial goals, such as accumulating the money for the down payment on a new house or for a special vacation. You also can have non-financial goals, such as spending more time with the family or beginning a recreational or charitable activity.

Designing a Game Plan

After you build a list of goals, you are ready to create a game plan to achieve these goals. As you work through the details, you undoubtedly will modify the goals and make compromises. If you describe the goals in general terms and include everybody's good ideas, you come up with a detailed list of the costs of pursuing and achieving your business or personal goals.

At this stage, you decide how much money you are going to spend on entertainment or a vacation, how much you can spend on housing, and other issues. As a rough yardstick to use to build a detailed game plan, table 16.1 summarizes, on the average, what percent of income most people spend in various spending categories. This list comes from the July 1990 issue of Survey of Current Business, published by the U.S. Department of Commerce. The survey is dated, but because the results show as percentages of total income, the data is still valid for planning and comparison purposes.

Table 16.1 Average Spending Based on After-Tax Income	
Spending Category	**Percent**
Durable Goods	
Motor vehicles and parts	5.43
Furniture and household equipment	4.50
Other durables	2.29

(continues)

Planning for the Future

Table 16.1 Continued	
Spending Category	**Percent**
Non-durable goods	
Food	5.74
Clothing and shoes	5.38
Gasoline and oil	2.13
Other non-durables	6.57
Services	
Housing	14.34
Utilities	5.46
Transportation	3.47
Medical care	12.12
Other services	14.71
Interest	2.74
Savings	5.12

If you are budgeting for a business, you can visit the local public library to obtain similar information. Dun & Bradstreet and Robert Morris Associates annually publish financial information on businesses grouped by industry and business size. For business or personal budgeting, however, don't interpret the averages as anything other than general guidelines. Seeing other companies' spending numbers can provide a useful perspective on your spending, but your goals should determine the details of your financial game plan.

After you finish setting your goals, write your spending game plan. Now that you know how much time and money you can allocate to each goal, you often can expand the list of goals to include estimates of costs and time.

Notice a few things about the relationships between goals and budgets. First, some goals represent plateaus you can achieve almost immediately; other goals may take longer to achieve. Second, some goals don't directly affect the budget, like spending more time with your family or starting an exercise program. Third, some expenditures don't tie to formal, or stated, goals but still represent implied goals. You don't list feeding the children or staying in business, for example, but these actions may be your most important goals.

Monitoring Your Progress

The third and final step in budgeting relates to monitoring your progress in achieving personal or business goals. Periodically every month or quarter, compare the amount you budgeted to spend with the amount you actually spent. Often, people view these comparisons as negative, but the idea is that, when following a budget, you are moving toward your goals. If you get through the first month of the year and are operating under the budget, you can compare what you spent with your budget. If you see from the numbers on the budget that you are having difficulty setting aside extra money for some of your goals, you know that your spending or your goals need to change.

> **Note**
>
> In Chapter 17, "Saving for Your Future with Quicken," you learn about Quicken's new Savings Goal account that you can use to earmark funds for savings. When you use the Savings Goal account, at any given time you can see the progress you're making (or not making) toward some financial goal.

Using Quicken To Set Up a Budget

Quicken provides two related features that enable you to budget more effectively for personal finances and for small businesses: categories and reporting.

With categories, you can assign each check that you record to a spending category, such as housing, contribution, entertainment, or taxes. You also can assign an income category to each deposit you record, such as wages, gross sales, or interest income. The steps and benefits of using categories are discussed in greater detail in Chapter 4, "Organizing Your Finances."

By assigning the category into which every check and deposit you record belongs, you can produce reports that summarize and total the inflows and outflows by category for a specific period. If you decide to tap the power of budgeting, Cash Flow Reports are invaluable. Figure 16.1 shows an example

Tip

You also can produce graphs that enable you to visually compare actual dollars with budgeted dollars. For more information on creating graphs, refer to Chapter 19, "Using Graphs To Analyze Your Finances."

III

Planning for the Future

of a Cash Flow Report that shows what is actually spent during a specified period. (You learn how to create a Cash Flow Report in Chapter 18, "Creating and Printing Reports.")

Fig. 16.1

A cash-flow report shows what you actually spent during a specified period.

```
                          Cash Flow Report
                      1/1/93 Through 8/18/93
8/18/93                                                          Page 1
PERSONAL-First Nat'l
                                              1/1/1993-
              Category Description            8/18/1993

    INFLOWS
       Div Income                              250.00
       Int Inc                                  52.19
       Salary                                5,000.00

    TOTAL INFLOWS                             5,302.19

    OUTFLOWS
       Activities                              75.00
       Auto:
          Fuel                    150.00
          Lease                   250.19

       Total Auto                             400.19
       Clothing                               150.25
       Dining                                 132.18
       Groceries                              400.00
       Int Exp                                812.50
       Tax:
          Fed                   1,000.00
          Medicare                 70.98
          Soc Sec                310.00
          State                  200.00

       Total Tax                            1,580.98
       Utilities                              200.00
       TO Mortgage                            135.73

    TOTAL OUTFLOWS                           3,886.83


    OVERALL TOTAL                            1,415.36
```

Quicken also enables you to enter any amount budgeted for a category. With this information, Quicken calculates the difference, or *variance*, between the total spent on a category and the budgeted amount for a category. Quicken performs the arithmetic related to monitoring how closely you follow the budget and how successfully you are marching toward your life goals.

With Quicken's graphing capabilities, you also can produce a graph that shows the difference between budgeted and actual amounts. Figure 16.2 shows an example of a Quicken Budget Report, and figure 16.3 shows an example of a graph that shows budget variances. For information on creating a budget report, see Chapter 18, "Creating and Printing Reports." To learn how to create the Budget Variance Graph, refer to Chapter 19, "Using Graphs To Analyze Your Finances."

```
                        Budget Report
                   8/1/93 Through 8/31/93
8/18/93                                                Page 1
PERSONAL-All Accounts
                           8/1/1993        -      8/31/1993
         Category Description    Actual     Budget      Diff

   INCOME/EXPENSE
     INCOME
       Salary            5,000.00   5,000.00        0.00

   TOTAL INCOME          5,000.00   5,000.00        0.00

     EXPENSES
       Activities           75.00      75.00        0.00
       Auto:
         Fuel              136.82     150.00      -13.18
         Lease             250.19     250.00        0.19

         Total Auto        387.01     400.00      -12.99
       Charity              50.00     100.00      -50.00
       Christmas             0.00       0.00        0.00
       Clothing            375.18     400.00      -24.82
       Dining              132.18     150.00      -17.82
       Groceries           402.19     350.00       52.19
       Home Rpair            0.00      25.00      -25.00
       Household             0.00      50.00      -50.00
       Insurance            98.16     100.00       -1.84
       Medical               0.00      25.00      -25.00
       Misc                 75.69     100.00      -24.31
       Mort Int            812.50     850.00      -37.50
       Subscriptions         0.00      10.00      -10.00
       Tax:
         Fed              1,000.00   1,000.00        0.00
         Medicare           70.98      71.00       -0.02
         Soc Sec           310.00     310.00        0.00
         State             200.00     200.00        0.00

         Total Tax       1,580.98   1,581.00       -0.02
       Utilities           198.52     250.00      -51.48

   TOTAL EXPENSES        4,187.41   4,466.00     -278.59


   TOTAL INCOME/EXPENSE    812.59     534.00      278.59

   TRANSFERS
     TO Mortgage          -135.73    -130.00       -5.73
     FROM Mortgage           0.00       0.00        0.00

   TOTAL TRANSFERS        -135.73    -130.00       -5.73

   OVERALL TOTAL           676.86     404.00      272.86
```

Fig. 16.2
You can create a Budget Report for any given period that shows actual data, budgeted data, and the difference between the two.

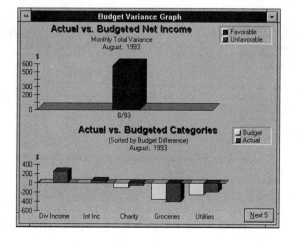

Fig. 16.3
The Budget Variance Graph shows the differences between actual data and budgeted data for any given period.

CPA TIP: Analyzing Budget Differences

When you review the Budget Report, don't worry about immaterial differences; instead, focus on large and unusual differences. Try to find out why a difference is large. Maybe you paid utility bills for the current month and in advance for next month, or perhaps you had some unexpected car repair bills or medical bills. Because some expenses are unexpected and therefore impossible to plan, you always should have a cushion in your budget for those items.

Setting Up a Budget in Quicken

After you determine how much you want to spend on what, you're ready to enter your budget data into Quicken's budget spreadsheet. The budget spreadsheet includes a row for each category set up in the Category & Transfer list. If you want to enter budget amounts for subcategories, you can select to include subcategories in the budget spreadsheet as well.

CPA TIP: Budgeting for Transfers

You can budget for transfers to other accounts. If you contribute to a 401(k) plan and have an asset account set up in Quicken to track the value of that account, for example, you can enter a budgeted amount each period to be deducted from your salary and transferred to a 401(k) account.

To display the budget spreadsheet, choose **S**et Up Budgets from the Activities menu. Quicken displays the budget spreadsheet that you see in figure 16.4.

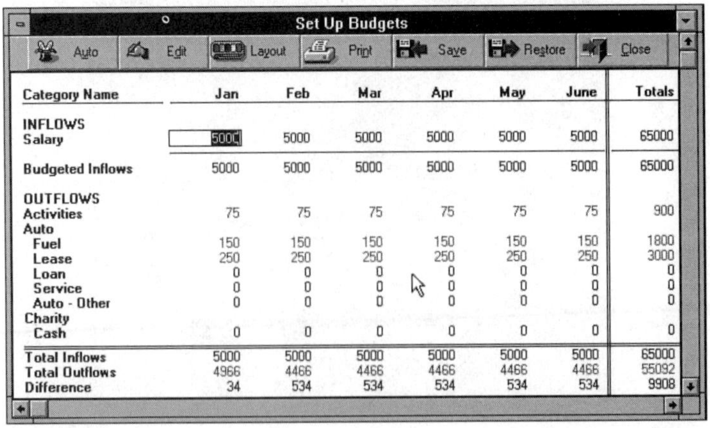

Fig. 16.4
The budget spreadsheet includes a button bar at the top of the window so that you can perform budgeting tasks quickly.

At the top of the budget spreadsheet is the budget button bar, which makes using the budget spreadsheet quick and easy. Table 16.2 describes each button on the budget button bar.

Table 16.2 The Budget Button Bar	
Button	**Function**
Auto	Enters budget information based on actual data
Edit	Displays the Edit menu, which includes the following options for editing data in the budget spreadsheet: ■ *2-Week.* Sets up a budget for an item that occurs every two weeks (such as a paycheck) ■ *Copy to Clipboard.* Copies the current budget spreadsheet to the Windows Clipboard ■ *Clear Row.* Clears budget data from the current row ■ *Clear All Budgets.* Clears all budget data from the current spreadsheet ■ *Fill Row Right.* Fills all subsequent periods (to the right) with the same budget amount as the current text box ■ *Fill Columns.* Fills all subsequent categories (below) with the same budget amounts as the current text box
Layout	Displays the Layout Budgets dialog box, which includes the following options for changing the layout of the budget spreadsheet: ■ *Columns.* Sets the interval on which you base your budget to Month, Quarter, or Year ■ *Rows.* Determines the rows that are shown in the budget spreadsheet: Show Subcats, Show Transfers, and Hide Zero Budget Cats
Print	Prints the current budget spreadsheet
Save	Saves the data in the current budget spreadsheet
Restore	Deletes all changes made to the current budget spreadsheet since the spreadsheet was last saved
Close	Closes the budget spreadsheet and gives you an opportunity to save your changes

When you first display the budget spreadsheet, the income categories appear in the top portion of the spreadsheet, followed by the expense categories. You need to scroll down the spreadsheet to see all your income and expense categories. If you drag the scroll box in the scroll bar to move through the

III

Planning for the Future

spreadsheet, Quicken displays a small box to the left of the scroll bar with the name of each category as you scroll through the spreadsheet.

The last three rows of the budget spreadsheet shown in figure 16.4 display the total budget inflows, the total budget outflows, and the difference for each period. These three rows remain at the bottom of the budget spreadsheet even when you scroll through the spreadsheet. The Total Inflows line shows the total of all income category budget amounts for each period. At the end of the expense categories section of the spreadsheet, the Total Outflows line shows the total of all expense category budget amounts for each period. The Difference line shows the difference between total inflows and total outflows.

Entering Budget Amounts

One way to enter budget amounts is to enter amounts directly into the budget spreadsheet into a selected cell. Select a cell by moving to the income or expense category for which you want to enter a budget amount, and then moving to the intersection of the appropriate period, such as Childcare for January. Quicken puts a box around the selected cell. You then can type the new budget amount.

> ### CPA TIP: Keeping Expenses in Line with Your Income
>
> As a general rule, your budgeted expenses shouldn't exceed your budgeted income. If expenses are more than your income, you're deficit spending. People who deficit spend usually rely on credit cards or bank loans to finance their lifestyle, which means they are spending now based on money they plan to make in the future. In most cases, deficit spending doesn't enable you to get ahead of the debt. Before you get in this situation, budget your expenditures wisely. Don't overextend. You should have a good idea of your income each month, each year, and so forth. Don't consistently spend more than that.

A second way to enter budgeted amounts is to copy amounts into the budget spreadsheet by using the AutoCreate Budget feature. AutoCreate Budget copies actual amounts for categories for a specified period to the budget spreadsheet, or you can fill in one cell or column and have Quicken copy the budget data that you entered into other rows or columns. For selected categories, you can enter budget amounts that occur every two weeks, such as a salary paid biweekly.

To enter budgeted amounts for a particular income or expense category, move to the cell at the intersection of the appropriate period and category in the budget spreadsheet. Type the amount and press Enter to move down one row or press Tab to move to the right one column.

The following sections explain how to create a budget automatically from actual data, how to fill in rows and columns quickly, and how to enter bi-weekly amounts.

Automatically Creating a Budget from Actual Data. If you want to set up a budget based on actual income and expense amounts, you can use the AutoCreate feature. AutoCreate copies actual data from a specified time period into the budgeting spreadsheet. You can tell Quicken to enter rounded values in the budget or to use averages for the period that you specify. When you use AutoCreate to enter your budget amounts automatically, Quicken uses information from all accounts in the current file; you can't choose accounts selectively from which Quicken can base a budget.

When you use AutoCreate to enter budget amounts from actual data in Quicken 3 for Windows, you can select the categories for which Quicken enters budget amounts from actual amounts. If, for example, you want to enter budget amounts based on actual amounts for all expense categories but not income categories, you can select only expense categories. Quicken copies actual amounts into the budget spreadsheet for only expense categories and leaves the income categories at zero until you enter budget amounts for those categories.

To create a budget automatically from actual data, follow these steps:

1. Choose Auto from the Budget button bar. Quicken displays the AutoCreate Budget dialog box, shown in figure 16.5.

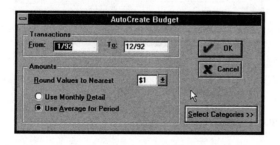

III

Fig. 16.5
Quicken displays the AutoCreate Budget dialog box when you choose Auto on the button bar.

Planning for the Future

2. Enter the date range of the actual monthly amounts you want to copy in the From and To text boxes.

3. From the Round Values to Nearest drop-down list box, select $1, $10, or $100 to indicate by how much Quicken rounds copied values before using them as the new budgeted amounts.

4. Select whether you want actual monthly detail used to enter budget amounts, or average amounts for the period. Select the Use Monthly Detail option button to copy the exact monthly amounts into the budget spreadsheet. If you select this option, however, you must set a maximum time frame of 12 months in the From and To text boxes in step 2.

   Select the Use Average for Period option button if you want Quicken to calculate the average for the copied actual amounts and use the result as the budgeted amount.

5. (Optional) To select the categories for which you want AutoCreate to enter budgeted data from actual data, choose the Select Categories button. Quicken displays all categories from the Category & Transfer list at the bottom of the AutoCreate Budget dialog box (see fig. 16.6).

Fig. 16.6

Quicken displays all categories in the AutoCreate Budget dialog box when you choose to select the categories to enter budgeted data from actual data.

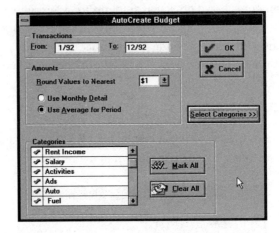

By default, all categories are marked. To clear all categories, choose Clear All. To mark all categories, choose Mark All. Click a category to mark one category at a time.

6. Choose OK when the AutoCreate Budget dialog box is complete. Quicken creates the budget (for the selected categories, if applicable) from the actual data for the period you specified.

Filling in Rows and Columns. Quicken enables you to fill in rows and columns of the budget spreadsheet quickly. Based on the amount in the selected cell in the current row, Quicken copies the amount to all cells to the right in the current row. If you enter **$25** as the January entertainment expense budget amount, for example, you can copy the amount to February, March, April, May, and so on. To copy a budget amount to rows to the right, follow these steps:

1. Select the cell that you want copied into rows to the right.

2. Choose **E**dit on the budget button bar and then choose Fill **R**ow Right.

3. Quicken asks whether you want to fill rows to the end of the year with the selected cell's budget amount. Choose **Y**es. Quicken copies the budget amount from the selected cell to each cell to the right of the current row.

Filling in columns works the same. If you fill in budget amounts for the July column, for example, you can copy amounts from the July column to the August, September, October, November, and December budget columns. To copy budget amounts from one column to all columns to the right of the current column, follow these steps:

1. Select any cell within the column that you want to copy to columns to the right.

2. Choose **E**dit on the Budget button bar and then choose Fill Columns.

3. Quicken asks whether you want to fill columns to the end of the year with the selected column's budget amounts. Choose **Y**es. Quicken copies the budget amounts in the current column to all columns to the right.

Budgeting for Biweekly Items. Quicken enables you to budget for items that you receive or pay on a biweekly basis. If you receive your paycheck every two weeks, for example, you can enter a biweekly gross salary budget amount for the Salary category.

To budget for biweekly items, take the following steps:

1. Highlight the category (or transfer account) for which you want to budget on a biweekly basis.

2. Choose **Edit** on the button bar, and then choose **2-Week**. Quicken displays the Set Up Two-Week Budget dialog box, shown in figure 16.7. The category for which you want to budget biweekly appears in the Budget For field.

Fig. 16.7
Use the Set Up Two-Week Budget dialog box to enter a biweekly budget amount.

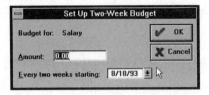

3. In the Amount text box, enter the amount you expect to spend or receive every two weeks.

4. Enter the first date of the first two-week interval in the Every Two Weeks Starting text box. If your first biweekly paycheck for the year is paid on January 6, for example, enter **1/6/***yy* in this text box.

Tip
You also can use the mini-calendar in the Every Two Weeks Starting text box to determine the starting date for biweekly items.

5. Choose **OK** to set up the two-week budget amount.

Clearing the Budget Spreadsheet

You can clear just a row in the budget spreadsheet, or you can clear the whole spreadsheet so that all budget amounts are zero and you can start over.

To clear budget amounts from one row in the budget spreadsheet, highlight the row that you want to clear. Then choose **Edit** on the button bar and choose **Clear Row**. Quicken asks whether you want to clear budget amounts for the category that you have selected. Choose **Yes**. Quicken zeros all budget amounts in the row.

To clear the entire budget spreadsheet, choose **Edit** on the Budget button bar and then choose **Clear All Budgets**. When you select to clear all budgets, Quicken asks you to confirm that you want to clear all budget amounts. Choose **Yes** to clear the budget spreadsheet, or **No** to retain budget amounts in the spreadsheet.

Changing the Budget Spreadsheet

By default, Quicken assumes that you want to budget on a monthly basis, so the spreadsheet displays a column for each month. You also can budget on a

quarterly and yearly basis, however. To change the periods shown in columns
in the budget spreadsheet, follow these steps:

1. Choose Layout on the button bar. Quicken displays the Layout Budgets
   dialog box, shown in figure 16.8.

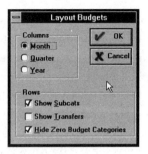

Fig. 16.8
The Layout Budgets dialog box includes options for changing the intervals on which to base your budget.

2. By default, Quicken sets up columns by month in the budget spreadsheet. Select the **Q**uarter option button to base your budget on quarterly amounts and display a column for each quarter in the spreadsheet.
   Select the **Y**ear option button to base your budget on annual amounts
   (only one column is displayed for the year).

3. Choose OK. Quicken changes the spreadsheet layout to include columns for the interval that you selected.

If you want to enter budget amounts for subcategories and transfers, you
must change the spreadsheet layout so that the spreadsheet displays rows for
each subcategory and each account in your Quicken file. You also can remove
categories that contain no budget amounts. If, for example, you have a category set up for music lessons but no budget amounts exist for this category,
you can select to hide, or not show, the category in the budget spreadsheet.

To include, or show, a row for subcategories and transfers, or to hide zero
budget categories, select one of the following options from the Layout Budgets dialog box and then choose OK:

■ Select the Show **S**ubcats check box to include a row for each subcategory in the budget spreadsheet.

■ Select the Show **T**ransfers check box to include a row for each account
   in the budget spreadsheet.

■ Select the Hide Zero Budget Categories check box to remove categories
with no budget amounts.

Saving and Restoring Budget Data

With Quicken 3 for Windows, you now can save your budget spreadsheet
after you make changes to it. In previous versions of Quicken, your budget
data wasn't saved until you removed the budget spreadsheet from the screen.
Now, you can work in the budget spreadsheet and save the data when the
budget is the way you want it. If you want to enter "what-if" scenarios by
changing budget amounts for selected categories, you can do so without
losing your original budget data. By restoring your budget data, you return to
the budget spreadsheet as it was the last time it was saved.

To save budget spreadsheet data, choose Save on the budget button bar.

To restore the budget spreadsheet to the way it was when last saved, choose
Restore on the budget button bar. Quicken warns you that restoring the budget overwrites the current changes you have made. Choose Yes.

Copying the Budget Spreadsheet to the Clipboard

Quicken 3 for Windows enables you to copy the data in your budget spreadsheet to the Windows Clipboard. You may want to use your budget data in a
spreadsheet program, for example, so that you can perform calculations using
the data, or you may want to use the budget data in a word processing program. With Quicken's new Copy to Clipboard command, you can copy all
budget data in the spreadsheet to the Windows Clipboard. You then can
paste the data to your Windows spreadsheet or word processor.

To copy the budget spreadsheet to the Clipboard, choose Edit on the budget
button bar and then choose Copy to Clipboard.

Printing the Budget Spreadsheet

In Quicken 3 for Windows, you can print a hard copy of your budget so that
it's easier to review.

> **Note**
>
> Before you print the budget spreadsheet, make sure that Quicken is set up to print reports and lists. Refer to Chapter 4, "Organizing Your Finances," to learn how to set up Quicken to print reports and lists.

To print the budget spreadsheet, follow these steps:

1. Display the budget spreadsheet, as explained earlier in this chapter.

2. Choose Print on the budget button bar. Quicken displays the Print Report dialog box.

3. In the Print To section, select where you want the budget spreadsheet printed. To print to your printer, select Printer. You also can save the budget spreadsheet to an ASCII Disk File, a Tab-delimited Disk File, a 123 (.PRN) disk file, or preview it on your Screen.

4. If you have a color printer, select the Print in Color check box to print the budget spreadsheet in color. You must have an installed color printer to print the list in color.

   Select Print in Draft Mode, if desired and if your installed printer supports draft mode printing.

5. Select the print range. Select All to print all pages of the budget spreadsheet; or select Pages and then specify which pages you want to print in the text boxes.

6. Choose Print or press Enter to begin printing the budget spreadsheet.

Closing the Budget Spreadsheet

When you finish preparing your budget, close the budget spreadsheet by choosing Close on the budget button bar. Quicken asks whether you want to save the budget data before exiting. If you want to save the changes you just made, choose Yes; otherwise, choose No. Choose Cancel to return to the spreadsheet.

III

Planning for the Future

Summary

This chapter outlined the budgeting process, told why budgeting is important in managing personal and business finances, and described how Quicken helps with the process. You learned how to do the following:

- Enter budget amounts in the budget spreadsheet

- Automatically create a budget from actual data

- Change the spreadsheet layout

- Clear budget data from the spreadsheet

- Save and restore budget data

- Copy budget data to the Windows Clipboard

- Print and close the budget spreadsheet

Chapter 17 shows you how to use a new feature in Quicken 3 for Windows—the Savings Goal account—to monitor your savings. You also learn how to use a few of Quicken's financial planners to calculate investment earnings, plan for your kids' college costs, and plan for your retirement.

Chapter 17

Saving for the Future with Quicken

You already know how to use Quicken to write checks, keep your Register, reconcile your bank account, track your assets and liabilities, manage your credit cards, create a budget, prepare for income taxes, and monitor your investments. But what about using Quicken for financial planning to save for your future? We all know the sacrifices we need to make to *save*, but what is financial planning?

Financial planning is the process of setting goals and developing plans to meet those goals. Then, when your goals are set, you must start saving to meet those goals. To retire with enough money to meet expenses (and have a little fun) through the rest of your life, for example, you first must determine how much money you will need, and then develop and implement a financial plan so that you have that amount of money at retirement age. You also need to develop a financial plan for the things that you want to acquire, such as a first home, new car, vacation home, trip to Europe, and so on. And if you have children, you will want to plan for college expenses *now*, even though your children are young.

You don't need other software programs to help you with planning your financial needs for the future. Quicken includes financial planners that are convenient and easy to use. Quicken's financial planners are easy to access from anywhere in the program and make calculations as quickly as you can enter the data.

In this chapter, you learn how to do the following:

- Set up a Savings Goal account

- Track savings in a Savings Goal account

- Use the Investment Savings Planner to calculate investment earnings

- Prepare for college tuition for your kids and use the College Planner

- Prepare for retirement and use the Retirement Planner

III

Planning for the Future

In Chapter 10, "Tracking Loans," you learned about the Loan Planner and the Refinance Planner. In this chapter, you learn about the remaining planners, as follows:

- *Investment Planner.* Calculates the expected growth of an investment, how much money you need now to have a certain amount in the future, or how much money you need to contribute periodically to an investment to have a certain amount in the future.

- *College Planner.* Calculates how much money you need to have today, or how much you need to save each year, to send your kids to college. You even can use this tool to help you determine how much annual tuition you can afford—state-supported school, Ivy League, or other.

- *Retirement Planner.* Calculates how much your current retirement account will yield in annual, after-tax income at retirement age given your estimated tax rate, yearly contributions, predicted inflation rate, and the expected annual yield. With the Retirement Planner, you also can determine how much you need to have now or how much you need to contribute to your retirement account on a yearly basis so that you have the money you need when you retire.

What about saving for a trip to Bermuda, new patio furniture, or a new boat? Quicken can even help you monitor your savings for the short-term expenditures that you don't necessarily transfer to another bank account. With Quicken's new Savings Goal account, you can track the money that you want to put aside for a special purpose. This new account is handy for gauging the progress you're making toward saving money, for whatever purpose.

Using the Savings Goal Account

With Quicken 3 for Windows, you can create a Savings Goal account to track money that you want to put aside for a special purpose—perhaps a vacation, a down payment on a new car, or an investment in a new business. Quicken treats transfers to Savings Goal accounts as paper transactions only. Money isn't actually transferred from the bank account to a Savings Goal account. The Savings Goal account is used to track the amount that you are *mentally* saving from your bank account.

> **Note**
>
> The Savings Goal account is unlike the other planners that you learn about in this chapter in that it doesn't perform calculations. However, the Savings Goal account does help you plan for the future by tracking your savings towards some future goal.

The Savings Goal account is set up as an asset account but is treated differently than other asset accounts. With the Savings Goal account, you periodically can make a paper transfer of money, or savings, into the account from your checking account. When you record a transfer transaction from your checking account to a Savings Goal account, the transfer amount increases the balance in the Savings Goal account but never really leaves your checking account. You can choose to show the balance in your checking account, however, with or without the transfer transaction to the Savings Goal account. When you reconcile your checking account, transfer transactions to your Savings Goal account don't appear because money wasn't actually transferred out of your checking account.

Setting Up a Savings Goal Account

Setting up a Savings Goal account is just like setting up any asset account. When you select to set up an asset account (refer to Chapter 3, "Defining Accounts"), Quicken displays the New Account Information dialog box, shown in figure 17.1. Select the Savings Goal Account check box to designate the asset account as a Savings Goal account.

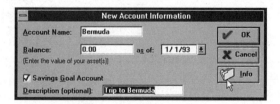

Fig. 17.1
Select the Savings Goal Account check box in the New Account Information dialog box to set up a Savings Goal account.

Tracking Savings in a Savings Goal Account

After you set up a Savings Goal account, you can begin to transfer savings periodically to the account from your checking or other bank account. To transfer amounts to the Savings Goal account, follow these steps:

1. In the Register for the bank account you're saving from (not the account you just created), enter the date that you're putting away money in your Savings Goal account.

III

Planning for the Future

2. In the Payee field, type a word or phrase that describes the transaction, like **August Savings**.

3. In the Payment field, enter the amount that you want to save at this time.

4. (Optional) Type a memo in the Memo field.

5. In the Category field, select the Savings Goal account. Entering the Savings Goal account creates a transfer transaction.

6. Select Record to record the transfer transaction.

When you use a Savings Goal account in Quicken, an additional option appears at the bottom of the checking or other bank account Register. When you select the Show Bank Bal. option (see fig. 17.2), any transfer transactions to a Savings Goal account are hidden. Savings transfers aren't included in the ending bank balance. If you want Quicken to show the transfer transaction in your bank Register and subtract the savings amount from the ending bank balance, remove the check mark from the Show Bank Bal. check box at the bottom of the Register.

Fig. 17.2

When you use a Savings Goal account, the Register for your bank account displays the Show Bank Bal. option.

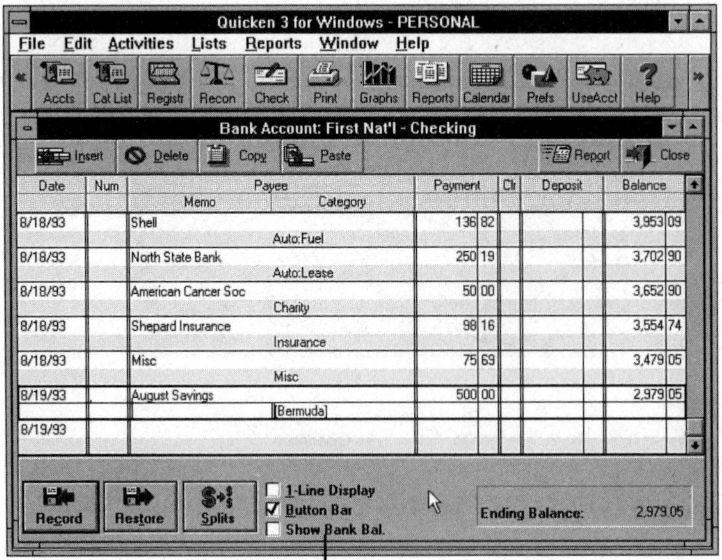

The Show Bank Bal. option

If you want to see how much you have "saved" in your Savings Goal account, select the account from the Account list to display its Register.

Planning Your Investments

Most of us have some amount of money saved or invested (no matter how large or small) that we would like to see grow. Whether you're saving for a new car, a down payment, or a European vacation, you want your money to grow quickly so that you don't have to wait so long to acquire the things you want.

Although Quicken can't make your money grow any quicker than the investment vehicle in which it's now maintained, you can monitor your investment growth and play out "what-if" scenarios using Quicken's Investment Savings Planner. You can see how much your investment will grow given different interest rates, inflation rates, and yearly contributions.

Using the Investment Savings Planner

With the Investment Savings Planner, you can calculate the following variables:

- The expected growth of the money that you now have saved or invested over a certain time period and based on a specific interest rate and expected inflation rate

- How much money you need *now* to accumulate a certain amount of money in the future

- How much money you need to save on a regular basis to accumulate a certain amount of money in the future

To access the Investment Savings Planner, follow these steps:

1. From the Activities menu, choose Financial Planners.

2. From the Financial Planners submenu, choose **S**avings. Quicken displays the Investment Savings Planner, shown in figure 17.3.

Performing Investment Planning Calculations

To use the Investment Savings Planner, follow these steps:

1. Access the Investment Savings Planner, as explained in the preceding section.

III

Planning for the Future

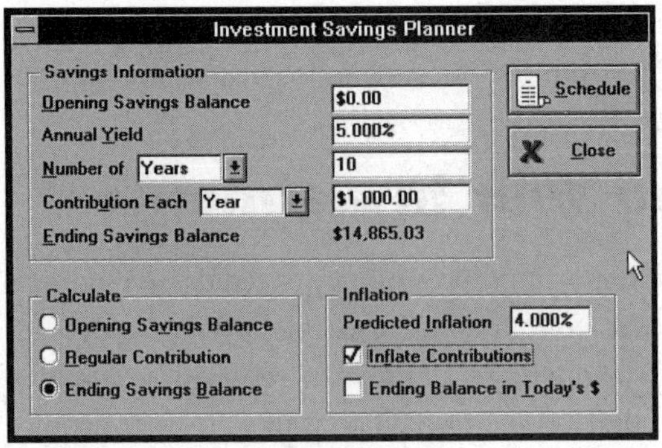

Fig. 17.3

The Investment
Savings Planner
performs several
calculations to
help you reach
financial goals.

2. In the Calculate section, select the calculation that you want to perform.

   To calculate how much money you need to start with to reach a certain goal, select the Opening Savings Balance option button.

   To calculate how much money you need to contribute each period if you start with a certain amount and want to reach a specified goal, select the Regular Contribution option button.

   To calculate how much money you will have at the end of a specified period if you start with a certain amount and make regular contributions, choose the Ending Savings Balance option button.

3. In the Savings Information section, enter the amounts needed for Quicken to perform its calculation. Use the drop-down lists provided for the Number Of and Contribution Each options to identify the type of savings periods you plan to use; Weeks, Months, Quarters, or Years.

   The information you are required to enter in the Savings Information section depends on the calculation that you select to perform in the Calculate section of the Investment Savings Planner. If you select to calculate the opening savings balance, for example, you must provide the annual yield that you expect to earn on your savings, the number of periods over which you expect to make contributions, the periods you plan to use to make the contributions, and the ending savings balance that you want to attain.

4. In the Inflation section, use the Predicted Inflation text box to enter the current or expected annual inflation rate.

5. Select the Inflate Contributions check box if you want Quicken to adjust the contributions that you make to your investment or savings account based on the inflation rate.

6. Select the Ending Balance in Today's $ check box if you want Quicken to convert the ending savings balance to its purchasing power today.

   As you enter amounts in the various text boxes and select options in the Investment Savings Planner, Quicken performs the calculation according to the option you selected in the Calculate section.

7. If you want to see a schedule of deposits or contributions that you need to make to attain your financial goal, choose the Schedule button. Quicken displays the Deposit Schedule, shown in figure 17.4. In figure 17.4, the schedule shows that if you contribute or deposit $1,000 each year, at an annual yield of 5% and an inflation rate of 4%, in 10 years your savings will grow to $14,865.03.

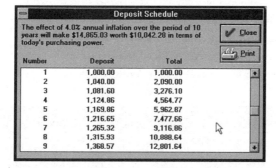

Fig. 17.4
The Deposit Schedule shows how your deposits or contributions to a savings plan grow over a specified period of time.

Note

If you want to print the Deposit Schedule, choose the Print button. The printed Deposit Schedule lists the data in the Investment Savings Planner (opening savings balance, annual yield, number of years, and so forth), followed by the deposits and a running total for each year contributions are made.

Make sure that you have set up Quicken to print reports before you choose to print the Deposit Schedule. Chapter 18, "Creating and Printing Reports," explains how to set up Quicken to print reports.

Choose the Close button to return to the Investment Savings Planner.

8. When you return to the Investment Savings Planner, perform as many calculations as you want. When you are finished, choose the Close button.

Quicken doesn't save your calculations when you close the Investment Savings Planner. If you need to retain the calculation information, print the Deposit Schedule, as explained in the preceding note.

Planning for College

Financing a college education is no small investment. You no longer can wait until your kids are in high school to start thinking about where you're going to get the money to send them to college. With rising tuition costs, most people must save and invest for several years to have enough money to pay for college.

With Quicken's College Planner, you can determine how much you need to save each year for college, as well as how much tuition you can afford in the future based on the amount that you can afford to save today. You also can calculate how much you need to have invested or saved now to have enough to pay tuition when your child reaches college age.

> **Note**
>
> Quicken's College Planner assumes that you will continue to save until your child graduates from college. If your child is 8 years old, for example, approximately 10 years remain until he or she starts college. But at least 14 years will pass until your child graduates from college. Therefore, the College Planner calculates present savings, current college costs, and yearly payments based on 14 years of savings, not 10.

Using the College Planner

To access the College Planner, follow these steps:

1. From the Activities menu, choose Financial Planners.

2. From the Financial Planners submenu, choose College. Quicken displays the College Planner, shown in figure 17.5.

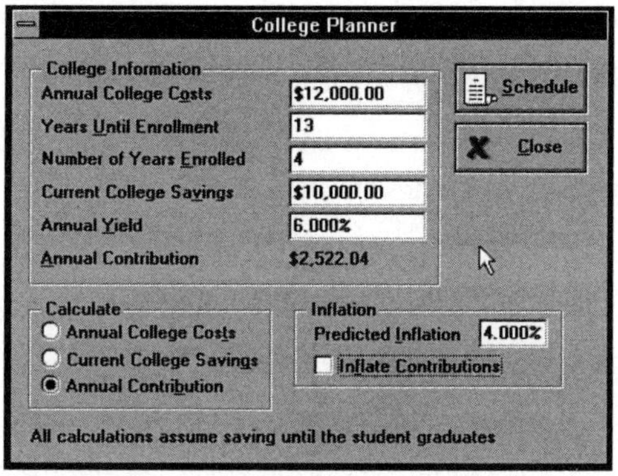

Fig. 17.5
The College
Planner calculates
how much you'll
need for your
child's college
costs.

Performing College Planning Calculations

To perform calculations with the College Planner, follow these steps:

1. Access the College Planner, as explained in the preceding section.

2. In the Calculate section of the planner, select the calculation that you want to perform.

   To calculate how much you need to be able to afford annual college costs if you make a specific contribution each period, given that you start with a certain amount of savings, select the Annual College Costs option button.

   To calculate how much you need to have saved *now* to have enough for college costs, given an expected contribution each year, select the Current College Savings option button.

   To calculate how much you need to put away each year to have enough to cover all college costs if you start with a certain amount of savings, select the Annual Contribution option button.

3. In the College Information section, enter the amounts needed for Quicken to perform its calculation. Check with the school's bursar's office to find out the current cost of tuition, room and board, and books.

   If you select to calculate annual college costs, for example, you must provide the annual yield you expect to earn on your contributions, the number of years enrolled, the number of years until enrollment, and the annual contribution you intend to make to your college fund.

4. In the Inflation section of the College Planner, enter the current or expected inflation rate in the Predicted Inflation text box.

5. Select the Inflate Contributions check box to have Quicken adjust your contributions by the predicted inflation rate.

As you enter amounts in the various text boxes and select options in the College Planner, Quicken performs the calculation according to the option you selected in the Calculate section.

6. If you want to see a schedule of deposits or contributions that you need to make to attain your college tuition goals, choose the Schedule button. Quicken displays the Deposit Schedule shown in figure 17.6.

Fig. 17.6
The Deposit Schedule shows how your deposits or contributions to a college fund grow over a specified period of time.

		Deposit Schedule		
				✔ Close
				🖨 Print
Year	Deposit	Tuition	Balance	
0	0.00	0.00	10,000.00	
1993	2,522.04	0.00	13,122.04	
1994	2,522.04	0.00	16,431.40	
1995	2,522.04	0.00	19,939.33	
1996	2,522.04	0.00	23,657.73	
1997	2,522.04	0.00	27,599.23	
1998	2,522.04	0.00	31,777.22	
1999	2,522.04	0.00	36,205.90	
2000	2,522.04	0.00	40,900.29	

In figure 17.6, the schedule shows that if you contribute $2,522.04 each year at an annual yield of 6 percent, in 13 years you can pay annual college costs of $12,000 per year (adjusted for inflation).

Note

If you want to print the Deposit Schedule, choose the Print button. The printed Deposit Schedule lists the data in the College Planner (annual college costs, years until enrollment, number of years enrolled, and so forth), followed by the deposits and a running total for each year contributions are made.

Make sure that you have set up Quicken to print reports before you select to print the Deposit Schedule. Chapter 18, "Creating and Printing Reports," explains how to set up Quicken to print reports.

7. Choose the Close button to return to the College Planner.

8. When you return to the College Planner, perform as many calculations as you want. When you're finished, choose the Close button.

Quicken doesn't save your calculations when you close the College Planner. If you need to retain the calculation information, print the Deposit Schedule as explained in the preceding note.

Tips on Saving for College

Tuition and fees at state colleges have risen an average of 9 percent a year since 1980. Costs have risen 10 percent at private schools. At these rates, a four-year degree for a newborn is estimated to cost between $95,000 and $290,000—or even more—by the time that child is 18. So there's no question that you must think about saving for college *now*, when your children are young, so that you can keep up with these rising costs.

The following are some things to consider to help you decide how you're going to meet rising college costs head on:

- If you're funding college for a young child, consider a multiphase investment plan. Phase 1, when your children are young, should include mutual funds that invest in stocks. Stocks are your best bet for growth at a level that exceeds the high rate of increasing college costs. Although the stock market can drop, it usually bounces right back, and over the long run, stock values rise.

  Begin phase 2 of your college investment plan as your child becomes closer to college age (12 to 14 years old, for example). You won't want the volatility of the market to impact your capital or earnings at this point. Consider gradually moving your money into capital preservation investments, such as Series EE Savings Bonds, Treasury securities, and certificates of deposit (CDs). You also could switch to a mutual fund that divides your money between stocks and bonds.

  Phase 3 should begin when your child reaches age 14 or so (then you know college is only 4 years away). At this time, preserving your investment becomes more important. Begin moving a portion of your funds (maybe 25 percent to cover the first year of college) into a guaranteed 4-year investment, such as a CD. The next year, move another 25 percent, and so on.

- Automated savings plans that take money directly from your bank account each month and deposit it into a savings plan or investment account are available. This setup makes saving a little less painful and virtually effortless. Consider the amount withdrawn from your bank account a fixed payment, like your mortgage or car loan payment. That way, you won't be tempted to think of other ways to spend it.

■ Don't get hooked into investing your money in bonds that don't mature until after your child reaches college age. If you buy a 30-year bond when your child is born, for example, you will be forced to sell it after only 18 years and risk losing some of your capital. Make sure that bond maturity dates coincide with the dates you will need the money for college.

■ Some states (about half) are offering special college savings bonds, also known as *baccalaureate bonds*, to be used to fund college costs to any state-supported school. These bonds are *zero-coupon bonds*, which means that they don't pay interest over the life of the bond, but sell at a large discount from their maturity value. The face value of college savings bonds increases from year to year. College savings bonds usually come in maturities of 5 to 21 years and are exempt from federal income tax and from state and local taxes if you live in the issuing state. Check with your state's finance department to see whether these bonds are being issued in your state and which brokerage firm you can call to place an order.

■ Remember that you can take out a home-equity loan to pay for college when the time comes. Hang on to your home rather than trade up. The longer you keep it, the more equity you will have.

Planning for Retirement

Most people aspire to stop working some day so that they can enjoy their later years. Just because you stop working, however, doesn't mean your expenses also stop. How do you plan to pay for living expenses after the paycheck stops?

You may believe this topic to be of interest only to readers who are retiring soon, but this isn't the case. The irony is that the easiest time to prepare for retirement is when the time you stop working is still a long way off, and the hardest time to prepare for retirement is when retirement is right around the bend.

Preparing a Living Expenses Budget

The first step in planning for retirement is to estimate living expenses. Obviously, the further away your retirement, the less precise are the estimates. Even if retirement is 20 years away, your current spending can provide a useful benchmark for estimating future expenses. The general rule of thumb is that retirement expenses are roughly 80 percent of current living expenses. Generally, three reasons account for this calculation:

- Housing expenses may go down because you owned a home and paid off your mortgage, or you moved to a smaller house or apartment.

- Children grow up and, usually, cease to be financial responsibilities.

- Work expenses, such as special clothing, transportation, tools, dues, and so on, stop because you stop working.

Be careful, however, that you don't drastically reduce your planned living expenses. Remember that certain expenses also may increase because you age or retire. Medical expenses—such as the insurance an employer paid previously—may increase. Entertainment and vacation expenses may increase because you have more free time on your hands. Consider also that retirement may mean new hobbies or activities with attendant costs.

In any event, the reports that Quicken provides should prove immensely helpful. In particular, Quicken's Itemized Category Report should be useful because the report shows the ways you now are spending money. (Read Chapter 18, "Creating and Printing Reports," if you have questions about how to print a particular report.)

Figure 17.7 provides a worksheet you can use to estimate the living expenses you may have during retirement. You can fill in the first column, the one that records your current expenses, by using the Itemized Category Report.

By using this information and the ideas already touched on, you can fill out the second column to come up with an estimate of retirement expenses. After you determine your estimated retirement living expenses, you have the number you need to enter as your after-tax income for retirement in the Retirement Planner.

Keep in mind two more things about estimating retirement living expenses. First, don't adjust the expense estimates for the inflation that probably will occur between now and the time you retire, because the Retirement Planner

Tip

Quicken's calculator provides a convenient way to compute the total expenses for retirement.

III

Planning for the Future

addresses the ravages of inflation by factoring the inflation rate that you enter into its calculations. Second, don't worry about taxes in your worksheet. The Retirement Planner also factors the tax rate entered into its calculations.

Fig. 17.7
Use the Estimated Living Expenses Worksheet to determine your expenses when you retire.

Estimated Living Expenses Worksheet		
Expense	Current	Retirement
Housing		
Mortgage or rent		
Property taxes		
Property insurance		
Maintenance		
Food		
Transportation		
Work		
Hobby		
Vacation		
Recreation		
Healthcare/Insurance		
Clothing		
Other		
Total Expenses		

Estimating Tentative Retirement Income

Estimating tentative retirement income is the second step in planning a retirement income. In general, a person's retirement income essentially consists of three components: Social Security, investment income, and pension income. To tally these three sources, you need to do the following:

1. Contact the local Social Security office and ask for the form called *Request for Earnings and Benefit Estimate Statement.*

2. Complete the statement by following the directions on the form. You need to enter your Social Security number, information about your earnings, and when you plan to retire. After you complete the form, send it to the address given. In a few weeks, you will receive an estimate of what you may receive in Social Security benefits when you retire.

3. If you qualify for an employer's pension, contact the pension fund administrator or trustee and ask for whatever information you need to estimate your future retirement benefits. The administrator should be

more than happy to give this information to you. In fact, the pension fund trustee is required to give you the information.

4. Add any other income sources that you may have when you retire, such as rental income from properties, annuities, and so on.

Now you have the information you need to determine your estimated retirement income. Add the amounts from steps 2, 3, and 4 for your total retirement income. You use this amount in the Retirement Planner.

Using the Retirement Planner

Now you're ready to use the Retirement Planner to calculate any of the following variables:

- How much your current retirement account will yield annually when you retire based on yearly contributions, expected annual yields, and estimated income tax rates

- How much money you need *now* to accumulate the money you will need when you retire

- How much you need to contribute each year to your retirement account to ensure that you have enough money when you retire

To perform the various retirement calculations with the Retirement Planner, follow these steps:

1. From the Activities menu, choose Financial Planners.

2. From the Financial Planners submenu, choose **Retirement**. Quicken displays the Retirement Planner, shown in figure 17.8.

3. In the Calculate section, select the calculation that you want to perform.

To calculate how much you need to have saved now to meet your annual retirement income goals if you contribute a specified amount, select the Current Savings option button.

To calculate how much you need to contribute each year to meet your retirement goals, select the Annual Contribution option button.

To calculate how much income you will have each year during retirement if you have a certain amount saved now and make specified

III

Planning for the Future

contributions each period, select the Annual Retirement Income option button.

Fig. 17.8
Use the Retirement Planner to calculate how much you need to save to retire comfortably.

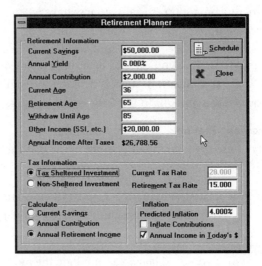

4. In the Retirement Information box, enter the amounts needed for Quicken to perform its calculations. If you select to calculate annual contributions, for example, you must provide the amount of your current savings (if any), the annual yield you expect to earn on your contributions, your current age, your expected retirement age, the age to which you expect to withdraw retirement income, and the amount of other income you have (Social Security, pensions, and so forth) that you determined in the preceding section.

CPA TIP: Choosing an Annual Yield

As a frame of reference in picking appropriate real rates of return, you may find several pieces of data helpful. Over the last 60 years or so, inflation has averaged a little more than 3 percent, common stocks have averaged 10 percent, long-term bonds have averaged around 5 percent, and short-term Treasury bills have averaged roughly 3.5 percent. Therefore, when you subtract inflation, stocks produced real returns of 7 percent, long-term bonds produced real returns of about 2 percent, and Treasury bills essentially broke even. Accordingly, if half of the retirement savings is invested in long-term bonds yielding 2 percent and the other half invested in common stocks yielding 7 percent, you may want to guess the return as somewhere between 4 and 5 percent.

5. In the Tax Information section, select the Tax Sheltered Investment option button if your retirement investments are invested in a tax-deferred account, such as an IRA or a Keogh. Select the Non-Sheltered Investment option button if your retirement investments are taxable.

6. In the Retirement Tax Rate text box, type your estimated tax rate when you retire. This rate may be tough to project because you really don't know where tax rates will be in the future. The best estimate, however, is today's tax rates, given your future level of income.

7. If you are calculating retirement income for non-sheltered investments, enter the applicable tax rate in Current Tax Rate text box. Quicken uses this rate to calculate the income tax effect on the earnings from your yearly contributions if your retirement account isn't tax sheltered. Type your current maximum tax rate without the percent sign. Because tax rates continually change, keep in mind that you may need to modify retirement planning results to take into consideration higher or lower tax rates.

8. In the Inflation section, enter the current or expected inflation rate in the Predicted Inflation text box. The *inflation rate* is the annual percentage rate that prices increase. The $2,000 that you contribute this year won't be the same as contributing $2,000 10 years from now.

9. Select the Inflate Contributions check box if you want Quicken to adjust your yearly contributions for inflation, or leave the check box blank to keep your contributions constant.

10. Select the Annual Income in Today's $ check box to have Quicken adjust the results of the calculation in today's dollars instead of their future value.

As you enter amounts in the various text boxes and select options in the Retirement Planner, Quicken performs the calculation according to the option you selected in the Calculate section.

11. If you want to see a schedule of deposits or contributions that you need to make to attain your retirement income goals, choose the Schedule button. Quicken displays the Deposit Schedule that shows how your retirement fund balance changes if you make regular contributions.

Tip

If part of your projected retirement income is tax-sheltered and part isn't, make separate calculations using the Retirement Planner.

III

Planning for the Future

> ### Note
>
> If you want to print the Deposit Schedule, choose the **P**rint button. The printed Deposit Schedule lists the data in the Retirement Planner (current savings, annual yield, annual contribution, current age, and so forth), followed by deposits and a running total for each year contributions are made.
>
> Make sure that you have set up Quicken to print reports before you select to print the Deposit Schedule. Chapter 18, "Creating and Printing Reports," explains how to set up Quicken to print reports.

12. Choose the Close button to return to the Retirement Planner.

13. When you return to the Retirement Planner, perform as many calculations as you want. When you're finished, choose the Close button.

Quicken doesn't save your calculations when you close the Retirement Planner. If you need to retain the calculation information, print the Deposit Schedule as explained in the preceding note.

More Tips on Retirement Planning

Planning for retirement can be frustrating and difficult. Before you decide that you can never quit working, however, consider the following suggestions and observations.

First, invest retirement money in tax-deferred investments, such as individual retirement accounts (IRAs), 401(k)s, annuities, and so on. Consider these kinds of investments even if you don't receive an immediate tax deduction because paying income taxes on the interest or investment income you earn greatly reduces the real interest rate you enjoy.

Suppose that you choose to invest in a mutual fund that you expect will return around 7.5 percent annually. If you don't have to pay income taxes on the interest, you may be left with a real interest rate of around 4.5 percent (calculated as the 7.5 percent minus the 3 percent historical inflation rate).

If you must pay income taxes, however, the story is different. Suppose that your highest dollars of income are taxed at the 28 percent tax rate. To subtract the income taxes you pay, multiply the 7.5 percent by (1 minus 28 percent). This means that the real *adjusted-for-income-taxes* interest rate is 5.4 percent. When you calculate the real interest rate by taking this 5.4 percent interest rate and subtracting the 3 percent inflation rate, the annual real interest rate amounts to a measly 2.4 percent—less than the amount you receive if you use an investment option that enables you to defer income taxes.

In this example, using investment options in which you can defer the taxes more than doubles the return, which makes a huge difference in the amounts you accumulate over the years you save.

A second consideration is that the longer you postpone retirement, the more retirement income you typically enjoy when you do retire. This tactic isn't much of a revelation, of course, because it makes intuitive sense. The difference postponed retirement makes may surprise you, however. If you postpone retirement, you have several things working in your favor:

- Social Security benefits may increase because you begin drawing benefits later or because the average earnings are higher.

- Any retirement savings you accumulate have a few more years to earn interest, and you probably can save more money.

- Pension plans usually pay benefits based on years of service, so working a little longer can increase this source of retirement income.

You can rework the numbers by using the Retirement Planner described in this chapter to see specific results for your case.

A third and final point to consider relates to a fundamental assumption of the Retirement Planner. The planner assumes that you live off only the annual investment income, Social Security, and pensions. This means that you never actually spend the money you save, only the interest those savings earn. If you have $100,000 in savings that earns $5,000 in annual interest, for example, you spend only the $5,000, and you leave the $100,000 intact. As a practical matter, however, you probably can spend some of the $100,000. The trick is to make sure that the $100,000 doesn't run out before you do.

Summary

This chapter explained how to use Quicken to save and plan for your future. You learned how to do the following:

- Set up a Savings Goal account

- Track savings in a Savings Goal account

■ Calculate the return on investments with the Investment Savings Planner

■ Use the College Planner to calculate how much money you need to save for your child's college tuition

■ Calculate the annual retirement income that you can expect to have given your current retirement savings and annual contributions

The next chapter begins Part IV, "Analyzing Your Finances with Quicken." The next chapter shows you how to create and print reports that show you the results of your work in Quicken. Quicken provides several types of reports that can help you assess your financial condition.

Part IV

Analyzing Your Finances with Quicken

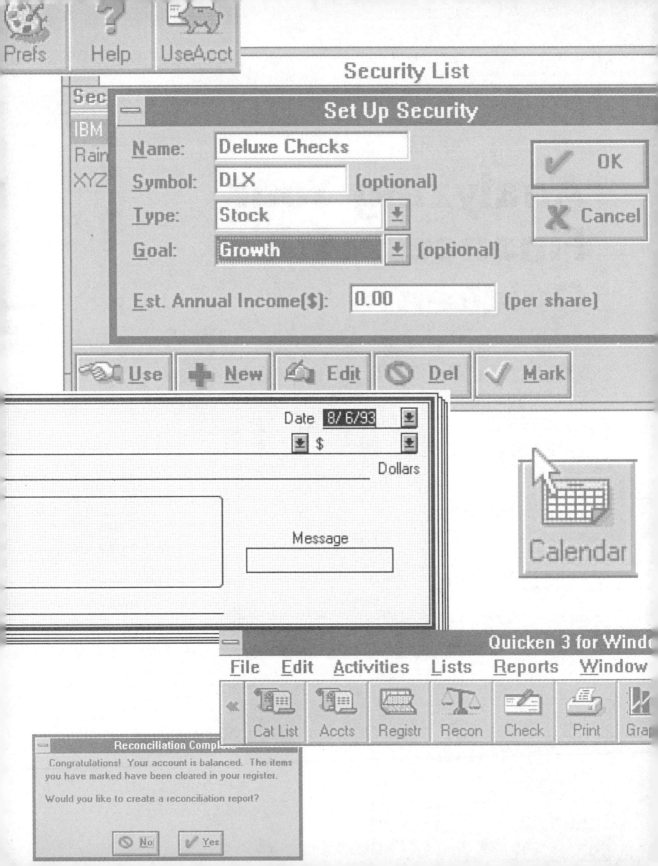

Chapter 18

Creating and Printing Reports

When you collect information about your finances in a Quicken file, you essentially construct a database. You can use the information in a financial database to determine cash flow, net income or loss, tax deductions, and net worth. But first you must arrange, retrieve, and summarize the data. To do so, Quicken provides a variety of reports. This chapter describes how to create and print the reports you need to analyze your finances.

Quicken 3 for Windows makes creating and customizing reports easier than ever. If you click the Reports button on the Iconbar, you instantly see the report list and a sample report. And with the new Customize button on the Report button bar, customizing reports is a breeze.

Quicken 3 for Windows also includes some new reports. Comparison Reports compare financial results from different periods, and Missing Checks Reports alert you when a check is missing from the sequence. Also, you now can view reports with percentages so that you can analyze the relationships of your data.

New QuickReports sort through transactions and lists and instantly display reports relative to the current window or list. If you want to see a listing of all checks for contributions to your church, for example, highlight one transaction in the Register that contains your church as payee and choose the QuickReport button. Quicken displays a list of all transactions in the current year payable to the church.

In this chapter, you learn how to do the following:

- Set up Quicken to print reports

- Use Quicken's new Quick-Report feature

- Create a report

- Print reports

- Customize reports

- Sort transactions in reports

- Examine report details with QuickZoom

- Memorize reports

- Copy a report to the Windows Clipboard

And to make Quicken even more Windows compatible, the new Copy command enables you to copy an entire report to the Windows Clipboard for use in another Windows program.

Creating QuickReports

QuickReport is a new feature in Quicken 3 for Windows that enables you to get instant transaction listings relating to the current window. QuickReports are available when you see the QuickReport button, as shown in the Register in figure 18.1. (Although the button that you see in the Register button bar is labeled Report, it is referred to as the QuickReport button.)

Fig. 18.1
Choose the QuickReport button in the Register button bar to create an instant report of all transactions that contain the same payee as the selected transaction.

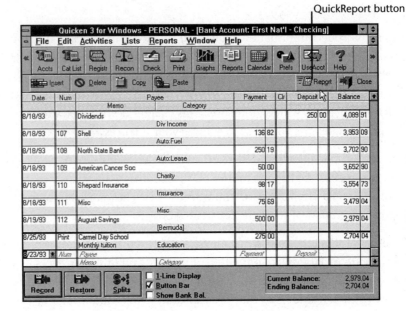

You can create a QuickReport from the following lists or windows:

- *Category & Transfer list.* Displays a list of transactions assigned to the selected category, subcategory, or transfer account. Refer to Chapter 4, "Organizing Your Finances," to learn how to create a QuickReport from the Category & Transfer list.

- *Class list.* Displays a list of transactions assigned to the selected class. Refer to Chapter 4, "Organizing Your Finances," to learn how to create a QuickReport from the Class list.
- *Memorized Transaction list.* Displays a list of all transactions that contain the selected memorized payee name. See Chapter 7, "Using Quicken Shortcuts," to learn how to create a QuickReport from the Memorized Transaction list.
- *Register window.* Displays a list of all transactions that contain the same payee as the selected transaction. Chapter 6, "Using the Register," explains how to create a QuickReport from the Register.
- *Portfolio View window.* For investment accounts, displays a list of all transactions for the selected security. See Chapter 15, "Monitoring Your Investments," to learn how to create a QuickReport from the Portfolio View of an investment account.

When you choose the QuickReport button, Quicken filters transactions in all accounts and displays a listing of transactions that match the list item (for QuickReports from the Category & Transfer list, the Class list, and the Memorized Transaction list), payee (for QuickReports from the Register), or security (for QuickReports from the Portfolio View of an investment account).

Figure 18.2 shows the transaction listing displayed when QuickReport is selected for a transaction in the Register that contains the payee Carmel Day School.

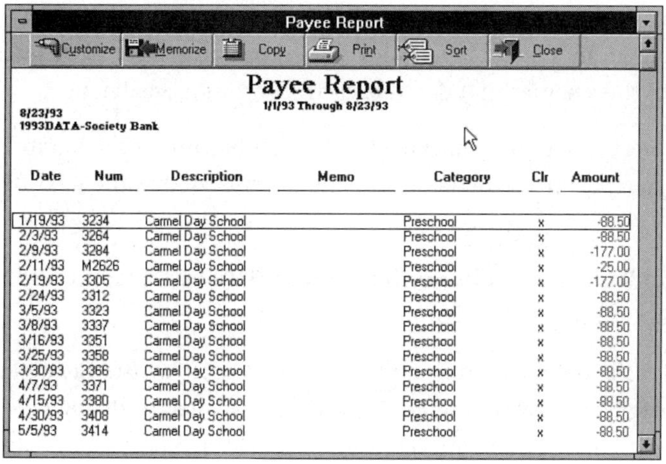
Payee Report

Customize Memorize Copy Print Sort Close

Payee Report
1/1/93 Through 8/23/93

8/23/93
1993DATA-Society Bank

Date	Num	Description	Memo	Category	Clr	Amount
1/19/93	3234	Carmel Day School		Preschool	x	-88.50
2/3/93	3264	Carmel Day School		Preschool	x	-88.50
2/9/93	3284	Carmel Day School		Preschool	x	-177.00
2/11/93	M2626	Carmel Day School		Preschool	x	-25.00
2/19/93	3305	Carmel Day School		Preschool	x	-177.00
2/24/93	3312	Carmel Day School		Preschool	x	-88.50
3/5/93	3323	Carmel Day School		Preschool	x	-88.50
3/8/93	3337	Carmel Day School		Preschool	x	-88.50
3/16/93	3351	Carmel Day School		Preschool	x	-88.50
3/25/93	3358	Carmel Day School		Preschool	x	-88.50
3/30/93	3366	Carmel Day School		Preschool	x	-88.50
4/7/93	3371	Carmel Day School		Preschool	x	-88.50
4/15/93	3380	Carmel Day School		Preschool	x	-88.50
4/30/93	3408	Carmel Day School		Preschool	x	-88.50
5/5/93	3414	Carmel Day School		Preschool	x	-88.50

Fig. 18.2
Select a transaction in the Register and choose the QuickReport button to display a listing of all transactions with the same payee as the selected transaction.

Creating and Reviewing Reports

In this section, you learn how to create any of the 22 preset reports that Quicken provides, such as the Cash Flow Report, Monthly Budget Report, and Net Worth Report. Quicken defines the format of preset reports, but you can customize any preset report to include the information you need. Quicken's preset reports are listed in the Reports menu as Home, Investment, and Business.

Quicken also enables you to create custom reports from scratch that do the following:

■ List specific transactions

■ Summarize transaction data by category, class, payee, or account

■ Compare data from one period to another

■ Compare actual data to budget data

■ List the balances in accounts

Custom reports are listed in the Reports menu as Other.

In the following sections, you learn how to create a basic report, review the report on-screen, and use the report button bar to perform actions on the report that you create.

Creating a Report

The following steps show you how to create a Quicken report. Although the reports may differ, the steps for creating reports are the same. If you want to learn about an individual report and what it contains, refer to the sections at the end of this chapter that describe each report in more detail.

You can create a report by clicking the Reports button on the Iconbar or by choosing a report from the Reports menu, as discussed in the next two sections.

Using the Reports Button on the Iconbar. To create a report using the Reports button on the Iconbar, follow these steps:

1. Click the Reports button on the Iconbar to display the Create Report dialog box, shown in figure 18.3. The Create Report dialog box includes the date range that Quicken uses to create the report and a listing of

each report by family: Home, Investment, Business, Other, and Memorized. (You learn about memorized reports later in this chapter.)

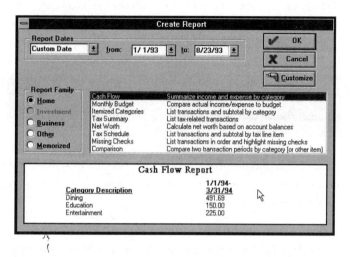

Fig. 18.3
Click the Reports
button on the
Iconbar to display
the Create Report
dialog box.

2. By default, Quicken creates a report from the first day of the current year to today. Or, if reporting on account balances as of a specific day (in net worth reports, for example), Quicken uses today as the default "as of" day. The default dates that Quicken uses to create the report appear in the Report Dates section.

If necessary, change the dates in the From and To drop-down list boxes to the date range you want the report to cover. If you are creating a report that shows account balances as of a specific date (like the Net Worth Report), change the As Of date. For comparison reports, change the date ranges that Quicken uses for comparison.

To change the dates in the Report Dates section, you can select a preset date range in the drop-down list box (such as Month to Date, Quarter to Date, or Year to Date). When you select a preset date range, Quicken automatically enters the appropriate dates in the From and To date boxes.

You also can select Custom Date from the drop-down list box and enter your own date range in the From and To date boxes.

3. From the Report Family options, select the report family to display the available reports. The following report families are available: Home, Investment, Business, Other, and Memorized.

Tip
Use + and – to
change the From,
To, and As Of
dates one day at a
time. Or click the
drop-down arrow
in the date boxes
to use the mini-
calendar.

When you select a report family in the Create Report dialog box, Quicken displays the reports in that family in the list box to the right of the Report Family options. For the highlighted report, Quicken displays an example of the report in the bottom part of the dialog box so that you can see the format of the report.

> **Note**
>
> The amounts that Quicken shows in the example report aren't actual data.

4. To create the report, double-click a report name, or highlight a report name and then choose OK or press Enter. Quicken creates and displays the selected report in a report window.

   Only part of the report may be shown, depending on its size. A button bar is displayed at the top of the report window. You learn how to view the entire contents of a report on-screen and how to use the report button bar later in this chapter.

   Figure 18.4 shows the report window for the Cash Flow Report.

Fig. 18.4
The report appears in a report window and includes a report button bar at the top of the window.

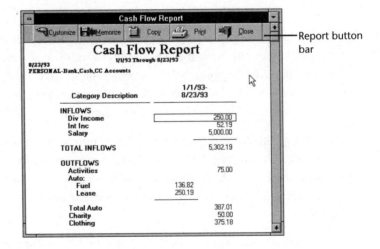

Report button bar

> **Note**
>
> You can choose the Customize button from the report button bar to custom-ize reports to include transactions that contain the same payees, memos, assigned categories, or classes. This technique is called *filtering* a report, which is explained later in the section "Filtering Transactions in Reports."
>
> You also can customize reports by changing other report options, such as the date range, the report organization (income and expense basis or cash-flow basis), row headings, and so forth. You learn how to change report options later in the section "Customizing Reports."
>
> You also can sort transaction reports in a different order by choosing the Sort button from the report button bar. See the section "Sorting Report Data" later in this chapter to learn how to sort transactions in reports.

5. To remove the report from your screen, choose the Close button from the Report button bar.

Using the Reports Menu. You also can create a report using the Reports menu, which includes a submenu with each report. Follow these steps to create a report from the Reports menu:

1. From the Reports menu, choose the report family for the report you want to create. Quicken displays a submenu for the report family that lists each report in that family. If you choose Home from the Reports menu, for example, Quicken displays a submenu that lists each Home report that you can create.

2. From the submenu, choose the report you want to create—for example, Cash Flow to create the Cash Flow Report.

Quicken displays the Create Report dialog box, with the report you selected already highlighted and a sample of the selected report in the bottom part of the window (refer to fig. 18.3).

3. Follow step 2 in the preceding section to change the date range of the report, if necessary.

> **Note**
>
> If you want Quicken to create a report instantly when you choose it from the
> Reports menu, you can set a report preference that tells Quicken to skip the
> Create Report dialog box. When this preference is set, Quicken creates the
> report using the default date range. Refer to the section "Setting Report Pref-
> erence" later in this chapter.

4. Choose OK to create the selected report (refer to fig. 18.4).

Viewing a Report

You have learned how to create Quicken reports so that they appear on-
screen. Most reports that you display, however, are too wide or too long to
fit entirely in the boundaries of your screen.

To view the entire length of a report on-screen, drag the scroll box in the
scroll bar on the right side of the report window up or down. To view the
entire width of a report, drag the scroll box in the scroll bar at the bottom
of the report window left or right. You also can enlarge the report window as
you would any window.

You also can use the keyboard to view reports on-screen, as follows:

Press	To View
→	One screen to the right
←	One screen to the left
PgUp	Up one screen
PgDn	Down one screen

Using the Report Button Bar

At the top of all report windows is a button bar you can use to perform activities after a report is created. The report button bar has the following buttons:

Customize   Displays the Customize Report dialog box, which you
can use to change the date range of the report, change
the report layout, choose the accounts to include in
the report, choose the amount and type of transactions to include, show information in rows, choose

the categories and classes to include in the report, and filter transactions. Refer to the "Customizing Reports" section later in this chapter to learn how to change reports.

Memorize | Memorizes the displayed report and its report settings so that you easily can recall the report the next time you need it. Refer to the "Memorizing Reports" section later in this chapter to learn how to memorize and recall a report.

Copy | Copies the contents of the displayed report to the Windows Clipboard. Then you can paste the report to another Windows application, such as Word for Windows, Excel, or 1-2-3 for Windows. To learn how to copy report contents to the Clipboard, see the section "Copying Reports to the Windows Clipboard" later in this chapter.

Print | Prints the displayed report. Refer to the later section "Printing Reports" to learn how to print a report you have created.

Sort | Changes the order of transactions in the displayed report by account, date, check number, amount, payee, or category. Note that this button is available for only transaction reports (reports that list transactions). Refer to the "Sorting Report Data" section later in this chapter to learn how to sort transactions in the displayed report.

Export | Exports the displayed report to a .TXF (tax export format) file so that you can import the report data to a tax-preparation program. This button is available only for the Capital Gains and Tax Schedule reports. Refer to Chapter 12, "Using Quicken To Prepare for Income Taxes," to learn how to export reports for use with a tax preparation program.

Close | Removes the report from your screen.

Tracking Personal Finances with Home Reports

You can select from eight reports in the Home reports family. To see a sample of each report, follow these steps:

1. Click the Reports button on the Iconbar to display the Create Report dialog box (refer to fig. 18.3).

2. Select the Home option button in the Report Family section. Quicken lists the following home reports by title and description:

   - Cash Flow

   - Monthly Budget

   - Itemized Categories

   - Tax Summary

   - Net Worth

   - Tax Schedule

   - Missing Checks

   - Comparison

3. Choose the report for which you want to see a sample. Quicken shows a sample report at the bottom of the Create Report dialog box.

The Cash Flow Report

The Cash Flow Report shows the total cash inflows and outflows by category. The home Cash Flow Report shows transfers to and from other accounts and includes transactions from all Bank, Cash, and Credit Card accounts in the current Quicken file.

The Cash Flow Report can be extremely valuable. This report shows the various categories of cash flowing into and out of your personal bank accounts, cash accounts, and credit card accounts. If you question why you seem to have a bigger bank balance than usual or you always seem to run out of money before the end of the month, this report can provide some answers.

The Monthly Budget Report

The Monthly Budget Report shows actual income and expenses and budgeted income and expenses over a specified period. The Monthly Budget Report also shows the comparison between the actual and budgeted amounts and calculates the difference (how much over or under budget you are, by category). This report includes transactions from all the bank, cash, and credit card accounts in the current Quicken file.

To produce a Monthly Budget Report, you must first set up your budget. Refer to Chapter 16, "Budgeting with Quicken," if you need information on setting up a budget. Chapter 16 also shows you an example of a Monthly Budget Report.

The Itemized Category Report

The Itemized Category Report shows each transaction in the current Quicken file sorted and subtotaled by category. This type of report provides a convenient way to see the detailed transactions that add up to a category total.

> **Note**
>
> You can replace the default report title, Itemized Category Report, with a more specific title (such as Personal Itemized Category Report) by typing a new Title in the Report Layout section of the Customize Report dialog box. (The Report Layout section appears when you select the Report Layout customize option in the Customize Report dialog box. See the "Customizing Reports" section for details.) You also can specify a range of months to be included in the report.

The Itemized Category Report resembles the cash flow report in purpose and information, except that the Itemized Category Report doesn't include account transfers. If you want to see your cash inflows and outflows grouped and summarized by category, this is the report you want.

The Tax Summary Report

The Tax Summary Report—a handy tax-preparation tool to use at the end of the year—summarizes the taxable income items and the tax deductions you need to report on your federal and state income tax returns. The Tax Summary Report shows all the transactions assigned to categories you marked as tax-related. Transactions are sorted and subtotaled by category.

> **Note**
>
> The Tax Summary Report summarizes tax deductions paid with only the Bank, Cash, and Credit Card accounts you choose to track with Quicken. If you write tax-deductible checks from two checking accounts but track only one of the accounts with Quicken, for example, you will miss some deductions. Refer to Chapter 12, "Using Quicken To Prepare for Income Taxes," to learn more about the Tax Summary Report.

The Net Worth Report

The Net Worth Report shows the balance on a particular date for each account in your Quicken file. If the file includes all your assets and liabilities, the resulting report is a balance sheet that provides an estimate of your financial net worth. (Balance sheets are described in Chapter 11, "Managing Your Assets and Other Liabilities.")

Net worth is the difference between your total assets and total liabilities. If you own more assets than liabilities, you have a positive net worth. If you own fewer assets than liabilities, you have a negative net worth.

Your net worth may include investments that produce regular interest or dividend income. Your net worth also may include your personal residence, completely paid for by the time you retire. Monitoring your net worth probably is more important than most people realize. Over the years that you work, one of your financial goals may be to increase your net worth. During your retirement years, you probably will look to your net worth to provide income and security.

When creating a Net Worth Report, you enter only one date instead of a range of dates. The Net Worth Report doesn't report on activity for a period of time. Instead, it provides a snapshot of the account balances in your Quicken file at a point in time.

The Tax Schedule Report

The Tax ScheduleReport summarizes tax-related categories in a way that makes preparing every common income tax schedule easy. By using category information, Quicken adds the transactions that go on each line of each tax schedule. Chapter 12, "Using Quicken To Prepare for Income Taxes," describes this handy report.

The Missing Checks Report

The Missing Checks Report displays a list of all checking account transactions in check number order with any gaps in the check number sequence identified. The gaps represent a missing check or checks you may need to investigate.

The Comparison Report

New to Quicken 3 for Windows is the Comparison Report, which compares income and expenses by category (or other items you select) for two time periods. You can compare, for example, your utility bills for December of last year and this year.

Tracking Investments with Investment Reports

You can select from five reports in the Investment reports family. To see a sample of each report, follow these steps:

1. Click the Reports button on the Iconbar to display the Create Report dialog box (refer to fig. 18.3).

2. Select the Investment option button in the Report Family section. Quicken lists the following reports by title and description:

   - Portfolio Value

   - Investment Performance

   - Capital Gains

   - Investment Income

   - Investment Transactions

3. Choose the report for which you want to see a sample. Quicken shows a sample report at the bottom of the Create Report dialog box. Refer to Chapter 15, "Monitoring Your Investments," to learn more about the information provided in investment reports.

The Portfolio Value Report

A Portfolio Value Report shows the estimated market value on a specific date of each security in your Quicken investment accounts. To estimate the market values, Quicken uses each security's individual price history (a list of prices on certain dates).

Quicken determines which price to use by comparing the date in the report to the dates that have prices in the price history. Ideally, Quicken uses a price for the same date as the date you specify. When the price history doesn't contain a price for the specified date, Quicken uses the price for the date closest to that date.

The Investment Performance Report

Investment Performance Reports help you measure how well or how poorly your investments are doing. These reports look at all the transactions for a security and then calculate an annual rate of return—in effect, the interest rate an investment has paid you.

The date range you use in the Investment Performance Report tells Quicken which time frame you want to use to calculate investment returns. You can subtotal rates of return by different time periods, by account, by security, by security type, or by investment goals. You also can specify whether you want rates of return calculated for just the current account, for a selected account, or for all accounts. Quicken notifies you if one or more of the total return calculations can't be completed and displays the value as NA.

The Capital Gains Report

The Capital Gains Report attempts to print all the information you need to complete the Schedule D federal income tax form. Taxpayers use Schedule D to report capital gains and losses.

Although income tax laws now in effect treat short-term capital gains the same as long-term capital gains, Congress may change this. Accordingly, Quicken enables you to subtotal by short-term and long-term gains and losses.

Now, gains and losses from the sale of capital assets are considered long-term if they are held for more than one year. Quicken enables you to change the default number of days it uses to determine whether a gain or loss is long-term, however.

The Investment Income Report

The Investment Income Report summarizes all the income transactions you recorded in one or more of the investment accounts.

Realized gains and losses result when the investment is sold and cash is received. Quicken calculates a realized gain or loss by comparing the cash received on sale with the original cost of the investment. Unrealized gains and losses result when the cost of the investment is compared with the market value to determine what the gain or loss would have been if the investment had been sold.

The Investment Transactions Report

The Investment Transactions Report lists each investment transaction in the Register. Use this report to review your transactions to make sure that you've accurately reflected all security transactions in your investment accounts.

Tracking Business Finances with Business Reports

You can select from nine reports in the Business reports family. To see a sample of each report, follow these steps:

1. Click the Reports button on the Iconbar to display the Create Report dialog box (refer to fig. 18.3).

2. Select the Business option button in the Report Family box. Quicken lists the following business reports by title and description:

   - P&L Statement
   - Cash Flow
   - A/P by Vendor
   - A/R by Customer
   - Job/Project
   - Payroll
   - Balance Sheet
   - Missing Checks
   - Comparison

3. Choose the report for which you want to see a sample. Quicken shows a sample report at the bottom of the Create Report dialog box.

The P & L Statement

The P & L (profit and loss) statement, also known as an *income statement*, shows the total monthly income and expenses by category for all accounts. Data from transactions from any account in the current Quicken file are included, but transfers between accounts aren't.

CPA TIP: Using a P & L Statement

The profit and loss statement is one of your business's most used and important financial reports. It reports your net income or net loss for a specific time period (month, quarter, year, and so on). Remember that the sales revenue and expenses on the profit and loss statement aren't the same as the cash inflows from sales and cash outflows for expenses for the period. Create a Cash Flow Report to show the cash position of your business.

The Cash Flow Report

A Cash Flow Report resembles a profit and loss statement. This report includes all Bank, Cash, and Credit Card accounts and shows the money received (inflows) and the money spent (outflows) by category for each month. The cash flow report also shows transfers between accounts.

The differences between the Cash Flow Report and the P & L statement are that the Cash Flow Report shows transfers to other accounts and groups cash inflows together and cash outflows together. The difference between cash inflows and outflows is the overall total, which may be positive or negative.

CPA TIP: Monitoring Cash Flow

Cash flow is just as important as profits, particularly over shorter time periods. In addition to making money, businesses need to have cash to buy inventory or equipment, to have as working capital while they wait for customers to pay their bills, and to pay back loans from banks and vendors. The Cash Flow Report, which summarizes your cash inflows and outflows by category and account, provides a method for monitoring your cash flow and pinpointing problems.

The A/P by Vendor Report

Because Quicken uses what is called *cash-basis accounting*, expenses are recorded only when you pay the bill. By not paying bills or by paying bills late, your net income or profit and your net cash flow may look better. The problem, however, is that this concept is illogical. Just because you haven't paid a bill by the end of the month doesn't mean the bill shouldn't be considered in assessing the month's financial performance.

To partially address this shortcoming, Quicken provides the A/P by Vendor Report, which enables you to see which bills haven't been paid. The A/P by Vendor Report lists all the unprinted checks, sorted and subtotaled by payee. Refer to Chapter 23, "Using Quicken in Your Small Business," to learn more about the A/P by Vendor Report.

Tip
A/P is an abbreviation for *accounts payable*—the unpaid bills of a business.

The A/R by Customer Report

The A/R by Customer Report shows the transactions sorted and subtotaled by payee in all asset accounts. The report doesn't include transactions marked as cleared, however—that is, transactions marked with an asterisk (*) or x in the Clr field of the Register. Refer to Chapter 23, "Using Quicken in Your Small Business," to learn more about the A/R by Customer Report.

Tip
A/R is an abbreviation for *accounts receivable*—the amounts your customers owe.

For businesses that extend customer credit (which is what you do when you allow a customer to "buy now, pay later"), monitoring the amounts customers owe is essential to profits and cash flows. Unfortunately, some customers don't pay unless you remind them several times, some customers lose invoices and then forget that they owe you, and sometimes customers never receive your bill. To make sure that these small problems don't become big cash-flow problems, you can use the A/R by Customer Report.

CPA TIP: Using Aging Reports

Good collection procedures usually improve cash flows dramatically, so consider using the customer-aging report as a collection guide. (See Chapter 23, "Using Quicken in Your Small Business," to learn how to create an aging report.) You may want to telephone any customer with an invoice 30 days past due, stop granting additional credit to any customer with invoices more than 60 days past due, and initiate collection procedures for any customer with invoices more than 90 days past due (in the absence of special circumstances).

The Job/Project Report

The Job/Project Report shows category totals by month for each month in the specified date range. The report also shows account balances at the end of the last month. If you are using classes, the report shows category totals by class in separate columns across the report page. The Job/Project Report helps business owners track income and expenses by job, project, customer, or client. This is called *job costing*. (Refer to Chapter 23, "Using Quicken in Your Small Business," for more information on job costing.)

The Payroll Report

The Payroll Report shows the total amounts paid to individual payees when the transaction category begins with the word *payroll*. The Payroll Report includes transactions from all accounts.

CPA TIP: Creating a Payroll Report for W-2 Forms

At the end of the calendar year, create a Payroll Report to help you complete your W-2 forms. Make sure that the time period covered by the report is for the full calendar year (1/1/93 to 12/31/93, for example). The Payroll Report shows the total gross wages paid to each employee and his or her total withholdings (federal, Social Security, state, local, and so on).

You must send a W-2 form by January 31 of the following calendar year to each person you employed at any time during the previous calendar year.

The Balance Sheet

The balance sheet shows the account balances for all accounts in the current Quicken file at a specific time. If the file includes accounts for all your assets and liabilities, the resulting report is a balance sheet that shows the net worth of your business. (Chapter 11, "Managing Your Assets and Other Liabilities," describes balance sheets in more detail.)

Even for small businesses, balance sheets are important reports. Because a balance sheet shows what a business owns and owes, balance sheets give an indication of the financial strength or weakness of a business. The smaller the total liabilities amount in relation to the total assets amount, the stronger the business. And the larger the total liabilities in relation to the total assets, the weaker the business. As a result of these and similar financial insights, banks usually require a balance sheet to evaluate loan applications from businesses.

CPA TIP: Using a Balance Sheet

The balance sheet measures the value of your business at one moment in time. Asset amounts represent values based on original cost rather than replacement costs or earning power (unless you entered any amount other than original costs for assets in Quicken). Liabilities represent the legal claims of creditors who have loaned you money or the unpaid goods or services provided to you. Owner's equity, or net worth, represents a claim resulting from the capital invested by the owners of the business and past profits retained in the business.

The Missing Checks Report

The Missing Checks Report displays a list of all checking account transactions in check number order with any gaps in the check number sequence identified. The gaps represent a missing check or checks you may need to investigate.

The Comparison Report

The Comparison Report, a new report in Quicken 3 for Windows, compares income and expenses by category (or by another item you select) for two time periods. You can compare, for example, revenues for the first quarter of this year to revenues for the first quarter of last year.

Examining Other Reports

You can select from five reports in the Other reports family. To see a sample of each report, follow these steps:

1. Click the Reports button on the Iconbar to display the Create Report dialog box (refer to fig. 18.3).

2. Select the Other option button in the Report Family section. Quicken lists the other reports by title and description as follows:

   ■ Transactions

   ■ Summary

   ■ Comparison

   ■ Budget

   ■ Account Balances

3. Select the report for which you want to see a sample. Quicken shows a sample report at the bottom of the Create Report dialog box.

You can use any report option as a template to create a specific report to meet your needs. You may want to list your Register transactions in an order other than chronologically, for example. You may find value in sorting and summarizing transactions by payee or by time periods such as a week or a month, for example. The Transactions Report enables you to see your account transactions in any of these ways.

Summary Reports extract information from the financial database you create in Quicken's Register. A Summary Report gives you totals by category, class, payee, or account, in addition to any other subtotals you request.

The Comparison Report compares income and expenses by category, class, payee, or account. Comparisons are made between two periods that you specify and the difference is shown in dollars or as a percentage.

Budgeting is a fundamental tool that businesses and individuals use to manage their finances better. One of the ongoing steps in using a budget as a tool is to compare the amount you received as income with the amount you planned to receive and to compare the amount you spent with the amount you planned to spend, or budgeted. The Budget Report enables you to create budget reports tailored to your business or personal needs.

The Account Balances Report shows the balance in your accounts for a specific date. If you have extensive investments with several brokers, for example, and want a report that specifies only those accounts, you can create an Account Balances Report (or a specialized version of this report).

Printing Reports

After you create a report, you can print it or save it to a disk file to be used in another application. Printing reports provides you with a hard copy of your data for the specified period. Reports that you create in Quicken can be useful in providing your bank, creditors, and even the IRS with important financial information.

Setting Up Quicken To Print a Report

Before you can print reports in Quicken, you must set up the program to print to your printer. Quicken includes different printer settings for reports (Report/Graph Printer Setup) and for checks (Check Printer Setup). This section shows you how to quickly set up Quicken to print reports.

To set up Quicken to print reports, follow these steps:

1. From the File menu, choose Printer Setup. Quicken displays the Printer Setup submenu.

2. Choose Report/Graph Printer Setup. Quicken displays the Report Printer Setup dialog box, shown in figure 18.5.

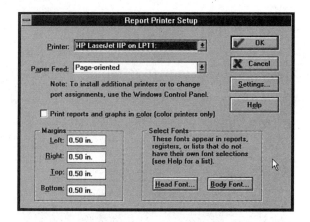

Fig. 18.5

The Report Printer Setup dialog box tells Quicken the printer, type of paper, report margins, and font you are using.

3. Select your installed printer from the Printer drop-down list.

4. Quicken uses Auto-detect to determined whether your printer is continuous-feed or page-oriented. If the paper feed isn't correct, select the appropriate paper feed for your installed printer from the Paper Feed drop-down list.

5. If you are using a color printer and want to print reports in color, select the Print Reports and Graphs in Color check box. You must have an installed color printer to use this option.

6. Check the Left, Right, Top, and Bottom margins. If necessary, enter larger or smaller values than the preset values that Quicken uses.

7. If you want to change the font for the heading or body of the report, choose Head Font or Body Font. Quicken displays the Report Default

Headline Font dialog box or the Report Default Font dialog box, from which you can change the font type, font style, and font size. When the heading and body fonts are the way you want them, choose OK to return to the Report Printer Setup dialog box.

8. You also can change other print settings, such as the paper tray, paper size, orientation, and number of copies. To change these settings, choose the Settings button. Quicken displays a dialog box for your installed printer. Make the necessary changes and choose OK to return to the Report Printer Setup dialog box.

9. Choose OK to save the printer settings.

Printing a Report

No matter which Quicken report you want to print, you must take the same basic steps, as follows:

1. Create the report you want to print, as explained earlier in this chapter.

2. With the report on-screen, choose the Print button from the button bar (or press Ctrl+P). Quicken displays the Print Report dialog box, shown in figure 18.6.

Fig. 18.6
Choose Print from the Report button bar to display the Print Report dialog box.

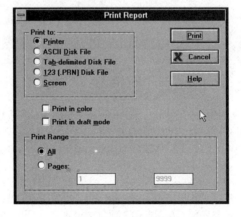

3. In the Print To section, select the Printer option button.

4. If you have a color printer and want to print the report in color, select the Print in Color check box.

5. Select the Print in Draft Mode check box, if desired, and if your installed printer supports draft mode printing.

6. Choose the print range. Select the All option button to print all pages of the report. Otherwise, select the Pages option button and specify the pages you want to print.

7. Choose the Print button to begin printing the report.

Note

If you want to see a preview of the report on-screen before you print, select the Screen option button and then choose Print. Quicken shows the report in the Print Preview window as it will appear when printed (using the selected fonts and type size). Review the report using the Prev page and Next page buttons at the bottom of the Print Preview window. Choose the Print button to begin printing the report or choose the Close button to return to the report window.

Saving a Report to a Disk File

If you want to use report data in a non-Windows program, you can save the report to an ASCII disk file, a tab-delimited disk file, or a Lotus 1-2-3 (.PRN) disk file.

Note

If you want to use report data in another Windows compatible program, such as Microsoft Word for Windows or Excel for Windows, use the Copy button from the report button bar to copy the report to the Windows Clipboard. (See the "Copying a Report to the Windows Clipboard" section later in this chapter.)

Complete the following steps to save a report to a disk file:

1. Create the report, as explained earlier in this chapter.

2. With the report on-screen, choose the Print button from the Report button bar (or press Ctrl+P). Quicken displays the Print Report dialog box (refer to fig. 18.6).

3. In the Print To section, choose one of the following file formats to save the report:

ASCII Disk File	Saves the report in standardized text format to be used in a word processing program, such as Microsoft Word or WordPerfect

Tab-delimited Disk File	Saves the report in tab-delimited text format (data items are separated by tab keystrokes to simulate ASCII file format), also to be used in a word-processing program
123 (.PRN) Disk File	Saves the report to a disk file that can be used in Lotus 1-2-3 or a Lotus-compatible spreadsheet.

4. Choose the Print button. Quicken displays the Create Disk File dialog box.

5. In the File Name text box, type the name of the file to which you want to export the report.

6. If necessary, change the directory and drive where you are sending the report in the Directory list box and the Drives drop-down list.

7. Choose OK to save the report to a disk file with the name you specified.

Customizing Reports

You already have learned how to create a report in Quicken. But what if you want to restrict transactions to those with a particular payee or assigned to certain categories, or what if you want to exclude certain accounts from the report? You can customize each Quicken report so that the report includes the information that is most useful to you. The Customize button on the Report button bar enables you to modify reports so that Quicken provides the information you want in the format you want.

You can perform the following actions when customizing a report:

- Change the report layout to rename the report, rearrange the report with different row and column headings, change the accounting organization (income and expense, cash flow basis, net worth format, or balance sheet format), or choose the way Quicken displays the report data (amounts in dollars or amounts in dollars and cents, for example).

- Choose the account to include in the report.

■ Choose the transactions to include in the report. You can exclude transactions whose amounts are below a specified level, for example, or you can include only payments, deposits, or unprinted checks.

■ Choose the information shown in rows in the report. You can exclude all transfers, hide all subcategories, or include only budgeted categories in reports, for example.

■ Choose the categories and classes to include in the report.

■ Filter or limit transactions in the report to include only the transactions that meet your criteria.

To customize a report, follow these steps:

1. Create a report, as explained earlier in this chapter, to display the report window.

2. Choose the Customize command button to display the Customize Report dialog box. Note that Quicken inserts the name of the report that you created in step 1 in the title bar. Thus, when you choose the Customize button from the Cash Flow Report window, for example, Quicken displays the Customize Cash Flow Report dialog box. You can also choose to customize a report by choosing the Customize button from the Create Report dialog box (refer to fig. 18.3).

3. The default report dates are entered in the Report Dates section. Change the date range, if necessary, as explained earlier in the section "Creating a Report."

4. The left side of the Customize Report dialog box lists the customize options available for the selected report. Select the appropriate option from the Customize section.

On the right side of the dialog box, Quicken displays the settings you can change for the selected customize option. As figure 18.7 shows, if you select the Report Layout option from the Customize section, Quicken shows the report layout settings you can change.

> **Tip**
> When you select an option, a message appears at the bottom of the dialog box telling you what the option does.

5. Change the report settings as desired. The following sections explain how to change report settings for each customize option in the Customize Report dialog box.

6. Choose OK to redisplay the report using the report settings you entered.

Fig. 18.7

When you select Report Layout, Quicken displays the report settings you can change.

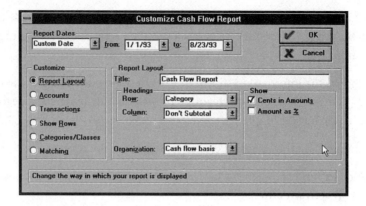

Changing the Report Layout

As mentioned, when you select the Report Layout customize option button, the right side of the Customize Report dialog box displays the Report Layout box with the report settings you can change (refer to fig. 18.7).

Depending on the type of report you are customizing, Quicken enables you to change the settings shown in table 18.1.

Table 18.1 Report Layout Settings

Report Setting	Options
Title	You can enter the title that you want to appear at the top of the report. The title can include numbers, letters, and other characters (up to 39 characters). If you don't enter a title, Quicken uses the report type title, such as Cash Flow Report or Net Worth Report.
Row Headings (for summary reports only)	Category Class Payee Account
Column Headings (for summary, budget, and account balance reports)	Don't Subtotal Week (Sunday through Saturday) Two Weeks (starts on Sunday) Half Month (the 1st through the 15th) Month Quarter (includes three consecutive months) Half Year (starts on the starting date and ends on the last day of the month five months later) Year (starts on the starting date for 365 days or 366 days in a leap year) Category Class Payee Account

IV

Report Setting	Options
Subtotal By (for transaction reports only)	Don't Subtotal Week (Sunday through Saturday) Two Weeks (starts on Sunday) Half Month (the 1st through the 15th) Month Quarter (includes three consecutive months) Half Year (starts on the starting date and ends on the last day of the month five months later) Year (starts on the starting date for 365 days or 366 days in a leap year) Category Class Payee Account Tax schedule
Interval (for account balances reports)	None Week (Sunday through Saturday) Two Weeks (starts on Sunday) Half Month (the 1st through the 15th) Month Quarter (includes three consecutive months) Half Year (starts on the starting date and ends on the last day of the month five months later) Year (starts on the starting date for 365 days or 366 days in a leap year)
Sort By (for transaction reports only)	None Date/Acct Acct/Chk # Amount Payee Category
Organization	Income and expense Cash flow basis Net worth Balance sheet
Show Cents in Amounts	Select to show amounts in dollars and cents
Show Amount as % (for summary reports only)	Select to show amounts in relative terms, as percentages of the total
Show Difference as a % (for comparison reports only)	Select to show the difference as a percentage from the first category comparison to the second
Show Difference in $ (for comparison reports only)	Select to show the difference as dollars from the first category to the second

(continues)

Table 18.1 Continued	
Report Setting	**Options**
Show Totals Only (for transaction reports only)	Select to display only the total dollar amount of transactions that meet the criteria you specify
Show **M**emo (for transaction reports only)	Select to include a column for memos
Show Category (for transaction reports only)	Select to include a column for categories
Show **S**plit Transaction Detail (for transaction reports only)	Select to include the detail from the Splits window

Selecting Accounts To Include in Reports

Although Quicken preselects the accounts used in reports, you can customize the report and select the accounts you want to use.

To select the accounts to include in reports, follow these steps:

1. From the Customize Report dialog box (refer to fig. 18.7), select the Accounts customize option button. Quicken displays the Accounts Used section with the list of accounts, as shown in figure 18.8.

Fig. 18.8
When you select Accounts, Quicken displays the list of accounts you can choose to include in the report.

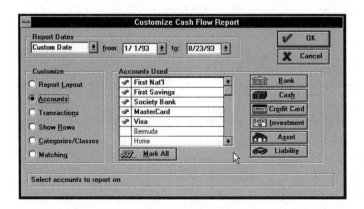

2. Quicken preselects accounts based on the report you create. For a Cash Flow Report, for example, Quicken selects all Bank, Cash, and Credit Card accounts. Accounts selected are marked with a check mark to the left of the account name.

To select an account, click it, or highlight the account and press the space bar. To select all accounts, choose the Mark All button.

3. Choose OK to redisplay the report using the accounts that you selected.

Selecting Transactions To Include in Reports

Normally, Quicken searches all transactions in the selected accounts to create a report. You can customize the report, however, so that Quicken uses only transactions you specify.

To select transactions to include in reports, follow these steps:

1. From the Customize Report dialog box (refer to fig. 18.7), select the Transactions customize option button. Quicken displays the Select Transactions section with the report settings you can change, as shown in figure 18.9.

Tip
To select all accounts in an account type (such as all bank accounts), choose the account type button to the right of the Accounts Used section.

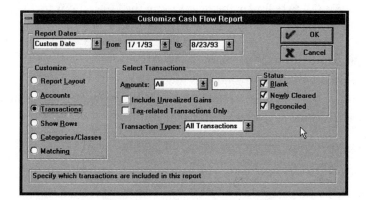

Fig. 18.9
Choose the transaction criteria for a report in the Select Transactions section.

2. To include transactions in a report based on the transaction amount, select All, Less Than, Equal To, or Greater Than from the Amounts drop-down list box. Then enter the amount you want transaction amounts compared to. If you want to include only transactions over $25, for example, select Greater Than and type **25**.

3. If you have investment accounts, select the Include Unrealized Gains check box if you want Quicken to include the impact of price increases and decreases for securities in a report.

4. To include only transactions that have been assigned to a tax-related category or subcategory, select the Tax-Related Transactions Only check box.

5. Select the transaction types you want to include in the report in the Transactions Types drop-down list box: Payments, Deposits, Unprinted Checks, or All Transactions.

6. In the Status section, select Blank to include transactions without an entry in the Clr field, Newly Cleared to include transactions with an asterisk (*) in the Clr field, or Reconciled to include transactions with an X in the Clr field.

> **Note**
>
> Quicken includes all transactions in reports, regardless of their cleared status. You shouldn't change the status settings for a report unless you are creating a report to show specifically the cleared status of transactions.

7. Choose OK to redisplay the report using the transactions that you selected.

Changing Row Information in Reports

You can change the items included as rows in a report by customizing the report. If you select to report on categories, for example, Quicken includes all the category names as row headings in the report.

To change row information in reports, follow these steps:

1. From the Customize Report dialog box, select the Show Rows customize option button. Quicken displays the Show Rows section with the report settings you can change, as shown in figure 18.10.

Fig. 18.10
Select the information you want to appear as row headings in the Show Rows section.

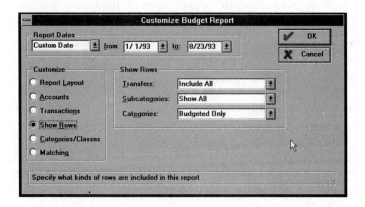

2. From the Transfers drop-down list, select Include All, Exclude All, or Exclude Internal (excludes transfers between accounts included in the report).

3. From the Subcategories drop-down list, select Show All, Hide All, or Show Reversed (displays subcategories with the main categories grouped under them).

4. For budget reports only, select Include All, Non-Zero Actual/Budgeted (includes only categories you already have assigned to transactions and categories with budget amounts), or Budgeted Only (includes only the categories with budget amounts) from the Categories drop-down list box.

5. Choose OK to redisplay the report using the rows that you selected.

Selecting Categories and Classes To Include in Reports

To select the categories and classes included in a report, follow these steps:

1. From the Customize Report dialog box, select the Categories/Classes customize option button. Quicken displays the Select to Include section, which lists the categories and classes (see fig. 18.11).

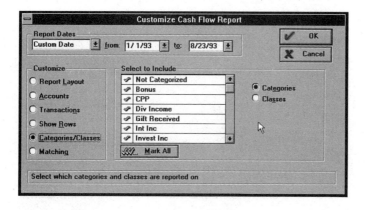

Fig. 18.11
Select the categories and classes you want to include in a report in the Select to Include list box.

2. Select the Categories option button to show categories in the list. Select the Classes option button to show classes in the list.

3. Select a category or class from the list. To choose all categories or classes, choose the Mark All button. To select a single category or class, click the item or highlight the item and press the space bar. To deselect a category or class, repeat the select procedure.

Tip
Select only the Not Categorized item from the category list to include only transactions without a category assigned.

> **Note**
>
> When choosing categories, you also can move to the bottom of the category
> list and select or deselect accounts so that transfers between specific accounts
> and the accounts included in the report are included or excluded.

4. Choose OK to redisplay the report using the categories and/or classes
that you selected.

Filtering Transactions in Reports

Quicken enables you to specify which transactions to include in a report by
specifying criteria that transactions must meet before being included in a
report. You can tell Quicken to include only transactions that contain a certain payee, category, class, or memo.

To filter transactions in reports, follow these steps:

1. From the Customize Report dialog box, select the Matching customize
option button. Quicken displays the Include Transactions If section
with the settings you can specify when filtering transactions (see
fig. 18.12).

Fig. 18.12

In the Include
Transactions If
section, define or
limit transactions
in reports by
setting the criteria
a transaction must
meet to be
included.

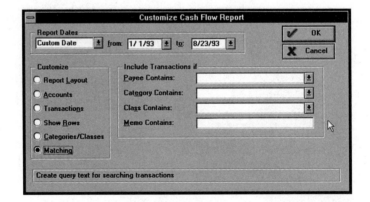

2. In the Payee Contains, Category Contains, or Class Contains drop-
down list box, enter or select the name of the payee, category, or class
you want to limit transactions to. If you want to report on transactions
with the payee Carmel Day School, for example, select or enter this
exact name in the Payee Contains drop-down list box. If you want to

IV

report on transactions assigned to the Utilities category, type or select Utilities in the Category Contains drop-down list box.

You can include more than one item to limit transactions to. For example, you can enter criteria in the Payee Contains and the Category Contains boxes so that Quicken limits the report to transactions that contain the payee that you specify that are assigned to the category that you enter.

> **Note**
>
> For categories and classes, Quicken searches entries in the Splits window for split transactions assigned to the specified category or class.

3. In the Memo Contains text box, enter the memo you want to limit transactions to. If you want to report on transactions that contain the memo *Gymnastics lessons*, for example, type this entry in the Memo Contains text box to limit the report to transactions with the same memo entered in the Memo field.

4. Choose OK to redisplay the report filters that you specified.

You can use the following match characters to limit a report to transactions that match the criteria you specify:

= (equal sign)	Includes only transactions that exactly match the text you enter (=**Carmel Utilities** finds *Carmel Utilities* only)
.. (two periods)	Includes transactions with unspecified characters where you type .. at the beginning, middle, or end of the text (..**Jones** finds *Nancy Jones, David Jones,* and *Scott Jones*)
? (question mark)	Includes transactions with one unspecified character where you type ? (?**ax** finds *tax* and *fax*)
~ (tilde)	Excludes all matches for the text that you type after the ~ character (~**tax** excludes *state tax, federal tax,* and *local tax*)

> **Note**
>
> If you type a tilde followed by two periods, Quicken excludes all transactions except those that are empty in the specified field. If you type ~.. in the **Memo Contains** text box, for example, Quicken includes only the transactions without a memo entry in the Memo field.

Sorting Report Data

For non-investment transaction reports, you can change how transactions are ordered in the report. You can sort transactions by amount, by payee, by account and then by date, or by account and then by check number.

To sort transactions in a report, follow these steps:

1. Create the report, as explained earlier in this chapter.

2. Choose the Sort button from the button bar. Quicken displays the Select Sort Criteria dialog box.

3. In the Sort Transactions By drop-down list, choose how you want to sort transactions.

4. Choose OK. Quicken searches transactions and redisplays the report in the sort order you selected.

Using QuickZoom To Examine Report Detail

QuickZoom enables you to examine the transaction detail behind an amount in a report while the report is on-screen. If, for example, you create a cash flow report and want to see the transaction detail behind the amount shown for the category Charity (for charitable donations), you can use QuickZoom to search the Register for all transactions that make up the total amount shown in the report. Quicken displays a QuickZoom Report that shows a list of those transactions. If you want to examine a transaction further or edit a transaction in the QuickZoom Report, you can go to the Register where the transaction was entered.

Note

You can use QuickZoom in only summary, transaction, budget, comparison, invest-ment income, and investment transaction reports. You can't use QuickZoom in account balance type reports, such as the net worth report or the balance sheet.

To use QuickZoom to examine the transaction detail in a report, follow these steps:

1. With the report on-screen, put the mouse pointer on the report item you want to examine. The mouse pointer changes to a magnifying glass icon to show that you can examine the report item (see fig. 18.13).

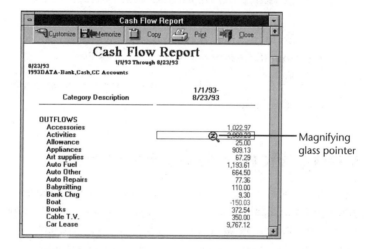

Magnifying glass pointer

Fig. 18.13
When you point to an item in a report, the mouse pointer changes to a magnifying glass icon to show that you can examine the report item with QuickZoom.

2. Double-click the report item. Quicken displays a QuickZoom Report window listing the transactions that make up the report item you se-lected (see fig. 18.14).

Note

If you double-click a report item in a transaction report, Quicken goes to the Register where the transaction was entered and highlights the transaction.

3. If you want to see the Register entry for a transaction listed in the QuickZoom Report window, double-click the transaction. Quicken goes to the Register and highlights that transaction. From here, you can make any necessary changes to the transaction.

Fig. 18.14

When you examine a report item, Quicken shows the list of transactions that make up the report item in the QuickZoom Report window.

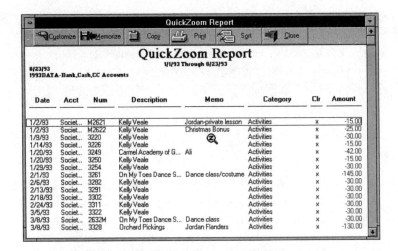

To return to the QuickZoom Report window from the Register, choose Close from the Register button bar or press Esc.

4. To return to the original report from the QuickZoom Report window, choose the Close button.

Using Memorized Reports

If you have spent considerable time customizing a report to include specific information in a particular format, you will want to save the report settings so that you don't have to customize the report again. Quicken enables you to have a customized report *memorized* so that you can simply select it from a list the next time you want to use it.

Memorizing a Report

You can have Quicken memorize a report after you customize the report and the report is on-screen. To do so, follow these steps:

1. Create and customize the report you want Quicken to memorize.

2. Choose the Memorize button from the Report button bar (or press Ctrl+M). Quicken displays the Memorize Report dialog box, shown in figure 18.15.

3. In the Title text box, type a unique title for the report. Quicken uses this title only to identify the report, but doesn't display it as the report's title.

Fig. 18.15
Enter the report
dates and a unique
title for the report
in the Memorize
Report dialog box.

4. In the Report Dates section, select the dates you want the memorized
   report to cover. Select the Named Range option button if you selected a
   preset date range in the Create Report dialog box. (This option is available only if you selected a preset date range for the report.) To memorize the dates used in the report, select the Custom option button. To
   use the preset starting and ending dates that Quicken enters in the
   Create Report dialog box when you recall the report, select the None
   option button.

5. Choose OK to have Quicken memorize the report.

Recalling a Memorized Report

Recalling a memorized report with the exact report settings you specified is
easy. To recall a memorized report, follow these steps:

1. Click the Reports button on the Iconbar to display the Create Report
   dialog box (refer to fig. 18.3).

2. Select Memorized from the Report Family section. Quicken displays
   memorized reports, by title, in the report list to the right.

3. Double-click the memorized report you want to recall, or highlight the
   report and press Enter. Quicken displays the report.

You can recall a memorized report also from the Reports menu, as follows:

1. From the Reports menu, choose Memorized. Quicken displays the
   Memorized Reports window, which lists all memorized reports by title
   (see fig. 18.16).

2. Double-click the memorized report you want to recall, or highlight the
   report and choose the Use button. Quicken displays the memorized
   report.

Fig. 18.16

Choose Memorized from the Reports menu to display the Memorized Reports window.

Editing and Deleting Memorized Reports

You can change a memorized report's title (perhaps to a name that's more meaningful to you now) or delete a memorized report, if you won't be using the report again.

To edit a memorized report title, follow these steps:

1. From the Reports menu, choose Memorized. Quicken displays the Memorized Reports window, which lists all memorized reports by title (refer to fig. 18.16).

2. Highlight the report that you want to edit and then choose the Edit button. Quicken displays the Rename Memorized Report dialog box.

3. Type the new title in the Report Title text box.

4. Choose OK to save the change.

To delete a memorized report, follow these steps:

1. From the Reports menu, choose Memorized. Quicken displays the Memorized Reports window, which lists all memorized reports (refer to fig. 18.16).

2. Highlight the report that you want to delete and then choose the Del button.

3. Quicken displays a warning that you are about to delete a memorized report. Choose OK to delete the memorized report.

Setting Report Preferences

You can set preferences to change the report defaults that Quicken uses to create reports. For example, Quicken creates reports using the Year to Date report date range by default. Although you can change the date of any report as you create it, you may want to change the default setting, or the report preference, to the date range you use most often. So, if you usually create monthly reports and use Month to Date as the date range, you can change the default to Month to Date so that Quicken automatically creates reports using this date range.

To set report preferences in Quicken, follow these steps:

1. From the Edit menu, choose Preferences, or click the Prefs button on the Iconbar. Quicken displays the Quicken for Windows Preferences dialog box.

2. Select the Reports preference button to display the Report Preferences dialog box, shown in figure 18.17.

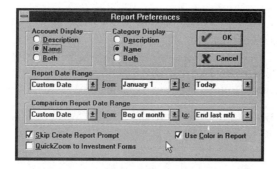

Fig. 18.17
You can change preference settings for reports in the Report Preferences dialog box.

3. From the Account Display options, select how you want Quicken to show account names in reports. Select Description to show only the account description, Name to show only the account name, or Both to show the account name and the account description in reports.

4. From the Category Display options, select Description to show only category descriptions, Name to show only the category name, or Both to show the category name and the category description in reports.

5. In the Report Date Range and Comparison Report Date Range sections, select the initial date range that you want Quicken to use for all reports. This range should be the dates you use most often when you create reports.

> **Note**
>
> If the date range that you most often use isn't included in Quicken's list, you can create a default date range. To do so, select Custom Date from the Report Date Range drop-down list. Then select the start and end dates in the **From** and **To** drop-down list boxes.

6. Select the **S**kip Create Report Prompt check box if you want Quicken to create a report immediately when you choose the report name from the **R**eports menu (rather than display the Create Report dialog box first).

7. For investment income and investment transaction reports, select the **Q**uickZoom to Investment Forms check box if you want to go directly to the entry forms instead of the Investment Register when you use QuickZoom.

8. Select the Use Color in Report check box if you want to display report text in blue and negative report amounts in red.

9. Choose OK to save the report preference settings and return to the Quicken for Windows Preferences dialog box.

10. Choose **D**one to close the Quicken for Windows Preferences dialog box.

Copying Reports to the Windows Clipboard

Now you can copy a report from Quicken to the Windows Clipboard. Then you can paste the report contents to another Windows program, such as Microsoft Word for Windows or Excel.

To copy a report to the Windows Clipboard, follow these steps:

1. Create the report that you want to copy to the Clipboard.

2. Choose the Copy button from the report button bar. Quicken copies the contents of the report to the Windows Clipboard.

To paste the report to another Windows program, follow these steps:

1. Switch to the other program.

2. From the other program, move to the field where you want to enter Quicken report data.

3. Choose the Paste command (usually found in the Edit menu). Windows copies the data from the Clipboard and enters it into the other program. The report data is pasted as unformatted text without the title or column headings.

Summary

This chapter reviewed the basics of creating and printing a Quicken report. These reports use the information stored in your Quicken file to provide a wealth of financial information that you can use to manage your personal and business finances better.

In this chapter, you learned how to do the following:

- Use the new QuickReport feature to get instant transaction listings

- Create a report

- Use the Report button bar

- Print reports

- Customize a report

- Filter transactions included in reports

- Sort report data

- Use QuickZoom to examine report detail

- Memorize reports

- Copy a report to the Windows Clipboard

In the next chapter, you learn about graphing. You learn how Quicken analyzes your financial data and puts it into graph format so that you can view your income and expenses, your assets and liabilities, actual and budget amounts, and the relative value of your investments.

Chapter 19

Using Graphs To Analyze Your Finances

In previous chapters, you learned how to enter transactions and write checks, track your assets and liabilities, create budgets, and monitor your investments. In Chapter 18, "Creating and Printing Reports," you learned how to produce reports so that you could analyze the information and data that you enter in Quicken. Creating reports is an excellent way to summarize your financial information, but not the only way.

You can create on-screen graphs to show relationships between your income and expenses, assets and liabilities, actual and budget amounts, and individual investments and total portfolio. If you have an installed graphics card, you can create graphs in Quicken. You can create graphs in just seconds based on the transactions that you enter and categorize, the account balances, budgeted data, and investment transactions entered.

In the case of your finances, assessing your financial situation is sometimes easier when you can see a graph that shows an overview or summary of your finances. Graphs show you, for example, the relationship of individual expense categories to your total expenditures. Therefore, you quickly can see what percentage each individual expense category is to your total expenses. Although reports show you information in a format that is useful in financial analysis, graphs are a visual means for analysis that sometimes have more effect than a list of categories or accounts in a report.

Understanding Quicken Graphs

Depending on the type of graph you select to create, Quicken displays the following graph formats:

- Bar graphs

- Pie charts

- Stacked bar graphs

- Line graphs

> **Note**
>
> You can't choose the graph format that Quicken uses to compare data. If you want to use a different format than Quicken uses, you must export the data to another program with graphing capabilities.

Each graph format compares financial information or shows information in a different way. In the following sections, you learn about the different graph formats and what they represent. Each graph that you create includes a *legend* that tells you what each bar or piece of pie represents.

Bar Graphs

Quicken can create *bar graphs* (like the one you see in fig. 19.1) to compare data within a specified period. The items the graphs compare appear as bars and are shown on the horizontal axis, side by side. The dollar amounts or values of the items being compared are shown on the vertical axis.

In figure 19.1, you see the comparison of income to expenses. The legend in the upper right corner of the graph shows that one bar in the graph represents income and the other represents expenses.

Pie Charts

Pie charts show the composition of each individual item to the whole. If you graph your income composition, for example, you see the percentage that your salary contributes to your total income from all sources. You also can use a pie chart like the one shown in figure 19.1 to help you determine whether you are spending too much in a particular expense category or earning too little as compared to your total income.

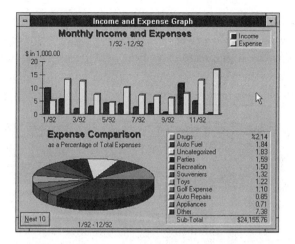

Fig. 19.1
Quicken creates bar graphs to compare data, like income and expenses, within the same period. The second graph, a pie chart, shows the composition of expenses.

IV

Analyzing Your Finances

Stacked Bar Graphs

A *stacked bar graph* shows two trends simultaneously (see fig. 19.2). First, the graphs show the composition of items in the stacked bar, such as the composition of total investments. In this case, a different color or pattern within each bar represents each security. That's why this graph format is called *stacked bar*—it stacks the items that comprise the whole in a single bar.

Stacked bar graphs also show how items are comprised to the whole over time. In figure 19.2, you see how the composition of security investments changes over a period of eight months.

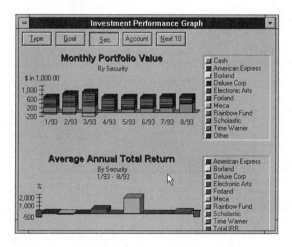

Fig. 19.2
Stacked bar graphs show two trends simultaneously: the composition of items in the stacked bar and how items are comprised to the whole over time.

Line Graphs

A *line graph* shows net values over time or trends. Line graphs in Quicken are superimposed over bar graphs to show how net values change over time. Figure 19.3 shows the Net Worth Graph window with a line graph that plots net worth value (assets minus liabilities) over an eight-month period.

Fig. 19.3
Line graphs show net values as they change over time.

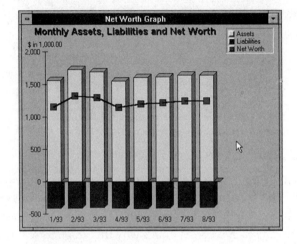

Setting Graph Preferences

You can set graph preferences so that graphs appear the way you want them. To set graph preferences, follow these steps:

1. Choose Preferences from the Edit menu or click Prefs on the Iconbar. Quicken displays the Quicken for Windows Preferences dialog box.

2. Choose the Graphs preference button. Quicken displays the Graph Preferences dialog box, shown in figure 19.4.

Fig. 19.4
The Graph Preferences dialog box provides settings that establish the way graphs appear on-screen.

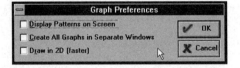

3. By default, Quicken uses solid colors to represent data in graphs. If you prefer black-and-white patterns, select Display Patterns on Screen.

> **Note**
>
> If you use a monochrome monitor, select **D**isplay Patterns on Screen. Other-wise, you may have difficulty differentiating the bars on-screen. You also should select **D**isplay Patterns on Screen if you are printing to a black-and-white printer so that you can see what the output will resemble.

4. Each Quicken graph that you create actually consists of two parts. The contents of the two parts vary, depending on the graph that you select to create. By default, Quicken displays both parts of the graph in one window. To display both parts of a graph in separate windows, select Create All Graphs in Separate Windows.

5. By default, Quicken displays all graphs in three dimensions. You can change the appearance to show two dimensions by selecting D**r**aw in 2D. Use this option if you find that your computer takes a long time to draw graphs in three dimensions. Be aware, however, that graphs that Quicken draws in two dimensions also print in two dimensions.

> **Note**
>
> Graphs that you create in 3-D in Quicken don't include a third axis; as a result, they aren't truly three-dimensional. 3-D graphs are actually 2-D graphs with shadows added to show depth within the graph.

6. Choose OK to save the graph preferences and return to the Quicken for Windows Preferences dialog box.

7. Choose Done to close the Quicken for Windows Preferences dialog box.

Creating Graphs

This section explains how to create and display graphs, in general. You learn how to select a graph type, display the graph, and remove the graph from your screen. The next section in this chapter explains each individual graph and how to use graphs to analyze your income and expenses, net worth, budget versus actual data, and investments.

To create a graph, follow these steps:

1. Choose **Graphs** on the **Reports** menu or click **Graphs** on the Iconbar to display the Create Graphs dialog box, shown in figure 19.5.

Fig. 19.5
Select the graph that you want to create in the Create Graphs dialog box.

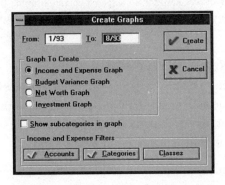

2. Enter the dates that you want to limit transactions to in the From and To text boxes. If you want to see your income and expenses for the first six months of the year, for example, enter **1/94** in the From text box and **6/94** in the To text box.

Tip
You can use the + (plus) and – (minus) keys to change the day or month by one.

3. In the Graph To Create section, select the graph that you want to create by selecting the appropriate option button. You can choose from the following graphs:

Income and Expense	Analyzes the items that make up your total income, items that make up your total expenses, and your spending and earning trends
Budget Variance	Compares your actual income and expenses to your budgeted income and expenses
Net Worth	Analyzes the assets that make up your total assets, the liabilities that make up your total liabilities, and how your assets and liabilities have changed over time; also compares your total assets to your total liabilities

Investment	Shows how your portfolio is distributed (stocks, bonds, options, Treasury bills, and so on) and the changes in your portfolio value over time

4. To include subcategories in the graph that you are creating, select the Show Subcategories in Graph check box.

> **Note**
>
> The filter buttons shown at the bottom of the Create Graphs dialog box are used to limit the data that Quicken uses to generate a graph to specific **Accounts, Categories,** and **Classes.** For investment reports, you can select the securities to include in a graph. Selecting accounts, categories, or classes to include in a graph is explained later in the section "Filtering Graph Transactions."

5. Choose Create to display the selected graph. Quicken always displays two graphs in the graph window for each graph that you select in the Create Graphs dialog box. (If you want graphs displayed in two separate windows, select the Create All Graphs in Separate Windows preference, as explained earlier in the section "Setting Graph Preferences.")

6. When you are finished reviewing the graph, double-click the Control menu box or press Esc to remove the graph from your screen.

Analyzing Income and Expense Graphs

You can use *income and expense graphs* to analyze the items that make up your total income, items that make up your total expenses, and your spending and earning trends. You also can use these graphs to compare your total income to expenses. Common questions you can answer by creating income and expense graphs follow:

- Has my income increased over time?

- By what margin is my income more than my expenses?

- Am I overspending?

- What sources make up my total income?

- What expenses make up my total expenses?

- Have my expenses increased or decreased over time?

After you create an income and expense graph, you will be able to answer these questions, and more.

Figure 19.6 shows an Income and Expense Graph window. The bar graph compares income and expenses over time. You easily can determine whether your income has been enough to cover expenses and how your income and expenses have changed over time.

Fig. 19.6

The Income and Expense Graph window displays a bar graph that compares your income and expenses and a pie chart that shows your top 10 expenses.

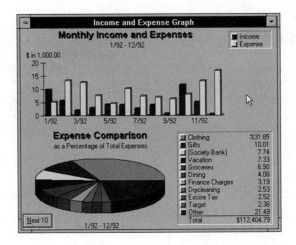

If your income was greater than your expenses in the time period covered in the bar graph, the pie chart shows the top 10 expenses relative to your total income. Quicken displays the difference between your income and expenses as the Net Savings because you didn't spend this amount.

Tip

To see the next 10 highest expense categories in the pie chart, choose Next 10 at the bottom of the Income and Expense Graph window.

If your expenses were greater than your income in the time period covered in the bar graph, the pie chart shows the top 10 expenses as a percentage of your total expenses. The Net Savings piece isn't displayed because you didn't generate savings.

Analyzing Budget Variance Graphs

You can use a *budget variance graph* to compare your actual income and expenses to your budgeted income and expenses. The budget reports that you learned how to create in Chapter 16, "Budgeting with Quicken," also tell you how your budget compares to your actual income and expense. The budget and actual graphs provide a visual comparison that enables you to assess quickly how successful (or unsuccessful) you are in sticking to your budget.

You can use the budget variance graph to compare actual amounts to budgeted amounts, identify areas where you are over budget, and identify areas where you are under budget.

Common questions that you can answer by creating a budget variance graph follow:

- Am I sticking to my budget?

- How much more can I spend and still stay within my budget?

- In which areas am I over budget?

- In which areas am I under budget?

Tip
With Quicken 3 for Windows, you can include subcategories in a budget variance graph by selecting the Show Subcategories in Graph check box in the Create Graphs dialog box.

IV

Analyzing Your Finances

After you create the budget variance graph, you will be able to answer these questions, and more.

Figure 19.7 shows a Budget Variance Graph window. The bar graph at the top of the Budget Variance Graph window shows actual net income less budgeted net income. The second bar graph shows the five categories with the greatest budget variances. To see the next five categories, choose Next 5.

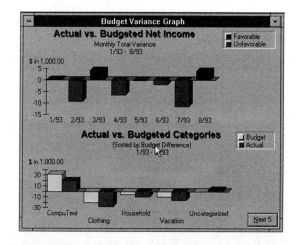

Fig. 19.7
The Budget Variance Graph window shows how your actual net income compares to budgeted net income and how each category's actual amounts compare to its budget amounts.

> **Note**
>
> You can't display budget and actual graphs without creating your budget first. Refer to Chapter 16, "Budgeting with Quicken," to learn how to create a budget. Budget variance graphs are created from the categories that you assign to transactions and the categories that you establish budget amounts for.

Analyzing Net Worth Graphs

You can use *net worth graphs* to analyze the assets that make up your total assets, the liabilities that make up your total liabilities, and how your assets and liabilities have changed over time. You also can use net worth graphs to compare your total assets to your total liabilities.

Common questions that you can answer by creating net worth graphs are as follows:

■ Do I have more assets than liabilities?

■ How has my *net worth* (assets minus liabilities) changed over time?

■ What assets make up my total assets?

■ Have my assets increased over time?

■ What liabilities make up my total liabilities?

■ Have my liabilities increased or decreased over time?

After you create the net worth graph, you will be able to answer these questions, and more.

Figure 19.8 shows the Net Worth Graph window. The net worth graph displays bars above the x-axis to represent your assets. The bars below the x-axis represent your liabilities. The line graph plots your net worth over time.

Fig. 19.8

The Net Worth Graph window displays a bar graph with assets shown above the x-axis and liabilities below the x-axis.

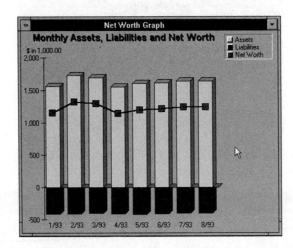

> **Note**
>
> To see the exact net worth amount for a specific point in time, point to the red box within the line graph for that time period (the mouse pointer changes to a magnifying glass icon) and press and hold down the left mouse button. Quicken displays the exact net worth amount within a small box. When you release the mouse button, the amount is removed from the graph.

Analyzing Investment Performance Graphs

You can use *investment performance graphs* to analyze your investment portfolio. With investment graphs, you can see how your portfolio is distributed (stocks, bonds, options, Treasury bills, and so on) and see the changes in your portfolio value over time.

> **Note**
>
> You also can create graphs from the Portfolio View of an investment account. You can create a graph that shows, for example, the price trends of your security holdings within an account. Refer to Chapter 15, "Monitoring Your Investments," to learn how to create graphs from an investment account.

Common questions that you can answer by creating investment graphs are as follows:

- Is my investment portfolio value increasing?

- How diversified is my investment portfolio?

- Are the prices of my individual holdings increasing?

After you create the investment performance graph, you will be able to answer these questions, and more.

> **Note**
>
> If you don't track your investments by using Quicken's investment accounts, you can't create investment graphs. Refer to Chapter 15, "Monitoring Your Investment," to learn how to use Quicken's investment accounts.

Figure 19.9 shows the Investment Performance Graph window summarized by **T**ype of security. Choose **G**oal to summarize the graph by goal, **Sec** to summarize the graph by security, or **A**ccount to summarize the graph by account.

Fig. 19.9

The Investment Performance Graph window displays a bar graph that summarizes the market value of each security and another bar graph that measures the performance of your securities.

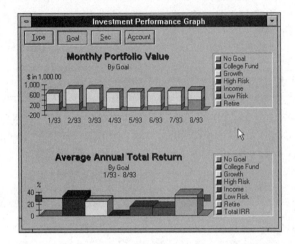

The stacked bar graph displayed at the top of the Investment Performance Graph window summarizes the market value of each of your securities. Each stacked bar shows the composition of the types of securities, security goals, individual securities, or accounts (dependent on how you select to summarize the graph). The second bar graph shows how well your securities are performing. The solid black line shows the total internal rate of return (IRR) during the time period you specified for the graph.

Using QuickZoom To Examine Graph Detail

Tip

To move the QuickZoom Graph window so that you can see the details in the original graph, drag the window toward one edge of the screen.

Quicken's QuickZoom feature enables you to see the detail behind an item in a graph. QuickZoom works the same way in graphs as in reports (see Chapter 18, "Creating and Printing Reports"). When the mouse pointer changes to the magnifying glass icon, you can use QuickZoom to get more information about a particular element in a graph. Just double-click the graph element to display the QuickZoom Graph.

When you use QuickZoom to see the detail of a bar in a bar graph, Quicken creates a pie chart showing the composition of the bar. Figure 19.10 shows the QuickZoom Graph window displayed with a pie chart that shows the composition of a bar in a bar graph.

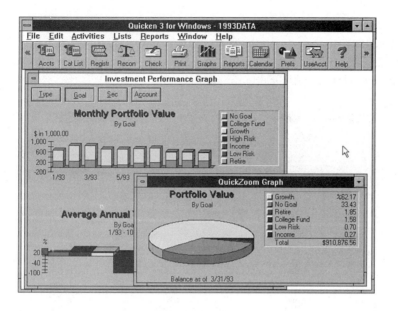

Fig. 19.10
When you use QuickZoom to examine the detail of a bar in a bar graph, Quicken creates a pie chart in the QuickZoom Graph window that shows the composition of the bar.

You also can use QuickZoom to investigate a pie slice or legend item. Just double-click the pie slice or legend item to display a bar graph showing the dollars (by month) of the pie slice or the legend item. Figure 19.11 shows the bar chart displayed when you use QuickZoom to investigate a legend item or pie slice.

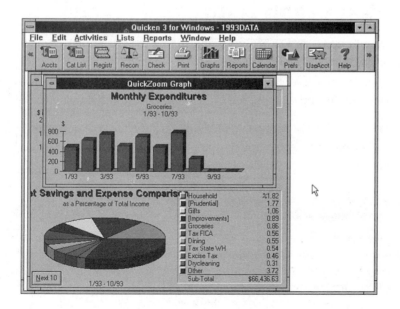

Fig. 19.11
When you use QuickZoom to investigate a pie slice or legend item, Quicken displays a bar graph that shows the dollars (by month) associated with the pie slice or legend item.

IV

Analyzing Your Finances

If you need to see transaction detail for an item in a QuickZoom graph, double-click the item to display a list of transactions, as shown in figure 19.12. From the transaction listing, you can go to the Register for a specific transaction by double-clicking the transaction.

Fig. 19.12
Double-click an item in a Quick-Zoom graph to display the trans-actions that make up the item.

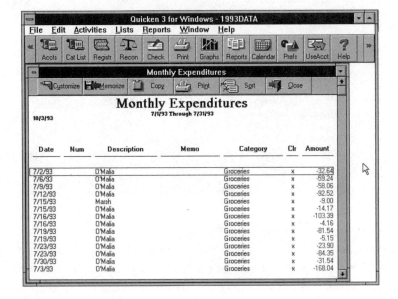

Hiding Graph Data

You can hide a pie slice or bar in a graph so that the remaining graph items appear bigger. If a category makes up a very large piece in a pie chart, for example, you may have difficulty seeing the other pieces. By hiding the larg-est piece, you free up space for Quicken to display the remaining pieces.

To hide a pie slice or a bar in a graph, Shift-click the pie slice or bar (press Shift as you click the left mouse button). To reveal the item, re-create the graph.

> **Note**
>
> Hiding a graph category isn't the same as selecting not to include a category in the graph when it's created. When you filter categories (see the next section) by dese-lecting a category from the graph, Quicken doesn't include the category in its analy-sis as it creates the graph. When you hide a graph category, Quicken still calculates the category value but doesn't display the value.

Filtering Graph Transactions

You can choose which transactions Quicken includes in graphs by *filtering* them. For income and expense, budget variance, and net worth graphs, you can select the accounts, categories, and classes that Quicken uses to display the graph. For investment performance graphs, you can select the accounts and securities that Quicken uses to display the graph.

To filter graph transactions, follow these steps:

1. Click Graphs on the Iconbar to display the Create Graphs dialog box (refer to fig. 19.5).

2. Enter the date range and select the graph type that you want to create.

3. Select the following buttons to filter transactions:

Accounts	Displays the Select Accounts to Include dialog box, where you can select the accounts that you want to include in the graph.
Categories	Displays the Select Categories to Include dialog box, where you can select the categories that you want to include in the graph. If you select the Show Subcategories in Graph check box in the Create Graphs dialog box, you also can select the subcategories that you want to include in the graph.
Classes	Displays the Select Classes to Include dialog box, where you can select the classes that you want to include in the graph.
Securities	Displays the Select Securities to Include dialog box, where you can select the securities that you want to include in the graph (only for investment performance graphs).

4. In the appropriate dialog box, select the items from the list that you want to include in the report by double-clicking the item, or by highlighting the item and choosing Mark or pressing the space bar. When you include an item, Quicken enters the word Include in the Include in Graph column in the dialog box. To include all items, choose Mark All. Choosing Mark or Mark All a second time excludes the item or all items.

5. When you are finished making your selections, choose OK to return to the Create Graphs dialog box.

> **Note**
>
> If you filter graph transactions by selecting accounts, categories, classes, or securities, Quicken places a check mark on the appropriate button in the Create Graphs dialog box. If, for example, you select accounts to include in a graph, Quicken places a check mark on the Accounts button in the Create Graphs dialog box. The check mark shows you that the transactions in a graph have been filtered.

6. Choose Create to display the graph using the accounts, categories, sub-categories, classes, or securities (for investment performance graphs) that you selected.

Printing Graphs

After you select and display a graph and (if necessary) filter the transactions included in the graph, you're ready to print the graph.

Before you can print graphs in Quicken, you must set up the program to print to your printer. Quicken includes different printer settings for reports and graphs (Report/Graph Printer Setup) and checks (Check Printer Setup). To set up Quicken to print graphs, follow these steps:

1. From the File menu, choose Printer Setup. Quicken displays the Printer Setup submenu.

2. Choose Report/Graph Printer Setup. Quicken displays the Report Printer Setup dialog box, shown in figure 19.13.

3. Select your installed printer from the Printer drop-down list.

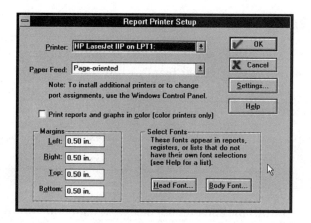

IV

Analyzing Your Finances

Fig. 19.13
The Report Printer
Setup dialog box
tells Quicken
which printer you
are using, the type
of paper you use,
the graph margins,
and the type fonts.

4. Quicken uses Auto-detect to determine whether your printer is continuous-feed or page-oriented. If the paper feed isn't correct, choose Paper Feed to select the appropriate paper feed for your installed printer.

5. If you are using a color printer and want to print graphs in color, select the Print Reports and Graphs in Color check box. You must have an installed color printer to use this option.

6. Check the Left, Right, Top, and Bottom margins. If necessary, enter larger or smaller values than the preset values that Quicken uses.

7. You also can change other print settings, such as the paper tray, paper size, orientation, and number of copies. To change these settings, choose Settings. Quicken displays a dialog box for your installed printer. Make the necessary changes and choose OK to return to the Report Printer Setup dialog box.

8. Choose OK to save the printer settings.

After the printer is set up, you can print graphs from Quicken. To print graphs, follow these steps:

1. Turn on your printer and make sure that it's on-line.

2. Display the graph that you want to print.

3. Choose Print Graph from the File menu (or press Ctrl+P). Quicken begins printing the graph.

Summary

In this chapter, you learned about Quicken's graphing feature. You learned about the different types of graphs that Quicken creates and how to create graphs to analyze your income and expenses, net worth, budget versus actual data, and investments. You also learned how to do the following:

- Set graph preferences so that graphs are displayed the way you want them

- Create graphs

- Analyze the income and expense, budget variance, net worth, and investment performance graphs

- Use QuickZoom to examine the detail that makes up a graph

- Hide graph data

- Filter or limit the transactions reflected in graphs

- Print a graph

The next chapter begins Part V of *Using Quicken 3 for Windows*, "Managing Quicken for Windows." In this part, you learn how to manage Quicken files and how to customize Quicken so that it works in a way that's best for you. The next chapter, "Managing Your Quicken Files," shows how to add another file to your Quicken system, how to open, rename, delete, and copy Quicken files, how to back up and restore files, how to transfer data between Quicken and another program, and how to handle your Quicken files at year's end.

Part V

Managing Quicken for Windows

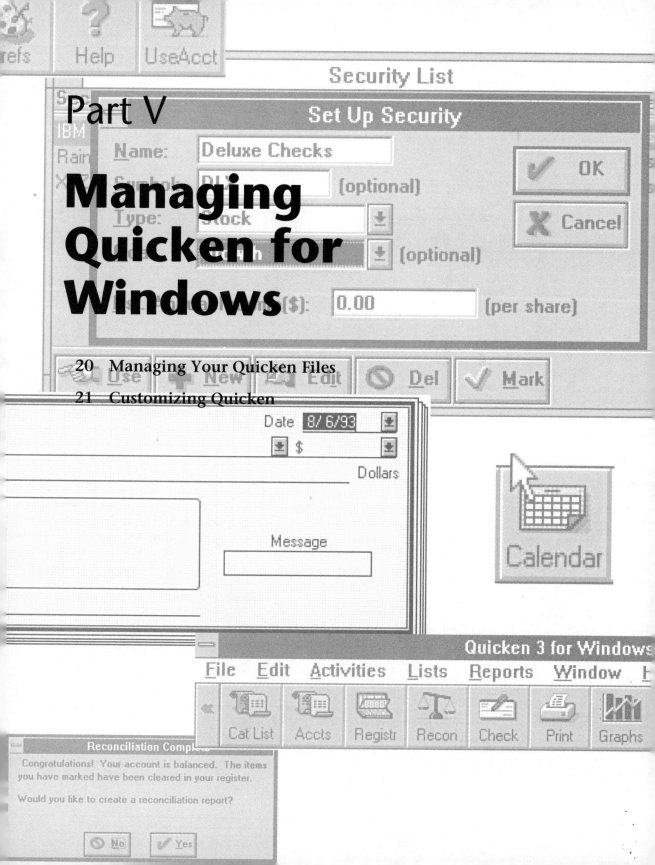

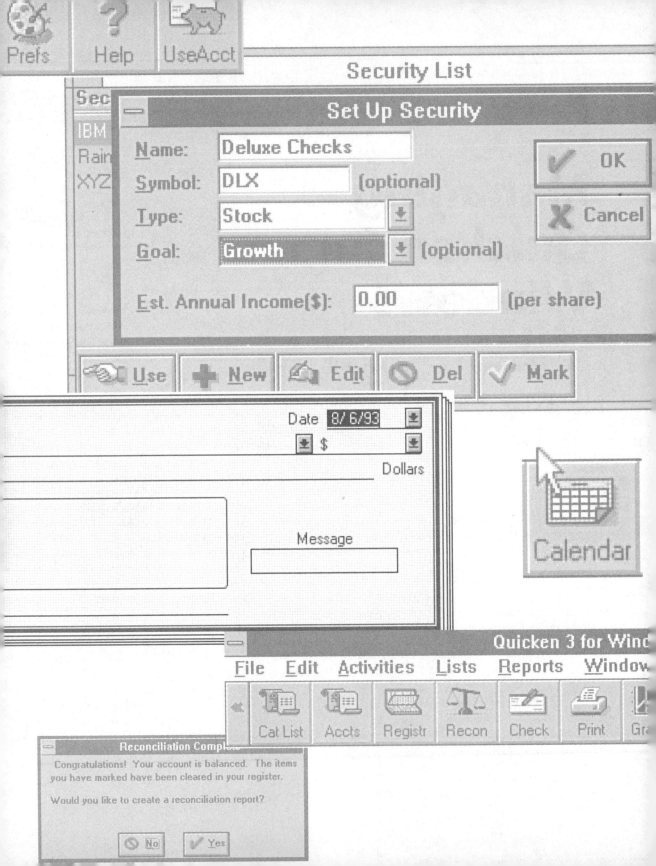

Prefs   **Help**   **UseAcct**

Security List

Sec

Set Up Security

IBM
Rain
XYZ

Name: Deluxe Checks
Symbol: DLX   (optional)
Type: Stock   ▼
Goal: Growth   ▼   (optional)

Est. Annual Income($):   0.00   (per share)

✓ OK

✗ Cancel

☞ **U**se   ➕ **N**ew   ✍ **Edi**t   🚫 **De**l   ✓ **Mark**

Date 8/ 6/93 ▼
▼ $ ▼
Dollars

Message

Calendar

Quicken 3 for Wind

File   **Edit**   **Activities**   **Lists**   **Reports**   **Window**

« Cat List   Accts   Registr   Recon   Check   Print   Gr

Reconciliation Compl
Congratulations! Your account is balanced. The items
you have marked have been cleared in your register.

Would you like to create a reconciliation report?

🚫 **N**o   ✓ **Y**es

Chapter 20

Managing Your Quicken Files

Until now, you have worked with only one Quicken file. Quicken enables you to add more files so that you can maintain separate files for more than one household or business. With multiple files in your Quicken system, you easily can work with several different files by switching from one to another. With Quicken, however, you can work with only one file at a time.

Working with Quicken Files

Quicken assigns a file name to each file. As you learned in Chapter 1, the name for the first file added to the Quicken system is QDATA. Each Quicken file consists of five data files with the same file name, but with different extensions—QDI, QDT, QMT, QNX, and QST. You can find these data files in the directory where you store Quicken for Windows data (such as C:\QUICKENW). Quicken stores in these data files the financial information you enter in the Register.

Quicken stores accounts you define in files and enables you to have more than one file. The obvious question, then, when you begin defining new accounts, is to which file an account should be added. You usually find these decisions fairly easy to make.

The general rule is that you store related accounts together in a separate file. Accounts are related when they pertain to the same business or the same household. If you use Quicken for home accounting and for a commercial printing business, for example, you use two files: one for home and one for

In this chapter, you learn how to perform the following tasks:

- Create a new Quicken file

- Open and close a file

- Copy and change Quicken files

- Delete a Quicken file

- Back up and restore your Quicken data

- Archive, export, and import file data

- Assign, change, and remove passwords

V

Managing Quicken

business. If you use Quicken for three businesses—a consulting practice, a small publishing business, and a restaurant—you use three files, one for each business.

Creating a New File

When you installed Quicken, you created at least one file, named QDATA by default (the QDATA file has five data files, as explained in the preceding section). Until you create a second file, any accounts you set up are added to QDATA. To add a new file to your Quicken system, follow these steps:

1. Choose New from the File menu to display the Creating New File dialog box, shown in figure 20.1.

Fig. 20.1

The Creating New File dialog box confirms that you want to create a new Quicken file, not a Quicken account.

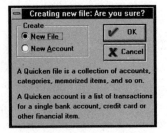

2. Choose the New File option button to create a new file.

> **Note**
>
> If you confuse the term *file* with *account*, and you really want to create a new account, choose the New Account option button and choose OK. Quicken displays the Select Account Type dialog box so that you can specify the type of account that you want to set up. For more information on setting up accounts in a Quicken file, refer to Chapter 3, "Defining Your Accounts."

3. Choose OK. Quicken displays the Create Quicken File dialog box, shown in figure 20.2.

4. In the File Name text box, type the name for the new file.

   The name you enter must be a valid DOS file name, which means any combination of up to eight characters, but no spaces. HOME, PERSONAL, BUSINESS, and LEGAL all are valid DOS file names. The space in PRINT 1, however, makes this name invalid, and RESTAURANT fails because this name uses more than eight characters. Refer to the DOS user's manual if you have questions about DOS file-naming conventions.

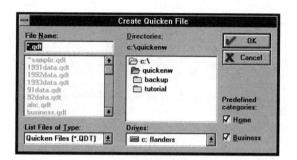

Fig. 20.2
Name your new Quicken file in the Create Quicken File dialog box. You also can specify the directory where you want your new file located.

5. (Optional) From the Directories list box, select the directory where you want your new Quicken file located. By default, Quicken stores data files in the Quicken for Windows program directory (such as C:\QUICKENW).

You really don't need to change the default directory name unless you have a personal preference where the new Quicken file is located. Quicken, however, does enable you to change the default directory.

6. In the Predefined Categories section, select the categories that you want to use in the new Quicken file. To use predefined home or personal categories, select the Home check box. To use predefined business categories, select the Business check box. To use home and business categories, select both check boxes. (By default, Quicken assumes that you want to use both predefined home and business categories.) Refer to Chapter 4, "Organizing Your Finances," for more on using predefined categories.

7. When the Create Quicken File dialog box is complete, choose OK to create the new file. The new file opens automatically, and Quicken displays the Select Account Type dialog box so that you can set up your first account in your new Quicken file. Refer to Chapter 3, "Defining Your Accounts," to learn how to set up your first account.

Opening a File

When you work with more than one file, you must open the file that you want to work with when you use Quicken. When you start Quicken, the last file that you used opens automatically.

To open a file, follow these steps:

1. Choose **O**pen from the **F**ile menu (or press Ctrl+O). Quicken displays the Open Quicken File dialog box, shown in figure 20.3.

Fig. 20.3

Select the file that you want to open in the Open Quicken File dialog box.

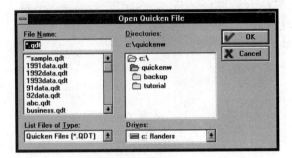

2. By default, Quicken lists the data files in the Quicken program directory (such as C:\QUICKENW). If necessary, change the directory in the Directories list box if the file that you want to open is located in a different directory.

3. Select the Quicken file that you want to open by typing the file name in the File Name text box or by clicking the file name in the list box. Just make sure that the file name for the file that you want to open appears in the File Name text box.

4. Choose OK to open the file. Quicken saves and closes the file you were working on, and then opens the file that you selected in step 3.

Closing a File

To close a Quicken file, just exit the program or open another Quicken file. When you exit Quicken, your work in the current session is saved automatically. When you decide to open another file, Quicken automatically saves and closes the file you were working on before opening the new file.

Copying Files

You can make a copy of your Quicken file, perhaps to give to your accountant to use with his Quicken program. You can copy all transactions from a file or select a date range of transactions to copy. You must open the file that you want to copy before you copy the file. Refer to the earlier section "Opening a File" to learn how to open a file.

To copy the current Quicken file, follow these steps:

1. Choose File Operations from the File menu.

2. From the File Operations submenu, choose the Copy command. Quicken displays the Copy File dialog box, shown in figure 20.4.

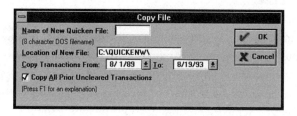

Fig. 20.4
Enter the name and location of the file to which you want the current file copied in the Copy File dialog box.

3. In the Name of New Quicken File text box, type the DOS file name for the new Quicken file.

4. In the Location of New File text box, type the path (drive and/or directory) to which you want to copy the file.

5. In the Copy Transactions From and To drop-down list boxes, select the beginning and ending dates for transactions to be copied.

6. Select the Copy All Prior Uncleared Transactions check box if you want to copy transactions dated before the dates in step 5 that haven't yet cleared the bank (as indicated in the Clr column in the Register). If you don't want to copy these transactions, leave this check box unselected.

7. Choose OK to copy the current file to the file name that you typed in step 3.

8. After the file is copied, Quicken displays the File Copied Successfully dialog box (see fig. 20.5). Select the Reload Original File option button to reopen the file that you just copied. To open the new file that you just created, select the Load New Copy option button.

9. Choose OK to open the appropriate file.

V

Managing Quicken

Note

If you choose to open the new copy of a file, your original file is saved and closed.

Fig. 20.5
The File Copied
Successfully dialog
box appears after
you copy a
Quicken file.

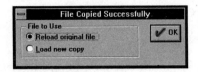

Renaming a File

You can edit the names of existing files, if necessary. You may want to edit a
file name, for example, if you named the file incorrectly. If you name files
based on the business name, changing the name of the business also may
mean that you want to change the name of the file. Suppose that the file
name for the business Acme Manufacturing is ACME_MFG. If the business
name changes to Acme Incorporated, you can change the file name to
ACME_INC.

To rename a file name, follow these steps:

1. Choose File Operations from the File menu.

2. From the File Operations submenu, choose Rename. Quicken displays
   the Rename Quicken File dialog box, shown in figure 20.6.

Fig. 20.6
The Rename
Quicken File dialog
box enables you to
change the file
name for any
existing file in the
File Name list box.

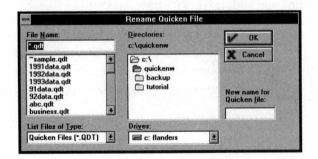

3. (Optional) To edit a file in some directory other than the default (such
   as C:/QUICKENW), select the directory in the Directories list box.

4. In the list box under the File Name text box, select the file that you
   want to rename.

5. Type the new file name in the New Name for Quicken File text box.
   Make sure that you use a valid DOS file name.

6. Choose OK to rename the file. Quicken returns to the file in which you
   now are working.

Deleting a File

Quicken enables you to delete files that you inadvertently added or that you no longer use. Deleting a file is almost always a bad idea because when you do, you essentially are deleting all the accounts in the file. After a file is deleted from your Quicken system, you may not be able to restore it.

If you no longer are tracking any of the accounts in the file, you can delete the entire file. This may be the case if you set up a special file for learning to use Quicken and no longer use the file. You also no longer need the file used for a business if you sell the business.

To delete a file, follow these steps:

1. Choose File Operations from the File menu.

2. From the File Operations submenu, choose Delete. Quicken displays the Delete Quicken File dialog box, shown in figure 20.7.

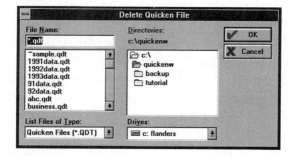

Tip
Make a backup copy of all files before you delete them to avoid losing data that you may need later.

Fig. 20.7
You can delete a Quicken file from the Delete Quicken File dialog box. Deleting a file removes it from your Quicken system.

3. (Optional) To delete a file from a directory other than the Quicken default directory (such as C:\QUICKENW), in the Directories list box, select the directory where the file is located.

4. In the list box under the File Name text box, select the file that you want to delete.

5. Choose OK.

6. Quicken displays the Deleting File message box to confirm that you want to delete the selected file. Type **yes** if you are sure that you want to delete the file.

7. Choose OK to delete the file.

V

Managing Quicken

Backing Up and Restoring Files

Although you may be a careful computer user, everyone loses data (this author once lost a whole three months' worth!) at one time or another. To avoid losing important financial data, you need to back up your files regularly.

Backing up means that you make a second copy of all Quicken data files (including Q3.DIR, QDATA.QDT, QDATA,QNX, QDATA.QMT, QDATA.QST, and QDATA.QDI). Back up these files so that if your original Quicken data files are damaged, you can use the backup copies to restore the damaged files to their original condition.

You can back up and restore files by using DOS file commands or one of the popular hard disk management programs. For convenience, you may find the Quicken backup and restore options easier to use. The following sections discuss these backup and restore options.

Backing Up a File

You need to make two important decisions about backing up files. First, you must decide how often you need to perform a backup. Although opinions on the subject vary, a good habit to form is to back up data files after you complete a session in which you enter or change financial data. When you finish entering the first set of account transactions, for example, back up all the data files.

Most people back up financial records daily, weekly, or monthly. After you spend time working with Quicken and become familiar with data file restoration procedures, you can estimate more accurately how often you need to back up files.

Second, decide how many old backup copies to keep. Usually, two or three copies are adequate. (This rule of thumb is the grandfather-father-son scheme.) Suppose that you back up the data files every day. On Thursday, a co-worker accidentally deletes the data file. If you keep two old backup copies in addition to the most recent backup copy, you have backups from Wednesday, Tuesday, and Monday. If the Wednesday copy is damaged (an unlikely but possible situation), you still have the Tuesday and Monday copies. The more recent a backup copy, the easier data is to recover, but using an old backup copy still is easier than re-entering all the data from the original documents.

Store these data file backup copies in a safe place. Don't keep all backup copies in the same location. If you experience a fire or if someone burglarizes your business or house, you may lose all the copies—no matter how many backups you keep. Store at least one copy at an off-site location. If you use Quicken at home, you can keep a backup copy in your desk at work; if you use Quicken for business, keep a backup copy at home.

> **Note**
>
> Without regular backups, you may lose financial records. Obviously, backing up files is important. Because backing up is so important, Quicken provides a backup message that periodically reminds you to back up the current file.

To back up your Quicken files, follow these steps:

1. From the File menu, choose Backup (or press Ctrl+B). Quicken displays the Select Backup Drive dialog box, shown in figure 20.8.

2. Select the Current File option button if you want to back up the file that is now open. If the file that you want to back up isn't open, select the Select From List option button.

3. From the Backup Drive drop-down list box, select the drive to which you want to back up the selected file.

> **Caution**
>
> Although you can choose to back up to your hard disk drive, you should back up to a floppy drive. If your hard disk fails, you risk losing the backup of your work, as well as the original.

4. Choose OK.

5. If you selected to back up the file that you are now working in, Quicken begins the backup process.

   If you chose to back up another file, Quicken displays the Back Up Quicken File dialog box. If necessary, select the directory of the file that you want to back up from the Directories list box and the drive containing the file from the Drives drop-down list box. In the list box

> **Tip**
> You can customize the Iconbar to include a Backup icon. Then, just choose the icon to begin backing up the current Quicken file. Chapter 21, "Customizing Quicken," explains how to add the Backup icon to the Iconbar.

V

Managing Quicken

under the File Name text box, select the file that you want to back up, or type the name of the file and path in the File Name text box. Then choose OK to begin the backup process.

Fig. 20.8

With the Select Backup Drive dialog box, you can back up the current file or select the file that you want to back up.

6. When the backup process is complete, Quicken displays a message box to confirm that the file was backed up successfully. Choose OK to return to the current file.

   If the file you are trying to back up can't fit on the disk, an error message alerts you that the disk is full, and Quicken enables you to choose to insert another disk.

7. Remove the backup disk from the disk drive and store the disk in a safe place.

Restoring Backed-Up Files

Eventually, someone or something may accidentally delete or destroy a data file. A computer can malfunction, or a co-worker may spill the contents of the pencil sharpener or a cup of coffee on the floppy disk that contains the Quicken data files. If you recently backed up these files and were diligent about printing copies of the Register, you should experience no serious setbacks. You can restore the Quicken files by using the backup copies.

To retrieve Quicken data from a backup copy, follow these steps:

1. Make sure that the Quicken file to which you want to restore data is open. If your QDATA file is damaged and you want to restore the backup copy data, for example, open the QDATA file.

2. Choose Restore from the File menu. Quicken displays the Restore Quicken File dialog box, shown in figure 20.9.

3. From the Drives drop-down list box, select the drive where your backup file is located. If your backup file is on a floppy disk located in drive A, for example, select a:.

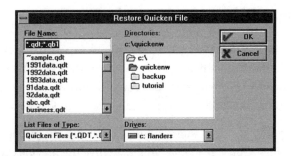

4. In the Directories list box, select the directory where the backup file is
    stored. If you backed up your data file to a floppy disk and the disk is in
    drive A, for example, select a: from the Directories list box.

5. Select (or type) the backup file name that you want to restore.

6. Choose OK. Quicken alerts you that if you proceed with restoring, you
    will overwrite the existing (or current) file. To proceed, choose OK.
    Choose Cancel to discontinue restoring the backup file.

7. After the restoration is complete, Quicken displays the File Restored
    Successfully dialog box. Choose OK to return to the current file.

8. Using the most recent printed copy of the Register, re-enter each trans-
    action that you entered for each account between the time you backed
    up and the time you lost the data.

9. Back up these files, as you learned earlier in this chapter, in case
    another accident causes you to lose the Quicken files again.

Note

If disaster befalls your Quicken data files that you didn't back up, you must re-enter
each Register transaction. The up-to-date printed copies of each Register show the
data that needs to be re-entered. If you don't have up-to-date copies of each Register, you need to re-enter each transaction from the original source documents—
checks, deposit slips, receipts, and so on. Regularly back up your Quicken data files to
prevent disasters from causing you to spend painful hours re-creating data.

Copying Files at Year's End

Theoretically, Quicken enables you to store up to 65,534 transactions in a file's Registers. Practically, these limitations are much lower. You may not be limited by space on your hard disk, but you probably don't want to work with thousands or tens of thousands of transactions in Registers.

Quicken provides a two-fold solution for dealing with the problem of ever-growing data files: Quicken enables you to archive the previous year's transactions to a separate file or create a new file that contains only the new year's data. When you archive data in the current file, the archive file contains data from the previous year and the current file is left untouched (contains both previous and current year data). When you create a file for the new year, Quicken saves a copy of your current file and then deletes any transactions from the prior year (before January 1st of this year) from the current file. This two-fold solution means that you can break large files into smaller, more manageable files.

For most users, the most convenient time to archive or start a new year file is after completing the annual income tax return and after any year-end reporting. At this time, all transactions from the prior year should have cleared the bank, and you have printed all necessary Quicken reports. Now, an archive copy of the files can provide a permanent copy of the data you used to prepare the year's financial reports. A new copy of the file also enables you to start a new year without a load of old, unnecessary data.

Archiving File Data

When you archive file data, Quicken copies the previous year's transactions to a separate file that is saved and can be used at any time. The transactions in the current file remain intact, for the previous year and current year.

To archive file data, follow these steps:

1. Because you can archive data from the current file only, you first must open the file whose data you want to archive.

2. Choose Year-End Copy from the File menu. Quicken displays the Year-End Copy dialog box, shown in figure 20.10.

3. Select the Archive option button.

4. Choose OK. Quicken displays the Archive File dialog box, shown in figure 20.11.

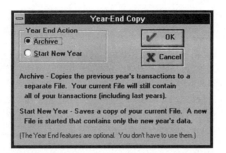

Fig. 20.10
Select an option button to archive file data or start a new year file in the Year-End Copy dialog box.

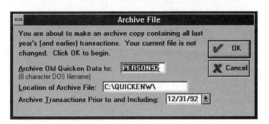

Fig. 20.11
Quicken enters default settings for the archive file in the Archive File dialog box.

5. If necessary, change any of the default settings in the Archive File dialog box. Choose OK to begin archiving data.

> **Note**
>
> By default, Quicken names the archive file using the current file name and the preceding year, locates the file in the Quicken program directory, and includes transactions only through the end of the preceding year.

6. When the archive process is complete, Quicken displays the File Copied Successfully dialog box. Here, select the Use Current File option button to continue using the current file, or the Use Archive File to close the current file and open the archive file.

7. Choose OK to use the selected file.

Starting a New File at Year's End

When you start a new file at year's end, Quicken saves a copy of the current file first. This copy becomes the "old" file, and its data isn't disturbed. Your current file then becomes the "new" file. Quicken then deletes any transaction data from the previous year (transactions dated before January 1st of the current year) from the new file. Therefore, your new file contains only current year data.

V

Managing Quicken

Note

If you start a new file, Quicken may include some transactions from previous years, such as investment transactions and any uncleared transactions. You need to keep these transactions in a working copy of a file because the investment transactions are needed for investment record-keeping and the uncleared transactions are needed for bank reconciliations.

To start a new year file, follow these steps:

1. Open the file from which you want to start a new year file.

2. Choose Year-End Copy from the File menu. Quicken displays the Year-End Copy dialog box (refer to fig. 20.10).

3. Select the Start New Year option button.

4. Choose OK. Quicken displays the Start New Year dialog box, shown in figure 20.12.

Fig. 20.12
With the Start New Year dialog box, you can delete transactions before a specified date to a separate file.

5. In the Copy All Transactions to File text box, type the file name you want Quicken to use for the new file.

Note

If you create a separate set of Quicken data files for each year, consider including the year number in the file name. You can name the data files from 1993 as QDATA93, the data files from 1994 as QDATA94, the data files from 1995 as QDATA95, and so on. Including the year number in data file names enables you to determine easily which year's records are contained in a particular data file.

---

6. In the Delete Transactions From Current File Older Than drop-down list box, select the date before which Quicken should delete transactions. If you want the file to contain only transactions dated from 1/1/94 to 12/31/94, for example, enter 1/1/94 in this field. All transactions dated before 1/1/94, such as 11/2/93 or 4/15/93, are deleted from the file.

7. Specify the location, if other than the Quicken program directory, for the new file in the Move Current File To text box.

8. When the Start New Year dialog box is complete, choose OK.

9. Quicken displays the File Copied Successfully dialog box. Here, you can select the Use Old File option button to use the file with the older transactions, or the Use File for New Year to use the new year's file.

10. Choose OK to use the selected file.

Exporting and Importing Files

Exporting is the process by which a software program makes a copy of a file in a format that another program can read. You may want to export the information stored in the Quicken Register so that you can retrieve and use the information in a database program, such as dBASE, or in a spreadsheet program, such as 1-2-3.

Importing is the process in which information created by one software program is retrieved by a second software program. You may want to import into Quicken the information created by an accounting program, such as DacEasy, so that you can use Quicken's reports to summarize the information.

Exporting and importing represent two sides of the same coin: exporting creates a file by using the information stored in the Quicken Register, and importing retrieves information from another file into the Quicken Register. Although most Quicken users never need to export or import files, Quicken provides the tools to do both.

Note

If you want to copy the Accounts, Category & Transfer, or Memorized Transaction list from one Quicken file to another, you can export the list to a QIF file and then import the QIF file to the other Quicken file. From the File menu, use the Import and Export commands to copy lists to other Quicken files.

V

Managing Quicken

Exporting Quicken File Data

When you export file data, Quicken creates an ASCII text file from the current account's Register transactions. You then can use this ASCII file in another software program. Most word processing, spreadsheet, and database applications enable you to import ASCII text files from Quicken.

To export file data, follow these steps:

1. Choose Export from the File menu. Quicken displays the QIF Export dialog box, shown in figure 20.13. (*QIF* stands for Quicken Interchange Format, which describes the special format in the ASCII file.)

Fig. 20.13

In the QIF Export dialog box, select the account or accounts, the export items, and the date range of transactions that you want to export.

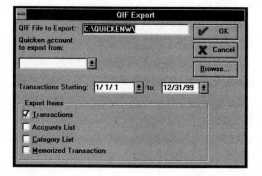

2. In the QIF File to Export text box, type the path and file name of the Quicken file that you want to export. If you're unsure of the file name, choose Browse to display files in a particular directory (from the Export to QIF File dialog box). Select the file in the File Name list box and choose OK to return to the QIF Export dialog box.

3. In the Quicken Account to Export From drop-down list box, select the account that you want to export. You can select <All Accounts> or an individual account.

4. If you want to limit the transactions exported to a specific date range, select the beginning and ending dates in the Transactions Starting and To drop-down list boxes.

5. In the Export Items section, select the check box for the item(s) that you want to export: Transactions, Accounts List, Category List, and Memorized Transactions.

6. When the QIF Export dialog box is complete, choose OK to start the export operation.

Quicken creates an ASCII file that contains the exported transactions. At the beginning of the file, Quicken inserts a line to identify the type of account from which transactions were exported. This information consists of an exclamation point, the word Type, a colon (:), and the actual type name. Transactions exported from a Bank account, for example, show !Type:Bank as the first line.

The following example is the ASCII information that Quicken uses to record each transaction in the Register:

```
!Type:Bank
D7/24/93
T-1,000.00
Cx
N550
PFirst National Bank
L[Savings]
^
```

The first line begins with ! and shows the type of account (Bank). The second line begins with D and shows the transaction date. The third line begins with T and shows the transaction amount as –$1,000.00. (The amount is negative because the transaction is a payment.) The fourth line begins with a C and shows the cleared status. The fifth line shows the transaction or check number. The sixth line begins with P and shows the payee. The seventh line begins with L and shows the Category field entry. (If you split a transaction, Quicken creates several L lines.) The last line shows only a caret (^), which designates the end of a transaction.

The ASCII file created when you export file data isn't the same as the ASCII file created when you print a report or list to a disk file (described in Chapter 18, "Creating and Printing Reports"). When you export file data, the ASCII file includes each transaction field on a separate line. You may use this option if you are trying to import the Quicken data into another software program that uses the information, such as an accounting program. When you print a report or list to a disk file, Quicken creates an ASCII text file that looks like a printed Check Register. You may use this option to create a list of certain Quicken transactions that you can retrieve by a word processing program, edit with the word processor, and then print or use in a document.

Importing File Data

You can import file data stored in the Quicken QIF format. This format is the same one Quicken uses when exporting data. The steps for importing parallel those for exporting data.

Tip
To move transac-
tions from one
account to another
account, you can
copy or export the
data from the
account and im-
port it into the
other account by
using the File
menu's Export and
Import commands.

To import file data, follow these steps:

1. Choose Import from the File menu. Quicken displays the QIF Import
   dialog box, shown in figure 20.14.

2. In the QIF File to Import text box, type the path and file name of the
   Quicken file that you want to export. If you're unsure of the file name,
   choose Browse to display files in a particular directory (from the Import
   to QIF File dialog box). Select the file in the File Name list box and
   choose OK to return to the QIF Import dialog box.

3. In the Quicken Account to Import Into drop-down list, select the
   account into which you want to import data. You can select <All
   Accounts> or an individual account. If you previously used another
   program to manage your finances (like Microsoft Money), for example,
   you can import all accounts into Quicken (select <All Accounts>) from
   the QIF file that you exported from the other program.

Fig. 20.14
The QIF Import
dialog box appears
when you choose
File Import.

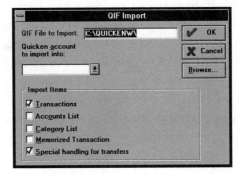

4. In the Import Items section, select the check boxes for the item(s) that
   you want to import: Transactions, Accounts List, Category List, Memorized Transactions, and Special Handling for Transfers.

   When you import transactions, Quicken duplicates transactions that
   involve transfers. Select the Special Handling for Transfers option,
   therefore, if you are importing data that previously was exported from
   multiple accounts or if you are importing CheckFree data (see Chapter
   13, "Paying Your Bills Electronically," for more information on
   CheckFree).

5. To import the file, choose OK when the QIF Import dialog box is
   complete. Quicken imports the file and records the transactions in the
   Register.

If the file in which you are importing data doesn't contain the appropriate categories, you may be prompted to add categories. Quicken also alerts you if duplicate transaction numbers, such as a check number, exist.

6. On completion, Quicken tells you that the import was successful. Choose OK.

Using Passwords

Anytime you deal with financial information, you must maintain the information's integrity and safeguard the system that stores the information from unauthorized entry. Using passwords in Quicken enables you to control the access or restrict transactions from being modified in your Quicken files.

Passwords represent an internal control mechanism. With Quicken, you can use passwords to limit access to the data files in which you store financial records.

You can use two kinds of passwords in Quicken: *file* and *transaction* passwords. The file password that you assign to the current file provides access to the accounts in the file. If you want each file in your Quicken system to use a password, you need to set up a file password for each file. The transaction password restricts anyone without access to the password from adding, changing, or deleting transactions before the date you specify.

Assigning a File Password

File passwords prevent unauthorized users from accessing any of the accounts in a Quicken file. To assign a file password to the current file, follow these steps:

1. Choose Passwords from the File menu. Quicken displays the Passwords submenu.

2. Choose File. Quicken displays the Set Up Password dialog box, shown in figure 20.15.

3. To define a file password, type the combination of letters and numbers you want to use as a password in the Password text box. You can use up to 16 characters, including spaces. Quicken doesn't display the characters as you type them; instead, it displays asterisks (*).

V

Managing Quicken

Note

When using passwords, consider the following precautions:

■ Make sure that you don't lose or forget the password. If you lose the password, you lose your data. Record the password in a safe place.

■ Don't share your password with anyone who doesn't need to know the password.

■ Someone may discover your password and you may be unaware that they have access. As a precaution, periodically change your password.

■ If you are worried about someone accessing Quicken and then writing computer checks, initiating electronic payments, or modifying the account information, use nonsensical passwords of at least six characters. The passwords you create with this procedure are extremely difficult to guess.

■ Make sure that you don't use a seemingly clever password scheme, such as month names or colors, as passwords. If you set the transaction password to *blue*, a curious user may not take long to figure out the main password.

Fig. 20.15

Assign a file password in the Set Up Password dialog box using up to 16 characters, including spaces.

Note

Quicken doesn't distinguish between the use of upper- and lowercase letters in establishing or using passwords.

4. Choose OK. Quicken displays the Confirm Password dialog box and asks you to retype the password to confirm that you know exactly what you entered. Type the password, exactly as you entered it in the Set Up Password dialog box, and choose OK.

When a file password is assigned, Quicken asks you for the password before opening the file. Figure 20.16 shows the Quicken Password dialog box displayed when attempting to open a file. Type the password and then choose

OK to open the file. (As an additional precaution, Quicken doesn't display the password as you type.) If the password was entered incorrectly, Quicken displays a message that you entered an incorrect password and access to the selected file is denied. You must select the file to open again and type the password correctly before Quicken will open the file.

> **Note**
>
> When you assign a file password, Quicken doesn't activate the password until you close the file or exit the program. When you try to open the file the next time, Quicken requires that you enter the file password.

Fig. 20.16
Type the file password in the Quicken Password dialog box to open a file.

Assigning a Transaction Password

Transaction passwords prevent unauthorized users from adding, changing, or deleting transactions dated before a date that you specify when you assign the password.

To assign a transaction password to the current file, follow these steps:

1. Choose Passwords from the File menu. Quicken displays the Passwords submenu.

2. Choose Transaction. Quicken displays the Password to Modify Existing Transactions dialog box, shown in figure 20.17.

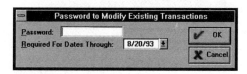

Fig. 20.17
Assign a transaction password in the Password to Modify Existing Transactions dialog box.

3. To define a transaction password, type the combination of letters and numbers you want to use as a password in the Password text box. You can use up to 16 characters, including spaces. Quicken doesn't display the characters as you type them, but displays asterisks (*) instead.

> **Note**
>
> Quicken doesn't distinguish between the use of upper- and lowercase letters in establishing or using passwords.

4. In the Required For Dates Through drop-down list box, select the date through which the transaction password is required.

5. Choose OK to assign the password and display the Confirm Password dialog box. Type the password to confirm the password that you entered in the Password to Modify Existing Transactions dialog box. Make sure that you type the password exactly as you entered it the first time. Choose OK.

> **Note**
>
> Quicken activates the transaction password immediately during the current work session. Unlike the file password, you don't have to exit the program or change to a different file and then reopen the file with the transaction password to activate the password.

If you want to record a transaction dated earlier than the date specified when you assigned the transaction password, Quicken requires that you enter the transaction password in the Quicken Password dialog box (see fig. 20.18). As with file passwords, Quicken doesn't display the transaction password as you type.

Fig. 20.18

You must type the transaction password in the Quicken Password dialog box before Quicken will allow you to enter or change a transaction.

Changing or Eliminating a Password

You can change the assigned password. You must enter the existing password, however, before Quicken enables you to change it. This precaution prevents unauthorized users from entering the Quicken system, changing the password, and then accessing your data file. You also can remove passwords to eliminate password protection from your file and transaction data.

To change or eliminate a password, follow these steps:

1. Choose Passwords from the File menu. Quicken displays the Passwords submenu.

2. Choose File to change or delete a file password; choose Transaction to change or delete a transaction password.

   Depending on the password type you choose, Quicken displays the Change Password dialog box (see fig. 20.19) or the Change Transaction Password dialog box.

Fig. 20.19
You change or eliminate a file password in the Change Password dialog box.

3. To change the file password, type the old and new passwords in the Change Password dialog box and choose OK. You now can use the new password.

   To delete the file password, type the old password in the Old Password text box and leave the New Password text box blank. Choose OK to eliminate the file password.

   To change the transaction password, type the old and new passwords in the Change Transaction Password dialog box. You also can change the date through which the transaction password is required. Choose OK to change the transaction password.

   To eliminate the transaction password, type the old password in the Old Password text box and leave the New Password text box blank. Choose OK to eliminate the transaction password.

Summary

This chapter described the steps and the logic for taking care of Quicken data files. In this chapter, you learned how to do the following:

■ Create a new Quicken file

■ Open a file

V

Managing Quicken

- Copy a Quicken file

- Rename a file

- Delete a file from your Quicken system

- Back up and restore your Quicken file data

- Archive file data at the end of the year

- Start a new file at the beginning of a new year

- Import and export data

- Use passwords with your Quicken files and transactions

In the next chapter, you learn how to customize Quicken to work the way you want the system to work. You learn how to change screen colors and background patterns, how Quicken displays the Register, and how to set general, check, and report preferences.

Chapter 21

Customizing Quicken

When you install Quicken, the program makes some assumptions about how the program ought to work and how elements within the program should appear. These assumptions are called *preferences*. Preferences control how the user enters transactions and checks, how the Register appears, how QuickFill works, how Quicken lists items in reports, and how the program works.

You can change these preferences so that Quicken works to suit your needs. If you don't want Quicken to display a confirmation message each time you edit a transaction, for example, you can turn off the **Request Confirmation** preference. If you want Quicken to memorize each new transaction you enter, you can select the **Automatic Memorization of New Transactions** preference. If you want to change the fonts and colors displayed in the Register, you can set the font type and style preferences and change the color of the Register for each account type.

Many preferences in Quicken have been explained elsewhere in this book. This chapter explains how to set preferences that haven't already been covered. This chapter also shows you where to go to learn about preferences that have been explained in other chapters.

Setting Quicken Preferences

When you install Quicken, the program presets all preferences to their default settings and values. You can change preference settings any time you want the program to work differently. The preferences you set in the current Quicken file are valid for only that file. If you use more than one Quicken file, you also must set preferences in the other files.

In this chapter, you learn how to perform the following tasks:

- Set general Quicken preferences

- Set QuickFill preferences

- Customize the Iconbar

- Turn Qcards off

- Save the desktop

- Customize the Register by changing colors and fonts

V

Managing Quicken

> **Note**
>
> When you change a Quicken preference, the change is in effect for the current session and all future sessions. You can change a preference setting at any time, however.

To set Quicken preferences, follow these steps:

1. Choose Preferences from the Edit menu or click the Prefs button on the Iconbar. Quicken displays the Quicken for Windows Preferences dialog box, shown in figure 21.1.

Fig. 21.1
The Quicken for Windows Preferences dialog box includes preference buttons that represent areas of the program that you can change.

2. Select the button for the preferences you want to set or change (table 21.1 describes the buttons). Quicken displays the appropriate dialog box.

3. In the dialog box, make your preference settings and then choose OK. Quicken saves your preference settings and returns to the Quicken for Windows Preferences dialog box.

4. Choose Done to close the Quicken for Windows Preferences dialog box.

Table 21.1 Preferences in the Quicken for Windows Preference Dialog Box	
Button	**Preferences Included**
General	Controls preferences for how users enter transactions, how Quicken behaves, and how the Register appears. The preference that controls whether Quicken beeps when recording and memorizing transactions, for example, is included in general preferences. You learn how to set general preferences later in this chapter.

Button	Preferences Included
Checks	Controls preferences on how Quicken prints checks. Refer to Chapter 5, "Writing and Printing Checks," to learn how to set check preferences.
Reports	Controls preferences on how Quicken creates reports. Refer to Chapter 18, "Creating and Printing Reports," to learn how to set report preferences.
QuickFill	Controls preferences on how the QuickFill feature works in Quicken. One QuickFill preference, for example, turns off QuickFill. You learn how to set QuickFill preferences in this chapter.
Billminder	Enables you to activate and schedule Billminder and Quicken Reminder messages. Refer to Chapter 14, "Scheduling Future Transactions," to learn how to set Billminder preferences.
Modem	Tells Quicken about the modem you use and how to initialize your modem. You use your modem in Quicken to download IntelliCharge credit card statements or to pay your bills electronically through CheckFree. Refer to Chapter 9, "Managing Your Credit Cards," and Chapter 13, "Paying Your Bills Electronically," to learn how to set modem preferences.
Iconbar	Enables you to customize the Iconbar displayed at the top of the Quicken application window. Later in this chapter, you learn how to set Iconbar preferences to add, edit, or delete an Iconbar icon.
Graphs	Controls preferences for how graphs are displayed. Refer to Chapter 19, "Using Graphs To Analyze Your Finances," to learn how to set graph preferences.
Qcards	Controls whether Quicken displays Qcards to help you fill out fields and windows. You learn how to turn Qcards on and off in this chapter.
Desktop	Determines how your Quicken desktop appears the next time you open the current file. You learn how to set desktop preferences later in this chapter.
Fonts	Enables you to change the font type and size shown on-screen in the Register and in lists. You also use a fonts preference to determine whether text appears in boldface type in the Register. You learn how to set the font preferences later in chapter.
Colors	Enables you to change the color of Registers for each account type. You can choose, for example, yellow for all Bank Account Registers, blue for all Cash accounts, and so forth. You learn how to set color preferences in this chapter.

V

Managing Quicken

Setting General Preferences

General preferences control the way Quicken performs and how the Register appears. General preferences also control the way users enter transactions in Quicken. To set general preferences, follow these steps:

1. Choose Preferences from the Edit menu or click the Prefs button on the Iconbar to display the Quicken for Windows Preferences dialog box.

2. Choose the General preference button. Quicken displays the General Preferences dialog box, shown in figure 21.2.

Fig. 21.2

You can change the default settings in the General Preferences dialog box to control how Quicken behaves when you enter transactions.

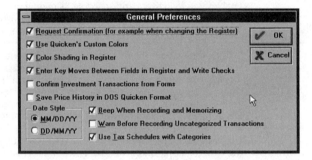

3. Change any of the General Preferences settings, which are described in table 21.2.

4. When you finish changing preference settings in the General Preferences dialog box, choose OK.

5. Choose Done to close the Quicken for Windows Preferences dialog box.

Table 21.2 Preferences in the General Preferences Dialog Box	
Preference	**Action**
Request Confirmation	Displays a confirmation message each time you change a transaction or list
Use Quicken's Custom Colors	Overrides the colors set in the Windows Control Panel and displays a gray background with a 3-D effect
Color Shading in Register	Displays transactions in the Register with color shading

Preference	Action
Enter Key Moves Between Fields in Register and Write Checks	Uses the Enter key and the Tab key to move between fields in the Register or the Write Checks window
Confirm Investment Transactions from Forms	Displays a confirmation message each time you enter a transaction in an investment form before entering it in the investment Register
Save Price History in DOS Quicken Format	Saves the price history in investment accounts to Quicken DOS format (select this preference if you plan to begin using Quicken for DOS)
MM/DD/YY	Displays dates in transactions in month/day/year format
DD/MM/YY	Displays dates in transactions in day/month/year format
Beep When Recording and Memorizing	Beeps after recording, editing, or memorizing a transaction
Warn Before Recording Uncategorized Transactions	Prompts you to enter a category in a transaction that you are recording
Use Tax Schedules with Categories	Adds a Form text box in the Set Up Category dialog box so that you can assign a tax form or schedule to a category

Tip
If you prefer to enter dates in Quicken using the Canadian or European date style, select the DD/MM/YY option button in the General Preferences dialog box.

V

Managing Quicken

Setting QuickFill Preferences

QuickFill is Quicken's automatic entry feature that works in the Register, Write Checks, and Splits windows to fill in various fields. (Refer to Chapter 7, "Using Quicken Shortcuts," for a detailed explanation of QuickFill.) You can change the way QuickFill works by setting preferences that control automatic memorization of new transactions, automatic completion as you type a transaction, automatic recall of a matched transaction when you press Tab, the automatic display of drop-down lists, or the appearance of drop-down buttons on all QuickFill fields.

To set QuickFill preferences, follow these steps:

   1. Choose Preferences from the Edit menu or click the Prefs button on the Iconbar to display the Quicken for Windows Preferences dialog box.

2. Select the QuickFill preference button. Quicken displays the QuickFill Preferences dialog box, shown in figure 21.3.

Fig. 21.3
The QuickFill Preferences dialog box contains preferences that control how QuickFill works.

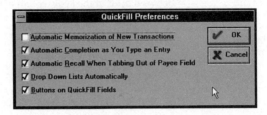

3. Change any of the QuickFill Preferences settings, which are described in table 21.3. (A check mark appears in the check box preceding an activated preference.)

4. When you finish changing the QuickFill Preferences settings, choose OK.

5. Choose Done.

Table 21.3 QuickFill Preferences

Preference	Action
Automatic Memorization of New Transactions	Memorizes each new transaction that you enter for a new payee
Automatic Completion as You Type an Entry	Fills in a field as soon as a matching item is found based on the characters typed
Automatic Recall When Tabbing Out of Payee Field	Fills in the rest of the transaction when you press Tab from the payee field
Drop Down Lists Automatically	Displays a drop-down list for each field that uses QuickFill
Buttons on QuickFill Fields	Displays a down-arrow button in each field that uses QuickFill

Customizing the Iconbar

The Quicken Iconbar enables you to select preset icons to perform frequently used functions. Such functions include displaying the Account list, the Category & Transfer list, the Register, the Write Checks window, and so forth.

You can change the icons displayed in the Iconbar by adding a new icon or by editing or deleting an existing icon. You can set up icons to open an account that you use frequently. You also can rearrange the order of the icons in the Iconbar.

Changing the Iconbar Display

If you want to change the way icons appear in the Iconbar, you can change the Iconbar display. By default, Quicken shows the graphic along with the label. You can set Quicken to show only the icon graphics or the icon label, or not show the Iconbar at all.

To change the Iconbar display, follow these steps:

1. Choose Preferences from the Edit menu or click the Prefs button on the Iconbar to display the Quicken for Windows Preferences dialog box.

2. Select the Iconbar preference button. Quicken displays the Customize Iconbar dialog box, shown in figure 21.4.

Fig. 21.4

The Customize Iconbar dialog box contains preferences that control how Quicken displays the Iconbar.

3. By default, the Show Icons and Show Text check boxes are selected in the Iconbar Display section so that both icons and text are displayed in the Iconbar. To show icons only, select the Show Text check box to remove the check mark. To show text only, select the Show Icons check box to remove the check mark. To hide the Iconbar completely, remove the check marks from both check boxes.

4. Choose OK to save the Iconbar settings.

5. Choose Done.

Rearranging Icons

You easily can change the order of the icons displayed in the Iconbar. To rearrange the icons, follow these steps:

1. Put the mouse pointer on the icon that you want to move.

Tip

You can return the Iconbar display to its default setting by choosing the Reset button in the Customize Iconbar dialog box.

V

Managing Quicken

2. While holding the right mouse button down, move the icon to the new position.

As you move an icon, the appearance of the mouse pointer changes to an empty box with a vertical arrow as you move along the Iconbar. If you drag the icon outside the Iconbar, the appearance of the mouse pointer changes to a circle-and-slash.

3. Release the mouse button to position the icon in its new location. Quicken shifts the other icons left or right to make room for the icon that you moved.

Adding an Icon

Quicken provides several icons that you can add to the Iconbar. Each icon represents a specific action of its own. The icon actions that you can select are predefined by Quicken, such as Open a Quicken File, Use a Memorized Report, Transmit Payments, and so forth.

To add an icon to the Iconbar, follow these steps:

1. Choose Preferences from the Edit menu or click the Prefs button on the Iconbar to display the Quicken for Windows Preferences dialog box.

2. Select the Iconbar preference button. Quicken displays the Customize Iconbar dialog box (refer to fig. 21.4).

3. Select the New button. Quicken displays the Add Action to Iconbar dialog box, shown in figure 21.5.

Fig. 21.5

The Add Action to Iconbar dialog box lists the actions that you can add to the Iconbar.

Selected icon——

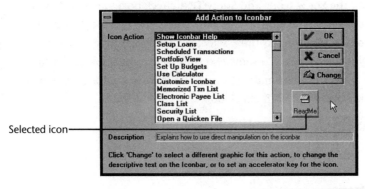

4. In the Icon Action list box, highlight the action that you want to add to the Iconbar. As you highlight an action, Quicken shows under the Change button the graphic that accompanies the selected action.

5. After you select the icon that you want to add to the Iconbar, choose OK.

To change the icon's graphic or label text, or to add a speed key, follow these steps:

1. In the Add Action to Iconbar dialog box (refer to fig. 21.5), choose the Change button. Quicken displays the Change Iconbar Item dialog box, shown in figure 21.6.

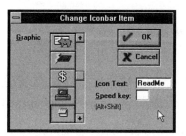

Fig. 21.6
In the Change Iconbar Item dialog box, you can change the graphic or label, or set up a speed key for the selected action.

2. To change the graphic, select a graphic in the Graphic list box (you can choose from more than 70 graphics).

To change the icon label, type a new label in the Icon Text text box.

To set up a speed key to perform the selected action, type a letter in the Speed Key text box. To use a speed key to perform an action, press Alt+Shift in combination with the speed key. If you assign *B* as the speed key to Set Up Budgets, for example, press Alt+Shift+B to choose the Set Up Budgets command.

3. After you select a graphic, change the icon label, or set up a speed key, choose OK to return to the Add Action to Iconbar dialog box.

4. Choose OK to return to the Customize Iconbar dialog box. Quicken adds the icon to the Iconbar. Choose OK again to return to the Quicken for Windows Preferences dialog box.

5. Choose Done.

Editing and Deleting Icons

You can change an icon displayed in the Iconbar or delete an icon. To edit an icon, follow these steps:

V

Managing Quicken

1. Choose Preferences from the Edit menu or click the Prefs button on the Iconbar to display the Quicken for Windows Preferences dialog box.

2. Select the Iconbar preference button. Quicken displays the Customize Iconbar dialog box (refer to fig. 21.4).

3. In the Current Iconbar list box, select the icon that you want to change.

4. Choose the Edit button. Quicken displays the Edit Action on Iconbar dialog box, which mirrors the Add Action to Iconbar dialog box in figure 21.5.

5. Choose the Change button. Quicken displays the Change Iconbar Item dialog box (refer to fig. 21.6).

6. To change the graphic, select a graphic from the Graphic list box.

   To change the icon label, type a new label in the Icon Text text box.

   To set up a speed key to perform the action, type a letter in the Speed Key text box. After you set up a speed key, press Alt+Shift in combination with the speed key to perform the action.

7. Choose OK to return to the Edit Action on Iconbar dialog box.

8. Choose OK to return to the Customize Iconbar dialog box. Quicken changes the icon. Choose OK again to return to the Quicken for Windows Preferences dialog box.

9. Choose Done to close the Quicken for Windows Preferences dialog box.

To delete an icon from the Iconbar, point to the icon that you want to delete and click while pressing the Shift key. Alternatively, you can delete an icon by selecting the Delete button from the Customize Iconbar dialog box (refer to fig. 21.4).

Setting Up an Icon To Open an Account

If you use a particular account frequently, you can set up an icon to open the account and display a window that you specify. If you have several credit card accounts set up but use your VISA account most often, for example, you can set up the UseAcct icon to open the VISA account Register.

To set up an icon to open an account, follow these steps:

1. Click the UseAcct button on the Iconbar. Quicken displays a message that explains how to set up the icon.

2. Choose OK to remove the message. Quicken displays the Assign Account to Icon dialog box, shown in figure 21.7.

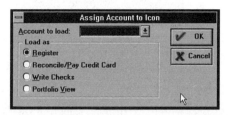

Fig. 21.7
Set up an icon to open an account in the Assign Account to Icon dialog box.

3. From the Account to Load drop-down list box, select the account that you want to open with the UseAcct icon.

4. From the options in the Load As section, select the type of window you want Quicken to load for the selected account.

5. Choose OK.

When you select the UseAcct button on the Iconbar, Quicken displays the window that you specified for the account.

Tip
To set up additional icons to open other accounts, add a new icon to the Iconbar and select Use a Specific Account from the Icon Action list in the Add Action to Iconbar dialog box.

Turning Qcards Off

Quicken provides Qcards that serve as on-screen "cues" to help you with each field in a window or a dialog box. Quicken displays Qcards within a window or next to a dialog box and explains each part of the window or dialog box as you go.

If you no longer need to use Qcards, you can turn them off by following these steps:

1. Choose Preferences from the Edit menu or click the Prefs button on the Iconbar to display the Quicken for Windows Preferences dialog box.

2. Choose the QCards preference button. Quicken displays the Qcard Preferences dialog box, shown in figure 21.8.

3. Choose the Qcards Off button.

4. Choose OK to return to the Quicken for Windows Preferences dialog box.

5. Choose Done.

V

Managing Quicken

Fig. 21.8
You can turn off
the Qcards feature
in the Qcard
Preferences dialog
box.

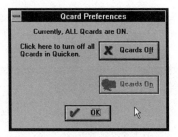

You can turn Qcards back on at any time by selecting the Qcards On button
in the Qcard Preferences dialog box.

Saving the Desktop

In Quicken, the term *desktop* refers to the arrangement of your screen with
respect to open windows and their position within the screen. After you have
the desktop the way you want it—with certain windows open and in the
positions you want them—you can save the desktop so that each time you
open your file, you have the same desktop arrangement.

To save the current desktop, follow these steps:

1. Choose Preferences from the Edit menu or click the Prefs button on the
Iconbar to display the Quicken for Windows Preferences dialog box.

2. Select the Desktop preference button. Quicken displays the Save Desktop dialog box, shown in figure 21.9.

Fig. 21.9
You can have
Quicken memorize
the current desk-
top by selecting
the Save Current
button in the Save
Desktop dialog
box.

3. Select the Save Current button. Quicken memorizes the current windows and their positions.

4. Choose OK to return to the Quicken for Windows Preferences dialog
box.

5. Choose Done.

The next time you open this Quicken file, Quicken displays the desktop that you saved.

You also can have Quicken display the desktop as it appears when you exit the program. If you must end a work session before you have finished working in open windows in Quicken, for example, you can instruct Quicken to save the desktop on exit. The next time you start Quicken, the same windows are open and in the same position as when you left.

To save the desktop on exit, follow the preceding steps, except select the Save Desktop on Exit check box in step 3.

Customizing Registers

You can change the font type and size in the Register, and determine whether text in the Register appears in boldfaced type. You also can change the color of a Register within a certain account type.

> **Note**
>
> When you change the appearance of the text in the Register, you also change the way text appears in lists (for example, the Account list and the Category & Transfer list).

Changing Fonts Used in the Register

To change the Register fonts, follow these steps:

1. Choose Preferences from Edit menu or click the Prefs button on the Iconbar to display the Quicken for Windows Preferences dialog box.

2. Select the Fonts preference button. Quicken displays the Choose Register Font dialog box, shown in figure 21.10.

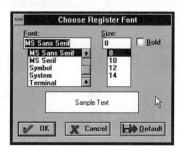

Fig. 21.10
Change the font type and size in the Choose Register Font dialog box.

Tip
You can return
fonts to Quicken's
default settings by
choosing the
Default button.

3. In the Font list box, select the font that you want to use.

4. In the Size list box, select the font size that you want to use for text.

5. If you want text in the Register to be boldfaced, select the Bold check box.

6. Quicken shows a sample of the selected font in the Choose Register Font dialog box. If the sample fonts are satisfactory, choose OK to return to the Quicken for Windows Preferences dialog box.

7. Choose Done.

Changing the Color of a Register

If you want to be able to quickly distinguish one account Register from another, you can change the color of each Register by account type. You can change the color of bank accounts to green, for example, and the color of cash accounts to blue. Subsequently, you know that all green Registers are Bank Account Registers and that you shouldn't enter Cash account transactions in them.

To change the color of a Register, follow these steps:

1. Choose Preferences from the Edit menu or click the Prefs button on the Iconbar to display the Quicken for Windows Preferences dialog box.

2. Select the Colors preference button. Quicken displays the Choose Register Colors dialog box, shown in figure 21.11.

Fig. 21.11
Change the color
of Registers within
an account type in
the Choose
Register Colors
dialog box.

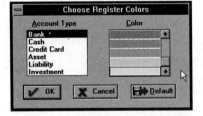

3. In the Account Type list box, select the account type whose Registers you want to appear in another color.

4. In the Color list box, select the color for the selected account type.

5. Choose OK to change the color of the Register(s) and return to the Quicken for Windows Preferences dialog box.

6. Choose Done.

Summary

You can customize the Quicken program so that it works and looks the way that best suits your working style. In this chapter, you learned how to do the following:

- Set general preferences that control the way Quicken behaves and how transactions are entered

- Change the way QuickFill works

- Customize the Iconbar by adding, editing, and deleting icons, and by assigning icons to open specific accounts

- Set Qcard preferences

- Save the desktop

- Customize Registers by changing fonts and colors

The following chapter begins the final part of Using Quicken for Windows: "Putting Quicken for Windows To Use." In this part of this book, you learn how to use Quicken for home finances or in small business. The next two chapters provide helpful hints for using Quicken to meet your needs.

Tip
You can change the color of Registers back to the default by choosing the Default button in the Choose Register Colors dialog box.

V

Managing Quicken

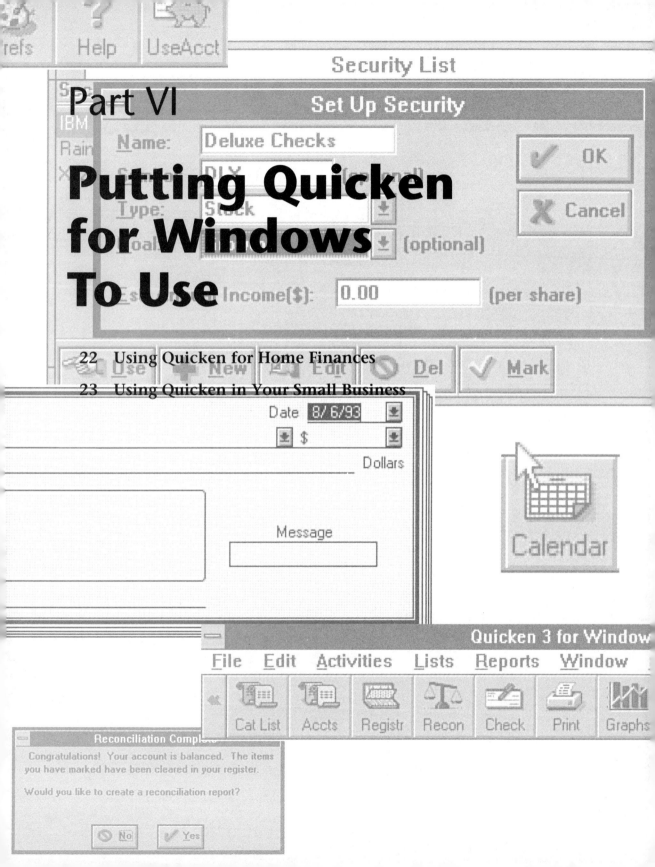

Part VI

Putting Quicken for Windows To Use

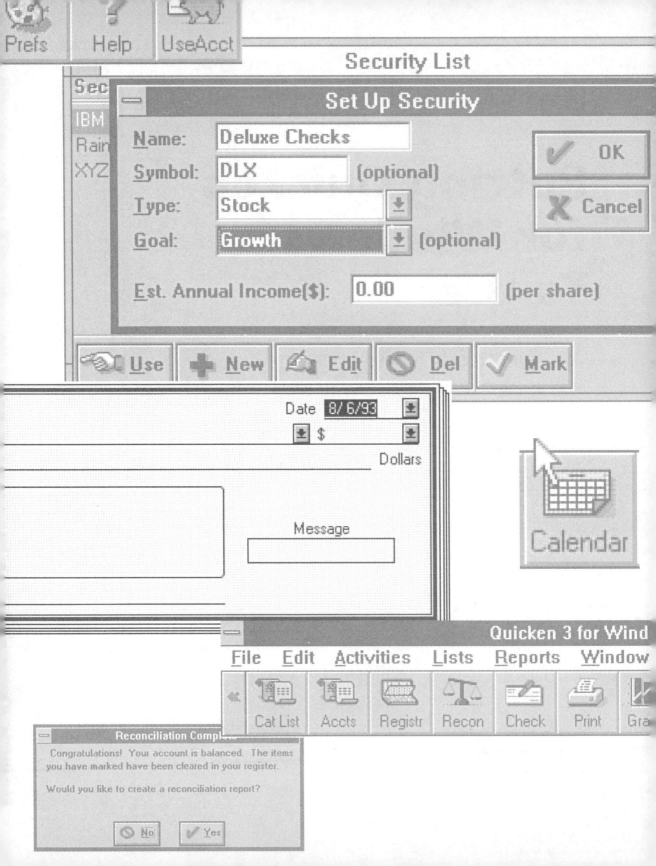

Chapter 22

Using Quicken for Home Finances

The first four parts of this book have supplied you with a firm grasp of the mechanics of using Quicken for Windows. You need more than an understanding of the mechanics, however, to use any software effectively—particularly an accounting program. Like most people, you probably have questions about where Quicken fits in, how Quicken changes the way you keep financial records, and when to use different Quicken options. Your financial planning needs determine where Quicken fits into your personal or home financial management.

Tracking Income-Tax Deductions

When you track income-tax deductions, you need to make sure that transactions producing an income-tax deduction are entered into one of the Quicken Registers. You also must to be sure to use a category marked as tax-related.

This process isn't as difficult as it may sound. Although you now may make payments (from a variety of accounts) that represent income-tax deductions, perhaps you can change the way you make payments and record such transactions in one or two accounts. If you now make charitable contributions in cash and with a credit card, for example, rather than set up a Cash account and a Credit Card account, you can start writing checks on an account you are tracking with Quicken. If you use Quicken for tracking income-tax deductions only, you need to set up only one account—a Bank account is probably the easiest method—and use this account only for charitable contributions.

In this chapter, you learn how to use Quicken for your home finances in these ways:

- To track income-tax deductions

- To automate record-keeping

- To monitor how closely you are following a budget

- To calculate "what-if" scenarios

- To track investment earnings

- To earmark funds for future goals

- To track in a bank account and credit card transactions

VI

Putting Quicken To Use

Further, you may not need the power of Quicken to track and tally income-tax deductions. The organization to which you make a tax-deductible payment may track and tally the tax deduction for you. Consider the case of a home mortgage. At the end of the year, the bank sends you a statement (Form 1098) that identifies how much you have paid over the year in interest, principal, and (if applicable) for items such as property taxes and insurance. Similarly, a charity may send a statement that shows all contributions for the year. A bank or brokerage firm also may indicate the total individual retirement account contributions. Although you may need to track and tally certain income-tax deductions, you can avoid the effort if an organization tracks these deductions for you.

Automating Record-Keeping

As a rule, any financial record-keeping you now perform manually is probably a candidate for Quicken. People go to different lengths in their efforts to keep clean, precise accounting records. The obvious candidate for Quicken is tracking activity in bank accounts—particularly checking accounts. You may be someone, however, who also tracks investments carefully, tracks personal spending in a precise manner, or keeps records of personal assets or liabilities. In all these cases, Quicken can make the job easier.

Consider the following when automating financial record-keeping:

- As with income-tax deductions, don't go to a great deal of effort to account for items that someone else already tracks for you. Why use Quicken if all your investments appear on the same monthly statements from a broker or a mutual fund manager? You also probably don't need to track other items, such as a monthly pension fund or 401(k) contributions, when your employer pays professional accountants to track these finances.

- Consider carefully whether you need to keep financial records for a specific asset or liability. You can track the value of a home or car, but often, tracking these values isn't worth the effort. Keep a detailed, transaction-by-transaction record of an asset or liability only when the resulting information enables you to manage your personal finances better. Keeping financial records isn't fun; it's tedious, requires attention to detail, and can take much time. If the information doesn't help you manage your finances, the data isn't worth collecting and storing.

■ Remember that in a Quicken Register, you record transactions that change the balance of an asset or liability. The values of possessions such as a home, stocks, or bonds can change without a transaction occurring; you can't point to an event and say, *This event needs to be recorded*. Not surprisingly, a lack of recordable transactions can make tracking changes in the value of something quite difficult. Accounts that are good candidates for tracking are your bank accounts (including checking, savings, and money market accounts), your credit card accounts that carry balances, and cash accounts from which you frequently pay expenses.

Monitoring a Budget

As suggested in Chapter 16, "Budgeting with Quicken," one of the program's most powerful home accounting uses is for monitoring how closely you are following a budget. Although the budgeting tools that Quicken provides are superb, the process of using Quicken to monitor monthly spending can be a challenge. Because you probably spend money in several ways—using checks, credit cards, and cash—the only way to really track your monthly spending is to record all three spending groups in Registers. Otherwise, you see only a piece of the picture.

To simplify monitoring a budget, consider several budgeting ideas:

■ Focus on discretionary items

■ Aggregate spending categories

■ Consider the spending method

Focusing on Discretionary Items

In Chapter 16, budgeting is described as a three-step process:

1. Setting financial goals.

2. Using financial goals as a guide to developing a financial game plan or budget that covers how you want to spend your money.

3. Using the financial game plan or budget to monitor spending so that you can track how closely you are progressing toward your financial goals.

VI

Putting Quicken To Use

Quicken helps you with the third step, using the budget to monitor spending. You then need to monitor only discretionary spending—not spending fixed by contract or by law. Keep this spending difference in mind when you define categories and set up accounts.

Tip
Use the Quicken Monthly Budget Report as the principal tool to monitor a budget. Refer to Chapter 16, "Budgeting with Quicken," for more information.

Some spending may not warrant monitoring. Consider, for example, a mortgage payment or a rent payment: although you certainly need to include these major expenditures in a budget, you probably don't need to monitor whether you are spending money on these payments. The spending is fixed by a mortgage contract or a rental agreement. You can't spend less than the budgeted amount, unless you want to be evicted from your home; further, you have no reason to spend more than the budgeted amount (unless you're trying to pay down your mortgage over an accelerated time schedule).

Other examples of fixed spending are loan or lease payments for a car, income and Social Security taxes, and child care. Each specific situation determines which expenses fit into fixed spending categories. In general, you don't need to monitor closely those categories that are fixed—or locked in— by a contract, by law, or by the terms of employment.

You still need to include fixed spending in the budget, because you want to make sure that you have enough money for the item; but this kind of spending doesn't need to be monitored. The rule is that for purposes of monitoring a budget, focus on monitoring discretionary spending.

Aggregating Spending Categories

When you monitor discretionary spending, working with a handful of categories is easier than working with a big clump of specific categories. Take the case of spending on entertainment. You can choose to track spending on entertainment by using just one category, named Entertainment. You also can break down the spending into all the various ways you spend entertainment dollars, as shown in the following list:

- Eating at restaurants

- Going to the movies

- Renting videos

- Going to the theater

- Playing golf

- Attending sporting events

Tracking exactly how you spend entertainment dollars takes a certain precision and usually requires effort. One reason this system requires effort is that you end up recording more transactions. If you use only one general category, for example, you need to record only one transaction for a credit card bill that contains charges for only the six spending groups in the preceding list. If you use all six specific categories, however, you must record a split transaction with six separate amounts.

A second reason that tracking a number of specific categories can be cumbersome is that because you budget by category, the more categories you use, the more budgeted amounts you must enter. If you feel you must have the detail that comes with using many specific categories, consider using subcategories that at least minimize the work of entering budgeted amounts.

Consider these general rules for aggregating spending categories:

- Lump together items that are substitutes for each other.

- Lump together items of similar importance, or priority, to you and other members of the family.

Both rules stem from the idea that if you overspend in a category, you need to consider further reducing spending in this category. Suppose that you lump together the six spending groups listed earlier into one general category. Further, suppose that you go golfing with friends over three straight weekends. As a result, you have no money left for restaurants and the theater—favorite activities of your spouse—and no money left for movies, videos, and sporting events—the favorite activities of your kids.

In this scenario, lumping all six categories together may be a bad idea, because eliminating spending in one category may not be a practical remedy for overspending in another category. A sensible solution is to budget for golf as one category, for the theater and restaurants as a second category, and for the movies and sporting events as a third category. You then can avoid over-spending on golf or any other single entertainment category. If your spouse overspends on the theater, a reasonable response is to minimize or curtail spending on restaurants. If the children insist on seeing two movies, they must forego a trip to the ball park and the video rental store.

Considering the Spending Method

Research has proven that the method people use to spend money—credit cards, checks, or cash—affects how they spend. In general, people spend more when they use a credit card than they do when spending cash or writing a check, and people often spend less when they use cash than when they write a check. This phenomenon has no direct effect on how you work with Quicken, but in terms of monitoring a budget, consider this information before you decide which accounts to set up to monitor spending.

Choosing an easily controlled spending method makes your budget more manageable. Recognize this reality when you set up accounts to monitor spending. Remember that Quicken enables you to set up special accounts for bank accounts, credit cards, and cash. For monitoring the spending categories over which you want tight control, choose a spending method that makes staying within a budget easier.

Reviewing What-If Scenarios

Quicken 3 for Window's financial planners and calculators enable you to use the program to review what-if scenarios for savings, retirement, refinancing, or college. Use the Investment Savings Planner to calculate the growth of an investment using various interest rates, over various time periods, and making various contributions each year. Refer to Chapter 17, "Saving for the Future with Quicken," to learn how to use the Investment Savings Planner.

The Retirement Planner can show you how soon you can retire. You can calculate the growth of your nest egg using various interest rates over various time periods. You also can vary the contributions you make each year until retirement. This feature is particularly useful in calculating the future value of an IRA or Keogh account in the year you retire. You learn how to use the Retirement Planner in Chapter 17, "Saving for the Future with Quicken."

And if you have children, you're probably concerned about saving money for college. With tuition rising annually at most colleges across the country, figuring out how much tuition will be by the time your children head off to the campus can be challenging. Use the College Planner to determine how much you need to save each year, given various interest rates, time periods, and tuition levels. Refer to Chapter 17, "Saving for the Future with Quicken," to learn how to use the College Planner.

The Refinance Planner helps you make the decision of whether to go through the hassles and expense of refinancing your home mortgage or staying with your current mortgage. The Refinance Planner shows you what you can save by refinancing and how long it will take to recover the closing costs and points you have to pay. Refer to Chapter 11, "Tracking Loans," to learn how to use the Refinance Planner.

If you're trying to decide whether to buy that new home or even a second home, use the Loan Planner to calculate your mortgage payment, based on the mortgage amount, interest rate, and length of the loan. The Loan Planner also can tell you how much house you can afford, based on a monthly payment that fits your budget. Chapter 11, "Tracking Loans," explains how to use the Loan Planner.

Monitoring Your Investments

You can set up an investment account in Quicken to monitor and report on each of your investments. You can set up a separate investment account for each account that you have with a broker, each mutual fund that you own interest in, each partnership or subchapter S interest that you own, or each individual security.

Traditionally, the investment features in Quicken have been a bit difficult to understand. (Investments by themselves present difficult concepts.) Quicken 3 for Windows simplifies entering investment transactions, however, through the use of on-screen forms that prompt you for the information the program needs to track your investment values and earnings. Quicken's investment tools enable you to monitor investment transactions, measure performance, track market values, and create reports for income-tax planning and preparation. Refer to Chapter 15, "Monitoring Your Investments," for an in-depth explanation of Quicken's investment features.

Earmarking Savings

If you're saving for that new car, European vacation, or down payment on a new home, you can use Quicken to track the money that you need to put aside for a special purpose. Quicken 3 for Windows' new Savings Goal account gauges how much and how often you should put money aside to achieve your goal.

Although the money never really leaves your account (checking, savings, money market, and so forth), it's accounted for in the special Savings Goal account. You then can create reports and graphs to check the progress you are making in saving for your financial goal. Refer to Chapter 17, "Saving for the Future with Quicken," to learn how to use the Savings Goal account.

Using Quicken in Common Situations

The preceding information helps you determine when and where to use Quicken for your home finances. This section covers a few tips that elaborate on the preceding discussion and covers reconciling bank accounts, tracking credit card spending, and recording tax-deductible cash outlays.

Using Quicken for Bank Accounts

As a rule, you can use Quicken for any bank accounts you want to reconcile on a monthly basis. You also can use Quicken for checking accounts for which you want to print checks. Finally, you may want to track certain bank accounts used for income-tax deductions or budget-monitoring reasons.

You unlikely will need to use Quicken—although you can—for bank accounts that you don't reconcile. You may not need Quicken to track certificates of deposit, for example, or for savings accounts with no activity other than monthly interest or fees. If you want to reflect your net worth accurately in Quicken net worth reports, however, you must set up an account for each bank account that has money in it.

Using Quicken for Credit Cards

You don't need to use Quicken to track credit card spending on credit cards for which you pay off the balance at the end of the month. When you write the monthly check to pay off the credit card company, you can record the spending categories by splitting the transaction.

> **Note**
>
> If you want to record credit card purchases as you make them, you must record the purchases in a credit card account. Then, when you pay your credit card bill, just write the check (or enter the transaction in the Check Register, if you write manual checks) and enter the credit card account in the Category field. This way, the check amount is subtracted from the balance in your credit card account.

For credit cards that you don't pay off on a monthly basis, however, you can set up and use Quicken accounts to track income-tax deductions or monitor spending. For credit cards for which you want to use the reconcile feature, you also need to set up and use Quicken accounts.

If you set up accounts for credit cards, you need to enter each credit card transaction into the Register. You need to collect the credit card slips, therefore, and periodically enter the amounts into the Register.

If you have a Quicken VISA card and want to use the IntelliCharge feature to track credit card activity (see Chapter 9, "Managing Your Credit Cards"), you must set up a credit card account and designate the account as an IntelliCharge account.

Using Quicken for Cash

If you spend cash on tax-deductible items, you can use Quicken to track these deductions. If you use Quicken to monitor cash spending, you can compare actual spending with budgeted spending and use Quicken to track this information. Essentially, every time you withdraw cash from the bank, you increase cash (and decrease your bank account balance). Every time you spend money, you need to collect a receipt for the expense. Then you periodically enter these cash transactions into the Register.

One problem with tracking cash spending is that you can't get receipts for small items, such as candy, a newspaper, or tips to a bellhop. You therefore must keep a record of these small transactions or periodically adjust the register's cash balance to match the actual cash on hand. You can give this kind of adjustment category a descriptive name, such as Sundries or Misc.

For credit card and cash transactions, collect in an envelope the credit card and cash receipts you need to enter. On a periodic basis (such as once a week or month), enter the receipt amounts in the appropriate Register, mark the receipts as entered, and label the outside of the envelope with a descriptive name, such as **Credit card and cash receipts from week beginning 4/1/94.** If you have a large number of receipts, number the receipts and then use these numbers as the transaction numbers in the Register so that you can tie a specific transaction in the Register to a receipt.

Tracking the Adjusted Basis of Your Home

By law, the gain on the sale of a home is taxable unless you purchase within a given time frame another home of equal or greater value, or unless you can use the one-time $125,000 exclusion to eliminate the gain. The gain on the sale of a home is calculated roughly as

(sales price) – (original cost + cost of improvements)

The sales price and the original cost are set and are connected to the purchase and to the sale. One way to reduce the calculated gain—and therefore minimize the income tax on the gain—is to track the cost of improvements.

Improvements don't include repairs or maintenance, such as fixing a roof, painting the walls, or sealing an asphalt driveway. These are simply repairs and don't increase the value of your home as an asset. Over the years, however, you likely will make a series of improvements that, if tracked, may reduce the gain. These improvements may include landscaping, adding bookshelves to the family room, and putting in an extra bathroom upstairs. Figure 22.1 shows an example of a Register used to collect this kind of information. (Remember that the account-transfer feature means you may never need to access the Register for the asset House because you can record the cost of the improvement when you write the check to pay for the improvement.)

Fig. 22.1

The House Register lists the initial cost of your house and the improvement costs. The ending balance shows your total investment in your house.

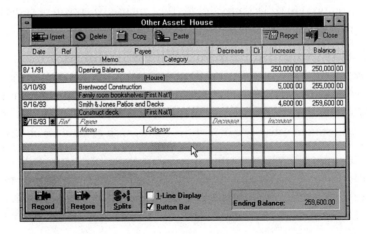

Tracking the Non-Deductible Portions of an IRA

One of the record-keeping nightmares from the last decade's ever-changing tax laws is the non-deductible individual retirement account (IRA) contribution. Although you may not qualify for an IRA deduction, you may have the option of contributing to an IRA. An IRA contribution can benefit you financially, because without the income taxes on the investment earnings, the account grows faster.

Over long periods, you can accumulate a great deal more money—even though the original IRA contribution didn't generate a tax deduction. If, for example, you contribute $25 a month over 35 years, you may accumulate $94,916 if you pay no taxes, but $47,231 if you pay the 28 percent federal income tax (these calculations assume a 10 percent annual yield).

In other words, you may accumulate almost twice as much money by not paying income taxes on the IRA earnings. Non-deductible IRA contributions enable you to defer income taxes on money earned until you withdraw the money.

The problem with non-deductible IRA contributions is that the non-deductible portion of your contributions isn't taxed when you withdraw the money; therefore, you need a way to track the non-deductible contributions. For most people, Quicken is an excellent solution. A basic approach is to set up an asset account for non-deductible IRA contributions. Whenever you make a non-deductible contribution, record the payment as a transfer to the account you use to track non-deductible IRA contributions. Over the years, this system builds a detailed record of all the non-deductible contributions you make. Figure 22.2 shows an example of the Register that tracks the asset Nondeduct IRA.

Knowing When To Perform Quicken Tasks

One final question that you may have about using Quicken is when to perform the various Quicken tasks. Table 22.1 divides these tasks into three groups: tasks to perform on a daily and weekly basis, tasks to perform on a monthly basis, and tasks to perform on an annual basis.

VI

Putting Quicken To Use

Fig. 22.2

The Register for the account Nondeduct IRA tracks the non-deductible contributions you make to your IRA account.

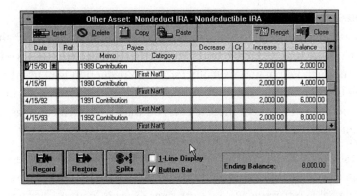

Table 22.1 When To Perform Quicken Tasks

Daily and Weekly Tasks

Record transactions in the Registers.

Print checks.

Print a temporary copy of the month's Register.

Back up files.

Monthly Tasks

Print monthly reports, including a budget report so that you can analyze actual versus budget results.

Reconcile accounts.

Print a final copy of the month's Register.

Throw away the daily or weekly copies of the Register (all this information is contained on the final copy of the month's Register).

Back up files.

File or store the month's bank statement, Register, reports, and backup files.

Annual Tasks

Print annual reports.

Print a permanent copy of the transaction report that subtotals by tax-deduction category. (This report is your permanent record for income-tax purposes.)

Back up files for the year.

Create new year's budget and enter the budget.

Make a year-end copy of files.

> **Note**
>
> Consider the information in table 22.1 as a rough guideline; as you use Quicken, you learn what works best for you.

Summary

This chapter covered information that you otherwise learn through trial and error. You have learned where Quicken fits in the management of your home finances, how to use Quicken for home accounting, and when to use the various Quicken options and features. You now have the information you need to incorporate Quicken easily into your personal financial management activities.

In this chapter, you learned some general ideas about using Quicken to do the following:

- Track income tax deductions

- Automate record-keeping

- Monitor how closely you are following a budget

- Calculate what-if scenarios, such as how much you will save if you refinance your home mortgage, or how much you need to save each year to send your 2-year-old to Harvard

- Track the earnings on your investments

- Earmark funds for future goals

- Track activity in a bank account

- Track credit card transactions

- Monitor cash spending

- Keep accurate financial records on a timely basis

You also learned how to track the adjusted basis of your home and track the non-deductible portion of IRA contributions.

The next chapter contains important information for small-business owners. In Chapter 23, "Using Quicken in Your Small Business," you learn how to use Quicken for business accounting.

VI

Putting Quicken To Use

Chapter 23

Using Quicken in Your Small Business

You may be surprised to learn that many people use Quicken as a business accounting package rather than a home finance package. The reasons for this usage are logical: with Quicken you don't need to know double-entry book-keeping (many other small-business accounting packages require that you do) and you can do most of your accounting with a simple and familiar tool—the Check Register. Although Quicken isn't a full-fledged business accounting package, this chapter covers some of the special techniques and procedures for using Quicken in business.

The procedures for using Quicken are well-documented in this book. For this chapter you are better armed if you know how to enter transactions into a Register, set up accounts, define categories, and print reports. If you aren't familiar with these features of Quicken, review the material covered in the first five sections of the book.

This chapter isn't intended to be an exhaustive list of all the business uses of Quicken. Different types of businesses require different accounting procedures, accounts, and reports. You need to modify your accounts, categories, subcategories, and so on to fit the needs of your particular business situation.

This chapter begins by discussing the overall approach for using Quicken in a business. This discussion is followed by short sections that detail the following basic accounting tasks:

- Tracking receivables

- Tracking payables

- Accounting for fixed assets

- Preparing payroll

- Tracking inventory

- Job costing

VI

Note

With the tools that you have been provided so far in *Using Quicken 3 for Windows*, you should be able to create a Quicken system that works for you. Notice, however, that Quicken isn't designed to track inventory on an item-by-item basis. If your business requires specific inventory tracking, you need to use a program other than Quicken.

When you combine basic bill paying and check writing—described throughout this book—with the details of the six basic accounting tasks described in this chapter, you should have the information you need to perform business accounting with Quicken. If you find that you need something more than Quicken to handle your business finances, read the section "An Introduction to QuickBooks." QuickBooks, also published by Intuit, is a program specifically designed to meet the needs of small businesses.

Understanding the Basics

Using Quicken for business accounting is easier if you understand the following three basic concepts: what Quicken accounts track, what should be recorded in a Register, and how categories are used. The following sections discuss these concepts in more detail.

Knowing What Quicken Accounts Track

Tip
When you track all your assets and liabilities in Quicken by setting up an account for each, you easily can determine the equity that you have in your business. Equity is the difference between total assets and total liabilities.

You can use Quicken accounts to track the values of business assets or liabilities. You need to set up one account for each business asset or liability you want to track.

A *business asset* is anything you own. Common examples of business assets include the cash in a checking account, the receivable a customer or client owes you, an investment in stock, inventory you resell, a piece of furniture, a piece of equipment, real estate, and so on.

A *business liability* is a debt that you owe. Common examples of business liabilities include the loan on a car or delivery truck, payroll taxes you owe the government, the mortgage on the building, the balance on a bank credit line, and so on.

Assets and liabilities have something in common: you can calculate their value at any time. Usually, you aren't interested in the day-to-day or week-to-week change in a particular asset but rather the value at a specific time.

All the accounts you set up for a business must be included in the same Quicken file. If you perform accounting for several businesses, each business requires a separate file. If you use Quicken at business and at home, you must create a file for each situation. (See Chapter 20, "Managing Your Quicken Files," to learn how to create multiple Quicken files.)

Note

Quicken enables you to define up to 255 accounts within a file.

Defining a Transaction

A *transaction* is any activity that affects the balance in an account or the value of an asset or liability. But no change ever affects only one asset or liability. Each time you record a change in the value of an asset or liability, you also need to record how that change affects other accounts (or income or expenses categories). You actually perform double-entry bookkeeping without concerning yourself with debits and credits.

If you transfer money from a checking account to a savings account, for example, you record the decrease in the checking account balance with one transaction and the increase in the savings account balance with another transaction. And if you write a check to pay for utilities, you record a decrease in your checking account and you assign an expense category—such as *Utilities*—to classify the transaction. To reflect your transaction activity accurately, you must assign a category or an account to all transactions.

This discussion of transactions may seem redundant, but you need to verify that all assets and liabilities are really things that you own or debts that you owe. You also need to verify that items you want to record as transactions in a Register are valid transactions.

If you want to track receivables and record customer payments on those receivables, you must set up an account each time you create an individual receivable. If you bill Johnson Manufacturing $1,000 for a service, for example, you must set up an account for this particular receivable (even if Johnson Manufacturing already owes you $750 for an earlier service).

The temptation with a group of similar assets, such as receivables, is to group them all together as one asset by using one account. But using the grouping approach obscures information on specific accounts. You can't tell whether Johnson Manufacturing still owes the $1,000 or how the $1,000 original receivable value has changed. Changes in the value of this asset, such as the change that occurs when you receive the customer's payment, need to be recorded as transactions in the Register.

The key to using Quicken as a small-business accounting system is knowing your assets, liabilities, and transactions. Throughout this chapter, you will find many tips and suggestions to assist you in your analysis.

Knowing What Categories Track

The term *bottom line* refers to the figure at the bottom of a profit and loss statement (also called an *income statement*) that shows whether you made a profit or lost money in business. You use categories in Quicken to track the income and expenses that, when added together, make up the bottom line. You then know whether your business is making or losing money. You assign two kinds of categories to transactions: Income and Expense. Income categories are assigned to business revenues, or *inflows*. Common income categories include sales of products or services, income from rental properties, interest and dividends from investments, and so on. Expense categories are assigned to the costs of doing business, or *outflows*. Examples of expense categories include the cost of advertising, insurance, utilities, and employee wages.

Income and expense categories have something in common: they enable you to accumulate business inflows and outflows over a period of time. You can use the income and expense category information, for example, to tell whether you made or lost money during the last week, month, or year. (Income minus expenses equals net income or net loss.)

If you use Quicken categories to track only cash inflows and outflows (bank and cash accounts), you are using *cash-basis accounting*. With cash-basis accounting, you record income only when you receive money, and record expenses only when you pay money. This system makes good sense. When you make the bank deposit or write a check, you categorize the transaction as income or expense.

If you use Quicken categories to track other assets and liabilities, however, you move toward *accrual-* or *modified accrual-basis* accounting. Accrual-basis accounting means that you record income when you earn it and expenses when you use the goods or services from which the expenses stem.

You may not always receive money when you earn income. If you extend credit to a customer, for example, you have delivered the goods or performed the service (earned the income) but you haven't yet collected the money. Similarly, you may not always pay money when you receive goods or services from a vendor. If a vendor ships you goods and encloses a bill, you have incurred the expense, but you haven't yet paid any money. If you use Quicken to account for fixed assets and depreciation, you categorize the expense of using the asset when you record depreciation.

CPA TIP: Using Accrual-Basis Accounting

Accrual-basis accounting gives you better estimates of income and expenses and a more accurate measure of profits. Accrual-basis accounting also results in better record-keeping because you keep Registers for all assets and liabilities, not just cash. If an accurate measurement of profits is important to your business, try using accrual-basis accounting.

Tracking Customer Receivables

To track customer payments and receivables, you first need to set up an Asset account for receivables. You can set up just one Asset account, aggregating all receivable activity, or you can set up a separate Asset account for the receivables of each customer or client. You also can set up separate accounts for each customer. You may name an aggregate receivable account **Receivables** or **Acc Rec**. With separate receivable accounts, you may use the customer name in the account name: **Jones Rec** or **Smith Rec**.

Each time you make a sale to a customer on credit (the customer doesn't pay for the goods or services at the time of sale), you must record an increase in the appropriate Asset account for receivables. The Receivables Register shown in figure 23.1 shows a transaction for a $1,000 sale to Johnson Manufacturing.

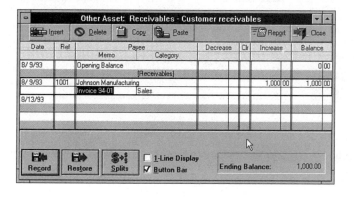

Fig. 23.1

Record a sale to a customer as an increase in the Register for the account you set up for Receivables.

VI

Putting Quicken To Use

After you record the receivable, you can record customer payments on the receivable and monitor receivables—topics covered in the following sections.

CPA TIP: Extending Credit

Although businesses prefer that customers pay cash at the time of sale (to the extent that they sometimes extend discounts for cash payments), business owners find that extending credit to their customers increases sales and is therefore good for business. Be cautious, however. One major cause of business failure is lack of control over accounts receivable. If you extend credit to everyone without investigating their credit history, you may get stuck with many bad debts and a large number of receivables on your hands. Remember that although receivables are an asset, they are of no value if they are uncollectible.

Recording Customer Payments

To record customer payments, select the bank account you use to deposit the check and record the deposit in the usual way. To categorize the transaction, record the deposit as a transfer from the actual receivable account. Suppose that you receive a $500 check from Johnson Manufacturing for partial payment of the $1,000 receivable created by Invoice 94-01 (refer to fig. 23.1). In this case, you would enter the deposit in the Register for your bank account, as shown in figure 23.2.

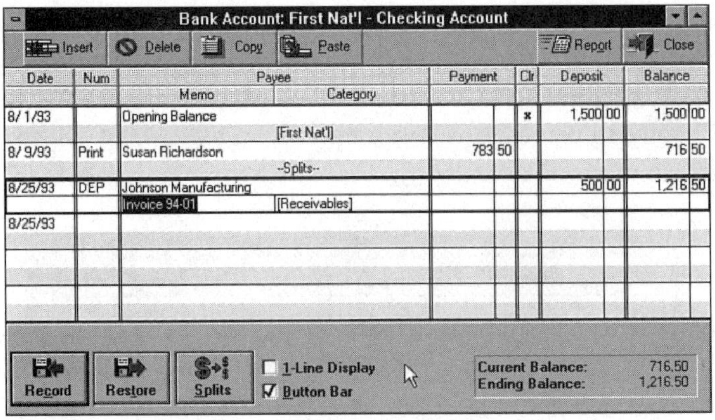

Fig. 23.2
Record a partial payment from a customer in the bank account Register into which you are depositing the money.

Quicken records a $500 reduction in the account you use to track the $1,000 receivable. Figure 23.3 shows the Register for the receivables account after you record the $500 partial payment from Johnson Manufacturing as a deposit to the bank account.

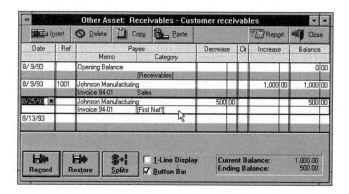

Fig. 23.3
Quicken enters a corresponding transaction to record the decrease in the receivables account when a customer makes a payment.

Tracking How Much Customers Owe You

Another basic receivables accounting task is tracking how much customers owe you and how long they have owed you. The age of a receivable usually determines the collection effort you make. You probably don't worry about receivables that aren't yet due. You may call customers with receivables more than 30 days past due. You may turn receivables more than 60 or 90 days past due over to a collection agency or an attorney.

> **Note**
>
> *Aging* refers to segregating receivables into different age groups. Aging receivables gives you information about how long receivable balances have been outstanding. Ages are calculated as the difference between the invoice date and the current date.

To create an accounts receivable report by customer, showing each customer's balance and the period in which the balance is outstanding, follow these steps:

1. Choose Business from the Reports menu.

2. Choose A/R by Customer. The A/R by Customer Report window appears.

By default, Quicken organizes the A/R by Customer Report by payee; each payee or customer is shown separately in the report.

VI

Putting Quicken To Use

3. Choose the Customize button to display the Customize A/R by Customer dialog box.

4. Change the dates covered by the report, if necessary, in the Report Dates From and To drop-down list boxes.

5. Choose the accounts to include in the report. Select the Accounts option in the Customize area to display the Accounts Used section, shown in figure 23.4.

Fig. 23.4

The Customer A/R by Customer dialog box displays the Accounts Used section when you choose to customize the accounts included in the report.

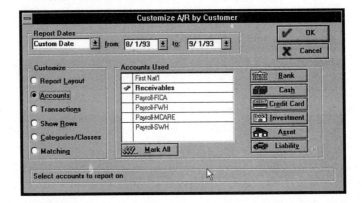

6. By default, Quicken includes all Asset accounts in the A/R by Customer Report, so all of them appear initially in the Accounts Used list box. Mark the receivables account(s) for your report by clicking the name(s) in the Accounts Used list. A check mark appears next to each selected account.

7. Choose OK to return to the A/R by Customer Report window. The report now is customized to include only your receivables account(s). Each customer, or payee, appears on a separate row (see fig. 23.5).

The report shows you how much money each customer owes you and the ages of the receivables. Johnson Manufacturing, for example, shows a receivable balance of $1,000 at the end of August. But Johnson's balance is only $500 at the end of September, because the partial payment was made during that month.

```
                      A/R by Customer
                  8/1/93 Through 9/30/93
  8/13/93                                              Page 1
  BUSINESS-Receivables

          Payee            8/1/1993      9/1/1993

  Bradford & Associates      2,000.00          0.00
  Johnson Manufacturing      1,000.00       -500.00
  Myers, Inc.                1,500.00          0.00
  Opening Balance                0.00          0.00
  Saxson & Reed              1,800.00          0.00

  OVERALL TOTAL              6,300.00       -500.00




                      A/R by Customer
                  8/1/93 Through 9/30/93
  8/13/93                                              Page 2
  BUSINESS-Receivables
                            OVERALL
          Payee             TOTAL

  Bradford & Associates      2,000.00
  Johnson Manufacturing        500.00
  Myers, Inc.                1,500.00
  Opening Balance                0.00
  Saxson & Reed              1,800.00

  OVERALL TOTAL              5,800.00
```

Fig. 23.5
A printed A/R by
Customer Report
shows receivable
balances for each
customer as well
as the dates that
the balances have
been outstanding.

Tracking Accounts Payable

Accounts payable are liabilities to vendors for goods and services used in a
business (and any other liabilities the business owes but that aren't due until
a future date). To record your payables, you must set up a Liability account
for that purpose in Quicken.

> **Note**
>
> If you're not using the accrual system of accounting (defined earlier in this chapter),
> don't worry about setting up accounts payable.

To set up an accounts payable account, first add a Liability account, name it
Accounts Pay or **A/P**, and then enter zero as the starting balance. Because
this account is a liability, it will appear in the Liabilities section of the balance sheet.

After you establish your accounts payable account, you can begin entering transactions for purchases or services. To track your accounts payable, follow these steps:

1. Access the Register for the accounts payable account.

2. By using your purchase invoices, enter a transaction for each credit purchase. Be sure to enter the purchase dates shown on the invoices. Enter the amount of the purchase in the Increase field. Use the Memo field to enter descriptive information about the credit transaction—invoice number, payment terms, and so on. Assign a category or subcategory to the transaction, and then record it.

Figure 23.6 shows the accounts payable Register with a credit transaction entered.

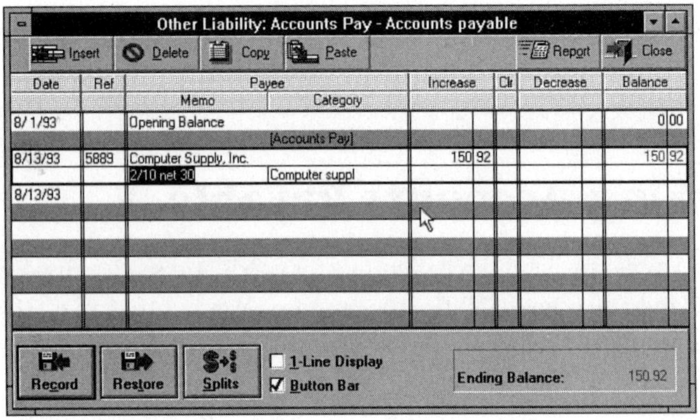

Fig. 23.6

Use an accounts payable Register to track all your credit purchases. Then you easily can monitor the outstanding balances that you owe vendors.

To record a transaction when you pay for credit purchases that you have entered in the accounts payable account, follow these steps:

1. Select the account that you use to write checks and display its Register.

2. Enter the payment transaction as usual. In the Category field, select the accounts payable account. Quicken enters the account in brackets to show that this is a transfer transaction (you're transferring funds from your bank account to decrease the balance in the accounts payable account). Record the transaction as usual.

Quicken enters the corresponding transaction in the accounts payable Register. Figure 23.7 shows the accounts payable Register after a payment is made.

Often, vendors provide incentives to their customers to pay their invoices early. Such incentives can include a 2 percent discount if the invoice is paid within 10 days of the invoice date. Otherwise, the full amount must be paid within 30 days. (Vendors provide many other discount terms as well.) If you take advantage of an early payment discount, split the transaction for the payment to the vendor and assign the discount to a subcategory called Discounts under the category Purchases (you need to add this subcategory to the Category & Transfer list).

CPA TIP: Taking Early Payment Discounts

Take advantage of all early payment discounts by paying invoices on the early payment date. Pay all other invoices so that the payment is received on the due date. You may even consider using aggressive accounts payable management by taking a 2 percent discount on any early payment, even if the vendor offers no such discount. Most vendors will be glad to receive 98 percent of the invoice amount early rather than wait for 100 percent in 30 or more days.

Accounting for Fixed Assets

Accounting for fixed assets represents another activity most businesses need to address. You may own furniture, equipment, and even real estate that needs to be depreciated. Although you can depreciate a number of different assets, the mechanics of recording depreciation are consistent.

Understanding Depreciation

Suppose that you buy a delivery truck for $21,000. You plan to use the truck for five years and then sell it for $6,000 (its salvage value). During that five-year period, you need to include the expense of the truck when measuring your profits. Depreciation provides you with a way to allocate the cost of an asset over two or more years. Several methods are available to make this allocation; one common method is *straight-line* depreciation.

Straight-line depreciation works in the following manner: If you buy the truck for $21,000, intending to sell it five years later for $6,000, the overall cost of using the truck over the five years is $15,000. To calculate the yearly cost, divide the $15,000 by five years; $3,000 is the annual depreciation expense to include in the calculations of profits.

On balance sheets, assets are listed at their adjusted basis (an amount equal to the original cost minus the depreciation already taken). With the delivery truck example, the balance sheet lists the truck at $18,000 (the $21,000 original cost minus the first $3,000 of depreciation) at the end of year one. Similarly, at the end of years two, three, four, and five, the balance sheet lists the truck at the original cost minus the depreciation taken to date. At the end of year five, when the truck is listed at $6,000, you stop the depreciation because you can't depreciate an asset below its salvage value.

Other depreciation methods exist, and the methods federal tax laws prescribe are often confusing. But in essence, Quicken works the same way to record depreciation no matter what depreciation method you use.

This chapter can't give you complete information about how to calculate the depreciation on assets. If you want more information on the tax laws, call the Internal Revenue Service and ask for IRS Publication 534. For more information on how to calculate depreciation according to generally accepted accounting principles (a different topic than depreciation calculated for tax purposes), consult a certified public accountant.

Recording Fixed Assets and Depreciation

To record fixed assets and the depreciation expense related to fixed assets, set up an Asset account for each fixed asset that must be depreciated. Enter a descriptive account name and enter the purchase price as the opening balance.

Figure 23.8 shows the New Account Information dialog box with the original cost of $21,000 entered in the Balance text box.

Fig. 23.8
Set up an Asset account for each fixed asset that you own in the New Account Information dialog box.

If you have groups of similar assets with similar life spans, you usually can depreciate these assets as a group. You probably don't need to depreciate each individual piece of furniture you buy during the year; you can aggregate and depreciate all the furniture together as a single asset.

To record depreciation, you can enter a decrease transaction for $3,000 each year. Assign the Depreciation Expense category to each transaction. If you haven't already set up a category for depreciation, Quicken displays the Set Up Category dialog box so that you can add the category as you assign it to the depreciation transaction.

Remember that Quicken doesn't include a transaction in its net income calculations unless the date of that transaction falls within the range you specify in the Customize Report dialog box. As a result, you can enter all five years of depreciation at one time by using transaction dates in each of the five years. Figure 23.9 shows the Register for the fixed asset account that was set up to record the cost and depreciation expense for the delivery truck. Note that depreciation expenses are recorded for 1993, 1994, 1995, 1996, and 1997.

VI

Putting Quicken To Use

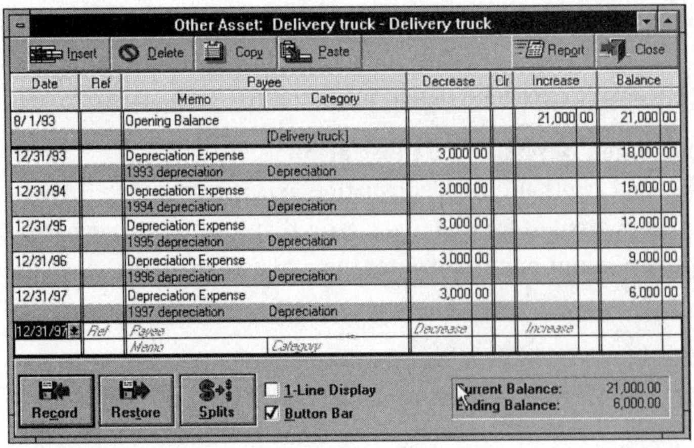

Fig. 23.9
Depreciation
expense is
recorded in the
Decrease column
in the fixed asset
account Register.

Preparing Payroll

One of the more common business applications of Quicken is to prepare
employee payroll checks and reports. Suppose that you want to prepare a
payroll check for an employee who earns $1,000 every two weeks. Each time
you prepare this employee's check, you must withhold these approximate
amounts: $62 for Social Security tax, $14.50 for Medicare tax, $100 for federal
income tax, and $40 for state income tax. You also must pay the employer's
matching share of Social Security ($62) and Medicare ($14.50), as well as
federal unemployment tax of approximately $10.

Note

If your payroll is becoming burdensome, consider using Quicken's add-on utility
program, called QuickPay. QuickPay calculates and processes your payroll; it even
enters the employee's paycheck information in the Write Checks window for you.
Refer to Appendix B, "Using QuickPay with Quicken," to learn more about this
payroll-preparation utility.

Getting Ready for Payroll

To record this payroll transaction, set up a Liability account for each payroll
tax payable account. To define each payroll tax account, select the New button from the Account list and enter the payroll tax account information. In
the **Balance** text box in the New Account Information dialog box, enter the
initial amount (the amount you already owe) as the starting balance. In this
example, the amount includes the federal income tax withholding, state

income tax withholding, the employee's Social Security and Medicare withholding, your matching Social Security and Medicare taxes, and the federal unemployment tax. (State unemployment taxes are also included, if applicable.)

The following is a list of suggested accounts to set up for payroll:

Account Name	To Record
Payroll-FICA	Social Security tax withholding
Payroll-FUTA	Federal unemployment tax liability
Payroll-FWH	Federal income tax withholding
Payroll-MCARE	Medicare tax withholding
Payroll-MED	Liability for medical insurance premiums
Payroll-SDI	State disability insurance liability
Payroll-SUI	State unemployment tax liability
Payroll-SWH*	State income tax withholding

*If you withhold state income taxes for more than one state, you should use the state's two-letter abbreviation at the end of the account name. For Indiana state tax, for example, use the name Payroll-SWHIN.

You also need to set up a category for payroll and a separate subcategory for the employer's payroll expenses: the employee's gross wages, the employer's matching share of the Social Security and Medicare tax, the federal unemployment tax, and any state unemployment taxes required by your state. You don't set up subcategories for the employee's withholding for Social Security tax, Medicare tax, federal income tax, or state income tax, however, because these amounts are expenses of the employee rather than the employer.

The following is a list of suggested subcategories to add to the Category & Transfer list for payroll transactions:

Subcategory Name	To Track
Comp FICA	Company's FICA tax contribution
Comp FUTA	Federal unemployment tax expense
Comp MCARE	Company's Medicare tax contribution

(continues)

Subcategory Name	To Track
Comp MED	Medical insurance expense
Comp SUI	State unemployment tax expense
Gross	Gross wages

CPA TIP: Keeping Up with Tax Rate Changes

Make sure that you keep up with the changing FICA (Federal Insurance Contribution Act) tax rates and the unemployment tax rates for your state. You also should be aware of limitations on 401(k) plan contributions each year. At the beginning of the year, consult with your accountant or tax advisor for this information.

Paying Employees

To record the payroll check, enter the payroll transaction in the Write Checks window or the Register. If you write payroll checks using the same bank account you use to write other checks, enter the Memo description as **Payroll** (including the pay date if desired). This technique enables you to use the contents of the Memo field to select payroll transactions for reports.

To assign multiple categories and accounts to the payroll transaction, choose the Splits button. First, enter the category that you use for gross payroll (like **Payroll:Gross**, where Gross is the subcategory of the category Payroll) and the amount (entered as a positive amount). In the next line, enter the account set up for federal income tax withholding (like **Payroll:FWH**) and the amount of federal taxes withheld (entered as a negative amount). Continue entering lines in the Splits window to account for each payroll deduction. When you are finished, the Remainder field should show zero (0.00).

You don't need to enter the net paycheck amount in the $ (Amount) field in the Write Checks window because Quicken calculates the net amount for you by subtracting any negative amounts that you enter in the Splits window for withholding from the positive amount that you enter for wages. If you use checks with vouchers (a good idea for payroll), the employee's gross wages and the employee's deductions should appear on the first 16 lines of the Splits window so that the payroll transaction can be detailed on the voucher (see fig. 23.10). Employees then can see how much of their gross pay was withheld for federal, state, Social Security, and Medicare taxes.

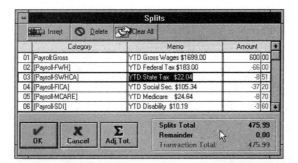

Fig. 23.10
The gross wages and employee deductions are entered on the first 16 lines of the Splits window.

> **Note**
>
> You can select the **P**rint Categories on Voucher Checks preference (from the Check Preferences dialog box) so that Quicken prints voucher information on checks. To learn how to use this preference, see Chapter 21, "Customizing Quicken."

Enter the other wage expenses (such as the employer's federal unemployment tax and matching share of Social Security and Medicare taxes) starting on line 17 of the Splits window so that these expenses don't appear on the payroll check's voucher (see fig. 23.11). (Entries made to lines 17 through 30 of the Split Transaction window aren't printed on check vouchers.) After you complete the Splits window, choose OK to return to the Write Checks window or the Register.

Fig. 23.11
The other wage expenses are entered in the Splits window, beginning at line 17.

Figure 23.12 shows a completed payroll check. The net wages amount is $475.99, which is $600.00 in gross wages minus $66 in federal withholding, $8.51 in state tax withholding, $37.20 in Social Security tax withholding, $8.70 in Medicare tax withholding, and $3.60 in state disability insurance withholding.

VI

Putting Quicken To Use

Fig. 23.12

A completed payroll check with the net amount entered in the $ (Amount) field.

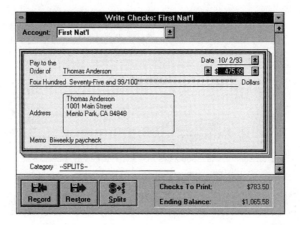

Paying Payroll Taxes

When you pay the government, you have recorded the expense of the taxes and are carrying, as a liability, the payroll taxes you still owe. When you write the check to the government, the entry made in the Category field should be the payroll tax liability account. If you write a check to pay the $10 in federal unemployment taxes, for example, enter the category as **[Payroll-FUTA]** (or whatever name you assigned to the Liability account that tracks federal unemployment tax obligations).

Use the same approach to record your payments on other payroll tax liabilities. Simply write a check to the government agency, categorizing the transaction as a transfer from the appropriate payroll tax liability account.

In real life you may have more payroll tax expenses and liabilities than the ones listed here (such as state and local income taxes, state unemployment insurance, and disability insurance). But you can use the same accounting procedures to record and pay each additional liability.

CPA TIP: Collecting Payroll Withholdings

You should segregate the payroll taxes that you withhold from your employees' gross wages. The best approach is to set up a separate account with your bank to collect and disburse payroll taxes. Don't, for any reason, *borrow* money from the payroll taxes bank account. Although the act may seem innocuous, this money isn't yours to spend. This money belongs to your employee or the federal government; you only hold the money in trust.

CPA TIP: Calculating Payroll Deductions

You probably know that most payroll deductions and taxes are calculated as a percentage of gross wages. Social Security deductions and matching payroll taxes are calculated at 6.2 percent of the gross wages up to a ceiling amount ($57,600 in 1993). Medicare deductions and matching payroll taxes are 1.45 percent of the gross wages up to a ceiling amount ($135,000 in 1993). With this feature of payroll preparation, you often can have Quicken calculate most of the payroll deductions and payroll taxes by using the percentage-split feature.

To use the percentage-split feature to calculate payroll deductions and taxes, follow these steps:

1. Begin the transaction as usual but enter the gross wages amount in the $ (Amount) field in the Write Checks window or the Payment field in the Register.

2. Choose the Splits button to open the Splits window.

3. Enter a line for each payroll deduction or payroll tax item. In the Amount field, enter the percentage used to calculate the deduction or tax (such as **6.2%** for Social Security tax and **1.45%** for Medicare). Enter the Payroll:Gross amount as **100%**.

   After you enter the percentages and press Tab, Quicken calculates the split amounts by multiplying each percentage by the amount entered in the $ (Amount) field or the Payment field.

4. For any deductions or taxes that you derive from withholding tables, enter the exact amounts in the Splits window.

A minor problem with this approach, however, is that the check amount remains the gross wages amount that you entered. The check amount, of course, should be the net of the gross wages minus payroll deductions and taxes. But this problem isn't difficult to fix. You may recall from Chapter 5 that to make the split transaction lines equal the check amount, Quicken adds another split transaction line to balance the transaction. Just delete this line by highlighting it and pressing Ctrl+D. Then choose the Adj. Tot. button to recalculate the check amount. The amount that now appears should be equal to the net payroll or paycheck.

Finally, Quicken enables you to create memorized transactions that use percentages rather than amounts. If you use the previously described approach, you can use this capability to make preparing payroll checks even easier. Refer to Chapter 6, "Using the Register," to learn how to split transactions using percentages.

Completing Quarterly and Annual Tax Reports

The final aspect of preparing payroll involves the filing of quarterly and annual payroll forms and reports to federal, state, and local governments.

VI

Putting Quicken To Use

A series of federal reporting requirements exists for forms W-2, W-3, 940, and 941. Depending on where you live, you also may have several state and local payroll forms and reports to complete. You may be able to retrieve the numbers for these forms by printing a Payroll Report based on the bank account you use to write payroll checks. If you select the Payroll Report, Quicken limits transactions included in the report to those with categories and subcategories or transfer accounts containing the word *payroll*.

To generate a report that summarizes your payroll withholdings and expenses, follow these steps:

1. Choose Business from the Reports menu.

2. From the submenu, choose Payroll. The Payroll Report window appears.

3. To define the time period that the report covers, choose the Customize button from the report button bar in the Payroll Report window. The Customize Payroll Report dialog box appears.

4. In the Report Date From and To text boxes, select the starting and ending dates for the Payroll Report.

5. Choose OK to limit transactions included in the report to those between the two specified dates.

6. Quicken displays the report for the specified date range. You can print the report by choosing the Print button on the report button bar. Quicken displays the Print Report dialog box. Choose Print to begin printing the report.

Figure 23.13 shows a printout of a sample Payroll Tax Report, which you may use to complete payroll tax forms.

Completing the W-2 and W-3 Forms

Use the gross wages figures on the report as the total wages amounts on employees' W-2 forms. Use the transfers from withholding figures as the federal income tax withholding amounts. Use the transfers from employees' FICA as the Social Security and Medicare taxes withheld amounts.

The W-3 form summarizes the W-2 forms you complete. Enter the employer totals for the individual amounts from each employee's W-2 form; you can use the totals from the summary report for these employer totals.

```
                      Payroll Report
                 1/1/93 Through 8/13/93
8/13/93                                              Page 1
QPSAMPLE-All Accounts

     Category Description      Fred Simpson     Sharon Miles

INCOME/EXPENSE
  EXPENSES
   Payroll:
     Comp FICA                    105.34           189.26
     Comp FUTA                     13.59            24.42
     Comp MCARE                    24.64            44.27
     Comp MED                       0.00             0.00
     Comp SUI                      20.39            36.63
     Gross                      1,699.00         3,052.50

   Total Payroll                1,862.96         3,347.08

  TOTAL EXPENSES                1,862.96         3,347.08


  TOTAL INCOME/EXPENSE         -1,862.96        -3,347.08

TRANSFERS
   FROM Payroll-FICA             210.68           378.52
   FROM Payroll-FUTA              13.59            24.42
   FROM Payroll-FWH             183.00           643.00
   FROM Payroll-MCARE            49.28            88.54
   FROM Payroll-MED               0.00             0.00
   FROM Payroll-SDI              10.19            18.32
   FROM Payroll-SUI              20.39            36.63
   FROM Payroll-SWHCA            22.04           186.83

TOTAL TRANSFERS                 509.17         1,376.26


OVERALL TOTAL                -1,353.79        -1,970.82




                      Payroll Report
                 1/1/93 Through 8/13/93
8/13/93                                              Page 2
QPSAMPLE-All Accounts
                                               OVERALL
     Category Description    Thomas Anderson     TOTAL

INCOME/EXPENSE
  EXPENSES
   Payroll:
     Comp FICA                    146.64           441.24
     Comp FUTA                     18.93            56.94
     Comp MCARE                    34.29           103.20
     Comp MED                      31.65            31.65
     Comp SUI                      28.38            85.40
     Gross                      2,365.38         7,116.88

  TOTAL EXPENSES                2,625.27         7,835.31


  TOTAL INCOME/EXPENSE         -2,625.27        -7,835.31

TRANSFERS
   FROM Payroll-FICA             293.28           882.48
   FROM Payroll-FUTA              18.93            56.94
   FROM Payroll-FWH             444.00         1,270.00
   FROM Payroll-MCARE            68.58           206.40
   FROM Payroll-MED              60.27            60.27
   FROM Payroll-SDI              14.19            42.70
   FROM Payroll-SUI              28.38            85.40
   FROM Payroll-SWHCA           122.91           331.78

TOTAL TRANSFERS               1,050.54         2,935.97


OVERALL TOTAL                -1,574.73        -4,899.34
```

Fig. 23.13
The Payroll Tax Report summarizes payroll tax transactions by account.

> **Note**
>
> One difference between the Payroll Tax Report shown in figure 23.13 and the one you use to prepare the W-2 and W-3 forms is that the range of transaction dates encompasses the entire calendar year.

Completing Other Forms and Reports

Federal and state governments have other tax forms and reports you must complete. You must use the 940 form to calculate and report annual federal unemployment tax liability, for example, and the 941 form (each quarter) to calculate and report federal income and Social Security taxes withheld (and your share of the Social Security taxes). Again, you may be able to use a Payroll Report similar to the report shown in figure 23.13 to complete the quarterly return.

> **Note**
>
> For the Employer's Annual Unemployment Tax (Form 940), the range of transaction dates must encompass the entire year. For the Employer's Quarterly Federal Tax (Form 941), the range of transaction dates must cover one quarter.

> **CPA TIP: Getting Help from the IRS**
>
> Typically, the Internal Revenue Service provides a great deal of help and information about federal payroll taxes. You may want to take advantage of the IRS help guides. Specifically, you need the Employer's Tax Guide (also known as Circular E). If you don't already have this document, call the nearest IRS office and request a copy. If you are a sole proprietor, you also may want to request the information packet "Your Business Tax Kit for Sole Proprietor," which provides information about the taxes you pay as a sole proprietor. Some IRS locations provide free small-business tax education seminars. You also can call the state revenue office and request all information they have on the state income and payroll taxes.

Preparing Inventory Accounting

A complete inventory accounting system answers two questions: how much inventory do you now hold, and how much inventory did you sell over the year? A perpetual inventory system can answer both questions. A *perpetual inventory system* tracks every change in inventory as the changes occur, in dollars and in units. As a result, you always know exactly how much inventory you hold.

Unfortunately, Quicken doesn't provide the tools to maintain a perpetual system. Because Quicken tracks only dollars, not units, you can answer only the second question: how much inventory did you sell over the year? You can answer this question with a simple periodic inventory system.

Understanding Periodic Inventory Systems

With a *periodic inventory system*, you count the inventory you are holding and add up the cost of the inventory at the end of each year. You can calculate the cost of the goods, or inventory, you sold by totaling the inventory purchases you made over the year and subtracting the change in inventory.

Suppose that you sell antique cars for $10,000 each. You held 3 cars in inventory at the beginning of the year, purchased 10 cars over the year, and have 4 cars in inventory at the end of the year. Using the equation described in the preceding paragraph, you can calculate the value of the inventory you sold over the year as follows:

Car purchases: ($10,000 * 10) = $100,000

Change over year:
Ending: ($10,000 * 4 cars) = $40,000
Beginning: ($10,000 * 3 cars) = $30,000
Minus change over year: –$10,000
Cost of inventory sold during year: $90,000

You know that during the year you bought $100,000 of cars and that you are holding $10,000 more inventory than you held at the end of the previous year, which means that you didn't sell all the cars you bought.

Implementing a Periodic Inventory System

You can use Quicken to construct a simple—but crude—inventory system that enables you to enjoy the benefits of periodic inventory. To implement a periodic inventory system using Quicken, follow these steps:

1. Set up an Asset account for the inventory you buy and sell. Give it a name (like **Inventory**) and enter your starting inventory balance as the starting balance. (If you are just starting a business and haven't begun to purchase inventory, the starting inventory balance can be zero.)

VI

Putting Quicken To Use

2. When you purchase inventory, don't categorize the purchase as an expense. Instead, transfer the total purchase amount to the inventory account. (Enter the inventory account in the Category field. Quicken enters it like this: [Inventory].)

3. To reconcile inventory, take a physical count and determine its value. Then display the account Register used for inventory and choose Update Balances from the Activities menu.

4. Choose Update Cash Balance. The Update Account Balance dialog box appears.

5. Enter the value of the physical count in the Update This Account's Balance To text box.

6. Select a Category For Adjustment, such as COGS (Cost of Goods Sold).

7. In the Adjustment Date drop-down list, select the date you want to use for the adjustment transaction. For end of year inventories, use 12/31/*yy*.

8. Choose OK to record the adjustment transaction.

Figure 23.14 shows an inventory account Register after a year of purchases and the adjustment transaction that determines the actual cost of goods sold.

Fig. 23.14
Record a balance adjustment transaction to update the value in your inventory account Register to the actual value of inventory on hand.

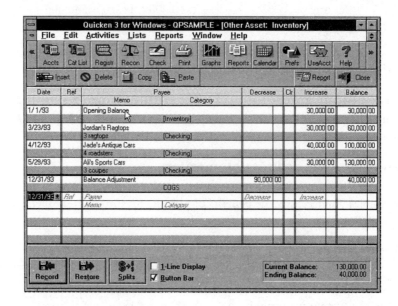

Reviewing the Problems of a Periodic System

As you know, a periodic inventory system isn't without problems. Make sure that you can live with the problems of a periodic inventory system before you spend a great deal of time and energy to implement this kind of system.

Although you have accurate measures of cash flow, you have an accurate measure of profits only through the last adjustment transaction. If you need to measure profits frequently, you must take frequent physical inventory counts and make the appropriate inventory adjustment transactions.

And you don't know the details or components of the cost of goods sold because you get the cost of goods sold from an adjustment transaction. As a result, you don't know the portion of cost of goods sold that stems from sales to specific customers or the portion that stems from breakage, shoplifting, or spoilage. This lack of information can be especially troublesome if your business sells more than one kind of item (books, tapes, and CDs, for example). You may have to set up a separate account for each kind of item in your inventory; if you do so, make sure that you segregate all purchases by splitting transactions.

This system also can't inform you of the amount of inventory you actually have on hand, except when you make physical counts of inventory, so you can't use it to keep track of your stock or to plan your reordering.

Understanding Job Costing

Job costing involves tracking the costs of a specific project, or job, and comparing these costs to the amount you planned to spend. Home builders, advertising agencies, and specialty manufacturers are examples of businesses that must monitor actual and planned costs for their projects.

One approach to job costing is to categorize each expense into a category and a class. If each class represents a job, you can get job cost totals by printing subtotals by class when you print a transaction or summary report. But this approach has many weaknesses. The following paragraphs describe alternative approaches that help you avoid two problems you encounter when categorizing expenses into categories and classes (see Chapter 4, "Organizing Your Finances," for a detailed discussion of categories and classes).

The first problem with using classes as the basis for a job-costing system occurs because within Quicken you must budget by categories, not by classes.

If you use the class approach, you have no way to handle one of the basic job-costing tasks: comparing the amount you planned to spend with the actual amount spent. Fortunately, you can solve this problem by setting up a group of categories that you use only for a specific job. You may even include a code or an abbreviation in the category name to indicate which job it represents.

Suppose that you are a home builder constructing a house on Lot 23 in Deerfield. Suppose also that you track expenses in three rough categories on all the homes you build: land, material, and labor. In this case, you can create three special categories named *D23 land*, *D23 material*, and *D23 labor*, which you can use exclusively to budget and track the costs of the house under construction. (You learn how to enter budget amounts for categories in Chapter 16, "Budgeting with Quicken.") Figure 23.15 shows the Budget Report that you can generate to monitor job costs if you do so.

Fig. 23.15

A sample budget report shows the actual expenses incurred on a job compared to budgeted job expenses.

```
                            Budget Report
                       8/1/93 Through 8/31/93
          10/2/93     Page 1
          BUSINESS-All Accounts

                                8/1/1993        -        8/31/1993
                Category Description   Actual      Budget        Diff

          INCOME/EXPENSE
            EXPENSES
                D23 Labor          16,753.00     20,000.00     -3,247.00
                D23 Land           30,400.00     30,000.00        400.00
                D23 Materials      23,456.00     25,000.00     -1,544.00

            TOTAL EXPENSES         70,609.00     75,000.00     -4,391.00


          TOTAL INCOME/EXPENSE    -70,609.00    -75,000.00      4,391.00
```

A second problem with using classes as the basis for a job-costing system is that you don't always have to categorize as expenses the costs you incur on a job. In some cases you need to treat these costs as assets. The costs of building the home on Lot 23 in the Deerfield subdivision should be carried as inventory until the home is sold. When the home is sold, the total costs of the home can be categorized as the cost of goods sold.

During the job, if you categorize the costs of building the home as expenses when you pay the costs, you overstate expenses (which understates profits) and understate assets (which understates net worth). These understatements of profits and net worth can become a real problem if you have investors or lenders looking carefully at your financial performance and condition.

To solve this problem, create a transaction in which you move cost dollars out of the job-cost categories into an Asset account at the end of your accounting year. The basic steps for moving amounts from expense categories to an Asset account are as follows:

1. Set up an Asset account for each job.

2. Create a Summary Report (choose **O**ther from the **R**eports menu and then choose **S**ummary), customizing the Col**u**mn headings to Class, to see costs by category and class.

3. Record an entry in the new Asset Register that increases the balance of the asset by the total amount shown in the expense category. Assign the expense category to the transaction. As a result, you increase your Asset account on the balance sheet and decrease your expense category in the profit and loss statement.

For more information on categories and classes, see Chapter 4, "Organizing Your Finances."

An Introduction to QuickBooks

If you like using Quicken but find that it just doesn't meet the needs of your small business (because you can't print invoices and statements, track accounts receivable and payable adequately, or create customer and vendor lists), you may want to look into Intuit's new small-business package called *QuickBooks*. You can convert your Quicken data to QuickBooks easily, so don't worry about having to re-enter anything in a new system. And even though you may convert your Quicken data for use in QuickBooks, your Quicken data remains intact after the conversion process if you want to use Quicken to perform tasks that QuickBooks doesn't handle (such as amortizing loans and tracking investments).

Although Quicken fully accommodates the needs of the individual user handling home finances and many small-business users, it doesn't offer some of the features that you may need to track your business finances adequately. QuickBooks offers small-business owners the ease of use that they're accustomed to with Quicken and also provides features that relate more specifically to business (such as invoicing and accounts payable tracking).

You write checks and enter transactions in the Write Checks window and the Check Register in QuickBooks just like in Quicken. You also can use QuickBooks to reconcile your bank account using almost the same steps that you use in Quicken. QuickBooks does several other things just like Quicken, but it also does many things that Quicken can't do. Some of those things include the following:

- Tracking your accounts receivable so that you know at any given time how much your customers owe.

- Enabling you to track reimbursable expenses so that you can bill clients and customers for reimbursable expenses on invoices.

- Applying customer payments to invoices and calculating early payment discounts.

- Calculating sales tax for taxable invoice items.

- Preparing a deposit summary that you can take to the bank when you deposit customer payments.

- Offering complete invoice-writing capabilities that enable you to enter line items with item codes that link invoice transactions to accounts.

- Determining when your bills are due and tracking your accounts payable.

- Using your chart of accounts to track income, expenses, and balance sheet accounts (instead of using categories and subcategories, like in Quicken).

- Using company lists to store data about your customers, customer types, jobs, vendors, vendor types, employees, invoice items, classes (or projects), payment and shipping methods, and payment terms. You even can store customer messages so that you don't have to retype them each time you write an invoice.

  Company lists speed up entry in many fields throughout the program. They also serve as a database of your customers, vendors, and employees; you can use these lists, for example, to print customer and vendor information on mailing labels or Rolodex cards.

- Using balance sheet accounts that are more representative of business, such as fixed asset and equity accounts.

- Enabling you to define jobs that relate to each customer so that you can track the work that you do for each client or customer.

- Enabling you to assign password protection to your QuickBooks activities. Three types of passwords are available:

Owner	Gives the user unlimited access to your company file
Data Entry	Allows the user to enter new transactions but doesn't let the user view registers, reports, or graphs or to edit transactions entered in prior periods
Transaction	Allows the user only to edit transactions entered in a predefined prior period

- Using terminology with which small-business people are familiar.

> **Note**
>
> You don't have to be an accounting expert to understand the terminology in QuickBooks. On the contrary—Intuit wanted to produce a program that wouldn't intimidate the user who wasn't an accountant. In QuickBooks, you don't see common accounting terms like *debit* or *credit*. You *do* see *accounts receivable, accounts payable, invoice, voucher*, and so on—the terms that you use or hear on a daily basis.

- Offering business reports and graphs that are designed to appear in the usual and customary business format.

- Enabling you to customize reports so that reports include comparison data in profit and loss statements, sales reports, and so forth.

- Creating an aging status schedule for each customer that shows the portion of the customer's balance that is current and the portion that is 0 to 30 days past due, 31 to 60 days past due, 61 to 90 days past due, and more than 90 days past due.

- Generating an accounts payable aging report that shows the status of your unpaid bills.

602   Using Quicken in Your Small Business

- Generating a 1099 report that you can use to fill out 1099 forms at the end of the calendar year for vendors or independent contractors to whom you pay more than $600.

- Tracking the sales tax that you collect for each government agency and accumulating sales tax data in a report that you can use when it's time to file sales tax returns and pay sales tax.

- Displaying a transaction history for transactions that you select in accounts receivable and accounts payable. A transaction history shows each transaction that is part of the transaction that you select.

- Enabling you to enter notes about customers, vendors, or employees in the QuickBooks program so that the notes are readily available.

As you can see, QuickBooks is designed to handle most small-business activities (with the exception of inventory control). If your small business has significant investments, however, you should know that QuickBooks isn't designed to do the following:

- Track individual investments, their market values, and their gains or losses. If you need to track your investments closely, use investment accounts in Quicken and use QuickBooks for everything else.

- Amortize mortgage loans. Quicken includes a loan amortization calculator that updates the principal and interest on outstanding loans each time a payment is recorded.

- Receive electronic credit card statements. In Quicken, you can receive an electronic statement that automatically assigns categories and subcategories to purchases.

- Specify accounts as tax-related. (This feature isn't as important in QuickBooks because most all business accounts and subaccounts are tax-related.)

Summary

This chapter provided you with a basic approach to accounting for any business asset or liability and gave specific suggestions and tips for performing basic accounting tasks. This chapter covered the following topics:

■ Quicken accounts and categories and what they track

■ Transactions and when to record transactions in accounts

■ How to use Quicken to track your accounts receivable

■ How to generate an A/R by Customer Report so that you can track your receivables by period

■ How to enter bills that you owe vendors for goods and services in an accounts payable account and how to record payments to vendors

■ How to track your fixed assets in Quicken and how to record depreciation expenses

■ How to prepare your business's payroll and generate the reports you need to determine payroll taxes payable (and how to use Quicken to help with payroll tax returns)

■ How to set up a simple periodic inventory system in Quicken

■ How to track the costs of specific projects and jobs

■ Intuit's QuickBooks program, which is designed specifically for small-business use

This is the last chapter of *Using Quicken for Windows*. In the appendixes that follow, you learn how to install Quicken 3 for Windows (which you probably already have done) and how to use QuickPay with Quicken.

Appendixes

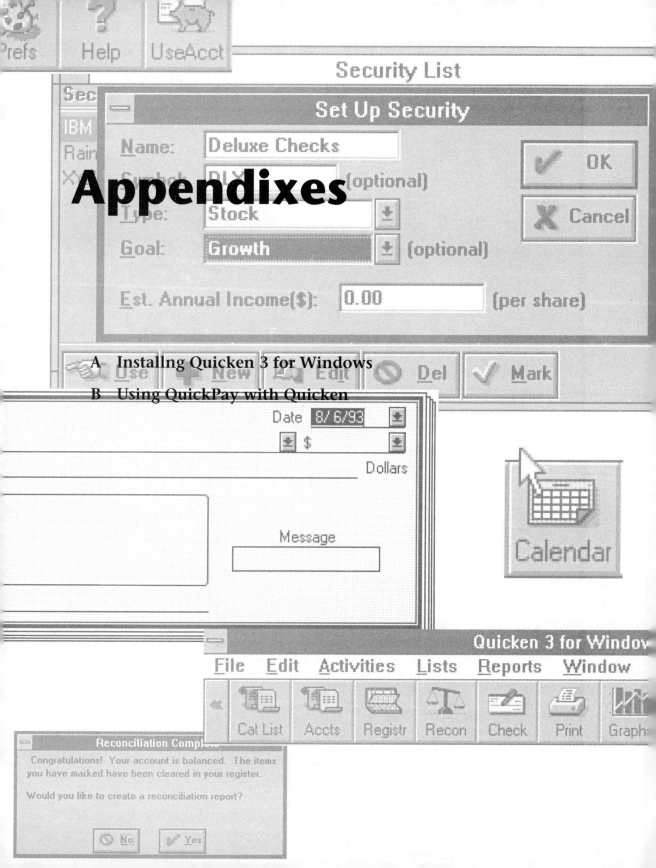

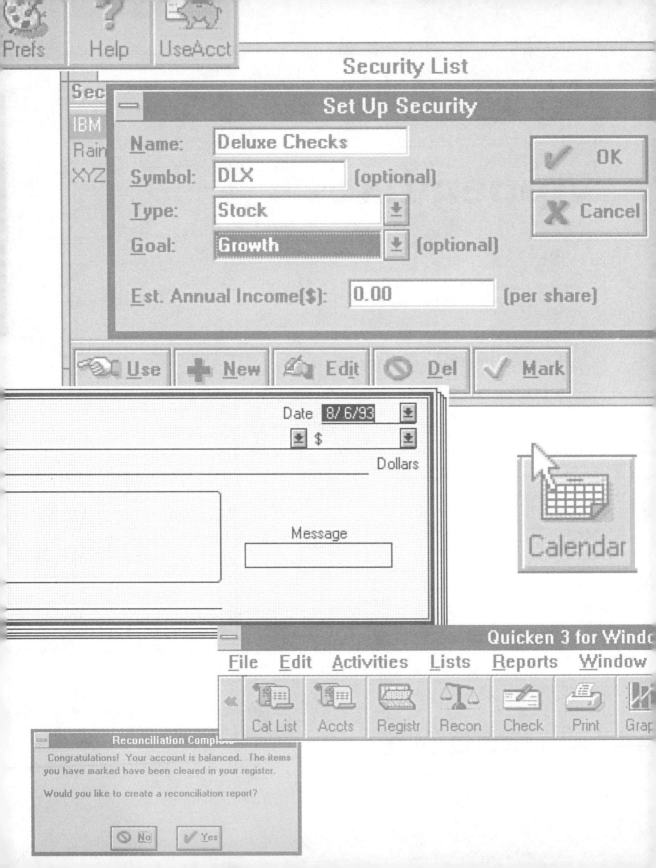

Prefs   **Help**   **UseAcct**

Security List

Sec

IBM

Rain

XYZ

Set Up Security

Name: Deluxe Checks

Symbol: DLX   (optional)

Type: Stock ▼

Goal: Growth ▼ (optional)

Est. Annual Income($): 0.00   (per share)

✔ **OK**

✘ **Cancel**

👉 Use   ➕ New   ✏ Edit   🚫 Del   ✔ Mark

Date 8/ 6/93 ▼

▼ $ ▼

Dollars

Message

Calendar

Quicken 3 for Windo

File   **Edit**   **Activities**   **Lists**   **Reports**   **Window**

Cat List   Accts   Registr   Recon   Check   Print   Grap

Reconciliation Comple

Congratulations! Your account is balanced. The items you have marked have been cleared in your register.

Would you like to create a reconciliation report?

🚫 No   ✔ Yes

Installing Quicken 3 for Windows

Before you can use Quicken 3 for Windows, you must install the program on your hard disk. This appendix explains the software and hardware requirements for Quicken and provides the steps you need to install the program.

> **Note**
>
> If you have a previous version of Quicken for Windows or Quicken for DOS 5 or 6 on your hard disk, installing Quicken for Windows will have no effect on these programs. To safeguard your data, however, you should back up your existing Quicken data files before you install Quicken 3 for Windows.

Reviewing the Program Requirements

The following sections review the software and hardware requirements to install and run Quicken 3 for Windows.

Hardware Requirements

You need the following hardware to work with Quicken 3 for Windows:

- IBM 386SX (or higher) or 100 percent compatible computer

- At least 2M of RAM

- One floppy disk drive, either 5 1/4-inch or 3 1/2-inch

- Hard disk drive with at least 3M of free disk space

- VGA or SVGA monitor, or better

- Microsoft mouse or compatible pointing device (optional)

- Microsoft Windows-compatible printer (optional)

- A modem that works at 300, 1200, or 2400 baud (if you plan to send payments electronically or receive your IntelliCharge statement electronically)

Software Requirements

You need the following software to work with Quicken 3 for Windows:

- MS-DOS or PC DOS, Version 3.1 or later

- Microsoft Windows 3.1 running in Standard or Enhanced mode

- Quicken 3 for Windows program disks

Installing the Program

Although not essential, knowing a thing or two about working with Windows helps before you step through the installation. You should know how to select menu options, click the mouse, enter data into text boxes, select command buttons, and work with scrollable list boxes. If you previously worked with Windows, you probably know how to do all these things. If you are new to Windows, however, learn the basics before you continue with this installation. You can use Quicken's Introduction to Windows Tutorial from the Help menu, after installing Quicken.

Installing Quicken 3 for Windows is easy and takes just a few minutes. You can install Quicken using Express Installation and have Quicken create the subdirectory and program group in which the program will be installed. You also can customize the installation so that Quicken is installed in a different directory or a different program group.

Using Express Installation

To use Express Installation to install Quicken 3 for Windows, follow these steps:

1. Type **win** at the DOS prompt and then press Enter to start the Windows program.

2. Make sure that the Program Manager window is active. If it isn't, double-click the Program Manager icon or press Ctrl+Esc to display the Windows Task List. From the Windows Task List, click Program Manager, or use the arrow keys to highlight Program Manager and then press Enter.

3. Insert the Quicken 3 for Windows program disk #1 in drive A or B.

4. With the Program Manager on-screen, choose **R**un from the File menu. The Run dialog box appears.

5. Type **a:install** (or **b:install**) in the Command Line text box.

6. Choose OK or press Enter. Quicken displays the Quicken Install window (see fig. A.1).

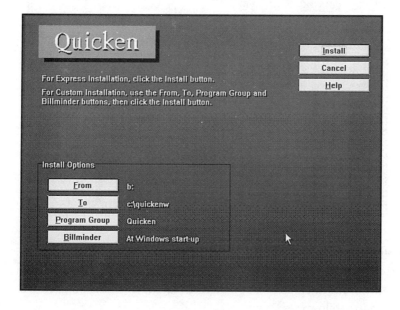

Fig. A.1
If you don't want to change any of the default installation settings, choose the Install button in the Quicken Install window for Express Installation.

7. To choose Express Installation, choose Install. Quicken for Windows displays a gauge to show you how installation of the program is progressing.

8. When prompted, remove the program disk from drive A or B and insert the next disk. Choose OK after you insert the next disk.

9. When installation is complete, Quicken for Windows displays the Quicken is installed… message shown in figure A.2. Choose OK to return to Windows.

Fig. A.2
Quicken for
Windows displays
a confirmation
message that the
program has been
installed.

The Quicken for Windows icon is placed in the Quicken program group, as
shown in figure A.3. Double-click the icon to start Quicken for Windows.

Fig. A.3
The Quicken for
Windows icon
appears in the
Quicken program
group.

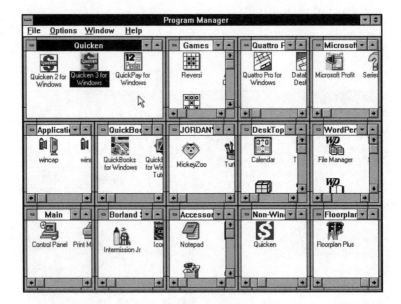

Using Custom Installation

To customize the installation of Quicken for Windows so that you can
change the directory, drive, or program group in which the program will
be installed, follow these steps:

1. Follow steps 1 through 7 in the preceding section to display the
   Quicken Install window.

2. To install Quicken for Windows in a different directory or on a different
   drive, click the To button to display the Destination dialog box shown
   in figure A.4. By default, Quicken creates a subdirectory named
   QUICKENW in the root directory of your hard disk (usually drive C).
   The Quicken program and data files are stored in this directory.

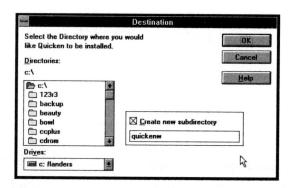

Fig. A.4
The Destination
dialog box enables
you to change the
directory and
subdirectory in
which Quicken
is installed.

3. To change the directory, select the desired directory from the Directories list box. (Use the scroll bar to scroll through the list of directories.)

   To create a new subdirectory other than QUICKENW, type the desired subdirectory name in the Create New Subdirectory text box.

   To change the current drive, click the down arrow in the Drives dropdown list to display other drives. Then click the desired drive.

4. When your changes are complete in the Destination dialog box, click OK or press Enter to return to the Install Quicken window (refer to fig. A.1).

> **Note**
>
> For most people, the default Quicken directory (QUICKENW) works fine. The one group of users who may want to specify a different directory are users who previously used Quicken for DOS. If you used Quicken 3, 4, or 5, for example, you probably want Quicken for Windows to use the same data files. To arrange this setup, install Quicken for Windows in the existing Quicken directory, probably QUICKEN3, QUICKEN4, or QUICKEN5. Thankfully, Quicken for Windows's capability to use existing Quicken files means that you don't have to worry about importing old data files.

5. To install Quicken for Windows in a different program group, click the Program Group button in the Install Quicken window to display the Which Program Group Should Quicken Be Added To? dialog box (see fig. A.5).

Fig. A.5
Change the
Windows program
group into which
Quicken places its
icon to start the
program.

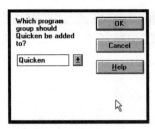

6. From the drop-down list box, select the program group into which you want to install Quicken for Windows. Then choose OK or press Enter to return to the Quicken Install window.

7. If you want to change the way Billminder (Quicken's on-screen reminder system) runs, choose the Billminder button. Quicken displays the dialog box shown in figure A.6, which asks when you want the Billminder program run. The three choices offered are never, when you start the computer, or when you start Windows. Indicate when you want the Billminder program run by clicking the appropriate option button.

    Choose OK to accept the Billminder setting and return to the Quicken Install window.

Fig. A.6
When you install
Quicken, you can
select when the
Billminder
program runs.

> **Note**
>
> When you turn on your computer or start Windows, Quicken's Billminder program reminds you of bills to pay and checks to write. This handy feature can save the price of Quicken and this book many times over by eliminating or minimizing late-payment fees. To run the Billminder program when you boot your computer, Quicken adds a line to the AUTOEXEC.BAT file. To run the Billminder program when you start Windows, Quicken adds a line to the WIN.INI file.

8. At the Quicken Install window, choose Install. Quicken for Windows displays a gauge to show you how installation of the program is progressing.

9. When prompted, remove the program disk from drive A or B and insert the next disk. Choose OK when you have inserted the next disk.

10. When the installation is complete, Quicken for Windows displays the `Quicken is installed…` message (refer to fig. A.2). Choose OK to return to Windows.

Appendix B

Using QuickPay with Quicken

If you're a business user of Quicken and the payroll tricks and tips described in Chapter 23, "Using Quicken in Your Small Business," don't give you the payroll horsepower you need, don't despair. Still another option is available that works seamlessly with Quicken: the QuickPay payroll utility. At the time of this printing, QuickPay 2.1 for Windows is the latest version of the program.

QuickPay is a payroll program that works with Quicken. In essence, the Quick-Pay program calculates the amounts you usually have to calculate outside the Quicken program—including the gross wages and the federal, state, and local taxes—and uses these amounts to prepare and record payroll checks.

The following sections briefly describe how to use the QuickPay utility. Quicken users considering the QuickPay utility may find the ensuing discussion useful in deciding whether to acquire QuickPay and in getting started with the program.

> **Note**
>
> The QuickPay utility isn't described in this appendix in great detail. This kind of discussion easily could require several chapters—perhaps even an entire book—to cover all the material necessary for every QuickPay user to prepare payroll in his or her state.

Installing QuickPay

Installing QuickPay is easy. You need just two other items to run the program: an installed copy of Quicken 3 for Windows, at least 92K of memory more than the minimum amount Quicken requires, and 1.2M of free space on your hard disk. If your computer meets these three requirements, insert the QuickPay disk into your A or B drive. Then, from the Program Manager File menu, choose Run, type **a:install** or **b:install** in the Command Line text box, and choose OK to begin installing QuickPay for Windows.

QuickPay's installation program displays the QuickPay Install window (see fig. B.1). By default, QuickPay installs from the drive in which you inserted the program disk, installs to the directory containing Quicken for Windows, installs the program files and the tax tables, and places the QuickPay icon in the Quicken program group. Choose the Install button to begin installation.

Fig. B.1
The QuickPay
Install window
shows the drive
that QuickPay is
installed from and
where QuickPay
will be installed.

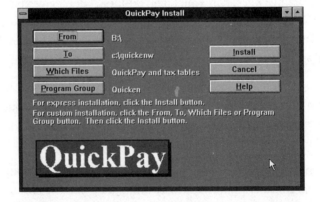

Note

If you use QuickBooks for Windows, QuickPay identifies its directory first and, by default, installs QuickPay in the QuickBooks program directory. To install QuickPay in the Quicken for Windows directory, choose To in the QuickPay Install window and then select C:\QUICKENW as the directory.

If you want to update only your QuickPay tax tables and don't want to install the QuickPay 2.1 for Windows program files, choose Which Files in the Quick-Pay Install window and select the Install Tax Tables Only option button.

After you install QuickPay for Windows, Quicken adds the QuickPay command to its Activities menu to start the program.

Starting QuickPay

To start QuickPay, just start your Quicken for Windows program as usual. Then, from the Write Checks window, choose the QuickPay command from the Activities menu or press F7 to display the QuickPay for Windows application window, as shown in figure B.2.

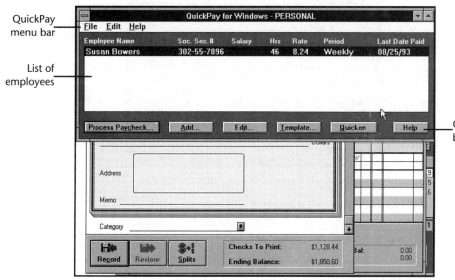

QuickPay menu bar

List of employees

Fig. B.2
The QuickPay for Windows application appears when you press F7 from the Write Checks window.

QuickPay activity buttons

The QuickPay for Windows application window includes a menu bar at the top of the window, an employee list in the middle of the window, and activity buttons at the bottom of the window. Use the menu bar to choose commands to set up passwords, back up and restore QuickPay data, set up your company, and exit the program.

Setting Up QuickPay To Process Payroll

After you access the QuickPay application window, you're ready to set up QuickPay for your payroll. You need to do the following before processing payroll with QuickPay:

■ *Set up your company or business.* From the File menu, choose the Set Up Company command. QuickPay displays the Set Up Company dialog box, shown in figure B.3. Enter your company's name, address, federal ID number, state ID number, the type of checks you are using, any miscellaneous employee deductions and the accounts to which the deductions should be assigned, and the bank account from which you write payroll checks. When the Set Up Company dialog box is complete, choose OK or press Enter to return to the QuickPay application window.

Fig. B.3

Enter information about your company in the Set Up Company dialog box.

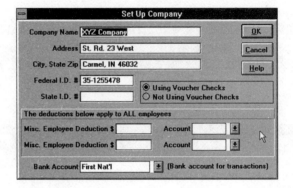

- *Enter general information about your employees.* Choose the Template activity button from the QuickPay application window. QuickPay displays the Edit Employee Template dialog box (see fig. B.4). Enter the information that is common to all your employees (such as pay rates, commission percentages, whether FUTA, SUI, FICA, or MCARE taxes are withheld, and so forth) and choose OK to save the employee information in the template. QuickPay automatically enters this information as you add an employee.

  If you need to edit the information about an employee (a new address, increase in salary, change in number of exemptions, and so forth), choose the Edit activity button from the QuickPay application window to display the Edit Employee dialog box. Edit the information about an employee and choose OK.

- *Add employees.* Choose the Add activity button from the QuickPay application window to display the Add Employee dialog box, shown in figure B.5. Enter the employee's name, address, telephone number, memo that you want to appear on payroll checks, the class of employee, Social Security number, hourly rates (if applicable), yearly salary amount (if applicable), commission rate (if applicable), and pay period. To define federal, state, or local taxes, or other deductions, choose the appropriate command button in the Add Employee dialog box. To add year-to-date amounts for the employee, choose the Year-to-Date button. When the Add Employee dialog box is complete, choose OK. QuickPay adds the employee's name to the list in the QuickPay application window (refer to fig. B.2).

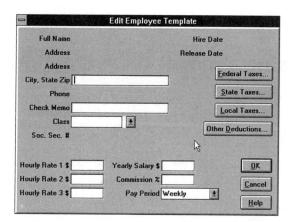

Fig. B.4
Enter information that is common to all your employees in the Edit Employee Template dialog box.

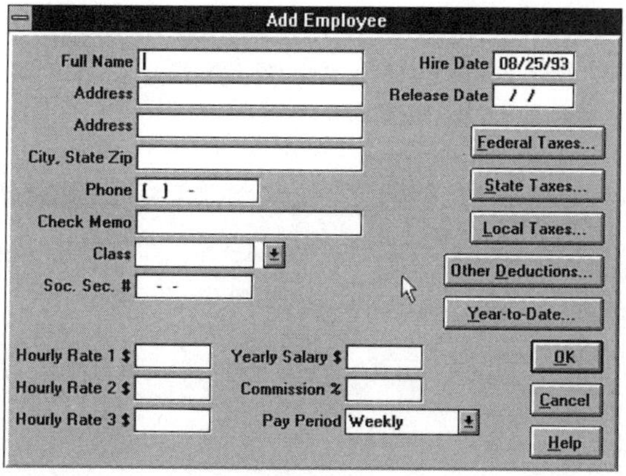

Fig. B.5
Enter information about individual employees in the Add Employee dialog box.

- *Set up payroll accounts and payroll categories and subcategories in Quicken.* Refer to Chapter 3, "Defining Your Accounts," and Chapter 23, "Using Quicken in Your Small Business," to learn how to set up payroll accounts. Refer to Chapter 4, "Organizing Your Finances," to learn how to set up payroll categories and subcategories.

- *Set up a year-to-date bank account to record payroll tax withholdings.* Refer to Chapter 3, "Defining Your Accounts," to learn how to set up a bank account.

Tip
To prevent unauthorized users from accessing your payroll records, set up passwords. From the File menu, choose Set Up Password to assign a password to your QuickPay files.

Note

If you have been using QuickPay 2 for DOS, QuickPay transferred those data files to QuickPay 2.1 for Windows. Your company and employee information is already set up for you, and you can begin processing payroll.

Processing Payroll with QuickPay

After you set up QuickPay with your company and employee information, you're ready to process payroll checks. To process payroll for an employee, follow these steps:

1. From the Write Checks window, press F7 to start QuickPay and display the QuickPay for Windows application window (refer to fig. B.2).

2. Use the up- and down-arrow keys to highlight the employee that you want to pay.

3. Choose the Process Paycheck activity button. Quicken displays the Process Paycheck for *xxx* dialog box (where *xxx* is the selected employee), as shown in figure B.6.

Fig. B.6
Enter information about the pay period in the Process Paycheck dialog box.

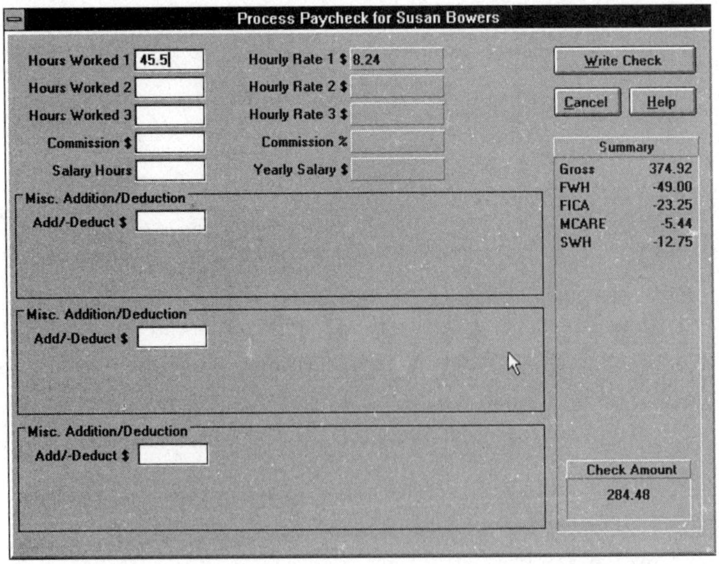
Process Paycheck for Susan Bowers
Hours Worked 1
45.5
Hours Worked 2
Hours Worked 3
Commission $
Salary Hours
Hourly Rate 1 $
8.24
Hourly Rate 2 $
Hourly Rate 3 $
Commission %
Yearly Salary $
Write Check
Cancel
Help
Summary
Gross 374.92
FWH -49.00
FICA -23.25
MCARE -5.44
SWH -12.75
Misc. Addition/Deduction
Add/-Deduct $
Misc. Addition/Deduction
Add/-Deduct $
Misc. Addition/Deduction
Add/-Deduct $
Check Amount
284.48

4. Enter information about the pay period for the selected employee. QuickPay displays the gross pay, payroll deductions, and the net pay (check amount) in the Summary section on the right side of the Process Paycheck dialog box.

5. When the Process Paycheck dialog box is complete, choose the Write Check button.

6. QuickPay displays a message that a check has been added to Quicken. Choose OK to return to the Process Paycheck dialog box.

7. Repeat steps 2 through 6 for each employee that you want to pay.

Returning to Quicken

After you finish processing your payroll, return to Quicken by exiting the QuickPay program (press Ctrl+X) or, if you want QuickPay to remain open, choose the Quicken activity button. You can also reduce the QuickPay for Windows application window to an icon by clicking its minimize button.

Note

If you don't exit QuickPay, the program can be activated by double-clicking the QuickPay icon or pressing F7 in the Write Checks window.

Tips and Suggestions for Using QuickPay

If QuickPay sounds like something you would benefit from using, great. Recognize, however, that QuickPay isn't the same thing as a payroll accountant or tax attorney. You can't expect the QuickPay program or its documentation to provide payroll tax knowledge or to answer your questions about how state unemployment taxes are calculated, for example.

Like every other payroll program, the QuickPay program only automates payroll processing. The bottom line is that if you need to prepare payroll but don't understand how the basic process works, you first need to acquire an understanding of payroll processing.

Several options are available if you need to acquire payroll processing know-ledge. The Internal Revenue Service and many state taxing authorities offer tax workshops that explain how to calculate federal and state payroll taxes.

The Internal Revenue Service also provides, free to small businesses, several well-written books and booklets that explain all kinds of accounting require-ments, including those related to payroll processing. Finally, in a pinch, you always can use outside service bureaus, such as ADP or PayChex, until you feel confident about tackling payroll on your own.

Index

B

X-Z